REVIEWS
WOKE DOESN'T MEAN BROKE

This book is a mental checklist. The analogies were great! Meditation and financial knowledge mixed in one.

Waka Flocka Flame - BET Music Awards Winner and International recording artist.

* * *

<u>Woke Doesn't Mean Broke</u> *explores the behavioral and mindset shifts that are necessary in order to manifest abundance in all areas of one's life. Billy does an amazing job of simplifying the steps for enlightened and conscious people to achieve their birthright of financial abundance and wealth while still living a purposeful life. The real world examples he shares throughout the book are relatable and practical that anyone can put into practice to see immediate shifts in their reality.* - Dawn Dickson, Light Worker, Serial Entrepreneur & Inventor. Entrepreneur Of The Year.

* * *

Woke Doesn't Mean Broke, by Billy Carson, is an absolute gem! This book is going to change the lives of many!

When given the right tools and knowledge to succeed in this simplified way in which the author ,Billy Carson delivers, you will already be successful before you have finished the book!

Billy Carson has taught me to keep a positive way of seeing all situations. By his example I have tripled my income this year (2020).

This is a must read if you are serious about becoming more successful. I am recommending this book to everyone!

Ashera Star Goddess - YouTuber and Blogger - Public Figure

* * *

This is truly the time to make changes. Do not wait for anything or anybody. Now is the time to make your move. You need to be ahead of the game with the right tools that this book will provide you on your journey into the future. Donny Arcade - International Music Artist and American Billboard Artist - DonnyArcadeWorld.com

* * *

In Woke Not Broke, Billy Carson provides the reader with the necessary tools and motivation for achieving a life of both financial success and higher knowledge. I recommend it to all those seeking wisdom and guidance in their life. -Matthew LaCroix - Author of The Stage of Time and The Illusion of Us.

* * *

The timing of this book's release couldn't be more important... the world is in the middle of the coronavirus pandemic, the economy is affecting every country on the planet, and everyone is waiting for things to take a turn and hopefully come to an end. This is truly the time to make changes. Do not wait for anything or anybody. Now is the time to make your move. You need to be ahead of the game with the right tools that this book will provide you on your journey into the future. Jimmy Church - JimmyChurchRadio.com - iHeart Radio and TV host.

* * *

This book is a must read. It definitely opened my mind and changed my relationship between finances and spirituality. Billy Carson did an excellent job of providing the information to make this book a captivating easy read. Mia X AKA Mia Young - Mia X, is an American rapper and author Things My Grandma Told Me, Things My Grandma Showed Me

Copyright © 2020 by Billy Carson

All rights reserved.

No part of this book may be reproduced in any form or by any electronic or mechanical means, including information storage and retrieval systems, without written permission from the author, except for the use of brief quotations in a book review.

First Edition

Library of Congress Control Number: NRC107337

ISBN: 978-0-578-78601-8

Although the author and publisher have made every effort to ensure that the information in this book was correct at press time, the author and publisher do not assume and hereby disclaim any liability to any party for any loss, damage, or disruption caused by errors or omissions, whether such errors or omissions result from negligence, accident, or any other cause. Likewise, the author and publisher assume no responsibility for any false information. No liability is assumed for damages that may result from the reading or use of information contained within.

Publisher info:

4biddenknowledge Inc

https://www.4biddenknowledge.com/online-store

Cover art by José Suárez

ALSO BY BILLY CARSON

Compendium

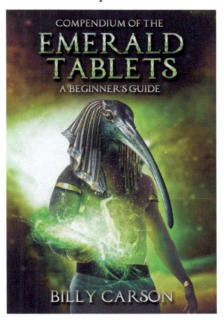

Billy Carson, the founder of 4biddenknowledge Inc. Billy Carson is the Author of 'The Compendium Of The Emerald Tablets' and is an expert host on Deep Space, a new original streaming series by Gaia.

The history of the Emerald Tablets is strange and beyond the belief of modern scientists. Their antiquity is stupendous, dating back some 36,000 years B.C. The author is Thoth, an Atlantean Priest-King who founded a colony in ancient Egypt, wrote the Emerald Tablets in his native Atlantean language which was translated by many famous scholars. This compendium of the Emerald Tablets gives unique insight and understanding of the content. Billy Carson breaks down each tablet for the reader. Because of the tablet's reference to the Egypt and sacred geometry they became a priority reference for those studying the Flower of Life and the Merkaba meditation. ORDER NOW.

Gaia & 4BIDDEN Knowledge TV

Deep Space, a new original streaming series by Gaia, explores the Secret Space Program, revealing extraordinary technologies. Billy Carson also serves as an expert host on Gaia's original series, Ancient Civilizations, in which scholars pieces together our forgotten history around the world.

Catch Billy Carson on 4BIDDENKnowledgeTV

Music

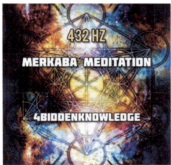

All songs are available on Spotify, Apple Music, iTunes, GooglePlay, Amazon, Deezer, Napster and more...

Billy Carson is a song writer, composer, and producer that hit Billboard in 4 categories for 8 weeks in 2018 with the album 'Return Of Enki' with artist Donny Arcade. Billy Carson's music can be found on 4biddenknowledge.TV, Which is a streaming TV network with conscious shows for the entire family.

Enjoy these and

other titles by

Billy Carson

https://www.4biddenknowledge.com/music

Unite the 99

Are you tired of the sites that block your content because it is less traditional than the other 99% of the population?

Your content is vital and should be seen by the world.

Unite the 99

will not shadow ban your content.

If you are looking for a place to share your content and expose hidden truths, then join this unique social media platform.

Join Unite the 99 Today.

DEDICATION

I dedicate this book to my father, Billy Carson Sr.

Billy Carson Sr.

Although we didn't always see eye to eye, he instilled a hard work ethic in me. From the early age of one years old, I was writing weekly book reports. By the age of twelve, my parents required me to pay rent to live in the family home. I was also required to use my own money to pay for most of my daily needs.

While this would have had an adverse effect on most children, it drove me. This work ethic pushed me to become an innovative thinker and entrepreneur.

For this reason, I thank you Dad. You saw something in me, and you used your own methods to extract it and teach me how to become my own savior.

I love you pops. Rest In POWER!

FOREWORD

There is a strange thing that goes on inside of the 'woke', 'awakened', and/or the 'consciousness' community... and it is this: *Money is bad and being broke is cool.*

I think that this generally stems from big corporations and the uber-rich people that run them. The hedge-fund CEO's that make their money, lots of it, from apparently doing nothing. The companies that dominate the world, health, economy, support wars, and entertain you are profiting from those who suffer the most. I understand where this mindset comes from.

There are also many successful individuals in this world today who are both financially stable and are 'awake'. They have compassion, empathy, and are fully engaged with making our community and planet a better place.

Yes, it is possible to have the mindset of *Woke Doesn't Mean Broke*.

I have been totally *broke* many times in my life. Struggling to pay bills, rent, feeding my family. I didn't like it. The last thing that this is, is, well, *cool*. Getting out of the seemingly endless months or years of worrying about my family wasn't easy at the time, but looking back, it was much more simple than I could have imagined.

One thing is for sure: If I had *Woke Doesn't Mean Broke* twenty years ago, my path to where I find myself and my family today would have been much easier!

The first 40 or so pages of this book lay it all out for you: You must be happy with yourself, be positive about your life and the life of others, and most importantly, be someone that others want to hang out with.

Find your Bliss.

People who have found their Bliss, who are happy with themselves and show compassion to the world, well, they just glow. You can literally see it. Once you achieve these things, complicated decisions become easy to make, life turns into something simpler, and negativity is no longer a part of your circle. Let's face it: People want to hang out with successful people who have integrity and a positive outlook on life.

There is no easy road... doing the right thing takes work. Doing the wrong thing is easy. If you want to stay where you are or sink even lower, well, keep complaining, blame others, point fingers at everyone and everything except you. Surround yourself with other negative 'friends' and see how far that gets you... or, you can make the changes that you know deep down inside need to be done and turn your world into one big, bright ray of sunshine.

Is there a secret to financial security? No, not really... except for this: Don't chase the money. Don't make money your goal to happiness. This is the trap that many fall into and ultimately, years and a lifetime are wasted.

Instead, you want to put yourself in the position of having the money chase you... and in the end, that is happy money.

The first step is simple and it's the real secret of *Woke Doesn't Mean Broke*: Be happy, find your bliss, and surround yourself with other positive individuals. It's really that simple.

The timing of this book's release couldn't be more important... the world is in the middle of the coronavirus pandemic, the economy is effecting every country on the planet, and everyone is waiting for things to take a turn and hopefully come to an end.

This is truly the time to make changes. Do not wait for anything or anybody. Now is the time to make your move. You need to be ahead of the game with the right tools that this book will provide you on your journey into the future.

And here is the other thing: This book is right for any point in history. It doesn't matter when you read it... everything presented here is timeless. The steps to your financial wellbeing and improvements to self are the same today as they will be fifty years from now.

Anybody that knows me personally, or that follows our network and broadcasts, can see that we surround ourselves with companies and sponsors who care about the planet, our community, and they are here to make a change in the world. We practice what we preach, we really do. It's this fundamental attitude of positivity that is the very fabric of everything that we are about. We live it.

In a perfect world, everyone would be giving, awake, conscious, happy, and, well, making money.

Billy Carson, and this book, will help make our world, your world, this big beautiful blue planet that we call home, a better place.

Jimmy Church, host, FADE to BLACK

The Game Changer Network, Inc.

November 1st, 2020

A NOTE FROM THE AUTHOR

If you are reading this, I want you to understand that this book is not about becoming a billionaire. Although, some people reading this will manifest that.

> The main purpose of this book is to teach you how to use your divine power coupled with knowledge of the financial matrix so that you can manifest abundance in the way that you choose is right for you.

Do not allow other people's opinions to discourage you from achieving your goals. People can't be trusted to always have your best interests at heart. This includes friends and family. Others will see your potential and try to destroy your POWER by focusing on your flaws.

Don't apologize for being who you are.
Use it!

Make your flaws into the part of yourself that you embrace, the core of your identity. When someone says, "You're an X," you turn around and say "Yes, I am, what of it? Being an X means I am better able to do Y or Z." Nobody can use a perceived flaw against you unless you let them. *So, don't let them.*

TABLE OF CONTENTS

Chapter 1 The Basics of Financial Health and Wealth

Chapter 2 Motivated

Chapter 3 Modeling

Chapter 4 Direction

Chapter 5 Habits

Chapter 6 Behavior

Chapter 7 Budgets

Chapter 8 Income

Chapter 9 Create Money

Chapter 10 Giving

Chapter 11 Living

Chapter 12 The Looking Glass

Chapter 13 Advantage

Chapter 14 Planning

Chapter 15 Tools

About The Author

Index Find all hot-links and Subtitles Here

PROLOGUE

Being Woke Doesn't Mean Being Broke

What's up, guys? Billy Carson here, with some 4bidden Knowledge.

Our mission as humans is to bring heaven to earth. We need to walk in full abundance 24 hours a day, seven days a week, non-stop.

> **Think about what abundance means to you.
> Whatever that is you can have.**

Don't allow any of these "conscious" people or "woke" people ever tell you that you can't live a happy, wealthy life in the third dimension. Don't let them trick you into believing if you're woke you got to be broke. They've told me for years I need to be a bicycle riding, tattered clothes wearing monk just to obtain a universal connection.

Don't listen to that garbage. *Don't listen to that garbage.*

I manifest abundance everywhere I go non-stop. I expect abundance in my life. To me, abundance means being able to help people. But to help people at the level I help people, I have to be stable. It is my job to be financially affluent because I help people with tens of thousands of dollars every year. I give tens of thousands, not a hundred dollars, not a five-dollar GoFundMe payment, but well-documented help of tens of thousands of dollars every single year.

Now, in order for me to give those kinds of funds away, I can't be out here making $10 an hour, it just won't work.

What does abundance mean for you?

What's Your Abundance?

If abundance means you want to buy pizzas on Saturday and taking it to the homeless people, you need a little extra money. Maybe abundance means your relationship is sound and things work properly, and everybody in your household is happy. Whatever abundance means to you, go for your goal.

No matter what abundance looks like to you, don't forget, you live in a world of money.

Don't allow people to hook you in the mindset of being poor and broke. Because if you're poor and broken up, your actions are telling people who you are. When you are woke, you can use the law of attraction to manifest the things you want in your life, but when you have a live with less attitude you can't.

Every day, too many people can't manifest their bill payments, and their lights are getting turned off, and the water's getting turned off, and their cars are being repossessed. If your life or the life of your family is constantly "having less than you need" you have a problem. *You have a serious problem.*

If you're broke, you're not utilizing the divine source energy within you. If you're caught up in being broke, you really need to seek some assistance and some help. Take the time to read some self-help books, read some financial books, learn how to do goal setting, and put into action your plans for short-term, medium-term, and long-term goals.

You need to be aware of what's out in the world, to look into alternative modes of investing. Learn to analyze your budget and figure out where you're wasting money you could take and invest in yourself. These are the things you need to be doing instead of being tricked into being broke! I'm telling you, don't be tricked into thinking that because you're woke you got to be broke. Don't fall for that garbage.

Plenty of people are out in the world who want you to do good for yourself, but many of them never want you to do better than them. Remember that. They want you to do good but never better than them.

Keeping It Real

So, like I have been saying, you need to be able to operate in this matrix. We're in a matrix and without the right knowledge. This matrix is deadly. Force must be met with force.

A revolution on this planet can not happen with a bunch of people sitting in robes on prepaid cell phones making Instagram posts. I mean, keep it real. Sitting around without action will not change the world.

To change the world, you have to be able to plug in with power people. You need to be able to flex a little and attract people into the system, into this conscious system we're trying to create to revolutionize the world.

Why do I move the way I move? Because I'm a person in this third dimension, I'm on a mission to plug in with power people. I attract people in key positions of power; people in athletics, people in government, people in entertainment, people in all different areas of life, all different walks of life who are in power positions.

Power positions are necessary so when we say, "Go, we need this done," things happen. The matrix bends to our will.

I can't hold $8 an hour minimum wage job, drive a beat-up Junker, and hope I can muster up enough money to give a guy a free sandwich. If this is me, I am not using the divine energy inside of me. I mean, bless the guy for caring and sharing, don't make me wrong, but I'm on a world-changing mission right now. I'm not on no 'give a guy a $5 sandwich mission.'

People start at all different levels. Today, I'm a top-level guy; you know what I'm saying. The world won't change with everybody being poor and broke and being woke; if you think it will, you're disillusioned. Don't let your energy go to waste, to waste. Yes, the world needs people at all different levels. You might have started on a lower level like me, but eventually, you must grow and graduate from being broke. Go ahead and gain a healthy ego and see what you can accomplish.

So, like I said guys, I'm telling you don't fall for these gypsies and their tricks- I call them gypsy tricks. Those are the fake woke people. They want you to do good but never better than them. As soon as they found out you got a little something, they are angry at you. Don't fall for the tricks. Guys, manifest abundance.

Try This

Start your own business. Start your own companies. Invest in yourself. Buy real estate. Find ways to help out your family. Change your attitude, your beliefs, and your effort you put into your daily living.

If you're a musician with a pile of produced music, you better have it out to be heard. If you don't upload anything on iTunes, Spotify, Apple Music, Tidal, Deezer, then your music is still sitting on your computer. What are you doing? Get that music out.

I own 120 songs in distribution. Don't contact me about how to make your music famous. Go to a distro kid, go to TuneCore, go to Engrooves, wherever you can go, and put your music in distribution.

Don't put out one song every month, or one song a year, put out a hundred songs, 200 songs, 300 songs as fast as you possibly can, all going simultaneously, and start making money. It may not be a lot, but it will start to grow. You could be seeing $2-3,000 a month. You could take that money out and reinvest it into something.

I own 120 songs in distribution, and I get a check; every month, a real live check in my hand.

Stop Playing Yourself

If you smoke weed and you don't suffer from any kind of PTSD, cancer, any kind of pains, stop smoking weed. Take that money and invest that money into a business. Stop smoking weed you don't need. Take the money and invest it.

Some of my acquaintances spend $500 to $800 a month on weed, and they aren't even sick. A complete waste of their money. Take that money and invest that money.

If you have kids, save up enough money to buy a rental property. Now, save all that rental income so that when your kids turn 18, they have money to work with. They could start a business. If they decide they want to go to school, that's great too. It is up to them to do whatever they want to do if money isn't an obstacle. You can do this, guys, you need to set your family up the right way to change the world.

Make Power Moves

You guys need to make power moves. Stop getting this mindset, "Oh, I'm conscious now so being poor is good. I'm just a humble being." If those are your thoughts shake your head and say, "No!" and stop and look up the definition of humble. I don't think you're going to like the definition of humble.

The definition of humble is a low person. Humble is seen like you're beneath the gutter. You need to understand what that word means. You need to understand that you shouldn't confidence confused with ego either.

I said the other day if I decide to play Michael Jordan, if I take the challenge to play against Michael Jordan, you best believe that I believe I'm going to beat him. Period.

That's not ego, it's self-confidence.

Now, are the odds against me that he'll beat me? Yes. And I'll lose? Yes. But if I take the challenge, I guarantee you in my heart of hearts, I believe I'm going to beat him. Period. Or I'm not going to take the challenge. Do you recognize it? Power!

Take the Challenge

I raised five kids and I have two grandchildren. Having a family is not easy. I'm not talking off the top of my head; I know what I'm talking about. Five kids raised in this world, and they're all grown adults. Nobody's locked up, nobody's in jail, nobody is on drugs. That's powerful, man.

If you take the challenge to start a family, you are going to step into a fight. Why? Because when you start a family, you enter a battle.

But wait, you're going to take the challenge to create a family and you don't have any plans to supply them with any means; what are you doing? Ah, you took the challenge with no confidence.

It's time to step up and take your challenge seriously. You have to leave something behind for everybody, leave your legacy. You need to find a way to break this cycle of suffering and begging. At some point, somebody has to step up and make the effort or nothing changes.

So, drop your anger for me, don't blame me because I stepped up. I came from underneath the gutter.

Where I came from, the crossing guards would rob you on the way to school. Everyone had holes in their sneakers because we couldn't afford shoes. I would put cardboard in my shoes to keep my feet from touching the street. One time, I had to wear football cleats because football cleats were on sale for $2.99 at K-Mart, and I had to wear football cleats to school as my school sneakers and kids laughed at me every single day.

I wore pants too small because I outgrew them so fast. They got so tight my crotch ripped open, and I had to sit with my legs closed to hide my underwear because of a hole in my crotch.

Eventually, I got more pants, but still only two pairs for the entire school week. Can you guess what I used to do? I used to buy the 79-cent pack of dye from the grocery store Winn-Dixie and I bleach them then dye them overnight to a different color.

The next day I went to school wearing a different colored pair of pants. As far as everyone knew, I had at least three or four different colored pairs of pants every week. These are the kind of things I went through.

The food situation was just as bad. If school was out, summer or winter break or whatever, Cairo syrup and toast was all I had for the whole day. The only other food I received was given to me when I got to school. Yeah, the kind of money I grew up with was the nonexistent kind.

So, I took the challenge. I made a guarantee to myself and by the time I turned 12 going on 13, I started selling newspaper subscriptions for the Miami News. I became the top newspaper subscription person, and I took all that money, 100 percent of it, and invested it into electronics. At 14 I started an electronics company and by 15 I was making more than my parents. By 16, I moved out of my parent's house, had two cars, an apartment, and still graduated from high school all the while running my own business.

So, when I come across these people saying they can't do this and "I don't have a clue how I'm gonna get this done," or "I can't figure it out," I don't have any time for them. I'm not an excuses man. I came from underneath the gutter, man, underneath the gutter!

Do the Research

Have you come across the poem by Tupac, *The Rose that Grew from Concrete*? I'm that guy, but I'm not the only one that can do that. Everybody can do it. It's inside of everybody. Every single one of y'all can do that; it's just a matter of if you want to.

Sometimes, people claim, "I don't know what to do." Well, do the work and the work is called research. When I was growing up, I had encyclopedias and dictionaries. I had real books you had to go pick up from the store, from the library. I'd go to the library or the bookstore and study.

In 1998, I met an exchange student in a building that I was living in. I had a health care company and I had just started a little discount health care program. Then came this guy, he was an Arabian guy, he says, "I need to do an internship with a business to build a website." I go "what is a website?" Remember this is 1998. I said, "what's a website?" He said, "Well, a marketing piece for your company is on the internet." Yep, you guessed it, I go "What's the internet?"

At that time, something like 20 websites existed. All the major companies were players- IBM had one and a few other companies, they were just really simple one-page sites. High-speed internet and all those other bells and tricked out sites hadn't been invented yet.

I said, "Sure, man, let's go, let's do it."

I went to this guy's house, started giving him the information, and I sat over his shoulder while he literally created with HTML a website for my company. Everything he did was incredible. The work was amazing and I thought this is the future. After he was done with the project, he went back to Arabia.

The Next Step

What did I do? I went to a rental center and I got a $19.95 a week computer, a Packard Bell, I used to call it a "Packard from Hell." It had a 2-gigabyte hard drive and it crashed all the time. Still, I did the work. I connected it with AOL dial-up and started an Internet company, Dot-Com Marketing Group, from scratch, ground zero.

How did I learn all the coding and programming? I used to go to the bookstore and read the books at the bookstore. I didn't buy them. Instead, I took my little notes, went home and duplicated the work at home.

Next, I said, "Okay, if I can create a nice website template for mortgage companies, this is something that they'll love, it's a permanent Ad online." These ads didn't require me to produce products; I didn't need any SKU numbers. All I needed to create a site for the next company was change the colors, change the names around, change the contact information, and some interest rates, and they were good to go.

So, what did I do? I got out the yellow pages. Without any cell phones, all these Google search options hadn't been invented yet either. I got out the yellow pages, the real thick book, and I would cold call. Monday, Tuesday, Wednesday you'd hear me, "My name is Billy Carson with Dot-Com Marketing Group, I'd like to talk to you about getting a website for your mortgage company."

Call, call, call, call, all day long, all day long. I pitched them the ad, and I set my appointments up for Thursday and Friday. Then I would go out to these appointments that I set for myself and sell them websites. Saturday and Sunday, I would make the websites. I was making 8-10 grand a week, eight to ten thousand a week!

Eventually, I got some people working for me, I doubled it, I tripled it, and I quadrupled it. Turned it into a multi-million-dollar corporation. I took that company and I sold it. I cashed out millions of dollars.

So, guys, don't buy into this concept of being woke you got to be broke.

Control the Matrix

You have to play in this matrix. Don't be disillusioned, thinking that you're going to walk around in this matrix and suffer. Suffering is an option. Don't believe the craziness. There's no need or reason for you to own all the power and knowledge that you own and choose not to consciously manipulate the matrix. How can you live with this power and not be able to pay your light bill, your water bill, or make a car payment? No need for that.

I am not saying you need to go out and be a multi-millionaire, but your needs should be met with ease. There should be no suffering, no anguish, no calling up relatives and begging for their help and asking for money. This behavior shouldn't exist, not if you really own the path of being conscious.

Abundance should flow to you instantaneously. Anything you need, boom, magically it becomes yours. Use your intuition to recognize and realize when opportunities are arising in your life. Jump on those opportunities and become a visionary. Grow to be able to realize what's coming next, to own the next big thing.

Find a Need and Fill It

You maybe trying to figure out what you are supposed to do in your life, how are you supposed to make money. The first thing you have to do is find a need and fill it. To do that, find your passion. Find something your like or can do really well. Now if you find a need for this thing, you can make money with it.

Whatever it is, whatever that passion you have is you need to own it.

If you have a passion for drawing or making art, say, "Okay, I'm art." Either you are already good at it or you need to perfect your art. The next step is now to find out what need is there for art **today**? Consider, there's a huge need for all these conscious accounts to get a lot of good graphic content out. There're millions and millions and millions of clients right there that you can tap into if you can create good graphic art.

Create an account and go Brand a look. Add that account to your resume. Maybe the first one you do for free and continue building your resume for a few months. You give them a test-run. Create all the artwork upfront they will need for the next three months. When they like it, then you can negotiate with them. Have them bring you on board. Finally, you get paid for your passion.

See, this is the kind of thinking you need to have out here, guys, in this matrix. Learn to manipulate this matrix and beat it up.

Fine the Loopholes

Have you figured out what you are supposed to do in your life, how you are supposed to make money? The first thing you do is find a need and fill it. Find something you are passionate about, something you can say, "I like this thing and I can do it really well."

Whatever it is, whatever that passion is you need to own it. This is the kind of thinking you need out here in this matrix. You must learn to manipulate this matrix and beat it up.

Fine the Loopholes

Find the loopholes in everything. In everything that exists, find all the loopholes in it. Find the loopholes in taxes, your ability to save and invest, loopholes so you can make time for your family while still having your personal success. Find all the loopholes; dig into it and dig deep.

I'm going to give you a loophole right here.

Let's say you want to buy a nicer car. If you do, you want to build your credit up. Car credit is very tricky. With car credit, you're only going to get a car for the same amount of money you spent on your last car.

So, if your last car was $30,000, then your next car credit is $30,000. Even if you can make the payments for a car with a cost over sixty or seventy thousand, you're not going to get it unless you put a lot of money down.

Well, this is what you do, guys. First, you get a small extra car, not your primary car, but a two or three-thousand-dollar Junker. You put down about a thousand dollars and the rest you finance. After four months of making payments, you refinance that car. Your car is now considered paid off.

You don't even need to drive these cars, you just need to build your car credit. Now you go back, and you double up on that first car. You pay that money, you refinance it, make a payment for four more months, refinance it again.

It's time to get a bigger car. You keep stepping it up until you can get a big, big car. Now if you got a car worth $30,000, you can refinance that one, now you can probably step up to a $45- or $50,000 car. Pay that for four or five months, refinance that car, then trade it in before you get negative equity in it for a car costing $80 to $90,000. There's your loophole.

Want an even larger matrix shift? I can tell you how to drive an exotic car for free.

One day I said to myself, "I'd like to drive Rolls Royce." But I didn't want to pay $3,000 a month out of my income for that, and an additional thousand dollars for insurance. How can I get this car for free? I can if I create an income source to cover the cost.

My end game? I bought myself a Rolls Royce, rented it out for 10 days a month, and drove it for the rest. The car is free for me. I'm driving a Ghost!

I did this by finding a reliable source that knew how to handle my car the way I liked. The source, an exotic car rental company. Our partnership agreement covered the car payment, insurance, and some profit. A win in every direction.

Come on, man, you got to play in this matrix, or it is no fun. You need to dominate this matrix. If you don't dominate the matrix, the matrix will dominate you. Every single thing I do, I find a way to beat this matrix down and bend it to my will. Everything I do, I'm looking with the intent for an opportunity to manipulate this system. I'm manipulating this system at every angle, every possible angle. I'm not inside the box thinking, "I can go and get a job, and this is what my income is for the week, and now here's my budget, and with this budget, this is what I can pay for."

No, I operate with power. If I want something new, I find an income source to pay for it. Period. Guys, think smart.

The False Control

Everything here in this system has you thinking it's a parameter that you must follow and live by. Parameters don't block me; they disappear for me; they don't even exist. I find a way where other people think there is no way. I can always find a way.

When you see people thinking a cup is half empty, remind yourself, "No, the cup is not." Some people say, "Well, the cup is half full." They are so proud of themselves. No, no, no, no. The cup is always full. You know why? On top of the liquid there are atmospheric gases. The oxygen that you're breathing in is a gas, and mixing with this oxygen is hydrogen, Krypton, helium, argon, and various other gases. These gases are mixing with what were you inhaling, and that gas is inside the cup too. The cup is always full.

My cup is always running over, there's no such thing as a half-empty cup.

You see, there's no such thing as 'the sky's the limit' because the sky for me doesn't exist either. The sky doesn't exist. This is the mindset that you need. If you want to dominate this matrix, if you want to make money, then you find a way.

Someone has to break the cycle. Stop falling for the foolishness from these gypsies, talking about you got to be broke to be woke. Stop walking around stinking in rot raggedy shoes, on raggedy pants, and all dirty riding bicycles everywhere. If you want that life, do it; but, if that's not what you want to do, realize there is a choice. Don't be afraid to do what you like. Don't be afraid to be who you like.

Live Your Best Life

I'll tell you what, I'm going to live my best life 24/7, seven days a week non-stop; non-stop. Why? Because my mission is to bring heaven to earth and I'm in heaven. I'm in heaven now. I'm not going to wait till I die to live, I'm going to live heaven now. You won't find me missing out on trips around the world, unable to enjoy this planet so that people can think I'm woke. That's stupid, absolutely dumb. Dumb.

I'm gonna live now.

I'm gonna live in the now and enjoy this life and when my spirit separates from this avatar body and recycles back into the system, I'm gonna come back and live again! You see what we do. I'm not going to live through five and six lifetimes, living poor and broke and suffering in agony and everything else. Forget that, I'm gonna be like Thoth.

I'm going to choose to incarnate at will. That's my goal. Do you see the mindset from me is different? Not, "Oh man, I wonder what's gonna happen when I die." That's the difference between my thought process and a lot of other people's thought processes.

This Universe Doesn't Recognize Weakness

I'm a power person. I deal in power--the power of my mindset, power of my thoughts. Everything is power. You can't come weak with this universe; this universe doesn't recognize weak frequencies. It doesn't recognize low frequencies. It doesn't recognize weakness, period.

What happens in the wild when a weak animal is found? The weak animals get devoured. If a lion is chasing a big thick fat wildebeest and sees an old sickly animal, that lion will cut the chase and grab the old decaying animal. The lion always looks for the weakest point.

You need to look for the weakest point and take your break, find your loophole. Be strong. Man, you need to be witty. If you don't think that you're witty or you don't know these kinds of things, you need to help yourself get on the witty level. Forget every reason you made up to be anything less.

You got smartphones in your pockets. Take it out. Everything you need is on YouTube. Everything you want to know is on Google. Pick any search engine. You can find a lot of blogs and articles that think outside the box. Find how to create wealth and alternative ways of making money. All this stuff is available right at your fingertips, so stop going, "Man, I wish I knew this."

There are about 10 million articles currently out there on the internet about alternative ways to make money. There are millions of them. You have no excuse. There is no excuse, so stop being complacent. Stop waiting for things to fall into your lap. Stop begging and pleading and hoping things happen to you and go out there and dominate this planet.

Dominate this world. Make things happen for yourself. Power gotta meet power. You can't move as weakness. If you move weak, you're going to get devoured out there.

Join Me at the Top

I'm just dropping a couple of tidbits on you guys. Man, I appreciate you guys. I love you all. I want to see everybody do good. Everybody needs to come up. I'm not one of these people that want to be the one on top and witness everybody else failing. Everybody can make it.

Everybody can reach whatever level of success in your mind that you think is good for you and your family. And when you reach it, I want to applaud you and I want to be happy for you. I'm not one of these haters out there that just wants to see everybody doing bad because they don't feel like they can do anything themselves.

Like one guy was commenting on my post regarding how I donated 12 million dollars since 2004 till now in the form of money, revenue, scholarships, building YMCAs and sports centers, and all kinds of support. His comment was that wasn't good enough, and his reason? Because I own a Rolls Royce!

He told me I shouldn't have a Rolls Royce. He told me I should be riding a bicycle. So, the 12 million wasn't enough? Do you see the mindset of the gypsies? I hate to use the term "gypsies" but that's the only thing I can relate them to. People, get out of that mindset. There is no revolution on this planet with a bunch of people thinking everybody needs to be broke and poor, it's not going to happen.

Jesus Christ

Some people don't believe he existed, Jesus Christ, but I know he existed. His name, though, was Yeshua. After all the research that I've done, my opinion is he was never crucified. Instead, he was a very spiritual person who traveled the world. He went to Tibet to learn the mystic arts, he went to India to learn Reiki healing, and he went to Egypt to learn the ancient Egyptian mysteries.

Yeshua taught reincarnation; the story in the Bible is actually largely inaccurate. But regardless of the point, the point of why I'm bringing him up is, everywhere he went, he manifested abundance.

This is a man who had no job, no income, no money, no financial resources whatsoever, but he manifested abundance everywhere he went. Everywhere he went, he had food, clothing, a place to stay. People rushed and flocked to him to give him whatever he needed wherever he went. You know why? Power to power. It's a power play. When I walk into a room, I expect the same thing. I expect power. I expect people to come up and say hi to me and shake my hand. And I give them the same "hey, I appreciate you" every time.

I feel my power. And you must gain that mindset. You got to get with people on your level and understand the power play. And when you have the power play mindset, everything comes to you. People will flock to you and give you stuff. If you need some help or assistance, people are going to look out for you.

People Take Care of Power

If I go on the internet and say, "Hey guys, I need a graphic designer to make me two images for this project I'm working on as a volunteer, I'm gonna have a hundred people do that right away". And it's not because I got a million followers and all this other kind of stuff, it's because people understand power to power.

They want to help out, they want to be part of power. You need to understand that, too.

So, when you change your mindset from weakness to power, when you stop begging and hoping, and you command greatness and abundance through power, it appears.

"I command that this need be met. I command that this opportunity be met. I command that this situation be taken care of." When you command greatness, you can relax and enjoy what happens in your life. Just like a snap of your fingers, just like that, things are going to flip around for you and you're going to recognize how much power you really is truly yours. Then it's just a matter of how you can control that power.

Just like the Jedi, you exist with the dark side and the light side. You are able to control both. You have the power inside of you. There's no need for suffering. There is no need to struggle with being broke and poor. Situations where you can't keep a car, you don't have bus money, no food in your house, all that should not exist. If you operate in power mode, in the law of attraction and in consciousness, and through helping other people, you can have whatever abundance is for you.

I've noticed something I do is I help people every single day. Every single day, I make it my business to do something to help somebody. I've been doing it for decades. Decades. So, if I get myself a nice car or a nice watch or a nice house, you know what, I deserve it. Plus, I understand that I deserve it.

If you don't love yourself, you can't love anybody else. Like I said earlier, you need to help yourself. If you're on an airplane having some kind of malfunction and those oxygen masks drop down from the ceiling, you have to put your oxygen mask on you first. After your mask is on and oxygen is flowing, then you can help somebody. You understand that. Don't forget it.

Peace and love from 4bidden Knowledge. I love y'all.

INTRODUCTION

Welcome to Financial Health and Wealth

This entire book is a series of stand-alone lessons. What this means is you can open the book to any unit and start reading. Each golden nugget of information will help you move towards your goal of being woke and Not Broke.

Through these articles, you will explore topics and details that:

- Support new information you need to create financial independence
- Addresses habits both good and bad
- How to develop and change unwanted habits into something useful
- Modify your behavior to share who you really are
- Making a budget that works to meet your short-term and long-term goals
- Live within your means
- Increase your means to create your dream life
- Teach you how to create money
- Build your passion to build your success
- Eliminate debt for your lifetime
- Successfully manage banking and credit card activity
- Understand how giving can improve your self-awareness
- Discover at what age you need to address each financial issue
- How to use circumstances to your advantage for wealth and personal growth
- What it means to make a plan and develop your personal financial health and wealth
- And much more

Even though you can start on any page, I suggest you go through the book first as a quick read. As you do, mark things that you want to go through again in more detail.

Do the Work!

At the end of each article, concept, and share is a section labeled *Do the Work!* These instruction sections are designed to help you dig in and do the work that moves you forward. Knowledge is a great support, but without the action that knowledge directs nothing in your life ever changes.

On your second pass through the book, make sure you *Do the Work!*

1

THE BASICS OF FINANCIAL HEALTH AND WEALTH

Before you can fly, you need to walk. It is important to learn to open up to possibilities, to understand your options, and to know that choosing to live a financially balanced life is often easier than you make it. A little knowledge can take you farther and faster than you thought possible.

Getting Started

You are here, you are ready to take your first step towards your financial health and wealth. Go ahead, start, and read the first unit, *Why It May Be Important to Be Wealthy*.

WHY IT MAY BE IMPORTANT TO BE WEALTHY

Few topics elicit such a wide range of opinions as wealth. It seems that we either pursue wealth with reckless abandon or downplay the importance of having money altogether. While money isn't the only thing that matters, there are few substitutes for those areas of life where money excels.

Wealth does have its advantages.

What are your current beliefs regarding money and wealth? Do you believe that money is the root of all evil or do you desire to have great wealth? Maybe you respect those with accumulated wealth. Have your beliefs in regard to wealth had an impact on your finances? Consider these advantages to being wealthy:

Solve challenges.

The fact that other qualities like love, family, friendships, and spirituality are important doesn't minimize the importance of wealth. Consider the many challenges that money solves quickly and easily.

- Cracked windshield
- Utility bills
- Toothache
- Hunger
- Career change
- Further education
- Ripped pants
- Your child wants to attend an Ivy League school
- A desire to own a motorcycle

Freedom.

With a sufficient level of wealth, you can quit your job and spend your days doing what truly fulfills you. You can live anywhere you choose and do nearly anything you desire. Money and wealth increase the options available to you. How would you spend each day if you didn't have to go to work?

Security.

Wealth provides security in different forms. It provides financial security against negative financial events, such as unexpected care repairs or medical bills. You can also better secure your home and care for your health. Money provides a safeguard in multiple ways.

Elimination of undesirable tasks.

If you loathe cleaning the house, mowing the lawn, shopping, doing your taxes, or even driving, you can hire someone else to do these for you.

Help others.

When you have more money than necessary for your basic needs, you have the option of applying the excess to enhancing the lives of others. Giving money to charity is one way to accomplish this. You could also provide funds in a more direct manner to those in need, including friends and family.

Take a break.

Wealth gives you the option of calling a timeout and realigning yourself. Life can become a series of projects or adventures with a healthy break in-between. The option to literally work hard and play hard exists.

There's a difference between the typical idea of playing hard and the "playing hard" options available to the wealthy. There's a difference between partying on the weekends after a long week at the office and spending a month in Hawaii learning to surf.

Status.

This goes beyond impressing the neighbors. The wealthy have advantages socially, politically, and when dealing with the legal system. There are many advantages, considerations, and niceties extended to the wealthy that are commonly unavailable to the average person.

It's true that money doesn't solve every hardship in life, but it does solve many challenges and provide a myriad of opportunities. The freedom that comes with wealth and the opportunity to help others are perhaps the most satisfying advantages.

Do the Work!

If any of these advantages are included in your life goals, then being wealthy would make them possible. Seek further education in the mindset and skills that could bring you wealth and work on them each day. Consistent action toward your goals over time yields positive results!

WEALTH IS FOR THE SMART!

Do you believe that being predisposed with the ability to become wealthy is the only way to earn good money? Fortunately, the reality is that wealth belongs to those who are smart in the ways they go about claiming and creating it.

Being able to make money even without having that background from the onset is definitely attainable, as long as you put some thought and creativity into your wealth making opportunities.

Making solid financial decisions and choosing sound investment options are simply the best ways to become wealthy once and for all.

Here are three simple, yet effective, tips you can apply to your life that can help to create the wealth you deserve:

Break down your big goal.

"I want to be rich!" Just about everybody you can think of has said this at one point or another in his or her life. Being wealthy is something that most of us dream about -- however very few are able to achieve -- because we look at it as a large, insurmountable goal. Remember:

- Looking at your desired achievement as an overwhelmingly huge goal makes it very difficult to obtain. In fact, it almost always amounts to a mere dream if we overlook setting smaller, attainable goals towards that major goal. Use this as one of the keys to becoming wealthy.
- Break your financial goal into smaller, more achievable ones that you can set reasonable time frames on. You'll be surprised to see how you progress towards your huge goal once you set smaller ones that are much easier to achieve.

Avoid using credit if you can't pay by cash.

One of the simplest and most effective tips for building wealth is to avoid credit. And what that means essentially is avoiding credit if you see no way to repay it in the short term. Remember:

- If it isn't possible for you to have the cash to settle your credit card expenses each month, then avoid making purchases with the card.
- By choosing to purchase only what you can afford to purchase with cash, you can undoubtedly start to create wealth for yourself.

Live within your means.

Sure, there will be things you see that you want to do, acquire, or simply accomplish. However:

- If it's not easy cash-wise for you to do something or acquire something, then perhaps you should leave it alone for the time being.
- It's very likely that something you aren't able to do this month or this year, will be more than possible in the near future.
- You should only focus on doing things and acquiring things that you are financially able to do without stress. The more often you practice that approach, the closer you'll be to having financial freedom.

Creating wealth requires very little money and quite a bit of financial "smarts." The more reasoning, common sense, and thought you put into your financial decisions, the sooner you'll find yourself becoming wealthy. Count yourself amongst the masters of wealth by applying some creative thinking.

Do the Work!

Achieve your financial goals by taking it in stride and believe that you are predisposed to the same wealth as anyone else!

THE WEALTHY MINDSET -- HOW YOUR THOUGHTS AFFECT YOUR FINANCIAL FUTURE

Surely, you've heard the saying that when you believe in yourself, you can do anything. It's a piece of advice that gets passed around for a reason -- because it's 100% true! It especially applies to having a wealthy mindset.

Even if you're starting from, with the right steps, the sky really is the limit.

Believing in Yourself

The first step is to believe that you can accomplish anything when you set your mind to it. You can prove to yourself that you believe you *can* become wealthy by making concrete plans.

Financially, where are you and where do you want to be? It doesn't matter how far you need to travel; you need to set out plans today.

The next thing you need to work on is the "how" of it all. What actions will you take to achieve the wealth you desire?

When you write these plans down, you'll be holding something concrete that you can believe. You're making yourself a promise for the future. You can refer to your plans often as you begin to use your wealthy mindset to take swift action.

Starting from Scratch

Having the correct mindset can be difficult if you're starting from nothing. However, this is when a positive attitude is needed the most! Just think about all the other people that would have given up and tell yourself that you're not going to be one of them.

It may help you to look up inspiring stories. There are plenty of people in the world that started with next to nothing who built extremely profitable companies and other streams of income. The difference between them and the average person wasn't a superhuman power; it was a simple will to achieve great things. They embraced a wealthy mindset, and they didn't take no for an answer.

Expanding Your Wealth

If you're looking to expand your wealth, a proper mindset can also help you do so. Check your plans. How far away you are from your ultimate goals?

When it comes to wealth expansion since you have some money you may want to take some risks. However, be careful and make sure you have back up plans and back up revenue just in case one of your risks don't pan out.

Wealthy Affirmations

Nothing gets you in the right mindset like a good affirmation. You can obtain a book on affirmations that pertain to wealth or you can write your own. Writing your own affirmations is a good idea because you can incorporate your personal life goals into them.

Tell yourself: "I am achieving my goals for wealth" or "I am making money," and you'll continue to do so.

Do the Work!

Keep an eye out for your future. Protect your financial future by being a forward-thinker. Developing a positive mindset *now* will help to ensure that you have a prosperous future. These strategies can help you develop and maintain a wealthy mindset and literally transform your life.

HOW TO DETERMINE YOUR FINANCIAL HEALTH

You probably have regular checkups from your dentist and doctor. Even cars and pianos require regular tune-ups. Most individuals fail to do the same for their financial health.

While experts can analyze your finances, most of us are entirely capable of measuring our own financial health.

However, we either don't think about it or choose to avoid it. Determining the financial health of a company requires looking at several things. The same is true for your personal finances. Follow these steps and give yourself a financial check-up:

Determine your net worth.

Your net worth is the number you're left with after subtracting your debt from your assets.

- The primary examples of assets are cash and other securities, the current market value of your personal property, and the equity in your home.
- Essentially all your debt is a liability--the balance remaining on your credit cards, automobile loan, mortgage, and student loans. Any other money you owe would be included.
- Note that high net worth isn't everything. You could have a painting worth $1 million on your wall, but still, be struggling to pay your bills. Your cash flow is important, too.

Determine your cash flow.

Consider how much money you're spending each month compared to the amount you're receiving.

- Tally your household income and subtract your spending. Exclude any amounts you're saving or investing.
- A larger, positive cash flow provides financial breathing room and psychological comfort. A negative cash flow suggests you're getting deeper into debt each month.

What is your savings rate?

Divide your monthly savings by your income. Include any contributions to your retirement accounts, too. Most financial experts recommend a 15% savings rate. Obviously, a greater number will result in more savings.

If you're saving less than 15%, strive to save more. Increasing it by just 1-2% each month will result in a healthy savings rate in short order.

Do you have the necessary insurance?

Different situations require different types of insurance. Asking yourself a few questions will help determine the types of insurance you need. If you ask yourself all the "what if" questions, you'll have the necessary answers.

Protecting your home, health, income, and valuable assets are reasonable places to start.

How much is in your emergency fund?

Could you weather the loss of a job, a major car repair, or any of life's other unpleasant surprises? Experts recommend an emergency fund equivalent to 3-6 months of living expenses. That might seem like a tall order, but you can chip away at it a little at a time.

How much do you expect to have at retirement?

A calculator will enable you to extrapolate the value of your nest egg well into the future.

Are you on schedule to retire with adequate financial resources?

Are you prepared for major expenses in the future?

If you are aware your car is nearing the end of its lifespan or major educational expenses are coming, are you in the position to handle them?

Do the Work!

Your answers to these questions will reveal the health of your financial situation. Pay close attention to your financial health. Putting a priority on your finances will result in choices that enhance your financial well-being.

2

MOTIVATED

Before you dig into the details of financial health and wealth, let's strengthen your motivation. How will you keep going when the path ahead is new and unknown? How will you make decisions about what to do next? Very important, how will you handle when you are overwhelmed with more information than you can manage?

Getting Started

Read through these inspiring shares. Each can give you a heads-up into what can happen when you are educated and prepared to make the best decisions possible during the different stages of your life's journey.

WHAT TWINKIES CAN TEACH ABOUT RESILIENCY

We all make mistakes, but you can still succeed as long as you know how to make a comeback. While snack cakes may not have all the answers to life's riddles, the humble Twinkie certainly knows how to pick itself up and start over.

You may remember the headlines last year when Twinkies briefly disappeared from the stores after their parent company went bankrupt. Soon, they were back on the shelves in a turnaround billed as "The Sweetest Comeback in the History of Ever."

Use these tips to stage your own revival:

Count on your friends.

Hostess couldn't have done it alone. The Twinkie comeback was driven by its loyal fans who campaigned on social media. To be resilient, you must develop strong friendships.

Simplify your message.

Twinkie advertising focused on their return date, affectionately known as Cake-Face Day. Identify your top priority and avoid getting bogged down in details.

Tap into nostalgia.

A few financial troubles couldn't dim people's fond childhood memories of Twinkies. Keep a hold of the good things in your past, even when making changes is necessary.

Pick a good name.

The words we choose to use have a powerful effect on our thinking. Twinkies might have disappeared forever if they were just another sponge cake.

Provide value to others.

Not everything in life can be deep-fried and full of sugar. Actually, it's better that way. The important thing is to concentrate on how your actions serve others and why they appreciate what you do.

Enjoy these Comeback Lessons. Keep your faith and strength will follow.

Learn from your missteps.

Building on your failures allows you to learn and grow. Any experience can make you a better person if you handle it constructively.

Hold yourself accountable.

You may need to clean up before you can move on. Repair any harm you cause to others and yourself. Inform your boss you missed a deadline, but you're restructuring your work. You'll be quicker the next time.

Spot patterns.

Common behavior is to make the same errors over and over. Figure out what conditions sabotage your diet or make you late for work. Then, you'll be able to make the necessary changes.

Take risks.

Live your courage. You may make a few blunders while you're seizing valuable opportunities.

Seek inspiration.

The world is full of role models even better than Twinkies. Nelson Mandela and Martha Stewart both put their lives back together after prison.

Forgive yourself.

Others will be influenced by the attitude you adopt. If you pardon yourself, you're likely to find more acceptance all around you.

Offer second chances.

Extend mercy to others too. They're likely to return the favor.

Acknowledge the past.

Of course, questions may linger about your previous conduct. Be forthright about the facts. Let your current actions prove that you've matured.

Build up your capabilities.

For more promising results the second time around, you may need to beef up your resources. If you struggled in your last job, consider going back to school for an additional degree or certification. Talk with a therapist to help your second marriage last longer than your first.

Start now.

Stop dwelling on all the reasons why it would be difficult for you to make a comeback. Decide to do your best from this moment on. You may be pleasantly surprised by the results.

Do the Work!

Why let the past hold you back? With a positive attitude and enough effort, you can put any setback behind you and build a brighter future. Twinkies taught us that!

WHAT AN OLYMPIC BRONZE MEDALIST CAN TEACH YOU ABOUT HEALTHY COMPETITION

Would you believe Olympic athletes who win bronze medals tend to be happier than those who win the silver? Research on the world's biggest sporting spectacle offers lessons on how to deal with winning and losing.

Studies show that second place winners rate their experience as being less satisfying than those who came in third. It appears that silver medalists focus on nearly missing the gold, while bronze medalists take pride in their performance. Try these tips for coping with the thrill of victory and the learning that comes with temporary defeats.

Learn how to enjoy the game of life whether you win or lose on any given day.

Of course, you're more likely to work in an office than play Olympic sports, so your issues may look a little different from the average gymnast. Still, you may find it important to distinguish between friendly rivalry and being cutthroat.

Accept your feelings.

Maybe you feel embarrassed by your competitive drive. Remember that competition and ambition are natural, and you decide how to best channel it.

Have fun.

You can have a good time while you're earning a living. Look for the humor in office politics and turn routine tasks into a game.

Help each other.

While you're pursuing your own objectives, pay attention to the rest of the team. Volunteer your assistance when a colleague is carrying a heavy load. Praise a coworker for their contribution to successful group projects.

Be specific.

It's easier to evaluate your progress when you have a clear definition of success. Examine your values and focus your energy on your top priorities.

Keep learning.

Competition benefits you when you're increasing your skills and knowledge. Sign up for training opportunities at work. Take online courses and subscribe to the leading publications in your industry.

Lighten up.

Are you in a high-pressure field? Make time for cooperative activities where you can relax without feeling judged.

While competition may be more intense in your career activities, competition can color your personal life too. Protect your peace of mind and relationships with these ideas:

Compare down.

Thinking about how you measure up to those with more money or fame can leave you feeling depressed. Try considering those less fortunate so you can recognize your blessings and put things in perspective.

Put forth effort.

If the idea of competition makes you feel nervous, fix your mind on your own hard work. You may find yourself taking on adventures you once shied away from.

Try again.

You're a winner as long as you find satisfaction in persevering. Use setbacks as an opportunity for learning and growth.

Make back-up plans.

It may be time to shift gears if you're feeling burned out. You may want to give yourself five years to write a novel or travel the world before you turn to other options.

Provide a role model.

Our attitude about competition starts in childhood. Think about what you're teaching your sons and daughters. Share you love them regardless of their performance. Build their confidence and curiosity.

Rejoice for others.

The downside of competition disappears when you can enjoy other's victories as much as your own. Celebrate when a friend wins a promotion or lucks out on the lottery.

Do the Work!

Strike a balance between competitive drive and team spirit. Create your own definition of success where you help each individual feel like a winner while you work to beat your previous record.

QUICK RELIEF FOR INFORMATION OVERLOAD

If you feel like you're drowning in information, it's not just your imagination. According to a recent Forbes article, we've created more information in the last 10 years than in all the rest of human history. Consider the 300 exabytes of information today compared to 30 exabytes 10 years ago. Meanwhile, that deluge is more than an annoyance.

Studies show that being bombarded with too many facts and choices can increase stress and impair your judgment.

Take back control of your time. Learn how to make this growing body of information work for you. Lighten your load. Filter out messages that have little use or significance for you.

Cancel your subscriptions.

How full is your inbox? Ask to be removed from mailing lists for newsletters you have no time to read.

Minimize interruptions.

Brief interruptions may be more troublesome than you realize. A study by Microsoft found that it takes about 24 minutes for you to restore your attention to your previous task. Try designating some hours of the day as your do-not-disturb time. Check your email and texts less frequently.

Be prepared.

Polish off brief tasks during those interruptions you can't avoid, such as online video ads. File your nails or read a magazine until the commercial ends.

Recognize recent bias.

Our brains are programmed to focus on the latest news regardless of its merits. Wait a few weeks before you rush out to watch a new movie.

Set limits.

The convenience of the internet may make you want to go on searching for your topic forever. Determine your priorities and the sources you want to rely on.

Simple habits can help you accomplish more in less time.

Now that you've cleared away the clutter, you can start to organize the knowledge that's meaningful to you.

Write it down.

Your brain can only keep track of a few items at a time. Free up mental energy by making lists of things you'll deal with later. That way you can concentrate on reading to your children instead of thinking about what's going on at the office.

Finish what you start.

As much as possible, complete a task in one sitting so it's off your mind. If necessary, break the task down into smaller steps.

Work in batches.

Bunch your similar activities together. Pick a time to stay focused on managing your finances or working on your hobby.

Stop multitasking.

Science has overwhelming evidence that multitasking is a myth. Your brain winds up switching rapidly between tasks. That scattered approach of multitasking wastes your energy, increases physical tension, and lowers the quality of your performance.

Take a break.

Scheduling frequent short breaks is more efficient than pushing yourself beyond your capacity. Stand and stretch every hour. Go for a walk or chat with a friend every few hours.

Adjust your expectations.

Decide how much time and effort will suffice for any undertaking. You probably want to find out all you can before purchasing a house while 10 minutes may be the most you want to spend on researching deodorants.

Daydream more.

Successful companies give their employees room for experimentation and innovation. Disconnect for a while each day to observe your thoughts and indulge your creativity.

Trust your intuition.

Your subconscious is extremely powerful. In addition to gathering facts and analyzing data, listen to your inner voice and emotions to discover your purpose and passions.

Do the Work!

Information is valuable when you can filter out the noise and manage your resources. Protect your creativity and productivity by staying focused on what you need to reach your goals.

WHAT TO DO WHEN YOU HAVE NO IDEA WHAT TO DO

Sometimes the right choice is obvious. Other times, the solution is a little less clear. When you are the most uncertain, you're often in a situation with great potential. This type of confusion is common when you come to a crossroads in life. The biggest decisions are often the most intimidating.

The ability to make challenging decisions increases with experience. Try these techniques to deal with uncertainty and make intelligent decisions:

Be clear regarding your values.

A wise choice might be easier if you're aware of your values. Whenever you're stuck, return to your values and take another crack at the situation. If you've never considered what your values may be, take the opportunity to make a list and describe what's most important to you.

Gather more information.

Do you have enough information to make a good decision? Take the time you need to gather the information needed to make a wise choice. Utilize every possible resource.

Avoid indecision as a decision.

Find the difference between taking your time and being indecisive. Make no mistake: failing to make a decision is a decision. It's a decision to rely on luck and forces outside yourself to decide your fate. When you don't make a decision, you lose control of your future.

Ask a mentor for advice.

Maybe a friend or partner has faced a similar dilemma. Experience counts for a lot. Seek guidance if it's available to you. Avoid blindly following the advice of others. Make your own decision. A mentor guides, but he doesn't decide.

Relax.

Your brain works better when it's relaxed. An overly stressed state results in the inhibition of the higher functions of your brain. Your best ideas come when you're mentally at ease. Take a long, hot bath and ponder your situation.

Exercise.

Physical exertion can change your chemistry and provide a new perspective. Hit the gym for an hour and then reconsider your dilemma. Don't be surprised if you have a few new ideas.

Meditate or pray.

The choice is yours. The mental state achieved through meditation and prayer can be highly creative. You'll be in a better place to make a good decision.

What would you tell a friend in the same situation?

Dealing with the challenges of others can be clearer than dealing with your own. What would you tell a friend or family member? It may be wise to take your own advice!

Review your goals.

Each action you take will make achieving your goals either more or less likely. How do your choices mesh with your goals? This can be an effective way to find an intelligent solution. Make a list of goals if you don't already have one.

Consider the downside.

Look at your choices. Maybe you have more than one choice with the same potential benefits. But consider the possible downside to each option. Manage your risk. When two or more options have the same potential benefit, the choice with the least risk is often the best.

When you're stuck, likely, all your choices seem equivalent. After you've done everything you can to reach a decision, choose.

Do the Work!

Even if you're still uncertain, make a choice and move forward until you're certain you made a wrong choice. Even a poor decision is usually better than no decision at all. Taking action might show you a new idea for a better approach. And you'll be moving forward, instead of stuck in the quagmire of indecision.

CHAPTER TWO, SUPPORT
MOTIVATED

Which Beliefs Can You Turn Around Fast?

Throughout the book you will find these support sections that are designed to help you use self-affirming language in your daily thoughts and habits.

It is as important to train your thoughts in your new understanding as it is to educate yourself with the knowledge.

Getting Started

Read through each section:

· For any sections that present you with new information, spend time each day until you are comfortable with the idea of thinking this new way.

· It can be beneficial to read through the self-affirming thoughts out loud.

· Pick the ideas that you need the most and implement them first.

After you have all this accomplished, go back and read through your notes every three months to make sure you haven't strayed from the work you need to get done.

Guided Meditation: Wealth

In a guided meditation, your meditation session is led by an outside source -- whether that's another person or a recording you made for yourself. Also, there is a specific purpose for a guided meditation. Your goal might be to manifest something like better health, wealth, or deep relaxation.

One of the hallmarks of a good guided meditation sequence is that it's open-ended.

A point is reached where the subconscious is allowed to take over and insert its own images and symbols. In the following example, the guided part of the imagery is stopped at the point of walking through the doors. This is where the subconscious could take over.

With some practice, the images that arise from beneath the conscious mind can become clear and easy to interpret.

You can use this guided meditation for wealth to help manifest wealth in your life by making a recording of yourself reading it aloud and then playing the recording as you meditate.

Guided Meditation for Wealth

Imagine walking in a field, in the soft glow of the moonlight on a pleasantly warm summer evening. The gentle wind causes the tall grass to sway in rhythm. The pleasant scent of the nearby shrubs and flowers intoxicates you as you deeply inhale the moist air.

After holding your deep in-breath for couple of seconds, you slowly release and continue to walk through the field.

As you're walking you notice many signs of abundance; piles of gold and diamonds are scattered throughout the field. You think to yourself that there is enough for everyone to be wealthy beyond his wildest dreams.

From a long way away, you can hear the gentle hooting of an owl. As the wind begins to pick up, you can feel the warm air blowing through your hair. You notice a light in the distance that appears to grow larger as you continue walking towards it. You realize that it is a temple -- a glorious temple made of gold and lit spectacularly by the full moon.

As you approach the temple, you are filled with a sense of awe. You realize that something amazing is about to happen; this is obviously a place of great prosperity and abundance. You feel that the key to wealth is going to be revealed to you.

When you finally reach the temple, you start up the long, winding stairs. You move quickly and easily up the stairs with minimal effort. The movement is so fluid that it reminds you of an escalator, only much smoother.

After a few moments you reach the top and see a set of large doors made of wood. With tremendous anticipation and excitement, you push against the doors with all your might.

The doors open slowly and with a gentle creaking sound. You walk into the temple, which is filled with light streaming down from the ceiling. What do you see in the temple?

How to Make Your Own Guided Meditation:

You can make your own guided meditations quite easily.

The most important thing to keep in mind is to emphasize the senses. Describe what you see, hear, feel, and smell. Also, you should feel safe and comfortable. For example, you don't want to imagine being in your bathing suit while in a snowstorm.

Comfort and sensory detail will help you project yourself into the imagery.

The images you give yourself and your thoughts around them should be centered on the topic -- wealth, in this example. As previously stated, leaving the imagery open-ended will allow you the space to find the answers you're looking for.

When you're finished, make notes of what you felt and saw.

Examine your meditation to determine what you can learn from it. The answers aren't always immediately obvious, but they are there.

Guided meditation can be a powerful tool in your self-development arsenal. Used regularly, it can provide tremendous insight and be used as a problem-solving tool.

Do the Work!

Try writing your own guided meditations based on your desires, goals, or challenges, and do it regularly. You'll be amazed and thrilled at the results you see in your life.

Wealth is within your grasp. Meditate on it.

Abundance Flows Freely

Today, I trust that abundance flows freely toward me.

Use this self-affirming language to teach your thoughts a new habit:

- My life is full of blessings. I have people around me who care for me. All my needs and most of my wants are met.
- I am full of gratitude. This is the natural order of things, today and each day. Therefore, I trust that abundance flows freely toward me.
- I live my life with a thankful heart. I regularly express my gratitude because I have a good life that I love. Even if situations seem challenging at times, I am sure to count my many blessings.
- What I focus on, I draw toward myself, so I choose to focus on allowing abundance into my world.
- I have great confidence that my life only gets better, day by day. All that I want in the world is coming toward me -- sometimes quickly, sometimes slowly, but moving, nonetheless.
- I know that my dreams are within my reach, so I reach for the stars! And time after time, my vision is made real. No dream is too outrageous.
- My happiness is paramount to me, so I cultivate it by practicing gratitude. If I begin to feel worry, fear, or resentment, I remind myself that nothing can stand in the way of natural abundance. Then, I am freed from negative emotion and can focus on enjoying the many blessings already in my life.
- Today, I trust that abundance flows freely toward me. I see and value all the blessings in my life, big and small. And I recommit daily to my gratitude practice.

Do the Work!

Take time for self-reflection:

1. What are five blessings in my life today?

2. In what way has abundance flowed toward me over the past year?

3. How can I increase my feelings of gratitude for the gifts already in my life?

I Have a Wealthy Life

Wealth is pouring into my life from all directions.

Use this self-affirming language to teach your thoughts a new habit:

- Each day, I am grateful for the way wealth flows toward me.
- I can hardly turn around without being given a gift of some sort. Sometimes these are material manifestations. At other times, wealth comes in other forms. I embrace them all!
- I remain open to the abundance constantly offered to me.
- The people in my life bless me with companionship, laughter, and compassion. My work provides me with a material abundance unknown in many parts of the world. And I am wealthy in my heart because of all the love I feel for my friends and family.
- If I ever start to feel that something is lacking in my life, I remember that all the resources are at my fingertips. All I have to do is ask, and whatever I need comes my way. In fact, I usually get not only what I need, but many things I may not yet know I want!
- I am so blessed to be alive today, with this healthy body and mind that serve me so well. Today, all my needs and many of my wants are met. Because I have so much going for me, I share my wealth wherever I can. By offering what I have to others, my gifts are returned to me a hundredfold.
- Today, I pay close attention to all the ways in which wealth is pouring toward me. At this very moment, all my needs are all met. Each day, I take a few minutes to pause and feel gratitude for all the abundance in my life.

Do the Work!

Take time for self-reflection:

1. What are some unexpected ways I have been blessed recently?

2. In what way does wealth manifest the most in my daily life?

3. How can I best remember to cultivate gratitude for all the ways that wealth is pouring into my life?

I Work Towards Financial Freedom

I know financial change is possible.

Use this self-affirming language to teach your thoughts a new habit:

- One of my main goals in life is to be financially free. Everything I do now in my personal and professional life is geared towards achieving the financial freedom I desire. And I know it is on the horizon.
- I am excited about what is to come, about what I know I can easily achieve once I leave financial challenges behind. I anticipate being able to provide all the niceties that my loved ones deserve.
- I acknowledge that my past chronicles unwise choices and a lack of the discipline needed to maintain financial wellness. But I also recognize that the time has come to put aside such behaviors and focus on a financially healthy future.
- In my workplace, I focus on achieving the targets set for the company. I actively play my part in making the business successful, so I can, in turn, reap financial success. I look forward to the rewards in store for me.
- In my personal life, I eliminate unnecessary and wasteful expenditures, so I can put that money away in savings. I now truly understand the impact of being financially responsible. I know that I am in charge of my financial future.
- Today, I bring my financial freedom into being. The pride I feel as I make wise choices in managing my money keeps me focused on my goal.

Do the Work!

Take time for self-reflection:

1. Do I have the discipline to deny myself one of my favorite, more expensive treats?

2. In what ways can I work at building financial freedom?

3. Can I maintain financial freedom after I achieve it?

Money Is Not Everything

The money in my checking account cannot replace the joy, love, and happiness in my life's savings.

Use this self-affirming language to teach your thoughts a new habit:

- I am thankful that I have money and that I can use it to provide for my family. But money itself will never fulfill any need that I may have. My deepest needs are met by my loved ones.
- I appreciate my money and I know how to use it wisely. I use it to finance the better things in life. The best things in life are not things; the best things in life are relationships. I am not in a relationship with money. I do not love money, nor do I hate it. Money is simply a tool.
- My life is rich with joy and my joy is contagious. My positive attitude allows me to draw joy from various sources. I get joy from watching children play and laugh, and I am filled with joy when I see rays of sunlight peeking through the clouds.
- Love is an essential part of my life. I am worthy of love and I know that I am deeply treasured. Unconditional love is the best gift I have received. To know that my faults are forgiven and that I am loved in spite of them is to experience genuine happiness.
- Reflecting over my life keeps me aware of my blessings. There are many memories that make my life great and I make a point of it to preserve my memories through photos and journals.
- I have a beautiful life!
- It does not matter whether my checking account is full or empty. Love, joy, and happiness belong to me. Whether I gain the world or lose it all, I know what my real treasure is.

Do the Work!

Take time for self-reflection:

1. How full is my life's savings account?

2. How do I preserve good memories?

3. What is my real treasure?

The Opposite Ornament Sisters

A story about being prepared.

Olivia and Olga Ornament thought differently about being prepared, until one holiday...

Twin sisters Olivia and Olga Ornament couldn't be more different! Only friends and family knew they were twin ornaments. Others didn't have a clue because of how different they looked and behaved.

At the end of every holiday, the Merry family would pack them away with all the other decorations. Olivia would ensure she was stored in a cushioned section of the ornaments box, so she would retain her brilliance for the next holiday.

Olga, on the other hand, was a free spirit who never gave much thought to planning for the future. *"It's all about the here and now for me,"* remarked Olga as she rolled around playfully with the lights and tinsel. *"A little fun never hurt anybody!"*

Every day, as Olivia sat still and socialized with nearby ornaments, Olga romped around nonchalantly. She rolled, bounced, and got entangled with the other decorations. In no time, she was tarnished, scratched, and dented.

"Oh my!" she exclaimed. *"I'm not looking as beautiful as I used to. Maybe it's time to take a break because the holidays are just around the corner!"*

But Olga was a tad too late. Hanging around with her sister at the last minute didn't undo the damage that was already done.

When Mindy Merry opened the box of decorations, she said, *"Mom, look! This ornament is so old and tarnished. It looks like it rolled around all year."* Mrs. Merry replied, *"You're right, Mindy. Let's just leave that one in the box."*

When Olga realized that Olivia was used as decoration while she was left behind, she immediately became sad. *"If only I had stayed put like Olivia, I would have been chosen as a decoration for this holiday for sure."*

Moral of the story: Preparation produces favorable results.

* * *

The Opposite Ornament Sisters Self-Reflection

Olivia and Olga Ornament never had much in common. Of course, they were twin sisters, but their similarities stopped there. Olivia always thought about the future and planned accordingly. While, Olga never put much thought into preparing for anything.

If you think back, you'll probably identify a time when you were just as eligible for a great opportunity as a co-worker or fellow student. However, because you neglected to put in enough work beforehand, you lost out on the opportunity.

One thought is, "You can never be too prepared for anything. It's much better to be over-prepared and be thought overzealous than to under-prepare and lose something that's important to you."

It's always a good idea to think of an opportunity as something that's right in front of you. Regardless of how much time you think you have to get ready for it, do what you can today!

Laying the groundwork and foundation for anything makes implementation much more seamless.

You'd be surprised at how much of a head start you give yourself by preparing. You'll have plenty of time after you've earned the achievement to bask in your victory. Use the here and now to prepare.

Do the Work!

Take time for self-reflection:

1. Have I fallen short on the expectations of others?

2. Can I make myself more marketable for great opportunities?

3. Are there positive behaviors of others that I can emulate?

The Wise Young Owl

A story about the importance of being vigilant.

As a kid, Oscar the owl spent much of his time hanging out with older owls observing how they did things. He gained a lot of wisdom that way. One day, his vigilance came in handy when he needed to take quick action to save his family...

"You're so boring, Oscar!" his best friend Lester commented one day. "Why don't you come and fly around with us?"

But Oscar never took his friends' criticisms to heart. He knew that pretty soon he'd be old enough to have to rely on the wisdom he'd been gaining from the old folks. His favorite lesson was how to keep watch at night for predators.

While everyone was relaxing at home one night, he went to meet the senior owls who were on night watch. *"I want to learn as much from you guys as I can,"* said Oscar. *"Pretty soon, I'll be the one in charge of protecting my family."*

He had a good night of observation training with the senior owls and was on his way home when he noticed that something wasn't right. He put his lessons in vigilance to use and identified a cat lurking in the shadows of his family's home.

Without a second thought, Oscar released a loud alarm call that got the attention of the senior owls on duty.

"Sounds like the alarm is coming from near Oscar's home," announced one of the owls. And with that, they rushed to the location and scared the cat away.

"That was quick thinking, Oscar," remarked one of the senior owls. *"You bravely put your training to good use and protected your family from danger."*

Oscar felt proud that his lessons in vigilance paid off. "You're so boring, Oscar!" his best friend Lester commented one day. "Why don't you come and fly around with us?"

Moral: When wisdom guides your actions, it is easy to sense when danger is near.

* * *

The Wise Young Owl Self-Reflection

There was a lot that young Oscar liked about being a kid. But something told him that there was value in gaining wisdom from senior owls in the community. He believed that sooner or later, he would have to call on the lessons learned.

As he sensed, a potentially dangerous situation arose involving his family, and he used what he learned to keep them out of harm's way.

Like Oscar, it isn't always easy to tell when quick thinking is required. Sure, it's nice to have carefree days, but preparation for the unexpected is also important.

Wisdom comes from various sources that you encounter each day. From parent's advice to experiences you have on the train, there are always lessons from which to develop your own wisdom.

One wise piece of advice is to remain vigilant at all times, even when you feel comfortable in your environment.

When things are going smoothly it is easy to let down your guard and openly trust what is around you. But sometimes danger lurks where you least expect it. Keeping in touch with your instincts is a way to identify when something isn't right.

Just like in the fable, the lessons you learn will come in handy when you need them!

Just as you dedicate some of your time to enjoying your life, reserve some time for lessons in wisdom as well. They're there to guide you through those times when your instinct is needed to overcome a worrying challenge.

Do the Work!

Take time for self-reflection:

1. What are my primary sources of wisdom?

2. What are some lessons I learn from spending time with older people?

3. Am I to discern when someone means me harm? How?

3

MODELING

Great job getting through the opening concepts that will support your new views for a healthier financially independent you. Now that you can see change is possible, it is important to move in a direction that you can gather support for the financial future of your choice.

Having a role model in your life and being a great role model to others can help move you quickly through unexpected challenges.

> *"Find someone who has a life that you want and figure out how they got it. Read books, pick your role models wisely. Find out what they did and do it."*
> *~ Lana Del Rey*

Getting Started

You are on a journey to live your best life possible. One way to ensure you fulfill your goals and dreams is to understand the importance of role modeling. Role modeling is paradoxical, meaning, if you surround yourself with positive role models, you'll likely become an effective role model for your kids, co-workers, or someone else important in your life.

WHAT IS A ROLE MODEL?

A role model is someone who does something really well and is worth imitating. Others tend to look up to and admire them. People often select role models who excel in one or more areas of their lives.

Think of a role model as the ideal person--maybe they're the best father you've ever seen or the most patient and kind human being you've ever known.

Your role models teach you how to live better lives by being highly skilled at something, developing your knowledge, or putting forth more effort. Role models help you become better versions of ourselves.

If you want to create the life you deserve, use your listening and observational skills to notice others who are living the kind of existence you desire. You might say that a role model is an expert at being the type of person you hope to be.

> *"I know that being seen as a role model means taking responsibility for all my actions. I am human, and of course, sometimes I make mistakes. But I promise that when I fall, I get back up."*
>
> ~ *Jennifer Lopez*

WHO ARE YOUR ROLE MODELS?

You may have already met and established connections with people you believe to be talented, wise, and worthy of duplicating. Interestingly, you may truly admire and try to be like someone without identifying them as a role model.

It's comforting to know you have role models in your life that you can emulate. Look through these categories and identify a role model in each one:

A role model who makes you say, "I want to be just like them."

This individual appears to have it all together. They're hard workers, nice to others, loving, and effective parents. You'd feel pretty proud of yourself if you could live a similar life to your role model.

- You aspire to be like this person because you view them as a brilliant human being or a "best all round" sort of individual. This type of role model is likely someone like a grandparent, parent, aunt, or uncle to you.
- However, maybe when you were growing up there was a neighbor next door whom you tried to spend as much time with as possible. This person may have been your role model because you viewed them as kind, giving, and caring toward others.

An intellectual role model.

An intellectual role model could be one of your former teachers, a professor you had in college, or a famous author. For example, Maya Angelou has written some very wise words with great impact. Therefore, she has become someone to aspire to if we want to live thoughtful, meaningful lives.

Another individual that's intellectual and inspiring for many is Dale Carnegie. His books have taught about the importance of showing confidence, reaching out to others, and standing up to speak in front of others. Who wouldn't love to possess all those traits?

A role model who excels at their profession.

Regardless of whether you're a maintenance worker, an office manager, or a salesperson, it's important to have someone who you can look up to in your chosen profession.

- Your role model doesn't even have to be someone who works in your exact job. Consider the number of individuals who used to see ex-NBA basketball player, Magic Johnson, as a wonderful person to imitate.
- Magic Johnson was excellent at his job, kind to those around him, and continually tried to increase his "job skills." He was personable, hardworking, and he reached out to others. But mostly, he seemed to glow, exuding a feeling of positivity.
- Maybe you've met someone you admire in your line of work when you attended a seminar and saw them presenting about a specific topic. Seeing their zest for their work, incredible focus, and willingness to share their knowledge may have been very attractive to you.
- After their speech, maybe you went up and introduced yourself and asked for their business card. You began to learn as much as you could about them, read material they wrote, and talked to others who know them. Did they inspire you or make you feel motivated to perform your best at work?
- Maybe at your office, there's someone who's worked in your field for twenty-five years and seems to hold a passion for the type of work you do. You've endeavored to work as closely as possible with them because you're in awe of their approach to the job.
- Have you chosen someone in your professional field to emulate?

A parenting role model.

If you're striving to be the best parent possible, it's helpful to have another parent whose footsteps you can follow in.

- If you think your dad was the best dad you've ever known, then you try to parent just like he did. When a tough parenting challenge arises, you may even pick up the phone, explain the situation, and ask his advice.
- Or it could be the mother of your best friend in high school. Maybe you thought she was a great parent and have decided to model your parenting style after hers.

Having role models will enrich your existence in ways you have yet to consider. Some of your role models are likely people who are accessible to you. Perhaps you can drop in for a visit or make a quick call to run something by them.

Others, like celebrities or well-known authors, create books and websites you can access to seek answers to your questions. Maybe you've observed them being interviewed on television and try to soak up every word they say.

Do the Work!

Psychologically, you can "lean on" these types of role models, ponder how you think they'd resolve a particular difficulty, and then apply that method to your own life. Hopefully, you've now homed in on a couple of your role models. If you haven't selected a role model, there's no time like the present to get started.

WHY IT'S IMPORTANT TO HAVE ROLE MODELS

Regardless of the type of work you do, whether you're male or female, or where you live, having role models will make your life easier and more fulfilling.

There are plenty of reasons to have positive role models. Ponder the reasons why it's important to have role models:

You can choose whomever you want.

The freedom of deciding who to emulate and which qualities to reproduce in your own life is powerful. Who do you want to be like?

You'll feel a sense of support.

Even though you may be unable to speak to your role model because they're a celebrity or someone who's deceased, you can still think about what you've learned from observing the famous person in an interview or speaking to a deceased loved one in the past.

You'll have someone to turn to for advice.

Many role models are likely open and willing to be contacted.

You can learn about how to solve challenges simply by observing others.

It's helpful to see your role model "in action," dealing with struggles, so you can see what they do.

It's unnecessary to reinvent the wheel.

Someone has likely already done what you desire to accomplish. If you've selected your role models wisely, you can learn from how they were able to excel.

When you admire and look up to someone, you're sending out positive vibes.

When others realize you look up to and respect someone else, they'll feel inspired themselves.

It makes your life easier.

It relieves stress when you can call on someone in times of need.

You can be a better parent, an extra caring friend, and a more effective co-worker.

It's within your power to live your best life. And having great role models will help you do it.

Do the Work!

The advantages of having role models are great. Consistently having those you trust to turn to in a crisis or teach you how to live a better life ensures you'll make your own contributions to the world. For these reasons and more, having role models is the key to a happy and fulfilling life.

REASONS TO BECOME A ROLE MODEL

Because you're likely raising children, working with others, and involved with others socially, you may want to become a role model for others as they approach their own lives.

Being a role model is a valuable experience for you too. Consider the benefits of becoming someone's role model:

You'll have a stronger sense of direction in your life.

When you know someone else is counting on you, you'll have clearer goals. Because your commitment to your goals is strengthened, you'll strive to be an incredibly competent role model.

Your confidence will grow.

When we see our role models showing self-reliance and a sense of self-assurance about the choices they're making in life, it's infectious. And as you observe others watching and emulating you, your confidence will multiply.

Become a better human being.

If your goal is to become a decent, contributing member of society, then being surrounded by those you look up to helps you in your own quest to serve as a great example for others.

People will look up to you.

It's a wonderful feeling to know others see that you have integrity, deserve respect, and they admire your success.

Do the Work!

When you become a role model for others, you'll likely live a more enriched, fulfilling life than those who choose not to be concerned with modeling behaviors for others. Your own sense of self is strengthened in many complex ways when you strive to be admired and emulated by others.

AVOIDING NEGATIVE ROLE MODELS

When you think of role models, you're usually picturing positive role models. Yet, you've likely found yourself in a place or situation where you've been exposed to those who send out a negative vibe to others. You might have identified with the source of negativity and even started to follow their lead.

And that's the power of a role model.

You connect with other's opinions and behaviors, and you strive to be more like them. So, it's possible that you could end up following along with a negative role model. It is better to avoid modeling negativity.

Stay in touch with your own emotions.

If you feel uncomfortable or have a negative reaction to someone, dig deep and investigate what's triggering those emotions.

Listen to your own feelings.

When you identify why you feel uncomfortable around someone, take that information to heart. There's likely an important reason why you're reacting this way.

Decline involvement with the negativity.

When someone lacks a positive vibe, speaks negatively about someone else, or displays a poor attitude, refuse to join the conversation or give into those feelings.

Be aware of peer pressure and how you respond to it.

You may feel incredible pressure to follow along with someone's negative behavior. However, you can choose not to.

Prepare for how you'll handle negativity.

Those who have the charisma to lead others astray may trip an emotional trigger within you. Determine methods for responding to such behaviors before they occur.

For example, if you dislike being around cursing, think about how you'll respond if you're in a conversation where others start using a lot of profanity. Ponder what your options would be and choose a possible response.

Exit the situation.

If you find yourself profoundly affected by a negative role model and their comments or behavior, remove yourself from the situation.

Maintain a healthy perspective.

Tell yourself that even though you have fond feelings for someone who is now spreading negativity, you can avoid repeating the behavior and becoming a voice for their skepticism.

Take personal responsibility to turn the negativity into positivity.

Sometimes, all it takes is for one individual to avoid joining in. Instead, make some positive comments about something or someone to turn the tide.

Do the Work!

Although you may feel like you're surrounded with uncomfortable skepticism, remind yourself of what you can do to avoid being drawn into the tornado of a negative role model.

CHARACTERISTICS OF A POSITIVE ROLE MODEL

Positive role models often have an endless list of desirable characteristics. If you're interested in becoming a role model, it's wise to begin to cultivate all the best things about yourself. What do you do really well? How are your people skills? What do others compliment you about?

When you pay attention to your own thoughts and behaviors, you have a clearer concept of which areas you can enhance to become a positive role model for others. Take action and cultivate these positive characteristics:

Embrace a strong work ethic.

Taking a passionate interest in your work and applying yourself each day of your working life will build your professional future. It will also ensure that newbies and younger co-workers are drawn to your talents and will try to emulate your skills.

Present a neat, clean appearance.

Although expensive clothes are unnecessary to your role model status, clothing that's neat and unwrinkled will go a long way. Consistently ensure you're clean and fresh.

Keep in mind that a pleasant appearance tends to be preferred by most of us.

Exhibit stellar personal conduct.

How we behave reflects much on our character. The way you act towards others at home, work, or out in public reveals to the world the kind of human being you are.

In order for others to admire and emulate you, ensure your conduct is appropriate in all kinds of situations.

Foster loving and involved personal relationships.

When your personal life shows you can have and maintain quality relationships with depth, emotional intimacy, and mutual respect, others will be drawn to you. They'll wonder about your secret for relationship success.

Display an effective communication style.

When you communicate with others, you're establishing connections. You're allowing others the opportunity to get to know you and observe your style of relating.

If you can clearly get your message across to others in respectful ways, remain calm in difficult situations, and listen to others, you'll be a great role model.

Demonstrate compassion and understanding.

Do you show a true sense of caring towards others? Do you make a concerted effort to understand others' viewpoints, even if they're different from yours?

Expressing a sense of compassion toward those around you says a lot about you.

Taking the time to show care, acceptance, and understanding makes you serious role model material.

Illustrate a willingness to take time with others.

Although your life is probably cramped with things to do, a role model consistently makes the choice to take time to listen to others and help them with those vexing challenges.

Hearing the other side of things is often enlightening. It will either strengthen your own position or weaken it, which broadens your ability to understand the world. Plus, taking time with others is greatly appreciated.

State your expectations clearly.

When you know what you want and share it with others succinctly, they'll easily understand where you're coming from and look up to you.

Show the capacity for working through conflicts.

When you negotiate two or more sides to a dilemma and reach an agreement that achieves mutual acceptance, you're on the path to becoming a role model. Handling conflict is one of the toughest things for many of us.

See the opportunities during challenging times.

As difficult as it can be, if you can view the rough spots as opportunities, you're modeling a strong trait for others. Finding the silver lining is an incredible skill and one that can be passed on as a role model.

Do the Work!

As you reflect on your own viability to be a role model, think about the skills you possess that could help you be a wonderful example to others.

WHAT KIND OF ROLE MODEL ARE YOU?

When you're trying to determine whether you're seen as an effective role model, it's necessary to evaluate some of your character traits, actions, and attitudes.

Your responses to these queries will reveal much about your capacity for role modeling. Ask yourself these questions:

How effective am I at building rapport with others?

If you easily establish a rapport with others, it means you're comfortable in your own skin and can accept others as they are.

Do I support whatever "team" I'm involved with?

Whether your family members, friends, or co-workers are your team in a given situation, are you the first to step in and say, "Way to go!" or "Nice job!" when they need encouragement? Giving support to others on your team makes you a super role model.

How honest and open am I about learning something from others?

An effective role model isn't afraid to say, "Well, I learned about how to write a monthly operation report from Joe." If you're open to learning from others, they'll be open to learning from you.

When you freely give credit where credit is due, you'll be admired by others.

Do I promote cooperation among others?

If you show that you're cooperative and encouraging, you're sending a powerful message to everyone that working together is the best strategy.

Do I periodically reflect on my own behaviors and how I relate to others at home, work, and in social situations?

It's helpful to ponder the type of individual you are, the type of human being you strive to be, and what changes you plan to make ensures you're presenting yourself in the best light.

What is my attitude like most days?

A role model carries positivity within and approaches each day with an upbeat attitude. When you wake up in the morning, survey your own mood. Then, decide if you want to adjust your attitude or whether you're good to go.

Do the Work!

You have the tools now to shape yourself into the type of role model you want to become. Your ability to be an admirable role model can contribute to the world being a better place.

EFFECTIVE ROLE MODELING BRINGS ABUNDANCE

There are plenty of advantages to becoming a positive role model. If you believe in karma, then you know that the more positivity you put out, the more you receive back.

Being a positive role model sort of works in the same way as karma. Consider the following advantages of serving as a role model:

Your kids will look up to you.

It's cool for kids to see that others admire and like their parents. They might respect you a little more when they see others responding to you positively.

Your peers will respect your judgment.

It's a good feeling to know that those you work with honor your ideas and wisdom.

You'll feel more self-reliance and self-assurance.

It all boils down to confidence.

Few things will provide uncomfortable challenges to you.

That's because you've gathered so much experience in dealing with troublesome situations that you simply rise to each occasion with gusto.

The joy you'll experience by observing the success of others is pretty awesome.

It's an amazing feeling to realize that you share some small part of the achievements of others because you were their role model.

It's extremely rewarding when others stand taller, live a cleaner life, or put more effort into their work or home because of something you may have shown them.

Do the Work!

The rewards that you can reap from being a role model are great. To live life knowing you've connected with many others and presented an example that helped them is pretty amazing.

CHAPTER THREE, SUPPORT
MODELING

The knowledge of role modeling can be solidified for you through this self-affirming language section.

Instead of repeating the same negative thoughts over and over replace those thoughts with some new self-talk, do the work!

Getting Started

Remember, read through each section:

- For any sections that present you with new information, spend time each day until you are comfortable with the idea of thinking this new way.
- It can be beneficial to read through the self-affirming thoughts out loud.
- Pick the ideas that you need the most and implement them first.

After you have all this accomplished, go back and read through your notes every three months to make sure you haven't strayed from the work you need to get done.

I Seek Out Role Models

My role models inspire and motivate me. I study the actions of others to help me grow.

Use this self-affirming language to teach your thoughts a new habit:

- I choose friends who share my values and embody qualities that I admire.
- We guide and support each other. Spending time with them helps me to build my confidence. I change my perspective and learn how to respond differently to challenging situations.
- In my faith community, I find spiritual guides who share their wisdom and insights. I discover new ways to put my beliefs into action.
- At the office, I team up with mentors, so I can sharpen my skills and stay up to date in my field. I work smarter and deepen my job satisfaction.
- At the gym, I notice the members who come in regularly and put their heart into their workouts. I admire their attitude and effort regardless of how much weight they can lift. They remind me to appreciate my body instead of criticizing it.
- In airports and waiting rooms, I appreciate those who remain calm and pleasant when their luggage goes missing or 15-minute delays turn into hours. They show me how patience reduces discomfort.
- Today, I give thanks for my role models and the impact that they have on my life. I copy the good example of others and adapt their teachings to leverage my own personal strengths.

Do the Work!

Take time for self-reflection:

1. How have my role models changed since I was a child?

2. How do I feel when I provide a positive role model for others?

3. What is one example of a role model I found in an unexpected place?

I Search for Opportunities to Grow

When I wake up each morning, I think back to my life of the previous day.

Use this self-affirming language to teach your thoughts a new habit:

- The person I am today is an improvement on the person of yesterday. I constantly look for opportunities to keep growing and celebrate when that growth is achieved.
- Growth comes in various forms, so I pay close attention to even minute changes. Spiritual, emotional, and physical evolution are all important.
- Positive resolution of daily circumstances helps me to develop wisdom to handle future situations. When I consider my handling of yesterday's challenges, I quickly recognize my growth in courage and patience.
- I seek out opportunities to engage in similar situations because I know I am that much more able to handle them today.
- Keeping my mind engaged is a sure way to achieve continued growth. I use every chance I get to learn a new skill or experience a new adventure. Exposing myself to something new helps to expand my scope and knowledge. When I am more knowledgeable, I am more marketable in the working world.
- Today, I recognize that my growth is only limited by the opportunities I choose to take advantage of. I commit to expanding my horizons by taking part in as much self- development as I possibly can.

Do the Work!

Take time for self-reflection:

1. How creative am I in finding cost-effective ways to add to my education?

2. What activities can I take part in to promote spiritual growth?

3. How does spending time with influential people help me grow?

I Learn Through Listening

Listening to others gives me greater knowledge and fresh insights.

Use this self-affirming language to teach your thoughts a new habit:

- I open up my ears and mind. The more I listen, the more I learn.
- I work on my listening skills. I attend lectures and engage in lively conversations. I study role models who have mastered the art of listening. I ask others for feedback, so I can target the areas where I want to grow.
- I value what others have to say. I remember that each individual I meet has something valuable that they can teach me. I make eye contact and ask relevant questions. I let them know that I am paying attention.
- I reflect on what I hear. Critical thinking helps me to find the truth and focus on lessons that are helpful for me.
- I listen to my loved ones. I enjoy hearing their stories and value their perspective. I encourage my children to put their thoughts and feelings into words. I empathize with their experiences and find out about new trends.
- I listen to my friends and coworkers. I share their struggles and benefit from their input.
- I listen to my inner voice too. I notice how I feel when my actions align with my values. I examine my reservations when I am considering something that makes me uncomfortable.
- Today, I talk less and listen more. Lifelong learning builds my confidence, makes me more interesting, and opens up new opportunities. My life becomes richer when I put my heart into listening.

Do the Work!

Take time for self-reflection:

1. How do I feel when someone gives me their full attention?

2. What is the difference between hearing and listening?

3. Why is listening an art?

Consistent Change

I am consistently growing and developing.

Use this self-affirming language to teach your thoughts a new habit:

- While others might be content with living the same way day after day, I choose a life of growth and development. Life is short, and I want to reach my full potential.
- There are many beautiful and amazing things in the world. I want to learn and experience as much as possible. I feel invigorated as I become a more complex and complete person.
- I value new opportunities and experiences. I love to learn! It is only when I change myself that I can change my life.
- I use my free time constructively. I have a list of skills and experiences I desire. When I have a free moment, I use that time to better myself. I know that a little time each day can have a huge effect. I am free from time-wasting activities.
- I schedule time each day for my development and I stick to that schedule. I do this each night before falling asleep.
- I am excited about who I am becoming. Each day, I take another step closer to realizing my full potential. But I also enjoy the process. The journey is just as important as the destination. I enjoy spending time on my personal growth.
- Today, I embrace the opportunity to grow and develop. I am using my time efficiently and effectively. I am consistently growing and developing.

Do the Work!

Take time for self-reflection:

1. What would I like to learn and experience?

2. What is my plan for accomplishing my goals and who can help me?

3. How am I currently wasting time on a regular basis?

4

DIRECTION

End the Blame Game

Imagine, if you had advanced knowledge of your financial picture. What decisions would create a better future? Instead of falling into the common traps, you would choose to avoid most of the financial stress you have suffered.

Whether you lost a job, experienced a drop in the economy, were faced with death or divorce, you spent more than you should, saved less than you needed to, none of these things control your future. In the end, the only person who suffers from your lack of knowledge is you.

Getting Started

If you could go back in time and eliminate all of your financial errors, your life would be very different. Though it is never too late to make improvements, it is much easier to prevent challenges than it is to solve them. You can help yourself and your loved ones avoid similar financial challenges through knowledge.

You are getting to the foundation of your financial success. What directions can you take to ensure you stop creating financial pain and start building financial gain? Dig in and do the work!

IMPROVE YOUR SELF-IMPROVEMENT EFFORTS

There's no shortage of self-improvement books, courses, manuals, videos, and concepts. The information needed to be fit, wealthy, healthy, famous, confident, and likable is readily available.

The challenge isn't information. It's implementation.

It's frustrating to feel everything you need to know is available, yet you still can't create the change you seek. You're not alone in your frustration. Make your self-improvement efforts more successful with these strategies:

Keep reasonable goals.

Sure, your mother told you that you can be anything you want to be, but she lied to you. If you're 5' 5", awkward, and 50 years old, you're never going to play in the NBA. You're also probably not going to be the prime minister of Japan, an astronaut, or co-star in a blockbuster with Brad Pitt.

You can do amazing things, but if you set your sights too high, frustration occurs and you may lose your motivation to continue. Set self-improvement goals you believe you can attain. You can always set bigger goals after achieving some success.

For example, you might want to earn $10,000 per week, but starting with a goal of earning $2,000 per week could be exciting without the stress of the larger goal.

Make reasonable timetables.

Losing fifty pounds is a reasonable goal but accomplishing it in a month is not.

You can do a lot if given enough time. Changing your life is entirely possible. Doing so at a breakneck pace is less possible.

Be enthusiastic about small steps forward.

It takes time to gain momentum, so keep a positive outlook about all of your progress. Your positivity is the only thing that keeps progress coming.

If you need to lose fifty pounds, the idea of losing three pounds might not excite you. Likely, you may struggle to be motivated after saving $1,000 when your goal is to save $1 million. Stay focused on your reason! Encourage yourself to keep up the momentum with a reward.

Reward yourself for even the smallest improvement. Rewarded behavior is more likely to occur in the future. Reward yourself for a day of healthy eating or saving an extra $10. Be generous with your rewards!

Create daily habits that move you forward.

Typically, it is not a single, monumental action that changes your life. It is the little things you do each day, day after day.

Create new habits that guarantee you can reach your goals. Then make sure you stay compliant with those goals.

Consider your obstacles.

What thoughts or beliefs are in the way of your self-improvement objectives? It might be your attitude, a close friend, your lack of skills, or your lack of time.

Making an effort to reduce or remove these obstacles can make a big difference in your success.

Patience is key.

Setting reasonable timelines and sticking to them requires patience. When you're motivated, it can be hard to be patient. However, if you lack patience, you may never last long enough to experience significant gains.

Make one change at a time.

You can work on several self-improvement objectives at once but introduce only one at a time into your current routines.

Making too many changes at once is overwhelming and a fast track to nowhere.

Give yourself a little room to breathe and get one self-improvement project well underway before starting a new one.

Do the Work!

You are at the best time and in the best position to work on improving yourself or your life! So much information in so many formats is now available on how to change your life. The only tricky part is applying the information consistently and reaping the rewards.

For your best results, develop the habits necessary to ensure success, enjoy your progress, and be patient. With time, you can do almost anything!

DO WHAT YOU DON'T WANT TO DO

The things that matter are often disagreeable to do. The easy things can be done by anyone, and that's why they often don't matter too much. That's why sipping lemonade on your front porch doesn't pay as well as handling nuclear waste.

Find the value in getting yourself to do the things you don't want to do. Consider these ideas:

Often, the things you need to do are things you don't want to do.

You might need to pay your taxes, clean the basement, visit your mother-in-law, go to the gym, or find a new job. Few of us want to do those things. Yet, they must be done if you want a great life.

It builds character and discipline.

Everyone could use a little more character and discipline. Regrettably, misery is part of the cost. Develop yourself by tackling those high-return tasks. You'll become more capable as a result.

Other people don't want to do them.

Your greatest successes include doing things others aren't willing to do. Larry Bird would shoot baskets in the snow while everyone else was watching cartoons. Be excited when faced with a task you don't want to do. It might be your ticket to the big time.

Your competitors might be doing the things you don't want to do.

Few people take on those disagreeable tasks. Some of them may be your competitors. Work smart and hard if you want to be successful, which means you do what needs to be done.

Take time to practice mindfulness.

Those hard-to-do tasks are hard because you think about how awful you believe they are going to be. If you're mindful, those thoughts stay out of your mind. Every task is just a matter of putting in the time if you keep your focus on the task. Just breathe and do it.

Your self-esteem gets a boost.

You might not be happy while you're doing something, but you often reach levels of greatness afterwards. You will enjoy when you are able to check a tough task off your to-do list. Good feelings about yourself follow and you walk a little taller.

You can do many things to help you complete those challenging tasks.

You don't need a strategy to sit on the couch and take a nap but getting yourself to change your clothes and drive to the gym when the weather outside is rain can be a little more challenging. Practice these strategies:

Get started.

Without giving the task too much thought, take the first step before you have a chance to stop yourself. Just walk down in the basement and move a box or put on your workout shoes and grab your keys.

Start small.

Tell yourself you only need to spend 10 minutes on the task. That's enough to build some momentum.

Think long-term.

Don't think about how awful it is to paint the deck. Think about how great it is to sit outside with your friends and grill hamburgers.

Do the Work!

You bring yourself greater success when you do things the average person is unwilling to do. Think about the most successful people you know. They all spend more time doing disagreeable things than the least successful people you know. If you can make yourself do those things you don't want to do, you gain more from yourself, and from your life.

DELIBERATE PRACTICE: HOW TO USE IT TO YOUR ADVANTAGE

You can find much in the news regarding "deliberate practice." In theory, 10,000 hours of deliberate practice is necessary and sufficient to gain mastery. This mastery might be playing chess, playing the piano, a sport, or becoming an expert on a topic. However, deliberate practice is very different from the practice most people engage in.

Deliberate practice might be the missing link in your attempts to achieve mastery in any endeavor.

Be warned, deliberate practice isn't easy!

Use these key actions to discover the power of deliberate practice:

Keep a set schedule.

Make your practice a priority. Whether your interest is mastering the violin or learning how to dominate the stock market, create a schedule you are willing to keep.

Avoid the trap of only practicing when there is free time. Make time.

Remove all distractions.

Imagine you're strumming your prized banjo while watching your favorite movie from the couch. You might be pretty pleased with yourself, but contrast that with locking yourself in the spare bedroom and focusing 100% on improving your banjo-playing technique.

A key component of deliberate practice is 100% focus. The hours you accumulate must be of high quality.

Choose the most effective action.

If you're great at dribbling a basketball, you may enjoy furthering your skills in that area. However, it might be your 3-point shot that's really holding you back. Human nature is to avoid activities we don't do well. Find the optimal activity and leave your emotions out of it.

Have a goal for each practice session.

While studying your chess books for an hour is good, your experience is much more effective when you make a specific goal for your study session.

- In what areas do you need the most work?
- What are you trying to learn?
- What is the best way to accomplish your learning objective?
- How does this fit into your mastery in the long term?

Feedback is required.

If you're a budding writer, you can't just practice your writing each day. You need a qualified person to review your writing and provide feedback. A baseball player can practice alone in a batting cage, but some endeavors require a coach, teacher, or mentor for the best results.

Understand that all deliberate practice is demanding.

Whether your practice is physical, mental, or both, practice is work. The focus required for deliberate practice can be exhausting.

The amount of deliberate practice that you can accomplish in a day is limited. Studies suggest that 4-5 hours is about the limit. Make a point to break the time up into multiple sessions.

Get enough sleep.

Studies show that musicians in training programs sleep more than those who are not actively training. Experts believe that greater levels of concentration require more rest and recovery. Be sure to focus and get your rest. The experts recommend naps, too.

Realize your limits.

If you're 50 years old or under 5-feet tall, no amount of practice permits you to play professional basketball. You can do far more than you realize, but there are limits in life. To become an expert in everything is impossible.

Do the Work!

Are you ready to raise your expertise to the next level? Deliberate practice is the fastest way to mastering any field. Practice with a goal and without distractions. Ensure you can measure your results. Set aside a time to practice or learn on a regular basis. Deliberate practice is hard work, but the results are well worth it.

ACHIEVE AN ABUNDANCE OF WEALTH

Do you honestly believe you can achieve the financial prosperity you deserve? Without one set way to achieve an abundance of wealth, it is up to you to find your personal path.

Every path to personal wealth begins with the right frame of mind.

A Wealthy Mindset

A positive mindset is the most vital part of any plan for financial success. Before you can succeed in the world, you must see the success you seek in your mind's eye and believe you can achieve it.

One way to develop this mindset is to study what other wealthy people do. If possible, set up a meeting with someone you look up to. Ask about the steps they took to get to where they are today. You'll likely find that they're an ordinary person who took some specific actions that led to their success. If you take those steps, you can enjoy the same success.

Plan for Success

If you have no idea where to begin, start by brainstorming ideas about practical ways to increase your income. Read books about inspiring entrepreneurs. Find businesspeople in your community who can mentor you. Learn from those who have gone before you and found the success you seek.

If you have an idea about a business venture or additional income stream, brainstorm the next small steps you can take that move you in the direction of your dreams. What small step could you take today that can move you closer to your goal? How about tomorrow, and the next day?

Set clear goals and write them down. Plan out each small step and give a realistic time frame to accomplish it. Get moving toward your goal by achieving something small each day. If you do, you'll create unstoppable momentum that almost guarantees your success.

Be Flexible When Things Go Wrong

Things do not always go according to plan. When things go wrong, your response to the obstacles you face determine your level of financial success. If you miss a deadline or your results disappoint you, simply recognize what works and what doesn't. Change your approach until you get what you want.

Grow Your Wealth

As your income begins to grow, alter your plans so you can experience greater financial prosperity. As you near the completion of each goal on your list, set a more exciting goal to replace it. This approach helps you to grow both financially and mentally.

Continue to challenge yourself. Celebrate each success along the way but keep moving forward. Set goals for promotion in your career, sales in your business, and money in your bank account. Remember to set personal goals, too. Financial prosperity is worth little without a balance in your life that allows you to enjoy that prosperity.

Listen to the Right People

Have you ever noticed how people are quick to give advice about everything? Only listen to people who experience more financial prosperity than you. Why would you trust the advice of someone who's broke? This is true in every area of life. Why take parenting advice from people without kids? Or job advice from someone who's perpetually unemployed?

The people with the wisest of advice are the ones with practical experience backed by success. If you can imitate their actions, you can likely achieve similar results.

Do the Work!

Most importantly, pursue your financial dreams no matter what. If you set effective goals, envision your success, find wise mentors, and keep taking action, you can experience the financial independence you deserve.

CREATE THE LIFE YOU WANT

In your quest for personal development, consider technology that could help.

Regardless of the area of your life that needs help to develop, you likely can find a website or mobile application to assist you with your potential.

Examine these web resources and use them to grow into the person you want to be:

TED.

TED (Technology, Entertainment, Design) is a non-profit website and app version where individuals can go to view videos on a variety of different topics. Their slogan is "ideas worth spreading."

If you're seeking knowledge, inspiration, and an impressive list of talented speakers presenting first-hand information, TED provides all these things for you.

Mindbloom.

Mindbloom is a website that aims to help you enhance your life. Whatever area you want to work on, you can include as part of a "tree" you build for free.

Deepen your relationship with others. Get a grip on anger management. Find a different job. Increase motivation to exercise consistently. Complete college or the training you need for advancement.

Watching your tree grow on Mindbloom while you achieve life's greatest milestones is exciting and fun.

Udemy.

If you want knowledge, Udemy has it. Regardless of the subject, you want to study, Udemy likely offers at least one course in it. Some courses are free, like "An

Entrepreneur's Checklist," "How to Negotiate Salary," and "Astronomy--State of the Art."

Other more extensive courses range in price from $35 to $500. Many are under $100.

Lumosity.

Lumosity is a brain training website developed and maintained by neuroscientists. The goal of Lumosity is to enhance cognitive functioning by providing various brain games. Wouldn't you like to increase your brainpower?

Lumosity can help you if you want to increase your attention span or sharpen your memory. Basic membership is free while premium membership costs you.

43 Things.

Another great website is 43 Things, which allows you to list the goals you hope to accomplish and then give and receive support from others through the website, all for free. So, if you want to increase your water intake, finish your PhD, or become more financially competent, you can do it all with the help and support of others on 43 Things.

Vision Board Deluxe.

The Vision Board Deluxe app by Happy Tapper helps you create your life vision on a smartphone or electronic tablet. To design a collage of what you hope your life can look like in the future is exciting.

Look at your board each day to spur on your day-to-day efforts to construct the life you want. Draw up the existence you seek with Vision Board.

Pinterest.

What can we say? If you're a member of Pinterest, your life is touched by it in some way. Pinterest provides amazing exposure to unique ideas, stories, and photos.

Regardless of your interest, there are others on Pinterest posting photos and stories related to it. Pinterest is free online, but the app may cost $2.99 or less.

Do the Work!

Living a conscious life means having your eyes and ears open to all the surrounding opportunities. Today's technology expands your ability to enhance your life for greater personal satisfaction and a renewed interest in creating the life you desire.

FINANCIAL IDEAS TO KEEP YOU ON TRACK

When the year is about to end, parties often come to mind. There are important issues worth considering beyond the festivities.

The end of the year is a great time to go through your finances and find just what you need to do and work on for the coming year. When you do, you'll be better prepared for the upcoming year. You can save money and pay off debt, even if you make the same amount you made last year. There are usually ways to cut spending, save more money or pay down debt.

Complete a serious analysis of the money coming in and the money going out to see how to make changes.

Take a good, close look at your budget.

How much you're bringing in matters, of course, but so does how much you're paying out. If you're spending frivolously, a close look at the money going out will show you where changes need to be made.

Look carefully at your money.

Set up a budget. See exactly where you're spending. Pay attention to everything. More than just your bills, you spend money on cups of coffee before work and lunches out. You'll probably be surprised to find the amount of waste in your spending.

Cut back.

When you're examining what you're doing with your money, consider how you can cut back on some of those little things. They might not appear to be much, but

Use money for something more important.

Use money from cutbacks for savings or paying down debt. Turn wasteful spending into fuel for achieving your financial dreams.

Plan carefully for the New Year.

If you make New Year's resolutions, at least one of them could be financial. Follow up your goal setting with an action plan and begin to take action toward the successful financial future you deserve.

As you plan, consider all the issues you're facing. Is overtime going to be cut? Are you due for a raise? Is there something you need to plan for? Take your life into account as much as you're able. As you create your New Year's plan for your finances, consider:

- How much you have in savings and how much you would like at year's end
- What debts you have and how quickly you want to pay them off
- What kind of fund you need to for unexpected expenses
- Long-range goals like college, retirement, or a vacation home
- What little expenses you could cut out of your budget
- Ways you could reduce your bills to more manageable levels

It might be a little overwhelming, but when you break it down and come up with a plan that you can use long-term, things fall into place. Remember, you don't have to do everything in one day. A plan is just that--not designed to be all done at once. It can also be adjusted as your life changes.

Do the Work!

Financial plans are valuable and sticking to them can help you reach your goals. Be flexible enough to re-think and re-adjust if you need to, though. Make adjustments as necessary until your financial dreams become a reality.

HOW TO SET AND ACHIEVE FULFILLING PERSONAL FINANCIAL GOALS

One of the most important keys to living a fulfilling life is to know where you're going. Form goals that motivate you, excite you, and push you forward. Your goals can help you get the most out of yourself and experience a life that's worth living.

This is especially true for your finances. If your financial life is in order and you're headed toward accomplishing financial goals that support your greatest values and dreams, you'll be happier and more self-confident as a result. Use these tips to begin setting fulfilling personal financial goals today:

Brainstorm without editing.

Grab a pen and paper and sit in a room where you won't be disturbed for about 20 to 30 minutes. As fast as you can, write down as many financial dreams and goals as you can. Allow your thoughts to flow freely onto the paper without editing or judging them. The time to edit and limit your thoughts will come later.

As you brainstorm the possibilities, think about the financial difficulties that frustrate you and the financial dreams that you've been afraid to pursue. Think about how big you would dream if it were impossible for you to fail.

As you brainstorm ideas, think about every area of your life. Would you like to be free? Own your own home? Become financially independent? Help out a loved one who has a big financial need? Supply money for college for your children? The possibilities are endless.

Prioritize your list.

After about 30 minutes, your list of financial goals should cover a page or two. Once you do, begin to think about which of these goals is most important to you.

Which ones bring you peace inside? Which ones excite you the most? Those are the ones to put at the top of your list.

Write down all the challenges that stand in your way.

After you've chosen about 3 to 5 financial goals that excite you, create a new page for each one. Write the goal at the top of the page. Then, list all the reasons you think you can't achieve this goal. Write down all the challenges that stand in your way.

Your list of obstacles will provide you with the next concrete steps to help banish your fear of failure. Come back to this list later and ask yourself how you can overcome each of these challenges. Who can help you? What resources do you need? What information do you lack? What are the next steps you need to take?

Instead of denying that there are challenges on the road to any worthwhile goal, meet those challenges head-on by thinking through them in advance. When you do, nothing will stop you from reaching the financial goals you set.

Create an emergency fund first.

One of the simplest ways to dramatically increase your sense of excitement, peace, and joy in life is to be prepared for when things go wrong financially. An emergency fund of one month's income frees you from much of the financial stress you're currently under.

Once you save enough money for your emergency fund, commit to only using this money in the case of real emergencies. This fund ensures the train to your financial dreams stays on track. You may be surprised how much of your day is spent worrying about finances. This is banished with your emergency fund.

Focus on action steps.

The end result of your exciting financial goals should drive you to keep putting one foot forward. But it can also hinder you from progress by making increasing your anxiety. Instead, focus on one step at a time until you reach the financial destiny you were born to live.

Do the Work!

Finances are a source of stress for many people. However, if you put these tips into practice, your financial situation can be different. Instead of chasing your tail, you'll be excited about the future and about the peace of mind that comes with a healthy financial life.

BEFORE YOU TAKE REVENGE, READ THIS

Revenge is a common theme in movies. People find something satisfying about watching the wronged hero make everything right by destroying his enemy. You might even fantasize about doing the same in your own life, though on a smaller scale.

Revenge is not an intelligent solution. It solves nothing and creates additional challenges. There are several disadvantages to revenge:

Revenge extends the conflict.

Obviously, if you're considering revenge, an issue of some sort exists. Revenge doesn't put the issue to rest. It causes the issue to continue. Imagine if the other person then seeks his own retribution. Where does it end? Someone has to be willing to let it go.

Revenge won't make you feel better in the long run.

Revenge is satisfying for a few minutes, but nothing has really changed. Whatever was done to upset you still exists. You can't go back in time and alter the course of your history. Revenge accomplishes nothing in the long-term.

Revenge isn't free.

There is always a cost. The subsequent actions of the other person may cost you. You can lose sleep, your self-respect, or even your freedom if you take things too far. Your peace of mind is also at risk.

Revenge prolongs the pain.

Time can heal all wounds, but only if you don't reopen them. Allow your wounds to heal by moving on. Giving the situation too much attention only makes you more miserable and prolongs your misery.

Revenge isn't a good solution to any challenge or hurt. There are wiser and more effective ways to handle your anger and pain.

What to do instead of getting revenge:

Forgive.

This is easier said than done for most of us. But what other option do you really have? The only way to stop the pain you are experiencing is to let it go. You can forgive without the need to forget. After all, it would be a shame if you didn't learn anything from your negative experience.

It doesn't seem fair to let the other person off the hook, but forgiveness is for your own benefit.

Learn from the situation.

Did you do something foolish? Were you too trusting? Was it an issue specific to the other person? How can you avoid the same outcome in the future?

Do you need to exclude the other person from your life? Were you too naïve or without knowledgeable to make a smart decision? Determine the cause and then consider a reasonable method of prevention.

Take advantage of a negative situation by learning from it. You grow to be a stronger and more capable person for it.

Meditate or pray.

Meditation and prayer can put your head back in the right place. You can be calmer, relaxed, and centered. Clear your mind and get to a place of rational thought. You can't be upset unless you allow yourself to be.

Do something that you enjoy.

Remind yourself that good things are all around you. Spend an evening chatting with a friend, read a good book, or make your favorite dinner. What activities do you enjoy the most?

It doesn't make sense to spend any more time on the negative issue than necessary.

Do the Work!

Revenge has been a theme of movies, books, and plays. This common theme in history is a natural human reaction. However, revenge seems like a better idea than it really is. Revenge hurts you more than it does the other person. Leave revenge for the movies. Forgive others and enjoy your life.

WAYS TO DEVELOP YOURSELF

Rather than just spending your free time trying to amuse yourself, put your time to good use. To fully reach your potential, spend some time each day furthering your development. A few minutes each day can yield great rewards over the years.

Everyone else is wasting their free time. Be original and put yours to work for you.

Enhance your development by making your personal growth a priority:

Read.

Developing a reading habit can be one of the most rewarding things you can do for yourself. Probably everything you dream of doing has been done by someone else before. Think of how much time you can save yourself by reading for a few minutes each day.

Meditate.

Meditation can improve your health, self-control, focus, and perspective. There is nothing more relaxing than a good meditation session. A bonus, meditation is free.

Learn a second language.

This is a challenging undertaking but provides numerous results for your brain, worldview, and overall development.

Conquer a fear.

Most of us are run by our fears. We expend a lot of energy avoiding them at all costs. Free yourself by putting your energy into conquering a fear.

Create a new habit.

The right habits can guarantee your success. Think about what you would like to accomplish and then determine a supporting habit to make that happen. It can be that simple.

Break a habit.

Good habits propel you toward your goals. Bad habits are like shooting yourself in the foot. Eliminating a negative habit can make life a lot easier.

Write down your goals.

Writing your goals has several benefits. First, identify your goals. Second, writing them makes them real. Third, you can see your goals after they are written down. Figure out your five biggest goals and record them.

Take a course.

No matter what you want to learn, someone is teaching a course on that topic. You can even take courses online. It couldn't be easier to expand your knowledge and your mind.

Get up earlier.

Getting up earlier allows you to accomplish more and create momentum early in the day. You might need to cut back in the evening TV to make your early rise possible.

Create to-do lists.

How can you maximize your productivity if you are missing a plan for the day? Think about what you want to do the night before and make a list.

Work on a weakness.

Like your fears, your weaknesses can be hindrances. Look at your most damaging weakness and turn it into a strength.

Contact the top people in your field.

Sometimes, it really is all about who you know. Ensure that you know the people that matter the most. Find a way to make contact and begin a friendly relationship.

Learn to be a better public speaker.

Public speaking skills are highly prized and can do wonders for your confidence and career.

Start a new hobby.

Time is ticking away. Get started on that hobby that's always intrigued you.

Keep a journal.

Keeping a journal forces you to think about yourself and your life. You will enjoy looking back on this record of your life. You can learn a lot about yourself and see your flaws more clearly.

Do the Work!

How do you spend your free time? Is it spent amusing yourself in some meaningless way, or are you putting the time to good use? Ensure that you're making the most of your downtime by building your skills and addressing your weaknesses. You can accomplish a lot with consistent, daily effort.

LIFE LESSONS YOU WEREN'T TAUGHT IN SCHOOL

Our educational system is focused on math, science, reading, and writing. While these subjects are important, being great at geometry doesn't necessarily lead to a happy and successful life.

Although there are many life lessons that aren't learned in school, we all still own the responsibility of learning them.

Keep these important truths in mind. They can transform your life:

Forgiveness is something you do for yourself.

Holding a grudge and being unable to let go of anger can ruin your own happiness, rather than causing grief to others. By not forgiving those who wronged you, you're only prolonging your own misery.

Many health issues can be avoided with proper diet, exercise, and rest.

The medical community is becoming more and more certain that many diseases are caused by poor diet.

Simply dropping a few of the unhealthy foods you eat on a regular basis can significantly impact your health and sense of well-being in many positive ways.

Getting enough exercise and sleep is a good prescription for anyone. It is easier to stay healthy than it is to regain lost health.

Perseverance is the most critical component of success.

There are few feats in life that can't be accomplished, as long as you try. When things don't work out as hoped, change your approach and keep on going. How could you possibly fail if you refuse to quit?

Your happiness is your responsibility.

Although you may wish that everyone made your happiness a top priority, most people have other things on their minds. Besides, you're the only one who truly knows what's required for your own happiness and fulfillment.

Figure out all that makes you happy and create a life that supports those things.

Say what needs to be said while there is still time.

If anyone in your life has passed away, you've probably regretted not telling them certain things.

Whether you are telling them how you feel about them or sharing the fact that you stole their baseball card in third grade, you only have a limited amount of time. Make the most of it!

Failure is part of the process.

You can learn a lot from a book or from watching others, but the most significant learning comes from "failing" at something. Provided you learn from each failure and apply that knowledge, you're really just perfecting your route to success.

Live life like it's hard, and your life becomes easier.

Having an easy life is about doing all the annoying things other people aren't willing to do. You need to take the time to find a rewarding job and pay your bills on time. You have to follow good eating habits and go to the dentist twice a year. These "difficult" things actually result in an easier life.

Obsessing about the future or past creates anxiety and frustration.

Looking to the past to gain wisdom is great. Focusing on and regretting things that happened five years ago is a sure way to make yourself unhappy.

Worrying about your future won't make it different. Look ahead to see potential roadblocks and start working on solutions.

You don't know what you don't know.

We all hold beliefs that are untrue. Unfortunately, we're unaware of which beliefs are false. If you face any challenges in your life, you probably believe some things that just aren't true.

Figure out what's true and false in your belief system. Having a more accurate road map to life results in a smoother trip.

Do the Work!

Being successful in school doesn't guarantee success later in life. They are two different environments, with two different sets of rules. Examine your life and consider the life lessons presented. Think about how applying these rules could lead to success and happiness.

WAYS TO UNLOCK YOUR POTENTIAL

Do you wonder why you haven't accomplished more with your life? Do you feel your great potential is locked up inside of you? Most adults relate to this idea. No one ever fully reaches their potential, but it is discouraging that so many of us never even scratch the surface of our potential. Are you ready to find out what you can do?

Find out what you're really capable of accomplishing.

Be bold. This is the number one tip for unleashing your potential in the world.

Your limited achievements are likely due to the fact that you're timid. If you were out there doing your best each day, you would be too busy piling up successes to read an article like this. Stop caring about the opinions of others and show the world what you've got.

Have bold goals.

To live up to your potential, you need goals. Goals provide a direction for your energy and effort. Effective goals are motivating, which is great if you're going to set bold goals! Avoid overwhelming yourself. Goals should be bold, but not overwhelming.

Combine your strengths and interests.

Do you really care about maximizing your chess-playing potential if you don't enjoy playing chess? You have the most potential in the areas where you show natural strength and have a high level of interest. What are you good at that you also enjoy?

Get expert assistance.

Some leading experts in the world still have a coach or mentor. The right mentor can help you to reach your potential faster than you can do it alone. Spend the time necessary to find a good mentor. Mentorship puts your progress on the fast track.

Make progress each day.

A small amount of progress, accumulated over time, can result in amazing progress. Avoid overwhelming yourself by setting a schedule or goals that you can't maintain. But, be sure to make some progress each and every day. The amount of progress you can make in a year would be staggering.

Develop habits that help you accomplish your goals.

Keeping with the same theme of making progress each day, your habits are those things you do each day. An effective set of habits all but guarantees success.

Examine your goals and determine the habits that would make success likely. The hardest job you have is creating habits. Once the right habits are in place, there is little else to worry about. Create an effective routine and stick with it.

Determine your obstacles.

Something is always in the way. It might be a lack of time, money, or other resources. Maybe you have a spouse that demands a lot of your time. Maybe you live in the wrong place. After all, to maximize your surfing skills in Missouri can be difficult.

Create a plan for dealing with your obstacles. What can you do to overcome them, or at least minimize them? What do you need to stop doing? How can you alter your life to make success more likely?

Expect success.

If you expect failure, you're bound to fail. Why not give yourself the benefit of the doubt and expect good things? If you have solid goals, good habits, and a smidge of discipline, there is no reason to doubt yourself.

Do the Work!

Making a few decisions, acting boldly, and finding a mentor are just a few of the things you can do to unlock your potential. Make today the day you start living at your highest level. What are you waiting for?

SIGNS YOU'RE HEADED FOR FINANCIAL DISASTER

Many of us are good at ignoring the negative trends in our lives. Maybe we refuse to acknowledge a growing waistline or a relationship that's slowly deteriorating. Many people also ignore the signs of impending financial disaster. Most personal financial meltdowns happen over time. They're rarely the result of a one-time event.

The warning signs are quite clear. You simply need to look and be honest with yourself. Do you recognize any of these warning signs in your finances?

You overdraw your checking account more than once a year.

When you're already struggling to pay your bills with your available income, overdraft fees only make the situation more challenging. Overdrawing your account can be a symptom of these things:

Poor money management.

Some bills simply take longer to clear than others. Do whatever is necessary to stay on top of your pending balance. It can also be a matter of simply failing to pay attention. Having good finances requires regular attention.

Overspending.

Do you have a budget? Are you sticking to it? Ask yourself why you are running out of money before you run out of month.

You're at or near the limit of your credit cards.

Your credit score starts to take a hit when you're above 35% utilization. On a card with a $5,000 limit, that would be anything above $1,750. If you're in this situation, you may be tempted to acquire another line of credit. In most cases, this is only a short-term solution with a poor long-term outcome.

Relying on a future one-time financial event.

Counting on an inheritance or big tax return to balance to your financial situation is a sign of significant debt.

Arrange your finances so that your situation is under control without the need for periodic injections of extra income just to get by.

A failure to save any money.

A deposit in your savings account can be viewed as just another expense. If you're unable to make that payment, you're headed in the wrong direction financially.

All it takes is one unexpected bill or the loss of a job and you're in dire straits. Savings is a better financial cushion than credit.

Borrowing money from family and friends is another sign of impending financial challenges.

Not only is it a sign of financial struggle, it can also be a real strain on your relationships. Most of us loathe asking the people in our lives for money, so recognize the seriousness of the situation if you're considering it.

You're dipping into your retirement funds to pay your bills.

Stealing from your future is a good sign that the present is shaky.

You're killing the magic of compound interest and likely incurring penalties and taxes by making early withdrawals. You don't have an unlimited amount of time to replace those savings.

Using a home equity loan to fill the financial gaps.

Using a home equity loan to pay bills or to purchase something you can't currently afford is a dire warning sign. Not only are you financially struggling, you're also putting your home at risk. Think long and hard before borrowing from the equity in your house.

Do the Work!

If you recognize one or more of these financial warning signs, do yourself a favor and start working on a solution. When these financial conditions start to pop-up, it's usually only a matter of time before things get significantly worse. Make strengthening your finances a priority in your life.

DOES YOUR SPENDING REFLECT YOUR PRIORITIES?

When most of your money goes toward providing what's most important to you, you tend to live a more fulfilled life and gain more satisfaction with the way you spend your money. It is also easier to stick to your personal finance plan when its objectives are to get you what you really want out of life.

Because life priorities can differ drastically from person to person, you need to be aware of your personal values.

What do you really want from life? What kind of lifestyle do you seek? What are your life goals? Does your spending reflect those things? Follow these steps to help determine if your finances are in alignment with your priorities:

List your priorities.

You might notice different levels of priorities as you write yours down. Things like having a place to live and plenty of food to eat are your basic priorities.

However, you most likely need to include some "necessary" priorities to ensure a strong future for yourself and your family members, like maintaining good health or providing your kids with a good education.

Also, list things you love to do that seem more like "luxury" priorities, like reading, traveling or playing golf. These might be on a lower level of priority than your basic priorities, but, nevertheless, they're still important to you, so include these as well.

Now, write down how you spend most of your money.

Where does it go? Although you may get annoyed that much of your money goes toward the mortgage or paying rent, the fact is that we all require a roof over our heads.

You might consider the type, size, and expense of your home and whether you've gone too far in terms of house expenses. If so, the location of where you live, and the mortgage/rent payments might require re-evaluation on your part.

Maybe a good portion of your dollars goes to other necessary expenses like groceries and paying your utilities. But what else do you spend your money on?

Do you play slot machines on Saturday for fun and end up losing money? Maybe you love to shop and use shopping as a pastime that ends up costing quite a bit. Perhaps you spend $20 a week on coffee and snacks or $30 a week having drinks with your friends.

Thoughtfully consider where your money goes from week to week and write it down.

Finally, compare your lists.

Take a look at your first list, the one with your priorities. Ponder each item; does every item accurately reflect what's important to you? Now examine your second list, the one showing where your money goes. Do the lists appear connected? Does your money go mostly toward your priorities?

You might be shocked to learn that, even though you listed certain priorities like providing a good education for your children or having a comfortable home, you're spending $100 plus a week on eating out instead of starting an education fund.

What if you listed reading as one of your priorities, yet you spend nearly $100 a month on cable television you don't watch much? Or if you do, you watch the same 3 channels that you'd actually get on a basic cable plan costing less than $40 a month.

In either case, you've got to ask yourself, "What are my true and real priorities" and "Why am I not putting my money toward the things that matter most to me?"

Do the Work!

Having great clarity regarding your priorities and being conscious of how you spend your money helps you routinely place money toward what's most important to you. Then, as funds becomes available for your favorite things, you are joyful.

CHAPTER FOUR, SUPPORT
DIRECTION

End the Blame and Start the Gain!

You may not have had advanced knowledge of your financial picture, but you are gaining insight into how to create a healthy, wealthy foundation for your future.

Remember, your suffering is ultimately your own creation.

The only person who suffers from your lack of knowledge is you. Let go of the past issues and march strongly into your future.

Getting Started

You are creating the foundation of your financial success. What directions can you take to ensure you stop creating financial pain and start building financial gain?

Read through each section:

· For any sections that present you with new information, spend time each day until you are comfortable with the idea of thinking this new way.

· Pick the ideas that you need the most and implement them first.

After you have all this accomplished, go back and read through your notes every three months to make sure you stay focused on the work you need to get done.

Spiritually Coexist with Money

Money and spirituality coexist in my life.

Use this self-affirming language to teach your thoughts a new habit:

- I appreciate the value money has in society. Money provides many benefits. It can resolve many of the challenges that life presents. I have a positive opinion of money and appreciate the money I have. I am grateful for any boost in my income.
- Spirituality is also very important to me. I am able to enjoy the benefits of wealth and be a very spiritual person at the same time.
- My wealth and spirituality are growing simultaneously.
- My spirituality continues to grow regardless of how wealthy I become. In fact, it is easier to be spiritual when money is abundant in my life. I have less to worry about when I have enough money.
- I can be wealthy and spiritual at the same time.
- Many people believe that money is the root of all evil. I believe that money provides freedom. My life has more potential when I have more money.
- Money provides the opportunity to explore my spirituality with complete freedom.
- Today, I allow money to flow into my life. I experience spiritual growth, too. I am a perfect example of how money and spirituality can coexist.

Do the Work!

Take time for self-reflection:

1. What are my attitudes about money? Is my perception of wealth interfering with my ability to create more financial wealth in my life?

2. What are five ways in which having more money would benefit my desire to be more spiritual?

3. Do I believe that having more money would interfere with my ability to grow spiritually?

Money as a Tool

Money is a powerful tool for helping myself and others.

Use this self-affirming language to teach your thoughts a new habit:

- I accept the idea that money is highly useful. There are many obstacles in life that can be easily resolved with money. Although money often comes with issues of its own, having money makes life easier in many ways.
- While many people choose to downplay the importance of wealth, I choose to be realistic and acknowledge the many benefits of money.
- I accept all the money that flows into my life. I am open to receiving the highest levels of abundance. I welcome financial wealth.
- I am comfortable with wealth. I am at ease with the idea of being a wealthy person. Having a lot of money just feels right to me.
- Some people have a negative opinion of wealth. I am the exact opposite. I know that the more money I have, the better able I am to care for myself and others.
- I care about people, and having money allows me to be more generous and thoughtful. When I have more money than I need, others benefit, too.
- Today, I am opening myself up to all the wealth the world has to offer. I remind myself that I become a more helpful person when I have more money than I need. I am using money as a tool to better my life and the lives of others.

Do the Work!

Take time for self-reflection:

1. Do I have any negative feelings when I think about being rich? If so, why?

2. What could I do for myself if I had more money? What would I do for others?

3. How would my life be enhanced if I were wealthy? Am I comfortable with the idea of being wealthy?

Self-Nourishment Supports You

My soul deserves nourishment.

Use this self-affirming language to teach your thoughts a new habit:

- In times of great uncertainty, I look after my spiritual health. My soul deserves nourishment because it keeps me grounded through difficult times.
- Spending time with my family is good for my soul. When I share laughs and stories with my loved ones, I enjoy a lightness inside. That positive support gives me the strength to push through challenges.
- My family reminds me that I have a lot to live for. Their well-being is one of my priorities, so I ensure that I remain mentally healthy for them.
- Nourishment also comes in the form of video calls with my best friends across the world. Seeing them virtually is the next best thing to having them physically close. I look forward to hearing about the wonderful things happening in their lives.
- I read books and magazines that make me warm inside. Stories of heroism and charity make me proud to be human. I gain strength from the strength of others.
- When I surround myself with positive energy, my spirit thrives. I am capable of tackling any difficulty that life throws my way. Conversation is a great way for me to keep my mind occupied. It rids me of destructive thoughts that occupy my solitude.
- Today, my soul is nourished and well because I seek out positivity. Taking care of my inner well-being makes way for a strengthened mind. I have what it takes to weather the challenging storms that come my way.

Do the Work!

Take time for self-reflection:

1. What is my favorite type of content to read when I find myself uninspired?

2. How do I allocate my time each day to ensure that I renew and refresh my soul?

3. What coping skills do I rely on to deal with unexpected challenges?

Building a Sturdy Life

Life is a house, and I choose to use building materials.

Use this self-affirming language to teach your thoughts a new habit:

- When I think of building my life, I compare it to building a sturdy home. There are many ways to build a house, but some last longer than others. I want my life to withstand the greatest calamities, so I choose to build it like a castle.
- A home built on a concrete slab with a wooden frame has a solid foundation, but the structure is not sound. It may resist inclement weather, but it is easily demolished by natural disasters. I choose to build with stone because it is sturdy, and able to withstand the test of time.
- Each piece of my life is like a stone I carefully choose, and then work to shape and stack.
- I envision the connections I make, and the relationships I build, as being the same as the materials I choose. If I intend for the relationship to be strong, it should be founded upon elements that endure.
- Building a life stone by stone takes time.
- I learn patience, and I begin to see the value of my craftsmanship. While others haphazardly throw together a life of wood, which can burn to the ground in minutes, I am meticulous and methodical. I know that what I build can withstand a disaster.
- Today, I continue to build. I search for ways to enhance my longstanding castle and strengthen my new relationships.

Do the Work!

Take time for self-reflection:

1. How do I help others to build their lives?

2. What are the benefits of quickly building relationships?

3. Who do I look to for support, and why?

Prosperity is My Destiny

I am destined to prosper!

Use this self-affirming language to teach your thoughts a new habit:

- I know that living consciously, focusing my thoughts and actions on what I value most, can only bring success, understanding, and happiness.
- Prosperity can be achieved in many ways, and every day I can find at least one way that I am prosperous. When I sit and reflect at the end of each day, I smile because I recognize how I have flourished.
- I take care of my body by eating right and getting lots of rest. When I look in the mirror, I see how my skin thrives from my healthy lifestyle. I pass my medical examinations with flying colors each time. I know I am prosperous from the point of view of my health!
- I work on building strong relationships with those around me.
- When I spend time nurturing my relationships, they grow more solid each day and thrive from the attention I lavish on them. I have prosperous relationships with others.
- Today, I claim prosperity in my life. I know that I am destined to flourish continually because I consciously make choices that are conducive to my prosperity.

Do the Work!

Take time for self-reflection:

1. How can I increase my feelings of prosperity from my health, relationships, finances, and more?

2. How can I teach my children that prosperity means more than having financial wealth?

3. Do I try to reassure others around me when things aren't going as well as they want?

5

HABITS

Which Habits Help You the Most?

Success takes more than just knowledge. It takes a way of thinking, habits that create your success patterns, and mental support for your success.

To create habits, you have to pay close attention. If a habit is given more power than what holds importance for you then you constantly struggle to accomplish what you want.

Instead of being comfortable suffering with the habit that you have created, do the work!

Getting Started

Read through each section regarding different habits that can improve your life.

· First, find the ones that you are utilizing, and pat yourself on the back.

· Next, see if these habits you have need any tweaking based on the new knowledge you are gaining.

· After you have that done, study things not included and that may be needed to develop your healthy financial lifestyle

· For the new information, spend time each day until you are comfortable with them.

· Pick the habits that you need the most and implement them first.

Finally, after you have all this accomplished, go back and read through your notes every three months to make sure you stay focused on the work you need to get done.

MAKE LIFE EASIER AND INCREASE YOUR SUCCESS

Beliefs determine your actions, and your actions determine your results. If you're not getting the results you desire, your beliefs deserve some examination. Your beliefs are the core of your results.

Life and success are both easier and more consistent when your beliefs are supportive.

Adopt these beliefs and your life will change:

There is a way.

If you don't believe you can succeed at a particular task or goal, you never completely start. It just wouldn't make any sense. You're much more likely to chase those big goals if you believe there is a path that works for you.

Everyone is doing the best they can.

It's easy to take things personally when people are cross or let us down. In many instances, you aren't the issue. The other person could be having a bad day or maybe had a rough childhood.

This belief doesn't imply that everyone is operating at the limit of their potential. But given a person's experiences, present circumstances, and belief system, they believe they're doing the best they can at this moment.

Failure is a learning tool.

At some point, it's necessary to stop learning, thinking, and planning, and pull the trigger. Your results determine your next step. See what happens and adjust your aim. The only way to avoid failure is to never do anything. Failure is part of success.

I can do anything, but I can't do everything.

There are few limits to what you can do. You could climb Mount Everest, be a movie star, astronaut, or neurosurgeon. You can do one or two major accomplishments, but it's unlikely you can do all of them. Select the most important objectives in your life and let the others go or make them a hobby.

Small improvements are enough.

Fast results require big changes, but those big changes can occur over a long period. Trying to change too much, too fast, is unlikely to work in the long-term. It's too uncomfortable. Introduce changes slowly. A small change that's maintained and built upon has a huge effect over time.

I don't need to be the best.

Your lawyer, third-grade teacher, doctor, and mechanic are almost certainly not the best in their respective fields. You can achieve a high-level of success without being the best at anything.

It will all be over someday.

Not to be morbid, but no one lives forever. A time will come when you're gone, and there will be no one left that remembers you. That might sound depressing, but it can be very liberating. None of your mistakes will matter in the end. Enjoy your life and take a few chances.

Good things often take time.

Our society is impatient. We want everything yesterday. Most good things take time to create. If you want something spectacular in your life, be patient. It's important to work hard and temper your expectations in regard to the timing of it all. Learn to enjoy the process.

I already have everything I need to get started.

Getting started is perhaps the biggest obstacle in life. For whatever reason, we have 100 excuses why we should put things off. Some of us wait to start diets on the first day of the month. Or we always need to acquire or learn one more thing before the time is right.

You already have what you need to take the first step today. You can make adjustments and learn a little more tomorrow.

Do the Work!

Can you see how these beliefs would enhance your life? A few, simple beliefs can make all the difference. Enjoy your life more and celebrate more success. Consider the impact your beliefs are having on your life.

ENHANCE THE QUALITY OF YOUR LIFE

When you decide to make a better life for yourself, you often tend to focus on huge changes, but this isn't necessary. Big changes are too intimidating for most of us to even take the first step.

Small changes are easy to integrate into your regular routines.

Luckily, accumulating these small changes over several months can completely transform your life! The secret is to get started as soon as possible. Try these small changes that lead to big results:

Spend 15 minutes each day decluttering your home or office.

decluttering is a bit like pulling weeds. You can't just do it once and forget about it. decluttering works the best if done each day. Choose a room and set a timer for 15 minutes. See how much you can get accomplished before the timer runs out.

Create a budget and follow it.

Everyone knows they should have a budget, yet few actually create one. There is an entire section in this book about how to make a budget. Make a budget that works for you and then stick with it.

Eliminate the unhealthiest food you eat most often from your diet.

What do you often eat that you know you shouldn't? Eliminate the worst offender from your life. Replace it with a healthier food that you would enjoy.

Eliminate one expense from your spending.

What is one monthly expense that adds little to your life but continuously drains your bank account? It might be the monthly termite service that you're not sure how you were roped into, or the monthly bill for the alarm system you haven't turned on in the last six months.

Make a daily schedule. Conscientiousness is the trait most associated with high levels of success.

Creating a daily schedule or to-do list is a great start. A short list of the 3 most important things to accomplish is sufficient to change your life for the better.

Make a list of things you like about your partner.

Keep a notebook and write down one thing each day that you like about your partner. You may be surprised how much more you appreciate them after a month.

Make a list of things you enjoy doing.

Do you think that you spend too much time watching TV? Are you bored on a regular basis? Make a list of things you enjoy doing — from small activities to more elaborate. Do at least one of them each day.

Make a list of the things that annoy you repeatedly and begin fixing them.

It's all the little annoyances in life that can really wear on your nerves. It's the closet door that won't shut all the way, the garbage can with a broken wheel, or the screen door with a hole that lets flies in the house. Start fixing those things.

Make one goal.

Just one little goal is enough to make a difference in your life. Choose something that is challenging but meaningful and work toward it each day for the next month or two. What do you want to accomplish?

Meditate.

Many people report that meditation was the most important thing they've ever done for themselves. Buy a book or enjoy a few videos online. Make a habit of meditating for 10-15 minutes each day. Try it for at least a month.

Do the Work!

You can begin enhancing the quality of your life today. You might not notice a change by the end of the day, but by the end of the month obvious changes occur. Make the most of each day and your life moves in a positive direction. Now is the time to start.

BREAK AWAY FROM SELF-LIMITING THOUGHT PATTERNS

Have negative thoughts hindered your efforts to live, learn, and grow? Your personal beliefs about yourself and your life matter more than you realize. In fact, those beliefs become the very foundation upon which you build your life. Take steps to recognize self-sabotaging thoughts.

Some common self-limiting thoughts are:

- I'll never be able to save any money for retirement.
- I guess I won't ever fall in love again.
- Why can't I find any trustworthy friends?
- I'll be fat forever.
- I'm sure Pat will get that promotion over me.
- I wish I could take a vacation to Europe, but I know I could never afford it.
- How will I ever live the life I want earning what I earn now?

If you identified some of your limiting thoughts while reading the above examples, take steps to break your cognitive ties to those thinking patterns.

How It's Done

Focus on these strategies to start thinking in a new direction:

Refrain from labeling yourself.

If you see yourself as money "poor," then you might unconsciously strive to match that label. Or if you think of yourself as "fat" you may be unable to imagine yourself as beautiful and thin.

Take baby steps.

When you move continuously towards your goals, you gain the momentum to keep on going. Rather than think you're unable to achieve success, make a plan of achievable steps to ensure you do.

For example, perhaps you'd like a European vacation. Instead of believing you can never get there, establish a small weekly goal of saving $20, and keep putting the money aside until you have enough.

Learn to be your own best friend.

Love yourself enough to be your own best friend. Do this by giving yourself the benefit of the doubt. Think positive thoughts such as, "I can do this." When you practice this, you begin to reject self-limiting thoughts.

Believe in yourself.

Instead of insisting you'll "never" do something, say that you can, and then do it. If you turn those negatives into positives, it boosts your self-esteem. Trust that you can accomplish, succeed, and prevail.

Assess the truth.

Ask yourself, "Is what I'm thinking really true?" For example, is it an absolute reality that you are unable to save any money at all for retirement? It doesn't have to be true, unless you strive for that.

Change your mindset by beginning your retirement fund today. At the end of the day, put all your change into a jar. See how simple it is to start saving?

Recognize how powerful your negative thoughts are.

You create who you are by what you think about yourself. Why not turn that power into positive energy that drives you towards the things that you want in life?

Learn from prior errors.

Instead of using your past against you, think about the knowledge you've gained from each experience. Maybe an important relationship dissolved a few years ago. The loss of that relationship doesn't mean you can never find another partner again.

Rather than getting bogged down with self-limiting thoughts, reflect on the shortcomings of your previous relationship. What part did you play? If you proactively learn from your past mistakes, you can make healthier choices in the future.

When you apply the these strategies to your life, you recognize possibilities are all around you. You can do anything you set your mind to. Extinguish those self-limiting beliefs right now so you can start embracing the good life that's yours for the taking.

Do the Work!

Question your self-limiting thoughts. When you realize they're unrealistic, untrue, and within your power to change, you'll be able to break away.

ASK EFFECTIVE QUESTIONS

You ask yourselves questions all day long. Where are my keys; what do I want for lunch; what should I do next? Sometimes the questions you ask serve you. At other times, they do you a disservice.

"Why can't I do anything right?" is an example of such a question. Your brain always attempts to answer your questions, even if it has to make up the answers.

Asking yourself better questions is a great way to improve your life. Better questions result in better answers.

Try these ideas to harness the power of asking more effective questions:

Develop a set of questions that you can ask yourself before you even get out of bed.

These questions should serve to motivate you and get you in the mood to have a great day. Consider these examples:

- What can I do to enjoy work today?
- What am I grateful for in my life right now?
- Whom can I help today?

Develop your own questions to inspire and motivate you!

Pay attention to the questions that you ask yourself throughout the day.

Make note of the questions that make your life more challenging. Correct yourself on the spot and come up with a better question. As an example, "Why can't I ever be on time?" could become, "What can I do to be on time more often?"

You will be surprised how many of the questions you habitually ask yourself are disempowering. We're all sabotaging ourselves! We can turn the tables and support ourselves.

Apply the same idea to your interactions with others.

Many of the questions we ask others make them defensive, and a solution becomes more difficult to find. Instead, ask questions that help you both.

For example, if one of your employees isn't getting along well with his co-workers, you could ask him, "What can we do to increase the level of harmony within our group?" This is more effective than asking, "Why can't you ever get along with anyone?"

The effectiveness of your communication increases dramatically simply by asking better questions and using the answers wisely.

Ask questions during challenging times.

When you first slip into a negative emotional state, use questions to find a solution. Questions focus our attention.

When your attention is on solutions, you tend to find solutions.

When your attention is on the challenge, the challenge tends to grow.

Ask questions that support your goals.

If you're trying to lose weight, ask yourself about healthy food choices. "What could I eat for lunch that would taste delicious and still support my weight loss goal?" Develop some questions that assist you in accomplishing your goals.

Create a set of questions to ask yourself at the end of the day.

Many of your morning questions might be suitable. Ask yourself about your day. What was great? What did you learn? How can you do better tomorrow?

Questions are a powerful aspect of language. They determine your focus and ultimately have a profound effect on your level of success. You can use questions to improve your relationships. They can even help you to have a good day and a restful night's sleep. Asking more effective questions is a powerful tool.

Do the Work!

Take the time to learn to harness the power of asking effective questions. Your life improves in surprising ways. Successful people ask questions that empower them.

CHOOSE POSITIVE SELF-TALK

Do you talk yourself out of being excited? Do you often start out feeling confident in yourself and your abilities, and then drop to zero confidence when your inner dialogue kicks in?

This negative thinking is something many people struggle with, but there's a better way.

You can combat negative thoughts with positive self-talk instead of letting an automatic negative thought process rule your life.

Many people lack the confidence to realize that they deserve to feel good about themselves. These people never pay attention to the fact that they are the ones telling themselves that they don't deserve rewards.

You can discover if you are sabotaging yourself by tuning into your thoughts and listening. What do you hear? Are you encouraging yourself with positive thoughts? Or are your thoughts filled with negatives?

You may not even realize how negative thinking may be dominating your life.

This may be something that you deal with daily and have come to see as normal. However, it's only normal if you allow it to be that way!

Positive self-talk is the practice of responding to negative thoughts that run through your mind. For example, when you tell yourself that you can't possibly land the job because you aren't good enough, you can respond with positive thoughts that do not leave room for negativity. These thoughts can be as simple or complex as you like. The important thing is that you continue to think positively.

Positive self-talk allows you to be the one controlling your thoughts!

Many people pair positive self-talk with affirmations. Affirmations are simple statements you can repeat to yourself over and over again. You can allow these thoughts to become true for you. The process is as subconscious as it is conscious.

When you continue to reaffirm the positive thought, you make it true for yourself until you eventually don't need to remind yourself to think that way.

You can change your life one thought at a time!

Try using affirmations. Affirmations are positive statements that replace your negative thought processes. When you are feeling low and thinking negatively about yourself or your future, try saying, "I give myself permission to be successful," or "I see myself in the winner's circle."

Strive to replace your negative statements with positive thoughts when you repeat your affirmations. Soon it becomes second nature to repeat your affirmations anytime that you start to think negatively.

With positive self-talk you can truly change the course of your life.

You can go from being a negative person with no hope for the future, to an optimist who can achieve anything you put your mind to.

Does this mean that there won't be challenges along the way, or that you never fail? No, because those things are a part of life. But what it does mean is that you can keep a better attitude, which allows you to grasp the very best that life has to offer.

Do the Work!

With practice, positive self-talk isn't difficult. It's worth the effort that is involved because it can truly change the way you view yourself and the world that you live in.

THE LIES YOU TELL YOURSELF

You lie to yourselves on a daily basis. These lies cover up the truth of who you are and keep you focused on your perceived shortcomings. They prevent you from taking risks. Ultimately, these lies limit your lives and your ability to enjoy life fully.

You may not even be aware of the lies you tell yourself. Stop lying to yourself and start living. Look at these lies and lock in your freedom to choose!

"I don't have a choice."

We all have an unlimited number of options available to us at any time. You might not be brave or capable enough to consider them all, but you do have options. Consider what advice you would give a friend in a similar situation. Or determine what your most capable friend would do. Can you do the same? Can you ask for support?

"If I do X or say Y, people will think less of me."

Though it's hard to believe, no one cares. Everyone is too preoccupied with their own lives or else wondering what your opinion is of them.

If you believe you're worthy, you won't have these types of thoughts. You're good enough to do and say what you want.

"It's too late for me."

People have graduated from medical school in their 60's. An 80-year old successfully climbed Mount Everest. Do you still think it's too late?

Many things become less convenient as we get older. For example, it's more challenging to return to school when you have a family and a full-time job compared to a single, 20-year old. But challenging and impossible are completely different.

"Anything short of perfect is failure."

If you have to be the best at something before you try it, you'll never get off the couch. Most of us don't have the potential to be the best at anything, but we can all be pretty good at just about anything. However, it requires time and effort.

Do you really need to be the best? That's another sign of feeling unworthy. There's no reason to be competitive with everything you do. Enjoy yourself without worrying about how well you're doing.

"I'd be happy if I had more money."

Studies have shown that happiness and income are only correlated up to a salary of roughly $70,000 per year. That means that millionaires are no happier than those that make $70,000 annually. If you can pay your bills each month, money isn't limiting your happiness, you are.

"I can change him (or her)."

Unlikely. Think about how hard is to change yourself, even when you want to change. Now imagine how difficult it is to change someone else. If that other person doesn't want to change, it isn't going to happen.

Learn to accept others as they are. If something about them is too disagreeable, distance yourself from them.

"I'm limited in my ability to accomplish anything."

It has been said that learning to walk and talk are far more challenging than anything else anyone has ever accomplished. You're probably saying to yourself, "Well, everyone can walk and talk." Exactly. You're infinitely more capable than you need to be.

You may have a few issues to resolve, but your inherent capability isn't one of them.

Do the Work!

You are a master at deluding yourself. You lie to the person in the mirror in order to protect yourself and others — to make yourself feel better. Avoid giving up your future in order to appease your emotions in the short-term. It could be argued that the purpose of all self-help is to learn how to lie to yourself less frequently. Try it! You could be the next marvel of your own universe!

WAYS TO DECLUTTER YOUR MIND

Our lives are filled with clutter, whether it's a desk covered with papers, a kitchen drawer stuffed with items that don't seem to belong anywhere else, or an overwhelmed mind trying to deal with too much. A cluttered mind is fatiguing and results in poor performance and poor decisions.

You can declutter your mind, just as you can declutter your kitchen drawer.

Start with your diet.

A poor diet can result in a foggy and confused mind. The main culprit is inflammation and unstable sugar levels. There are plenty of resources available on anti-inflammation diets. Avoid processed carbohydrates and all the foods that your mother told you were bad for you.

Exercise.

Few things can clear your mind as well as a good workout. It's great for your mind and body.

Simplify your life.

You might just have too much going. Cut out activities that don't add significantly to your life or your enjoyment. Clamp down on optional activities. It's easy to become bogged down by things that don't matter.

Create habits.

Habits eliminate the need for making decisions. It streamlines your thought process. Eating the same thing for breakfast each day is an example of a habit that avoids having to make a decision. Create daily and weekly habits that take care of your basic needs.

Use lists.

Creating mental notes to yourself to do something at a later day or time requires a lot of mental resources. It's always in the back of your mind, taking up part of your attention.

By writing it down, you're free to eliminate it from your awareness. It's right there on the paper instead.

Use single tasking as a strategy.

Multi-tasking is a mistake. Studies have shown that it's more effective to do one thing at a time. Complete it and move on. You then stay fresher mentally and accomplish more each day.

Make decisions quickly.

Decisions that you put off begin to pile up in your mind and take up valuable space and resources. Successful people make decisions quickly and stick with them. Unless you need more information, make a decision. You won't be any smarter tomorrow or next month, so get it over with and decide.

Rest your mind each day.

Reading, watching TV, or surfing the internet do not count as a rest. Meditation or sitting alone can be considered rest. Sit outside and enjoy nature. Stay focused on your surroundings and avoid allowing your mind to think about anything other than your surroundings.

Prioritize.

There's a limit to how much anyone can do in a day. The secret is to get the most important things accomplished. The easiest way to do this is prioritization. Decide what's most important and start working there.

Do something kind for someone else.

Your cluttered mind is too focused on your own challenges. Give it a break by helping someone else. The result is a clearer mind and a refreshed perspective.

Just two hours of volunteer activity per week has a profound effect on your attitude. It can change your life. It's a simple thing that can add a lot of value to your life.

Do the Work!

Clutter is everywhere. The clutter between your ears is under your control. Simplify your life as much as possible. The less you have to deal with, the easier it is to avoid mental clutter. Give your mind regular breaks through the day. Use your time as advantageously as possible. Prioritize. You may enjoy the peace and clarity that result.

* * *

Complete the *Declutter Your Mind, Questionnaire* in the Tools Section.

FINANCIAL HABITS THAT HELP YOU THE MOST

One of the many keys to effectively changing your life is prioritization. Everyone has limited resources, whether those resources are time, money, or energy. Since you're likely limited by your time and energy, it only makes sense to focus your resources on creating those financial habits that have the biggest impact on your situation.

Use the process of questioning to figure out and focus on your most important new habit.

Where are you feeling the most pain in your financial life?

What keeps you up late at night? Is it the lack of savings? Your non-existent emergency fund? Too little income to pay your bills each month? A bleak retirement future?

Addressing the most stressful financial challenge in your life can be an effective place to start.

Which new habit would have the biggest impact on your finances?

Knowing that you need to work on your savings doesn't necessarily highlight the optimal habit to adopt. Consider the impact each potential new habit would bring to your life.

Make a list of all the potential habits you could build that are related to your target financial concern.

Prioritize your list based on the likely outcome from incorporating that habit into your life. Eliminate the bottom 80%.

Reexamine the 20% that remain. Visualize the impact each of the remaining possibilities can have down the road 1 month, 6 months, 12 months, and 5 years down the road. How does the habit impact your life 25 years from now?

Choose the habit that makes the most sense after carefully considering the future.

If you're torn between 2 or more habits, consider which would be the easiest to implement. Never underestimate the power of momentum. You can swing back around and pick up the other habits in the near future.

Seek to be average at first.

Bring all the parts of your personal finances up to an average level before attempting to be a high achiever. The worst aspects of your financial life are causing your greatest financial discomfort.

In other words, eliminate consumer debt, have an emergency fund, save at least 10% of your income, have adequate insurance, and be consistently saving for retirement before worrying about the purchase of a vacation home or the installation of a swimming pool.

If your habit doesn't address a fundamental, personal finance issue, be certain your target habit is in your best interest.

On a 1 to 10 scale, bring each part of your finances up to a "5" before attempting anything on a grander scale.

Do you have what you need to put the habit into place?

If not, can you get what you need or start small enough that the habit is viable? If you're 75lbs overweight and spend every evening on the couch, you'd have to start small if your desired habit was to run 10 miles each day. You'd need running shoes, too.

Some financial habits might require you to gain a significant amount of knowledge or have a starting point that is currently beyond your reach.

Determine if the habit is possible with your available resources and expertise. It's possible another goal might be more appropriate.

Do the Work!

Time is a limiting factor for everyone, and there are only so many hours that can be applied to building and performing a new financial habit. Ensure you're spending your time efficiently. The most important habits are often the least appealing. Focus on positive habits to best enhance your finances.

CREATE A WEALTH MINDSET

Without a wealth mindset, it's unlikely that you can do the things necessary to build and preserve wealth. A wealth mindset is necessary, but insufficient on its own.

Even so, your mindset is a starting point. A wealth mindset creates the potential to change your financial life in a big way.

Most people have a mindset of short-term enjoyment. They spend money to make themselves feel better at the moment with little regard for the long-term ramifications. How many times have you been excited to purchase something that turned out to be less than exciting after you owned it for a week?

Avoid spending pitfalls and enhance your mindset and financial situation to ensure a more joyful and success filled life.

Take your spending seriously.

A wealth mindset requires taking your money and your spending seriously. Each dollar you spend has the potential to decrease your wealth by more than just a dollar. Consider this example of how this works:

If you purchase a $50,000 boat, the impact isn't just the price of the boat. You also pay for gas, insurance, maintenance, and so on. There's also the opportunity cost. You could've invested that money in something that would actually build your wealth.

You also lose the time you spend enjoying and dealing with your boat. That time could've been spent on creating more wealth. Is the enjoyment worth more to you than the money? Only you can decide what's right for you in the long-term.

A wealth mindset takes spending seriously and considers the short and long-term impact of each dollar spent.

Focus on creating value.

A job can be lucrative, but it can take years to reach the point in your career that you're making a very large salary. The wealthiest people create the most value and charge others for it.

Consider how you can contribute the greatest amount of value to the world and get paid for it.

Spend your time smartly .

One of your greatest powers is your ability to choose how you spend your time. A person with a wealth mindset uses their time effectively. How do you spend your free time? Are you building wealth, learning about wealth, or spending your time on something else?

Learn about wealth creation.

The more you know, the more you can do. Unless you are very fortunate, no one pulled you aside and taught you about wealth. You might not even know anyone who is wealthy. It's up to you to learn everything there is to know about wealth.

Think big. It's important to have big goals, ideas, and plans.

Conservative goals are for average people. Wealth and average don't go together.

Imagine that you could make steady progress for 25 years. Where would you end up? Now, create a plan to accomplish that in five years. That's thinking big.

Consider how your behaviors, thinking, and decisions relate to your wealth goals.

Before you do anything, consider how it impacts the achievement of your goals. Each dollar you spend can take you further away from or closer to your goal. Each person you date **is** either a help or an obstacle.

In a nutshell, ask yourself, "Is what I am about to do going to make me more likely or less likely to achieve my goals?"

Hang around wealthy people.

You become more like the people you hang around with. Wealthy people have a different way of viewing the world and making decisions. You can gain a lot of ground just by hanging out with wealthy people on a regular basis.

Do the Work!

If you want to turn your financial life around, your mindset is a great place to start. Do some research. You'll find that wealthy people don't view money in the same way that financially challenged people do.

When your mindset changes, the way you view the world changes, too. This is a powerful step to creating wealth.

FIVE SELF-HELP RECOMMENDATIONS TO IGNORE

Self-help advice is sometimes difficult to avoid. From comments about the best weight loss method to tips on how to handle relationships, these recommendations can be popular.

You don't have to follow every self-help recommendation that you hear.
Be choosy and don't let popular ideas sway you if they are not right for you or your situation. Consider these popular recommendations:

1. **Stay positive.** Self-help recommendations about staying positive are abundant, but they aren't always helpful. It's not okay to ignore your feelings and pretend to be positive. Negativity doesn't have to be embraced, but it also can't be ignored.

- The key is to recognize and acknowledge your feelings, even if they're negative or sad, and work through them.

2. **Believe that you can do anything.** At its core, this self-help recommendation is trying to encourage people to do great things and find confidence. However, it can be harmful for those who have real limitations.

- It's important to strive for greater things and believe in your abilities.
- However, it's also important to understand that you're human and have limits. For example, you may want to believe that you can work without sleeping for four days in a row, but your body suffers, and you burn out.
- Each person has unique talents and abilities, but this self-help recommendation makes it sound like anyone can do everything. On the contrary, it's better to recognize your gifts and focus on them.

3. **Just ignore the pain.** This self-help recommendation is used in several ways, including telling people to ignore the pain while working out. Blindly following this advice can lead to serious consequences.

- Pain while exercising can be a sign that you're pushing too hard. It's your body telling you to slow down before a serious injury occurs.
- This phrase is also used to tell people to ignore the pain from other things like bad relationships or unhealthy situations. Pain is your body and mind telling you something is wrong and needs to be changed or fixed. Pay attention to it.

4. **Embrace change.** Change can be a positive force, but it's not always necessary.

- Some self-help recommendations make it sound like embracing change is the only way to find happiness. Although change is necessary at times, it's most beneficial to love your current life.
- If changes are happening, and you can't control them, then do what you can to benefit from the change, or work through it, and move forward.
- However, you don't have to constantly change things and add variety to please others or follow a guru's advice. You can simply enjoy what you have at whatever level you are at and find joy.

5. **Follow a specific diet.** There are many self-help recommendations about following specific diets and only eating certain foods. Unfortunately, you can spend years trying diets and watching them fail without seeing results. This self-help recommendation forgets that each human body is unique.

- Although diet advice is popular and prevalent, it's important to find your own path.
- You can't pick up a diet book or online plan and expect it to instantly fix your body. Instead, you have to figure out what works for *you*. There's nothing wrong with reading about diets and using them as general guidelines, but they may not be enough.
- It's better to develop a diet and meal plan that fits your lifestyle, budget, allergies, and other concerns.

Do the Work!

Not all things are for all people. Even though some self-help recommendations are hard to ignore, keep in mind that each person's situation is unique. Pay attention to what works for you and what is best applied to your life.

CHAPTER FIVE, SUPPORT
HABITS

Which Habits Can You Turn Around Fast?

You have the knowledge, now it is time to lock in your success. Use this next section to help you change the way you think of yourself and what you can accomplish. Change your way of thinking, develop habits that create your success patterns, and give yourself the mental support for your success.

Getting Started

Read through each section. They are designed to help you change your stinking thinking into satisfying facts.

· First, find the ones that you are already utilizing, and pat yourself on the back.

· Next, see if yourself talk needs any tweaking based on the new knowledge you are gaining.

· After you have that done, study the self-talk that is new to you. Which ones are missing form your tools used to develop your healthy financial lifestyle?

· For the new self-talk concepts, spend time each day until you are comfortable with them, until you catch yourself replacing your old thoughts with your new and supportive ones.

· Pick the self-talk support that you need the most and implement them first.

Finally, after you have all this accomplished, go back and read through your notes every three months to make sure you have stayed focused on the work you need to make your life great.

My Experiences Are Perfect for My Growth

Life is wonderful. Your journey brings you each and every experience. These experiences serve in developing your space for personal growth. Good experiences are always enjoyable, but the experiences that appear to be negative are also beneficial.

Use this self-affirming language to teach your thoughts a new habit:

- I grow and develop more fully from each event I experience.
- Negative experiences only appear negative. The greatest growth comes from so-called negative events. I learn from each unpleasant experience in my life.
- I have come to look forward to experiences that some may view as negative. My perspective is that they actually bring something positive to my life. One only needs to find it. So, I proactively seek the positive aspects.
- I become better and stronger when I persevere and make it through challenging times.
- It feels like the universe is providing exactly the experiences I need in order to develop into the greatest possible version of myself. I am grateful for this.
- I know my personal growth is happening automatically and at the optimum rate. I face all experiences head-on and fully appreciate them. I am assured to grow in new and spectacular ways if I do my part.
- Every experience is perfect for my personal growth. Believing this is a core principle in my life. I can face anything when I hold this belief.
- Today, I welcome all new experiences, regardless of how challenging they may be. Every experience is an opportunity to learn and develop. I am ready for whatever life brings to me.

Do the Work!

Take time for self-reflection:

1. What could I learn from the biggest challenge I am currently facing?

2. What should I be doing that I have been avoiding?

3. Which life experiences have taught me the most? What have I learned?

Small Steps Lead to Results

New opportunities have the potential to be overwhelming. You can protect your peace of mind by taking a systematic approach to ventures.

Use this self-affirming language to teach your thoughts a new habit:

- Small and meaningful steps lead to a calm process and long-lived results.
- I take my time to think through the viability of new ideas. When something feels good in my gut, I move forward with it.
- I plan my approach, so I am sure to include all the necessary steps in the process. My mantra is to be prepared for anything to avoid unexpected delays down the road. Today's work creates tomorrow's smooth execution.
- New business endeavors get this same treatment. Before I commit my financial and time resources, I gain comfort that the venture is promising and appears to be profitable.
- I step away from business ideas that are overly risky. My peace of mind is my ultimate priority when going into entrepreneurial undertakings.
- When I set a solid foundation for my relationships, it results in long-term bonds. I take the time to get to know someone before committing myself to our relationship.
- Taking it one day at a time means learning what makes someone both happy and unhappy. It means understanding what they value.
- Today, I take a staged approach to anything that I consider worthy of my time and effort. The rules that guide how I approach business are the same ones that I use for personal endeavors.

Do the Work!

Take time for self-reflection:

1. At what point am I able to determine that something is a bad idea?

2. How do I measure the success of business ventures?

3. How do I ensure that I cover all the bases when looking at new opportunities?

Welcome Prosperity into Your Life

To live the life you desire, it is important to understand that you need to be open to whatever good fortune comes your way. Often, the habits of lying to yourself or distracting yourself with negative self-talk can blind you to prosperity that is in your life.

Use this self-affirming language to teach your thoughts a new habit:

- I choose to welcome prosperity into my life.
- I seek to stay aware of incoming abundance and golden opportunities. When I make myself available to all possibilities, positive things happen. I welcome prosperity into my life.
- To be ready to receive wealth, I say, "yes" when someone requests that I do a task. For example, when I am at work and my supervisor wants someone to take on an extra project or squeeze in another special report, I step up. Doing so sends the message that I am ready and willing to work extra hard to achieve a goal.
- Because of my readiness to step into a new project, my manager knows he can depend on me. His increased confidence in my skills improves my possibilities to receive material prosperity. Sometimes, I take a risk when I believe that doing so could lead to my increased good fortune and success.
- When I am open to prosperity, I stand to meet many wonderful people, to be involved in interesting situations, and to receive many blessings. I realize that a sincere effort on my part is required. Yet, ultimately the rewards of prosperity and success are mine.
- Today, I make it a goal to continue to welcome prosperity into my life. I reap the benefits of allowing good fortune into my home, work and social life.

Do the Work!

Take time for self-reflection:

1. Do I consciously invite prosperity into my life?

2. In what ways do I welcome abundance? Do I sometimes pass up opportunities for new experiences that could bring me good fortune?

3. How can I ensure that I stay ready and willing to bring prosperity into my life?

Financial Principles Guide My Transactions

Applying a set of financial principles assures that you can effectively manage your income and expenses.

Use this self-affirming language to teach your thoughts a new habit:

- Because I have done in a healthy way the work to create and understand my financial life, my financial principles guide my every transaction.
- The first principle is to only use credit when I have the equivalent amount available in cash. This approach keeps me from sinking deep into uncontrollable debt.
- Spending beyond my means is a thing of the past. I recognize that the necessities in life are adequately taken care of when I practice smart spending. My mind is constantly focused on what matters most.
- Budgeting makes it easy to monitor and manage my spending. When I allocate set sums for specific expenses, I am able to stay on track each month.
- Putting away savings is the first thing I do when I get paid. Doing this ensures that I am protected in the event of an emergency. I like knowing that my diligence with saving leads to true peace of mind and a less stressful life.
- I believe that committing money to charitable work results in continuous blessings. Sharing what I earn with the less fortunate is both my duty and my pleasure.
- Although I feel protected against the unforeseen by saving, I avoid becoming attached to money.
- Today, I am proud to live by financial principles that make my life easier. When I commit to living by those standards, there is less for me to worry about.

Do the Work!

Take time for self-reflection:

1. How do I decide where to invest my money?

2. What do I normally end up doing with excess funds each month?

3. What allocation do I make to personal growth and development?

Economic Challenges Inspire My Creativity

Tough times come in life even when you have done everything right. When they come, tough times call for more resolve. In tough economic times, do your best to resist the urge to be helpless and hopeless.

Use this self-affirming language to teach your thoughts a new habit:

- Economic challenges inspire me to be creative.
- I know I have the skill sets to be creative. I apply creativity in many areas of my life. This ability can also be exercised with my finances.
- When things get a little tougher financially, I think of ways to make extra money. I actively seek opportunities to earn. I look for things I know I am good at and can earn from.
- I am also creative with my spending. There is always room in my budget for cutting expenditure.
- I consider whether some things I want are actually things I need. I am mature and disciplined enough to know the difference between wants and needs. I remind myself that there is a time and place for everything.
- If I notice others around me folding under economic pressure, I encourage them to persevere. I help them find ways to cut their expenses or earn more.
- When I see something that I want but cannot afford, I sometimes feel disappointed. But I resist the urge to spend on it. I allow myself to sleep it off. From experience, I know that I may no longer feel for it the next morning.
- Today, I confront every challenge with determination to succeed. I am committed to staying one step ahead of economic challenges.

Do the Work!

Take time for self-reflection:

1. Do I consistently budget to prevent overspending?

2. What plans do I have in place to secure some kind of savings?

3. Do I allow myself to be indulgent when I know I can afford it?

Waiting Interrupts Doing

Ideally, the most opportune time to act on a plan is the present. When you wait to make a move, plans can get sidetracked.

Use this self-affirming language to teach your thoughts a new habit:

- Sometimes opportunities only come around once in a lifetime.
- I am steadfast in my commitment to seizing a good thing when it presents itself. This one blessed life I have deserves to be lived to its fullest.
- When fear presents itself, I refuse to let it take control. It is the intangible thing that stands between me and potentially amazing opportunities. I am resolute in overcoming it and going after what I want.
- Procrastination is another barrier that inhibits greatness. Instead of putting things off, I attack them the first chance I get.
- Getting my tasks done efficiently leaves room for more exciting things to happen in my life. The sooner I complete my research paper is the sooner I become qualified for more meaningful career options.
- Instead of waiting for what is considered the right time, I commit to making life-changing moves in the present. That is the quickest way to expose myself to opportunity.
- Today, I am on my way to doing great things and becoming more accomplished because I choose to act now. I realize that waiting is counterproductive. My choice is to make the current time the right time.

Do the Work!

Take time for self-reflection:

1. What value do I put on planning before making decisions?

2. How do I know when a decision is the ideal one for me?

3. What are some things that I am waiting to do? Can I get started on them?

Television is a Void I Avoid

Television is part of worldwide culture. Separating yourself for something so ingrained and so prevalent in society may be a hard challenge to accept.

Use this self-affirming language to teach your thoughts a new habit:

- Using time efficiently can make all the difference in my success and future.
- It is very easy to slip into my favorite television series. However, I know that television is like candy: good in moderation, better if completely avoided. There are numerous ways to entertain myself, and television is the least beneficial.
- When I want to experience a good story, I reach for a book. The imagery created in my mind is better than what I see on television because it is created by me. Reading keeps my imagination active and vocabulary sharp.
- If I feel the need to use my hands, I ignore the video game controller and pick up a pencil. Drawing is stimulating and provides a visual outlet for my creativity. Also, writing is an exercise in creating my own stories. Rather than watch rehashed plots and tropes, I develop original storylines.
- Sometimes music is enough to entertain me. My spirits are lifted when I sing along with my favorite songs. Other times, listening to talk radio enables me to catch up on current events while using my imagination to create the imagery of a talk show scene.
- Television is tempting, but with a myriad of other options, I can easily avoid falling into its hypnotic pull.
- Today, I would like to keep the television off. If the temptation is too great, I can step outside and go for a walk, because I know that it is ill-equipped to follow me.

Do the Work!

Take time for self-reflection:

1. If I know the television lacks benefit, why do I own it?

2. When I do watch television, what amount of time is acceptable?

3. What other forms of entertainment are more engaging than television?

I Spend Extra Income Wisely

What do you do when extra money comes into your life with no strings attached? Do you have a plan and know how to spend it on your benefit? Often, keeping a balance between wants, needs, and your future can help you spend extra money wisely while still enjoying it.

Use this self-affirming language to teach your thoughts a new habit:

- I use my money to help me achieve my goals.
- I know what to save and what to use right away.
- I understand how money works. I know how to divide my income, so I can buy what I need now and also save for other things that are important to me, like an emergency fund, vacations, and my retirement.
- I use extra bonuses and income wisely too.
- I know how to stretch my funds and help them grow. I make room in my budget for saving, spending, investing, and helping others.
- I have financial goals that are clear and easy to follow.
- I maintain effective money habits that help me reach my goals. I pay myself first for savings before I allocate funds for other items. I pay attention to bills and take care of them before due dates. I avoid late fees and penalties.
- I take action with my money. I pay off my loans and debts as soon as possible. I put money away for rainy days with a reliable emergency fund. I invest regularly.
- I make my family aware of our budget too. I teach my children to avoid extra debt. I give them lessons about using money.
- Today, I focus on how I handle money. I am proud of the way I deal with extra income.

Do the Work!

Take time for self-reflection:

1. How can I use extra income wisely?

2. What can I teach my children about money?

3. How do I balance saving and spending?

6

BEHAVIORS

Now that you have momentum in regard to your habits--how you think, what you do, and when you do it--it is time to dig deeper and work on how you behave each and every day. Remember, success takes more than just knowledge. It takes consistent effort to create these successful patterns as well as mental support for continuous application. Success always takes awareness, action, and effort.

The financial life you want takes discipline. You need to pay close attention to times you are less responsible. When you veer off course, you need to return to action and finish the job.

Instead of being comfortable not having the financial life you want, do the work!

Getting Started

Read each section and learn the behaviors that can improve your life.

· First, find the ones that you already utilize, and pat yourself on the back. You are on the right track.

· Next, tweak these behaviors with your newly acquired knowledge.

· After you are done, study the things you need to achieve and develop them to support your healthy financial lifestyle.

· For the new information, spend time each day until you are comfortable with the idea of these behaviors.

· Pick the behaviors that you need the most and implement them first.

Finally, after all this is accomplished, go back and read through your notes every three months to make sure your path remains steady.

PITCH OR KEEP: YOUR TAX DOCUMENTS

Clutter can wear you down. Though the topic is specifically your tax documents, you can apply this to many other forms of paperwork clutter.

What should you do with tax documents and the supporting paperwork? Your aunt says to throw it all away after 2 years. Your banker friend says to save everything for 7 years. What should you do? Are there reasons you should save tax documents forever?

This handy guide to help you determine which tax-related documents to save and which to pitch:

Save tax returns.

Many financial experts recommend to keep your tax returns forever. They might come in handy in the future when you need to reflect back to determine the cost basis of prior investment figures, if you wish to apply for loans, or if you want to file for disability insurance.

If there is no room to store tax returns, scan them and keep them in computer files. Be sure to back them up, though, in case your computer crashes.

File stock and mutual fund confirmations for safekeeping.

Because you are likely to someday sell your stock market purchases, keep the original information about your purchase of those items, such as the date of purchase, price per share, and how many shares you purchased.

As long as you own the stock, you need those confirmations. So, save -- don't pitch.

Throw away monthly statements from all financial institutions if you receive year-end reports or monthly online access.

Be careful with this one, though, because some major brokerage firms recently made a move to eliminate year-end summaries and expect their customers to save monthly reports for tax time.

Pitch salary pay stubs after the year's end.

If you save your pay stubs all year, it's okay to destroy them after you match your W-2 with your total yearly earnings. The only exception here is to keep your final pay stub of the year to claim your donations to charities through your payroll.

Before you dispose of copies of household bills, ensure you don't need them.

To support the deduction of your home office, keep your utility bills and other similar receipts. These receipts back up your ability to claim your office space on your tax return.

Electric/gas bills, internet connection fees, homeowners' insurance, HOA maintenance fees, and others may help you earn a hefty tax return for your home office.

Save credit card bills.

Although some financial experts recommend pitching them, many reasons to save them exist. For example, these days, credit card companies often insure anything you purchase with the cards.

Expect exceptions to these rules.

If the room is available, save all important records.

For instance, in 2010, the government offered the Longtime Home Buyers' Tax Credit to home purchasers who could furnish proof they'd resided in their previous home for 5 of the prior 8 years.

Sound easy? It wasn't, as many applied for and didn't receive this credit. Why? Many home buyers were unable to prove they'd resided in their home for 5 years to the satisfaction of the Internal Revenue Service (IRS).

One couple that did receive the credit got it because they had saved their monthly utility bills for the home and sent copies with their application for the tax credit. So, saving their utility bills ultimately helped them receive a $6,000 credit from the IRS.

Do the Work!

If you take this information into account, you will always have the receipts you need and eliminate the need to use up precious space to store papers you don't require.

Another proactive option is to scan all documents into an app or computer file then discard them. If you do this monthly, nothing piles up and you maintain access to what you need.

RECORDS TO KEEP, RECORDS TO SHRED

Are you determined to whip your home office into shape? It doesn't take long for financial records to overrun the best of us.

One of the most important steps is to organize what is worth keeping and what isn't. Pay stubs, credit card bills, mortgage statements, utility bills, and the endless stream of financial mail are enough to overwhelm anyone. There are several records that are important to save:

Save pay stubs for a year.

If you receive your paycheck via direct deposit, you can stop saving your pay stubs. Though errors are infrequent, the ability to double-check your W-2 form against your pay stubs can be useful. Run your stubs through the shredder the next year.

Keep investment records for as long as you own the investment.

Waiting 12 months after your taxes are filed is even more prudent. It's beneficial to double-check your gains or losses when selling. Remember that these records are frequently available online, so paper copies are redundant.

Keep tax returns for a minimum of four years.

For a standard audit, the IRS will go back 3-4 years. If you've underreported your income by 25% or more, they can go back further.

If you're an honest tax filer, four years is sufficient. If you're not, keep at least 7 years of returns.

Do you employ a nanny, housekeeper, gardener, or other domestic help that you hire directly? Keep 3-4 years of pay records.

Mortgage records are also worth saving.

This includes all the documents received at closing and records of payments. Also, keep receipts related to home improvement projects.

Fortunately, there aren't many records that require saving. While there are financial records worth keeping, most paperwork can be fed to your shredder. Avoid keeping these records:

Put your bills in the shredder.

Most bills aren't worth saving. Only keep bills that are necessary for tax purposes. Check your bills for accuracy and then pay and shred them.

Throw out all junk mail except preapproved credit card applications.

As annoying as junk mail can be, avoid the urge to throw it all in the trash. Shred preapproved credit offerings to avoid identity theft issues.

Computer media can have sensitive information.

Be aware of simply throwing away memory sticks, old computer disks, or hard drives. There are companies that will destroy these items for you. A hammer can serve well, too. Some experts recommend fire, but the fumes aren't exactly safe. A hammer is more environmentally friendly.

Unless needed for tax purposes, avoid saving receipts.

If you're very conscientious and go over your finances in great detail each month, keep your receipts for a month. Otherwise, throw all receipts in the trash except those that are for items that you might want to return. Keep these receipts until the return period has expired.

As a general rule, the more expensive the item, the longer a receipt should be saved. It makes more sense to keep a receipt for a new washer and drier than a pack of gum.

To determine which items should be shredded, shred items that you wouldn't want to fall into the hands of strangers. If an item contains your social security number or credit card number, shred it. Beyond that, it's up to you.

Do the Work!

Financial records are a part of everyday life. From ATM receipts to mortgage statements, financial papers accumulate at a rapid rate. It's important to know which financial records are worth keeping and which aren't. Avoid keeping records that serve no purpose. Keep your financial records neat and organized.

MANAGE JOB SEARCH EXPENSES

A job search can be expensive as well as time-consuming. There are ways to manage your expenses so that you achieve the maximum value out of your spending. These are strategies for keeping costs down and taking advantage of all the tax deductions you are entitled to.

Make the effort to reducing your job search expenses while moving closer to your success.

Network over coffee.

Face to face networking still matters even in the Facebook age. Inviting people out for coffee or breakfast is usually less expensive than lunch or dinner.

Choose your wardrobe.

Allow your wardrobe to reflect your personality and how you will fit into the the job market.

Buy your interview suits and tasteful accessories at consignment shops or on eBay for a fraction of the retail cost. Select separates that you can mix and match for more options.

Barter for services.

Some job coaches are worth their high fees, but you may know people who will help each other out for free. Offer to proofread each other's resumes. Share job leads and take turns rehearsing for interviews.

Access community resources.

Local government offices, nonprofits, and business groups often provide free and low-cost career services. Call your state employment office and check community calendars.

Evaluate your travel priorities.

In a tight job market, some employers may expect you to pay the travel expenses for long-distance interviews. Ask yourself if the position is worth it for you. Clarify how many candidates are being considered.

Deducting Job Search Expenses

Stay in the same field.

The IRS only allows deductions for job search expenses if you're looking for a job in your current occupation. On top of that, there cannot be any significant gap between your last position and the start of your job search.

Know the limit of 2 percent.

Allowable job search expenses are deductible if you itemize deductions on Schedule A and those miscellaneous expenses including your job search costs exceed 2 percent of your adjusted gross income.

Hold onto your receipts.

Good record keeping will help you stay on track. Keep receipts for everything from stamps to airline tickets. The IRS may want to examine more than your credit card statement. Mileage logs and odometer readings can be submitted if you travel by car.

Watch your phone minutes.

Phone bills only count if you incur extra charges. With an unlimited phone plan, the details are probably irrelevant to the IRS.

Calculate agency fees.

If a job search agency charges you a fee, you may be able to deduct it. If your new employer later covers it, you'll naturally need to make a reimbursement.

Keep business trips mostly business.

To be deductible, a job search trip must be primarily for business purposes. Keep a log of your time to confirm your activities.

Specify your coaching services.

Certain coaching services can be deducted while others fall outside the guidelines. Improving your interviewing technique is likely to be approved while counseling on making a career switch would be ruled out.

Consider your childcare needs.

Some experts question if childcare can be deducted. If you want to do so, document it like any other expense with receipts and details on why it was essential.

Stay up to date.

The tax code is complicated and changes all the time. Consult your tax professional or IRS Publication 529 on Miscellaneous Deductions to ensure your information is current.

Do the Work!

Keep expenses under control so you can focus your efforts on finding the right position for you. Your job satisfaction is worth making an investment, but a little knowledge and careful record-keeping can help you achieve excellent results for less.

EARLY TAX FILING

Do you rush to file your tax returns as soon as possible? If you have all your documentation, this might be as soon as January. But is filing early a good idea? Like many things in life, the answer is, "It depends."

Not every situation supports the idea of filing early.

In fact, filing for an extension and putting it off as long as possible makes sense for some filers. Let's look at the advantages and disadvantages of filing early.

Advantages

Receive your refund sooner.

If you're owed a tax refund, you might as well enjoy your money as soon as you can. If you're going to mail your return (30% still use the mail), the IRS is less busy in February than in April, so the processing time might be quicker.

Be free of the mental clutter.

End your clutter one way or the other. It makes sense to end your procrastination and free yourself. Life is easier if you don't procrastinate. Just do it.

The post office is less crowded.

Remember, 30% of the adult US population is a lot of people and most of them will be trying to use the post office at roughly the same time. A lot of people don't want to electronically file for a variety of reasons. Avoid the crowds.

You won't be late.

Many of us plan to do things at the last minute, but this is always risky. What if you find out that you're missing some key piece of information? What if you get sick? There are too many variables in life to put off something like filing your tax return until the last minute.

You'll be more accurate.

If you're not rushed for time, you'll be more likely to avoid errors. You'll be able to ensure that you maintain everything you need correctly.

Disadvantages

Why pay early?

If you owe the IRS money, you'll make more money in interest if you can keep your money as long as possible. It makes sense to keep your money as long as you can.

You might end up having to file a corrected return later.

Employers, banks, and investment firms commonly come back a month after sending your documentation and say, "Oops, we made a mistake." Taking a little time to file your return will help to ensure that you only need to do it once.

Greater chance of being audited.

It is commonly believed that early filers are more likely to be audited. The rationale being that if the vast majority of the population is filing at the last moment, then there are so many tax returns that the odds of being selected are minimal.

Some experts say that getting an extension lowers the odds even more since the IRS agents are continuously busy (and behind) with their audits.

Consider the above factors when deciding to file your tax return. If you're in a situation that makes it more likely that you'll be audited and you don't need your refund or copies of your return right away, it can be wise to wait.

Do the Work!

Assess your situation and make the smart choice for your circumstances. If your return is simple, you're due a refund, and you need the refund now, then file your return.

PAYING OFF DEBT IN THE NEW YEAR

Having debt is like carrying a huge boulder on your shoulders. Each time you finance another purchase or swipe your credit card, you're adding weight to that boulder.

Let this year be the year of removing that boulder of debt from your shoulders so you can live joyfully in the realm of financial freedom.

You can pay down your debt this year, whether your debt amounts to $3,000 or even $30,000. The single most effective way to do so is by creating an income stream and dedicate its earnings towards paying down your debt.

Yes, you may need to temporarily add quite a few hours to your workweek, but one year of long hours can lead to a life free of the many burdens of debt. Can you imagine what it would be like not having to make debt payments? Your paycheck would be yours to do with as you please!

Getting a Part-Time Job

If you can aquire a moderate to a well-paying part-time job, go for it! If you're able to land a 20-hour per week part-time gig paying just $12 per hour, that's over $1,000 each month. Granted, you'll inevitably need to pay taxes on this income, but even so, you're able to keep about $945 in your pocket by the end of each month.

Over the course of a year, you'll be able to devote over $11,300 to your debt. Imagine the relief when you remove the heavy boulder of debt from your shoulders! And if your spouse is willing to work a part-time job with the same pay, you'll be able to pay off your debt in the following amounts.

Total Debt Paid Off with Two Additional Part Time Incomes:

Month Debt Paid Off

Month 1 $1,890

Month 3 $5,680

Month 6 $11,340

Month 9 $17,010

Month 12 $22,680

How drastically would your life change if you were able to pay off over $20,000 worth of debt? Better yet, if you choose to keep the job even after you're done paying off debt, you'll be able to build a hefty savings account to protect yourself from ever needing to borrow money from lenders in the future.

Capitalizing on Your Hobby

Everyone has a hobby. Unless your hobby is habitual shopping, chances are you'll be able to capitalize on indulging in your hobby. You can flip furniture, sell knitted items, profit with sporting gear, or even sell your homegrown vegetables.

If you're talented in repainting furniture, purchase used furniture for pennies on the dime at Craigslist.org, yard sales, or a local thrift shop. Then, sand the piece, prime it, paint it with two coats of glossy white paint, apply a protective coat, change the hardware and then list it back on Craigslist.org for sale.

If you purchased the piece for $25, spent an extra $20 on supplies, and are able to flip it for $150, your profit is $105 with just a few hours of work! When you become accustomed to the process, you may be able to flip 3 pieces of furniture per week and end up with a nice $1,260 profit. Not bad for indulging in a hobby you enjoy!

While you may not be the Picasso of cabinet refurbishing, you can still develop another hobby. Below are 7 common hobbies that are easy to capitalize on.

- Knitting/sewing
- Cooking/baking
- Babysitting
- Painting
- Flipping collectibles
- Writing
- Party planning

Do the Work!

For some, there's no need to downsize, or even adjust your lifestyle to pay off your debt. Hard work was used to build everything that supports your life; why give it up now? Getting a part-time job or monetizing your hobby will allow you to pay down your debt considerably this year so you can start living the debt-free life you deserve!

LEASE OR BUY? FINANCING TIPS FOR AUTOMOBILES

There are two basic options when you need a new vehicle: Lease or buy. You can purchase a vehicle with cash or through financing or strike up a lease agreement with an auto retailer. Leasing a vehicle provides you with short-term benefits without ownership, while buying is a much more serious commitment, but with greater long-term value.

To get the most out of either financing option, become familiar with the benefits and drawbacks associated with each option.

Both options are viable when the right conditions are met, so leasing might be best for you at some point in time while buying is best during another point in your life.

Here are some things to consider before deciding to buy or lease a vehicle:

Leasing is similar to renting your car.

When you lease a vehicle, you make monthly payments on it, but you never really own it. This means that once the lease term is up, you either give the vehicle back or renew the lease. You never pay off or own the vehicle.

- Despite not owning the vehicle, you're still responsible for all aspects of maintenance during the lease term in most circumstances. This means new tires, oil changes, new fluids, and all general maintenance costs are your responsibility.
- Because you don't own the vehicle, you cannot make any modifications to it: no bumper stickers, aftermarket parts, window tinting, or other alterations that you might like to make on a car that you enjoy driving.
- Leasing is most ideal for individuals who want to drive a new vehicle

every few years. When your lease agreement ends, you can initiate a new lease agreement with a new vehicle.

Getting an auto loan means the vehicle is yours.

As long as you make the auto loan payments on time, you can keep the vehicle. Once the vehicle is paid off completely, your worry about making payments ends.

- As the owner, you're responsible for maintenance costs and repairs. However, you may enjoy the fact that you're maintaining your own vehicle. You can keep it as long as you like.
- When you own your car, you can use it as collateral for secured lending options. When you lease a vehicle, you cannot use it as collateral and there are many restrictions about how you can use it that may limit your enjoyment of the vehicle.

Interest rates affect whether one option is better than another.

Affordability is key when it comes to choosing between leasing and owning a vehicle. The affordability of one option over the other can change based on the market and current interest rates and other incentives.

- When interest rates on auto loans are low in general, lease payments may not be the most attractive option. Lower interest rates combined with incentives from auto dealers often make an auto loan a better opportunity.
- When interest rates go up and obtaining an auto loan is not always feasible, leasing may be a better option because it provides short term access to a car with lower monthly payments since you don't pay based on the interest rate.

Do the Work!

The bottom line weighs your options closely before deciding to buy or lease a vehicle. Different options provide different incentives, advantages, and disadvantages over time. Compare the opportunities for leasing or buying to your current financial situation to determine which is best for you.

FUEL-EFFICIENT CAR OR NOT

With the high price of gas these days, you may want to consider selling your car and purchasing one that's more fuel-efficient. If your current car is only delivering 17 miles per gallon, one of those hybrids gets 50+ miles per gallon might look pretty good!

If you start doing some quick calculations, it doesn't take long for excitement to increase about all the money you could be saving. Think about all the wonderful things you could purchase with that extra cash. Maybe you could take that vacation you've been dreaming of!

If you're driving an inexpensive paid off model, you might not be able to justify getting a new car, regardless of the great gas mileage.

Consider the car payments, insurance, taxes, and yearly registration fees if you're thinking about buying a more fuel-efficient car. Will the increase in those costs validate your decision to go from 20 mpg to 45 mpg? At $3.50 per gallon and 1,000 miles per month, you'd be saving less than $100 per month in fuel costs. As long as your car is in good condition, it's not worth all the extra expenses.

Complete these calculations to consider if purchasing a fuel-efficient car is a smart financial move in your situation:

How much are you going to spend on a more fuel-efficient car?

You need to know how much the new car will cost you. That increase in mileage isn't free.

For example, let's suppose you're interested in a 2011 Toyota Prius that costs $15,000.

How much is your current car worth?

Assuming you're planning to sell it, that money can go towards the "new-to-you" car.

Continuing with our previous example, perhaps you're selling your 2003 Ford F-150 that's paid in full and worth $5,000. That means your new car would cost about $10,000.

What are the other costs associated with owning that new car that are above and beyond the old car?

Take time to consider all those "hidden" new car costs you might forget about.

- Sales tax: $600 at time of purchase
- Insurance: An increase of $50 per month
- Registration Fee: Depending on your state, it might stay the same, but it could also increase by $200 per year. We'll use $100 per year for our calculations.
- Payments: A 4-year loan at 7% for $10,000 would come to $240 per month.
- If you're paying cash for your car, consider how much money you'd be losing by your inability to invest that money. This is called the opportunity cost. Ten percent per year on $10,600 (car + tax) is $1060 per year or $88 per month.
- Look at our total on a monthly basis (assuming a loan): $50 (insurance) + $100/12 (registration) + $240 (payment) = $298 per month beyond the cost of your current car.

What is the change in mileage per gallon?

Let's be optimistic and claim 50 mpg for the Prius and 15 mpg for the F-150.

How many miles per month do you drive?

The average driver puts about 1,000 miles per month on their car.

How much are you saving?

- Prius = 1,000 miles/50 mpg X $3.50/gallon = $70 per month for fuel costs.
- F-150 = 1,000 miles/20 mpg X $3.50/gallon = $233 per month of fuel costs.
- You would be saving $163 per month on gas.

Is it worth it?

In our example, it wouldn't be worth it from a financial perspective. Your spending increases by $298 per month in order to save $163.

Do the Work!

Take your time and do all the calculations before making a decision. In most cases, the old car will win if you're making a financially responsible decision. So, before you run out and buy that newer, more fuel-efficient car, do the math. The answer might be different from what you think.

FINANCIAL RULES YOU SHOULD RECONSIDER

There are many financial rules we've all heard over and over again. But many of these rules aren't perfect or don't apply to every person's individual situation. Instead of blindly following rules that someone else made, take the opportunity to consider a few counter-arguments. You might find a better alternative to what you're currently doing with your money.

Consider whether financial rules make sense to you. Consider the variables in your life that make the difference in each choice you make.

Cutting expenses is the key to long-term financial success.

Most of the well-known personal finance gurus focus on cutting expenses and saving money. While there's no reason to spend unnecessary money, there's only so much you can cut from your expenses. Then you're stuck with no further room for growth and a potentially less than enjoyable lifestyle.

Few of these financial gurus mention the other side of the equation. How about increasing your income? After a certain point, it's much easier to increase your income by $300 per month than to cut another $300 each month from your bills.

Take the time to trim your expenses to a reasonable level and then focus your efforts on creating more income. A promotion, a new job, or a second job can be easier to accomplish with less effort and grief than making further budget cuts at home.

Leasing a car is always the wrong choice.

Cars today last an average of over eleven years. That's a long time. If you like to keep a car until it's ready for permanent retirement, buying is the best option.

However, if you want to update to a new car every few years, leasing is a much better option.

Instead of following anyone's advice on this topic, pull out a calculator and do the math yourself. Be sure to consider all the expenses included with both options.

Do the same exercise in regard to housing. Renting is usually a better option in the short-term. If you're not going anywhere anytime soon, buying is likely to be the best bet.

Do what you love, and the money will follow.

This can be a great idea if what you love to do can provide an income and you're good at it. There are many hobbies and interests that would be exceedingly difficult to turn into a significant source of income.

You might also find that your hobby ceases to be enjoyable when you're forced to do it 40+ hours each week to earn money.

For example, you might love to go bass fishing. But professional fishermen fish standing up, rain or shine, in hot and cold weather, and make a certain number of casts per hour to be competitive. You will also be required to travel extensively. Many people that love to fish wouldn't enjoy fishing in that manner.

Always contribute the maximum amount into your 401(k).

If you don't have an emergency account, how will pay for a new transmission or the $4,000 deductible for your broken leg? What if you lose your job?

There are other expenses that should be considered before putting all the money into your 401(k) or other retirement accounts. Withdrawing money from a retirement account can result in both penalties and taxes. You can't always put the money back in, either.

Do the Work!

These are just a few of the common financial rules that you should consider breaking. No rule applies to all situations. Examine the rules you follow and evaluate if they make sense for your financial situation.

FINANCIAL HABITS THAT WILL KEEP YOU POOR

Are you continually facing financial challenges? You might be keeping yourself poor with habits you didn't even realize were contributing to your situation.

Drop the habits that keep you poor. Use this effective first step to move toward enhancing your security and financial future.

Make the decision to drop these financial habits from your life:

Failure to create an adequate emergency fund.

An emergency fund that covers at least 3 months of living expenses is the best prevention for financial disaster. A short period of unemployment or a single, unexpected, major bill can be economically devastating. It will happen.

Set aside whatever dollar amount you can manage and begin building an emergency fund. Even a few dollars each week is a start.

Habitually paying bills late.

Most consumers believe that credit card companies make most of their money from the high-interest rates they charge. This isn't true. They actually make the most money from the late fees they collect. Nearly every bill you pay each month becomes more expensive if you're late, even by a single day.

Develop the habit of sitting down once a week and paying the bills that are coming due. Pay them at least 7 days in advance.

Inappropriate use of credit cards.

Using credit cards to purchase unnecessary items you can't afford is the worst use. Putting charges on your cards up to their limits and then only paying the minimum due will put you in a precarious position, lower your credit score, and keep you in debt for a long time.

Resolve to limit credit card use to emergencies or to accumulate rewards if you're paying off your balance in full each month.

Failing to save money from each paycheck.

If you're struggling to make ends meet, saving money often looks impossible. But saving money now is critical. Start by saving 1% of your take-home pay and build from there. If you never save any money, how will your situation change?

Making impulse purchases.

How many times has making a big purchase caused you to run out of money at the end of the month? Impulse purchases are rarely satisfying after the initial glow has worn off. In fact, you're probably resentful of the purchase after the financial pain comes home to roost.

Take a few days to think about the purchase before making a final decision. You'll often find the urge has subsided.

Buying items you don't need.

After shelter, clothing, food, and medical care, most spending is optional to varying degrees. You probably don't want to feel like you're living in a cave and eating sticks, but you certainly spend money each month that could either be saved or spent more wisely.

Failing to contribute to your retirement.

After forty years of toiling to make ends meet, wouldn't it be nice to retire comfortably? Many seniors find themselves in challenging financial circumstances because they failed to contribute adequately to their retirement. It's never too late to start.

Do the Work!

Eliminating negative habits is the most effective way to start your journey to financial abundance. Choose one habit and make an effort each day to remove it from your life. The most powerful action you can take in regard to your finances is to eliminate your three most debilitating financial habits.

MAKING THE MOST OF A FRESH START

Fresh starts take place in your life every day. When you do something for the first time, you can consider that a fresh start. However, something new isn't always something you look forward to.

How can you make the most of a fresh start—especially when what you do proves to be difficult?

Try these techniques:

- Embrace it with an open mind. There are exciting new opportunities ahead!
- Conquer your fears with faith. Faith is stronger than any fear, doubt, or insecurity you experience, so by all means, rely on it when you need to. Believe in yourself.
- Liken it to an experience that you previously made it through.
- Begin by thinking of the end. Make a plan to get to your new destination.

Do the Work!

Looking to make a fresh start? Use every opportunity to your advantage.

AXE SELF-SABOTAGING BEHAVIOR

Self-sabotage is a uniquely human behavior. Many of you sabotage yourselves when you decide you want something by doing everything you can to ensure you don't get it. Sound familiar? Although self-sabotage is a subconscious behavior, you can get a handle on it.

When you're immersed in mediocrity, the idea of greatness may be frightening.

There are many reasons that you might sabotage yourself. It's an extremely common behavior, rooted in a fear of the unknown. Find out why you may self-sabotage.

Control.

You might self-sabotage because of a need to be in control of your circumstances. The easiest and most certain way to stay in control is to maintain the status quo.

If you put your all into something, you run the risk of becoming vulnerable. Fear can get the best of you and you will self-sabotage.

Low self-esteem.

Do you consider yourself to be unworthy of greatness?

For whatever reason, you may have decided that happiness ought to be forever beyond your reach. This is a self-limiting idea, and it becomes a self-fulfilling prophecy.

Excitement.

Perhaps you undermine your efforts because you're seeking excitement. You think you need to remain in a constant state of turmoil to distract yourself from painful memories or alleviate boredom.

If you see yourself in any of these descriptions, don't worry. There are steps you can take to put yourself on the path toward self-mastery. Consider this process for defeating your self-sabotage:

Observe your behavior.

First off, it's essential that you begin to observe yourself. You can do this by creating a self-sabotage journal. Make a journal entry every time you realize that your actions are self sabotaging. Describe the setting, circumstances, and end result. Avoid over-analyzing.

Most often, a person's true intentions are most evident in their actions, rather than their words.

Strive to be an impersonal observer in your journal. Eventually, you'll gain a better understanding of your motives in certain situations.

Envision success.

Keep in mind that success is neither black nor white. Cultivate the habit of envisioning what success means to you and remember how it feels to achieve it. If you do this consistently, you may find that what you envision changes over time.

Begin to see success as an integral part of your future but realize there will still be challenges. Just like with everyone else, your taxes still need to be paid and relationships might still include issues.

Let go of the notion of perfection.

As you visualize success, are you still thinking that success equals perfection? If so, it's time to realize that nobody is perfect.

This is what George Bernard Shaw would refer to as "doublethink." Perfection and life are mutually exclusive because perfection is unattainable. Your subconscious won't allow you to achieve success if you associate success with the impossible task of being perfect.

Think of your subconscious as a computer. It doesn't know how to execute a command called "do the impossible."

If you associate success with fear, your subconscious will fight you the entire way. Why? Your subconscious's primary function is to protect you from perceived threats.

Give yourself permission to anticipate success with excitement. Perhaps your subconscious has been receiving the message, "Don't give me success!" So, let's put your self-sabotaging behaviors in the past!

Do the Work!

Embrace the good life you deserve by picturing yourself as successful, and then refuse to talk yourself out of going for it. The journey to your ideal life starts now!

KEYS TO SURVIVE A ROUGH DAY

Everyone has good days and bad. When faced with a bad day, do everything you can to make the most of it. At the very least, avoid making it worse. A bad day doesn't mean you should just throw in the towel. Life is only so many days long, so take full advantage of each one.

You can accomplish something worthwhile, no matter how bad of a day you're experiencing.

Survive a bad day and make the most of it:

Avoid behaviors that make a bad day even worse.

Complaining, overeating, yelling at a coworker or loved one, or drinking are just a few ways you might make a bad day worse. Why throw gasoline on the fire? Keep your wits about you and hold on. Tomorrow is a new day. It might be your best day ever.

Maintain your perspective.

Maybe your boss hates your report, but it beats the heck out of living under a bridge. No matter how bad your day is, it could always be worse. And many are faced with far worse each and every day. Things will get better.

Meet with a friend for dinner.

People love drama as long as it isn't their own. Your friend would love to hear about your bad day over a delicious dinner. You can tell your story and unburden yourself, all while enjoying your favorite restaurant.

Remember that it's just one day.

You can handle one bad day, having already survive many in the past. Finish the day but look forward to tomorrow. Things can only get better, right?

Avoid making any important decisions.

A bad day isn't the best time to decide to quit your job, give up on your dream of law school, or end a relationship. All of those things can wait until your mood and circumstances normalize. Again, avoid doing anything that can make your crummy day horrible.

Make plans that excite you.

Decide to get away for the weekend or buy that new iPod that's been on your list the last few months. Give yourself something to look forward to in the near future.

Learn a lesson.

Is there anything you did to cause your bad day? Could your rough day have been prevented? Can you learn anything from this experience? A rough day isn't so bad if you learned something useful from it. Make the best of it.

Breathe.

Unless you're underwater, breathing is always a good idea to relieve tension and regain control of your emotions. Just breathe and get your work done. Completing everything that needs to be done is more challenging when everything appears to be going wrong, but you'll feel more satisfied at the end of the day if it wasn't a complete loss.

Take a nap.

Sometimes you can reset your day and your brain by taking a quick nap. Maybe you'll see your situation in a new light. A nap also provides a needed break.

Do the Work!

Deal with your bad days effectively. When you're experiencing a bad day, focus on survival and completing the most important tasks. Most importantly, avoid using a bad day as an excuse to do something stupid or you might find that it can get worse. Follow these strategies and you'll get through your rough days in the best ways possible.

THOUGHT PATTERNS CAN CLOUD YOUR JUDGMENT

Your thoughts impact your actions, and ultimately, the level of success you achieve. Your thought patterns influence your emotions and perspective of the world. If you can identify your unhelpful thought patterns, you can correct them and develop new ways of managing yourself and the world.

Your thought patterns influence multiple aspects of your life.

Making assumptions.

Good decisions require information. Too many of us jump to false conclusions because we are missing some of the facts. Before you reach a negative conclusion about a situation or person, delay your judgment. Gather all the available information and make an informed decision.

How many decisions were made too quickly and you later regretted it? Give yourself the chance to be right.

Applying the past to the future.

Maybe the most beautiful girl in high school ignored you, but that has nothing to do with your ability to appeal to the woman of your dreams today. The past doesn't equal the future.

We're too quick to believe we're experts regarding our abilities. One failure isn't enough to prove anything. Pharmaceutical companies aren't allowed to test a drug on just one person and then release it to the public. Many attempts are required to prove that results aren't due to random chance.

Would you believe that a flipped coin would only land on "heads" in the future after flipping it once or twice and getting that result?

Even if you lack natural skills in one area, you can always learn. You weren't born knowing how to walk or do algebra. You can learn to be a great public speaker, salesperson, or social butterfly, too.

Focusing too much on the positive or the negative.

Strive to be accurate. Consider when you start dating someone new. At first, you're too focused on their positive traits. As the relationship is failing, you're too focused on the negative. Neither is accurate.

Giving things too much or too little relevance.

Do you give your failures too much attention? Do you give your successes too little? Strive for a balanced view. Just because your boss ignored your morning greeting doesn't mean you're about to be fired. Give yourself the credit you deserve.

Taking something personally that has nothing to do with you.

People do and say things for many reasons that don't include you. They might be having a bad day or dealing with a personal issue. Your car breaking down doesn't mean the universe is out to get you. Others tend to be focused on themselves with more on their mind than just you.

Focusing on the past.

The past can provide lessons. However, most people don't use their past constructively. They focus on missed opportunities and mistakes. When used this way, the past creates feelings of regret. Let go of the past and avoid allowing it to cloud your future.

Focusing on the future.

Having goals and plans is great! But it's common to use the future as a source of worry. Stay focused on today. Today is the only time you can change your life. Allow the future to arrive. It will come soon enough.

Putting things off.

Is it easier to have your muffler replaced when you notice it's deteriorating or to wait until it falls off in the middle of the highway? If you wait until you're forced to deal with things, your solutions will be less elegant and less convenient. Do things in your time.

Do you indulge in any of these negative thought patterns? Noticing your tendencies is the first step to changing them.

Do the Work!

When you catch yourself thinking in a way that clouds your judgment, replace your thought pattern with one that serves you well.

IDENTIFY AND ADDRESS YOUR WEAKNESSES

Dealing with weaknesses is a challenging task for most of us. We instinctively don't want to think about our weaknesses or deal with them. It feels easier to just accept that we're not good at something and then avoid it. This isn't a very fulfilling way to live. You leave too much on the table with this strategy and limit your life severely.

There are simple techniques you can apply to gain mastery over yourself and the world by identifying and dealing with your weaknesses.

Follow this process:

Make a list of the weaknesses you know.

Let's face it: You can likely list several weaknesses right off the top of your head. That's a good place to start. So, start that list.

However, you also have weaknesses you're not aware of. Those can be the most insidious. It's the things that you don't know that sometimes cause the greatest challenges.

Ask a trusted friend and a family member.

A good friend will know you well. A family member will have known you for a long time. You can get some great insight from asking these people about your weaknesses. You're bound to hear something you never considered.

Ask your boss.

Some weaknesses are only weaknesses in the workplace. Ask your boss to identify your weaknesses. This information can be invaluable. It also shows your boss that you're a thoughtful employee.

Give it some serious thought.

With all that information, sit down and think. Take it all in and decide which weakness is most important to rectify. Also, consider how challenging each will be to address. Between those two criteria, it will be clear where you need to start.

Now that you're aware of your weaknesses, it's time to actually do something about them.

Understand that your weaknesses are often things outside of your natural ability. This means it might be challenging to make a significant amount of progress. Patience is key! Even a small amount of progress is worthy of celebration.

Let's suppose your most significant weakness is interacting with strangers. Meeting new people can be uncomfortable and awkward. This has been limiting your social life, career, and ability to enjoy your life. Try these strategies:

Learn.

Find three reputable sources of information on how to deal with this issue. Include at least two types of media. It might be a video course, a book, and an audio program. With our example, these programs might cover social skills, social anxiety, and how to make friends.

Three different sources provide three different perspectives. You can surround your challenge with different types of information. This is a well-rounded approach.

Develop a plan.

You know your weakness and you know a lot about how to address it. Create a step-by-step plan to eliminate your weakness. Your plan might start with something as simple as making better eye contact with strangers and end with asking a stranger out on a date.

Re-evaluate.

Once your plan is complete, take a look at yourself and evaluate your current situation. Is it time to move on to another weakness? Or is it necessary to create a new plan?

Identify your weaknesses, educate yourself, create a plan, and execute it. This can make your life simpler and more enjoyable.

Do the Work!

Few people are willing to address their weaknesses. Most of us avoid our weaknesses at all costs. It's much better to improve your skills than it is to spend your energy creating a little world for yourself that avoids your weaknesses. It's exhausting to build a life around your weaknesses.

YOU CAN TAKE CHARGE OF YOUR LIFE

Everyone wants a better life, but few are willing to take charge and make it happen. It's the accumulation of fears and a lack of responsibility that are to blame. You can take charge of your life and transform it into something exciting and fulfilling. It's never too late.

Are you sick and tired of feeling sick and tired?

Take control of your life and put yourself in the driver's seat:

Take responsibility.

The easiest way to deal with life is to accept full responsibility. That doesn't mean that everything is your fault, but it is your responsibility to deal with your life. Even if your parents abused you, it's your responsibility to deal with it and move on. Who else is going to do it?

Taking responsibility is powerful because you then have the power to change. If it's someone else's responsibility, all you can do is wait for someone else to fix it.

Raise your standards.

If you're content with making $50,000 per year, you'll never have a million-dollar salary. If you're content with your love handles, you'll never see your abs. People only improve until they are content, and then they relax.

The willingness to accept your current circumstances is a decision to maintain your current life. Set your standards accordingly.

Avoid being afraid of failure.

This is the primary obstacle for most people. They're afraid of failing. You fail all the time and don't think anything of it. When you're five minutes late for work or you cook the chicken five minutes too long, you don't normally take these things as personal. What about when you spill your coffee or misspell a word? For some reason, you don't take these failures personally.

But the prospect of having a script rejected or losing a competition is too much to handle.

The more you fail, the more successful you will be, as long as you learn from your failures and try again. If you only do the things you know you can do, you'll be stuck.

Stop caring what others think.

This is the other major obstacle. It seems silly to worry about the opinion of someone you barely know, but it happens all the time. No matter what you do, you're being judged by others. So, let go of it. Half of the world thinks you're wonderful. The other half doesn't.

Embrace discomfort.

Changing anything in your life can seem at first to be at least a little uncomfortable. The anxiety you experience is nothing more than a feeling in your body, like a sunburn. You don't have to allow it to stop you.

If you're uncomfortable, be excited. It means you're doing something that can make a difference in your life.

Be proactive.

Taking control of your life also involves avoiding unnecessary challenges. There's no better way to do this than being proactive. Look ahead for potential challenges and avoid them. Most negative experiences can be predicted and avoided. Avoid being reactive. By then it's too late.

Set goals.

The reason goals are so important is the decision-making aspect. You have to make decisions to set goals. Setting goals means making decisions about what you want. So, make a few decisions and decide on your goals.

Do the Work!

Are you finally ready to take charge of your life? Are you tired of pretending that you're a victim? You can choose the direction of your life. Take responsibility and work through your fears. A little discomfort is a small price to pay for a life that you enjoy.

INVITE ABUNDANCE INTO YOUR LIFE

Have you noticed that some people you know have more positivity in their lives than others? They overflow with goodness and abundance. Looking at them, you find yourself wondering, "What's their secret? They have such a great life. I want my life to be better, too."

You might have thought the people who have so much spiritually, physically, and emotionally are just lucky. Good things just happen to them.

Great things can happen to you. There are specific actions you can take to attract positivity and invite more prosperity into your own life!

Try these strategies to usher greater abundance into your life:

Get organized.

When you keep all the things you own in order, everyday living is easier and less stressful. There's a place for everything and everything is in its place. The art of organization leaves room in your life for abundance.

Throw out old stuff.

If you don't use it anymore, get rid of it. Clear out clothing, appliances, gadgets, and anything else you no longer need. Things that are old, broken, or unable to be cleaned up properly are just taking up space you could use for something that has more value to you.

Give away some of your possessions.

Whether you pass along magazines you've read or clothing that no longer fits, spread the abundance to others. When you give to others, your heart opens up and good things can more readily make their way into your life.

Find a place for possessions that are important to you.

Provide each of your cherished items with a "home" within your home. When you take care of what you have, you're acknowledging and showing respect for the abundance that's in your life.

Use what you have.

Take advantage of the items you've collected over the years. You obviously see them as having value, so why not put them to good use? Life will be more positive and you will get in touch with the abundance you have when you make use of your possessions the way they were meant to be used.

Stop mindless purchases.

Make a vow to avoid compulsively buying the next new gadget. If you always want the latest item on the market, look inside yourself and see what that's all about. Also, remind yourself of all the accumulated stuff that you don't use. After all, they were at one time the next new thing.

Take some time to figure out your desires whenever you want to buy another new item. Recognize that you'll hamper your efforts to invite abundance into your life if you keep spending money frivolously on random stuff.

Ask yourself what you need in your life right now.

Learn to distinguish between "wants" and "needs." If you do, you'll find it takes very little to live a good life with purpose and abundance. As you learn to determine when you need something or want it, you'll experience more confidence in your own abilities to usher in abundance.

Do the Work!

You may be surprised to learn that in order to invite abundance into your life, you can follow some fairly simple steps. There's no magic secret to happiness. Anyone can cultivate it.

As you begin to truly cherish your possessions and take care of your home, you'll find yourself loving your world and your circumstances more than ever. Your mind will be in tune with abundance and attract more of the same. You'll begin living the abundant life you always dreamed of!

DO IT TODAY: STOP WAITING FOR THE RIGHT TIME

Later is never a better time than the present. Too often, we wait for the perfect time to start losing weight, build a business, save money, or have children. Time is constantly passing, and there's no time to wait!

Also, stop your delays because a perfect time never comes. You can start working out today! You don't need to wait for Monday, or the first of the month, or the first of the year. There will never be a perfect time to have a child.

Instead of waiting for the perfect time, get started today and make the most of the present moment. Taking action is often better than waiting.

You can always find a way:

You can't control time, but you can control how you use it.

Rather than waiting, use your determination and ingenuity to find a way to make the present work for you. Take the opportunities you have and figure out how to bring them to fruition. You can always find a way.

Progress is often slow, so get started as soon as possible.

It can take a while to build momentum, so it only makes sense to begin building it today. Success can take time. How much time do you have? You really don't know. One thing is for certain: the sooner you get started, the sooner you'll taste success.

You learn more.

The sooner you start doing something, the sooner your education begins. You learn nothing from waiting. The more you know, the easier it is to be successful and to enjoy your life.

Ignore the excuses.

You can always invent an excuse to justify postponing action. Most people do this on a daily basis. Do you want the same results as the average person? A year from now, you'll still have plenty of excuses, but you won't be any closer to your goal. Forget the excuses and take action.

You'll be pleased with yourself.

Imagine you're old and at the end of your life. Do you think you'll regret the things you did, or the opportunities you failed to act upon? You'll regret your inaction much more than the actions you took. No one wants to die full of regret.

Taking action now is better than waiting for the perfect moment in the future. That time will never come. Begin making progress and building momentum today.

Begin taking action today with these strategies:

1. **Create a plan that you can begin executing right away.** Your plan should include actions that you can take either today or tomorrow at the latest.

2. **Consider the likely obstacles.** What roadblocks are you likely to run into? What can you do to prepare for them? Do you have any solutions? What resources do you have available to you?

3. **Create a reward system.** Obviously, you have some resistance to getting started, or you would've started the first time you realized there was an issue. Encourage yourself to take action by promising yourself a small reward after accomplishing a task or two toward your goal.

4. **Be persistent.** Make a habit of taking a small action each day. Small actions might seem like they accomplish little, but the effect is cumulative. Just keep going!

Do the Work!

Life can only be lived in the present. Waiting for some unspecified, magical time in the future is a waste of your life. You can get started right here and now! By this time next year, you could either change your life completely or still be stuck.

Take control of your life, starting today. You'll be glad you did.

DISCOVER TAKING CHANCES

One of the best ways to make positive changes to your life is to take more risks. Life is more exciting and rewarding when you're willing to put yourself out there and take a few chances. Plus, successful people take more risks than unsuccessful people.

With a little practice, you'll find that taking a chance or two adds immeasurably to your life.

Consider these benefits of taking a chance and reap the power it gives you:

Taking chances enables you to move beyond your comfort zone.

Nothing ever changes if you don't do something new. It's not easy to force yourself to do something that makes you feel uncomfortable, but it's necessary if you want to experience growth in your life. Imagine the new adventures you can have!

Taking chances gives you power over yourself.

Most people are risk-averse. It's not in our genetic makeup to take chances. We're like an antelope hiding in the tall grass, afraid to run out in the open for fear of being eaten by a lion. But there is tremendous power in taking chances.

When you can make yourself do things you don't want to do, you realize that you're conquering yourself.

This power extends to other areas of your life. You'll find that you'll do a better job of taking care of the mundane, but necessary, tasks in life. Taking action in the face of discomfort has a powerful impact on your life.

Taking chances gives you greater power over your life.

You can take control of your life by taking steps to build the life that you desire. This gives you greater control. You can determine how you want to move forward, how you can overcome obstacles, and then do it.

Think of the people that never take chances. They're much more susceptible to the randomness of life. External conditions have a greater effect. By taking a chance, you can avoid all this.

Taking chances reduces feelings of regret.

More people regret the things they didn't do than the things they did. Not taking chances in life leads to regret in your later years. You don't want to be one of those people that looks back on his life and wonders, "What if?"

Your life is more exciting when you take chances.

One of the most frequent complaints of adults is boredom. Do you live the same day over and over? The time flies by because there's nothing to differentiate one day from the next. There are no victories or defeats, just the dullness that comes from monotony.

Add some spice to your life and have a reason to get up in the morning. Take a chance or two.

You'll develop greater self-confidence and self-esteem.

When you have control over yourself and your life, you increase your self-worth. These qualities influence all the other parts of your life, too.

You have more opportunities.

Taking chances exposes you to even greater opportunities. When you're willing to act boldly, life meets you halfway. It can be a great boost to the amount of success you experience in life.

Do the Work!

Taking chances can be scary. Ask yourself what you have to lose. Whether it's approaching someone attractive or sending your resume to your dream company, what do you have to lose? Most risks have little potential for real loss. The threat is inside your head.

For your best results, start slowly. Decide to take one small risk each day for a month and measure the effect it has on your life. Then you can move up to taking bigger chances as your tolerance for discomfort improves.

REASONS YOU'RE NOT MAKING PROGRESS

Life can be frustrating, especially when you know you could be doing much better. You might be intelligent, friendly, and talented, but still fail to make significant progress in your life. Avoid confusing potential with results. No matter how talented you may be, it's still necessary to apply your time and effort effectively.

There are only a few reasons why you're struggling in your life, and they're all under your control. That's good news.

You can change anything you control. Make more progress in life by eliminating these errors:

You don't know what you want.

When the waitress brings out the dessert cart, you have to choose something or go hungry. Everything else in life is the same way. You might be stuck choosing between a career as a physician or a rocket scientist. But if you fail to make a decision, you might find yourself tipping garbage cans for a living.

Making a choice is more important than making a perfect choice. Weigh your options and be brave enough to pull the trigger. Choose something.

You change your mind too frequently.

Imagine if you started from Topeka, Kansas with the intention of driving to Los Angeles. But after 500 miles, you changed your mind and decided to drive to Miami, so you turned around. A thousand miles later, you change your mind and decide to go to Seattle.

You're then passing by your home when you realize that you don't have enough vacation time left to drive to Seattle, spend a couple of days, and drive back.

The amount of time you spent driving is a lot, but you changed your mind too much to accomplish anything. You're exactly where you started, but now you're exhausted, too.

It's important to choose a direction for your life and stay the course.

How much of your time do you spend productively?

The average office employee spends less than 25% of their time at work doing anything of value for their employer. How much of your time are you spending to enhance your life?

How much time do you waste each day? Playing on your phone, watching TV, surfing the internet, daydreaming, worrying, and hanging out with your friends will never help you to make progress in your life.

Time is the great equalizer. The better you can spend your time, the better your life will be. No other resource matters as much as your time. Keep track of your time for a week. Every 30 minutes record how you spend that time. You'll be surprised by how much time you waste each day.

You give up without a fight.

Good things take time. You can't lose 50 pounds or make a million dollars in a month. It will take time to make significant progress in your life. There will also be obstacles along the way. Perseverance is critical. Be patient and keep going.

You don't manage your negative emotions well enough to be successful.

Frustration, fear, boredom, anxiety, and impatience are common emotions, especially if you're trying to do something challenging.

Mastering yourself is the ultimate pathway to mastering life. If you know what you want, the only true obstacle you have is yourself. Everything things else is easy if you can control yourself.

Do the Work!

You can begin making meaningful progress in your life, no matter how long a rut has been dug. Recognize your contribution to your own struggles. Make a decision and stick with it. Progress comes from using each day adequately. If you persevere and manage yourself, you can accomplish anything.

WAYS TO BUILD SELF-RELIANCE

Self-reliance is the ability to use your own powers, ideas, skills and resources without the help of others. It's a fundamental part of independence. Right now, you are learning and growing rapidly as you add all the knowledge in this book to the ways you can improve your life and finances.

Take the time to understand and increase your self-reliance.

Take responsibility.

One of the key features of self-reliance is taking responsibility for your actions and words.

Pass up the chance to blame others.

Some things may be beyond their control. Instead of being a victim, leave the past behind and move forward in the best way you can with the situation as it is.

Stay informed.

It's easier to be self-reliant if you're aware of the latest news and potential issues.

Investigate solutions on your own.

Spend time investigating how to solve the challenge on your own instead of promptly asking others for help and advice.

Avoid expecting others to rescue you.

Your family and friends may not always be around to save you.

Look for opportunities to learn.

You can build self-reliance by constantly seeking out new skills and activities that will provide learning experiences.

Be observant.

Observation can provide valuable lessons about life.

Create goals.

Goals help you narrow down your focus and give you the chance to work toward an idea that makes you more self-reliant.

Make your own decisions.

Instead of allowing others to make your decision, investigate the pros and cons of your options, seek additional knowledge if necessary, and then choose the best option for you.

Avoid expecting challenges to magically vanish.

Challenges don't usually disappear on their own. Instead of waiting for others to fix them, take the initiative to find solutions.

Learn to manage your reputation.

Avoid waiting for others to praise or criticize you. Instead, learn to manage your own reputation by admitting mistakes and sharing your successes.

Learn how to network.

Networking can provide you with valuable ideas and suggestions, but it doesn't make you dependent on others.

Create a self-reliant mindset.

Focus on your thoughts and banish the ones that stop you from taking responsibility.

Manage your own finances.

Your family members don't want to pay your bills.

Create something.

Whether you make a drawing or cook dinner, the process of creation can boost your confidence and make you more self-reliant.

Learn to entertain yourself.

Find activities that keep you cheerful and occupied.

Steer clear of complaining.

Instead, focus on the positive aspects around you.

Avoid being needy.

Instead, focus on gratitude and helping others.

Handle your own chores.

If you're physically capable of handling your own chores, then use them as an opportunity to get exercise and become more self-reliant.

Take on new challenges.

Try new challenges and develop new skills.

Learn to be happy alone.

You don't have to rely on others to be happy.

Reject negative influences.

Protect your developing self-reliance by declining anything that pushes you toward dependence.

Monitor your emotions.

Recognize your feelings and choose appropriate responses without waiting for someone else to acknowledge them first.

Find internal motivation.

Find things that inspire you to persevere despite challenges.

Accept that change takes time.

Becoming self-reliant is a process. Take one step at a time.

Do the Work!

Practice these actions and you'll no longer consider yourself a victim, blown back and forth by the storms of life. Increase your self-reliance and enjoy greater control over your future.

CHAPTER SIX, SUPPORT

Which Behaviors Can You Turn Around Fast?

It is as important to train your thoughts in your new understanding as it is to educate yourself with the knowledge. This next section is designed to give you specific self-talk, questions, and support for creating behaviors to change your future and become a lasting part of your daily support.

Instead of repeating the same negative thoughts over and over replace those thoughts with some new self-talk, do the work!

Getting Started

Read through each section regarding different behaviors that can improve your life.

· First, find the ones that you are utilizing, and pat yourself on the back. You are on the right track.

· Next, see if these behaviors you have need any tweaking based on the new knowledge you are gaining.

· After you have that done, study things you neglected to include and that you may need to develop your healthy financial lifestyle.

· For the new information, spend time each day until you are comfortable with the idea of these behaviors.

· Pick the behaviors that you need the most and implement them first.

Finally, after you have all this accomplished, go back and read through your notes every three months to make sure you are reaching your goals.

My Income Is Increasing

Creating value from your employment can help you increase your bottom line, make you eligible for a higher paying job, and give you a sense of satisfaction and well-being.

It is important to realize your value at work and to strive to share that with others.

Use this self-affirming language to teach your thoughts a new habit:

- I am a valuable employee who works hard each day to earn an income. My work is marked by integrity and passion. I work above and beyond what is expected of me in order to prove my worth.
- My income is increasing because it is my time to eat the fruit of the seeds I have planted through the years. My income is increasing because I have learned to be faithful right where I am.
- My work ethic is a blessing to my employer. My hard work causes growth in the business. As a result, my income is increasing. I attract success into my life by working selflessly.
- I look for ways to increase my income beyond work. I am free from pride when it comes to doing whatever I need to do to provide for my loved ones. My heart is free from greed. I desire to increase my income so I can better serve my family and help those in need.
- I use my talents and creativity to draw more income. I am willing to take risks and push myself outside of my comfort zone to tap into new sources of income.
- My mind is at peace about my financial situation because I am a blessed individual, regardless of how much money I make. My life is full of things worth more than money could ever buy.
- Today, I choose to work hard and prove myself worthy of a raise. I work diligently and cheerfully, so I can attract great success in my life.

Do the Work!

Take time for self-reflection:

1. What seeds have I been planting at work?

2. Am I worthy of a pay increase?

3. Do I have a good attitude about my work?

Day by Day, I Decrease My Debt

I am on a mission to decrease my debt.

Use this self-affirming language to teach your thoughts a new habit:

- Each day, I challenge myself to minimize my spending, so I can apply my expendable income towards paying down my debts.
- So far, so good!
- I no longer charge purchases on my credit card. My only active "charge card" is my debit card. Due to my efforts, I am dramatically decreasing my credit card debt!
- Decreasing my debt provides me with instant gratification and peace.
- I make financial sacrifices every day. I buy the store brand and utilize coupons when grocery shopping. I settle for the basic cable package rather than the expensive plan with all the bells and whistles. My personal shopping is nearly nonexistent.
- Even so, I feel more satisfied than ever! I know my money is better spent going towards my outstanding balances rather than unnecessary things.
- Some days, my family finds my newfound frugality to be annoying. I pay no attention to the nagging comments. Not only am I helping myself by decreasing my debt, but I am also forming a better future for my family.
- I always write checks for substantially more than the minimum amount due when paying my mortgage, credit cards, and loans. When I receive my yearly tax returns, I apply at least 75% of the money towards paying down my debt.
- I am disciplined in my ways and determined to pay off my debts. Few feelings are more fulfilling than the liberation of being debt-free!
- Today, I write my checks with joy. I am already reaping the emotional and financial benefits of unloading this weight off of my shoulders.

Do the Work!

Take time for self-reflection:

1. In which areas can I afford to minimize my spending?

2. How do I visualize my life when I am fully debt-free?

3. Am I comfortable hiring a financial planner to assist me in my journey?

My Investments Are Flourishing

In the midst of a financial future that is shaky for many, my investments are flourishing.

Use this self-affirming language to teach your thoughts a new habit:

- I am blessed beyond my comprehension. I use wisdom when making financial decisions. My investment choices are based on factual research instead of emotional whims.
- Before I make an investment, I research the published facts as well as the truths that can only be uncovered through personal research.
- I refrain from blindly trusting offers that seem too good to be true. I ask people whom I trust about their experiences, so I may learn from their advice.
- I am patient with my investments. I have the necessary courage to hold on to an investment and ride the wave. Timing is an art for me. I know when to buy and when to sell. Giving an investment time to mature, rather than trying to get rich quickly, is the right way to go.
- My investments are thriving because they are varied. I spread my money throughout several types of investments to secure my treasure. If one investment sinks, there are others that rise to give me great profit.
- Another reason I experience a boost in my finances is that I am faithful to give to others. When I give to others, I get more in return. I reject greed and embrace generosity. Sharing my wealth makes me rich.
- Today, I choose to take the necessary risk with the appropriate caution to make my investments flourish. I use wisdom and patience, so I may take care of my family's finances.

Do the Work!

Take time for self-reflection:

1. Are my investments varied?

2. Do I have the patience necessary to give my investments time to grow?

3. How can I give to others?

I Train My Mind

I control my feelings, thoughts, and actions.

Use this self-affirming language to teach your thoughts a new habit:

- I train my mind to stay strong and healthy.
- I focus on the positive. I count my blessings and express my gratitude. When faced with challenges and changes, I remind myself of what I have to gain. When I run into setbacks and delays, I find something to laugh about in the situation.
- I monitor my self-talk. I reframe my doubts and fears. I give myself credit for making an effort. I accept me for who I am now.
- I adopt healthy habits. I work at making constructive choices automatic.
- I engage in activities that sharpen my mental skills. I study foreign languages and play word games with my children. I register for online courses and shake up my daily routines.
- I take care of my body. My physical well being affects my mental strength. I eat nourishing whole foods, exercise daily, and go to bed early.
- I stay connected. Spending time with family and friends reduces my stress. I learn by listening to others and sharing my opinions and experiences.
- I live mindfully. I help my brain to function productively by organizing my schedule and minimizing distractions. I use meditation and prayer to help me concentrate on the present moment.
- Today, I give my mind a workout. I maintain a positive outlook and cultivate the kinds of thoughts and behaviors that help me to succeed.

Do the Work!

Take time for self-reflection:

1. How do I define mental strength?

2. Where can I learn more about exercises that can help my brain?

3. How is training my mind similar to training my body?

Making Mistakes Is Part of Learning

Learning without ever making mistakes is highly unlikely.

Use this self-affirming language to teach your thoughts a new habit:

- Humans are designed to learn from their missteps. Mistakes, errors, and failure are all just forms of feedback.
- I choose to learn from my mistakes and use them to change my approach.
- I expect to make errors when I learn something new. I am able to stay focused and positive, regardless of the outcome. I use my results to propel myself to a greater level of expertise. The more slip-ups I make, the greater my skill level becomes.
- Everyone I know makes mistakes on a daily basis. Even the greatest baseball hitters in the world are successful less than 40% of the time. I am free from unreasonable expectations. I know mistakes are inevitable, and I am confident in my ability to learn and succeed.
- Mistakes can be developed to produce positive results.
- I am learning to enjoy making mistakes. They are signs that I am getting closer to my success. When I make a mistake, I smile, learn, and move on.
- Today, I look forward to making a few mistakes. I use my missteps to increase my wisdom and knowledge. Mistakes are just a part of the learning process.

Do the Work!

Take time for self-reflection:

1. Why is it difficult to learn anything significant without making mistakes?

2. When have I had unreasonable expectations of perfection for myself?

3. How would my life change if I were able to stop worrying about making mistakes?

My Financial Future Is Bright

I am destined to be stable.

Use this self-affirming language to teach your thoughts a new habit:

- The thought of being financially stable brings me immense excitement. Knowing that at some point in the future I can achieve financial wellness gives me the drive to work towards it.
- I cultivate the intelligence needed to build a solid path to a bright financial future.
- I spend a lot of time understanding the best financial decisions to make and the best ways to allow my money to grow. I rely on the advice of experts in money management to help guide my direction.
- Some of my choices may not bring immediate returns, but I am okay with that because good things come to those who exercise patience.
- I am patient with the journey to financial wellness because I know the rewards always appear sweeter when I push myself harder to achieve them.
- My commitment to saving is solid. I treasure the success I gain through my finances because of the effort I put into achieving it. I know it is much easier to lose money than make it, so I am mature and sensible with my spending decisions.
- Today, I look forward with excitement to a sunny and bright financial future. It is my reward because I take the correct route to achieve it. I commit to working hard to reap financial success.

Do the Work!

Take time for self-reflection:

1. Do I avoid making impulse purchases of things I desire to not get into the habit of overspending?

2. What plans are in place for me to maintain financial wellness?

3. How can I teach others to achieve financial success?

My Finances Are Organized and Easy to Track

My personal finances are organized to fit my lifestyle.

Use this self-affirming language to teach your thoughts a new habit:

- I manage my money efficiently with easy to track tools. At any point in time, I know how much money is available for daily expenses, bills, and luxuries.
- My organization skills help me stick to my budget. I keep my receipts to avoid challenges at the end of the year. I file copies of my bills to make reports easier.
- I know the status of my financial health because I am organized.
- I keep track of my checking account balance, savings, investments, bills, debts, and other obligations. I know what each transaction means on my statements.
- I maintain accurate payment schedules and know the exact amounts for each bill.
- I know where every penny of my money is located. My tracking tools are straightforward and easy to use. I use charts and graphs to note changes in my budget.
- Today, I am in control of my finances, so I can avoid uncomfortable money surprises. My financial future is secure because I make it a point to keep my money organized.

Do the Work!

Take time for self-reflection:

1. What procedures can I set up to help organize my family's finances?

2. What tools can be used to make managing my finances easier?

3. Does my budget fit my lifestyle? How can I make it more realistic?

Financial Freedom

I tread the path to financial freedom.

Use this self-affirming language to teach your thoughts a new habit:

- One of my main goals in life is achieving financial freedom. I excitedly look forward to the day when I have all my finances under full control.
- Each day brings a new opportunity to make responsible decisions about money. I treat financial wellness with the same importance as other daily priorities. I structure cues to remind me that I am committed to be a wise spender and saver.
- My main cue is to weigh whether something is a want or need. Before spending a cent, I ask myself questions about the purpose of the purchase.
- When I determine that something is a want, I avoid making the purchase. I know that it is important to make myself happy. But I also know that something for my happiness still has the same effect when I purchase it later on.
- I am also committed to only acquiring what I am able to buy with cash. The credit monster is my greatest foe. I avoid using credit cards when I am unable to repay them.
- I ensure I clear my debt each month, so I maintain a good credit score. This approach makes me eligible for significant facilities like a mortgage or my kids' education.
- Today, I acknowledge that the path to financial freedom is sometimes challenging. But I am dedicated to keeping navigating it as smoothly as possible. My strategies for staying on the right side of debt are effective enough to guide me.

Do the Work!

Take time for self-reflection:

1. How do I convince myself to avoid making emotional purchases?

2. How do I get back on track when I lose my financial wellness bearings?

3. What are some strategies I can use for clearing old debt?

Freedom Is Within My Reach

I have the power to liberate myself.

Use this self-affirming language to teach your thoughts a new habit:

- Freedom is within my grasp.
- I control my decisions. I shape my life by the way I choose to think. I manage my emotions and respond constructively to any events that come my way. My attitude helps me to remain at ease.
- I look for ways to serve others. Taking the focus off myself reduces my anxiety. I am happier and encourage more cooperation.
- Mindful living enables me to break out of old patterns. I pay attention to the present. I determine my actions instead of automatically repeating what is familiar. I make time for fun as often as possible. I play ball with my children and run around with my dog. I call up a friend and laugh about the ups and downs of our dating experiences.
- I let go of expectations. I accept that uncertainty is a part of life. I am strong enough to persevere until I reach my goals.
- I take responsibility for my decisions. I hold myself accountable for my impact on myself and others.
- I practice forgiveness. Grudges are a burden that I want to throw away. I wish others well even when I am disappointed by their behavior. My compassion extends to myself as well. I reassure myself that each mishap teaches me how to learn and grow.
- Today, I celebrate my independence. I am the architect of my life.

Do the Work!

Take time for self-reflection:

1. What are 3 words that I associate with personal freedom?

2. What is the relationship between freedom and responsibility?

3. How does freedom help me to live authentically?

My Beliefs Can Be Adjusted

I recognize the difference between facts and beliefs.

Use this self-affirming language to teach your thoughts a new habit:

- I transform my life by adjusting my thinking.
- I examine my assumptions. I accept my emotions without giving up rational thinking. I probe the limitations that have held me back and decide to move forward. I celebrate me and my abilities.
- I live in the present moment. I focus on how I am performing now instead of regretting the past or creating expectations about the future.
- I embrace change. I know that I can handle uncertainty. I learn and grow by adapting to challenges. I experiment with new approaches. If I have become used to thinking I am slow with numbers, I sign up for a business math course and play games that sharpen my skills.
- I give myself a pep talk. I choose words that inspire and motivate me. I look on the bright side. I see the upside of each situation. I reframe obstacles so that I can take charge of my destiny.
- I ask my loved ones for support. I welcome feedback as I break free from patterns that I have outgrown.
- I rely on repetition. My new beliefs become stronger the more I put them to the test. I look for opportunities in my daily life to practice changing my habits.
- Today, I turn my thinking around. I shift my point of view and adopt beliefs that bring me health, happiness, and peace.

Do the Work!

Take time for self-reflection:

1. How do my beliefs influence my experiences?

2. How does changing my beliefs help me to change my actions?

3. What is one limiting belief that I would like to let go?

7
BUDGETS

The Balancing Act Perfected

If you knew of a tool that could bring your mind, family, and finances into harmony, dramatically reduce stress, and make the challenges of life much more manageable, would you use this tool for your advantage? Such a tool does exist.

A Budget!

A budget allows you to take control of your finances, instead of your finances controlling you. You can create a budget that supports your dreams while making sure you are taking care of your necessities.

Getting Started

Budgeting doesn't have to be depressing and minimalist. However, it can give you an accurate picture of what you're spending. Then, you can decide how to spend less-- or if you even want to spend less --and make changes that will benefit you in the long run.

Good luck and get started.

MANAGING MONEY BY USING A BUDGET

Even when the economy is good and you're living comfortably on the money you're making, it's a good idea to use a budget. Many people cringe when they hear that word because they think it means you can't have any fun or spend any money. That's far from the truth. Even a tight budget leaves room for fun and a little extra spending from time to time.

When you plan a budget, you must be realistic about what you're spending and saving. Don't say you spend $10 per week on lunches if you know you *really* spend $40. You can change the amounts later and cut back if necessary, but the first step is to get everything down on paper just as it is now. That way, you can see what you're really spending.

You Might Be Pleasantly Surprised the Changes You Can Easily Make

Usually, people who create an honest budget by tracking their spending each month and writing everything down find that they're shocked at how much they're paying out. It's not just the bills, but also the little things like lunches and dinners out, coffee in the morning, and small purchases that add up.

For one month, keep track of every cent you spend. Avoid hiding anything or sweeping it under the rug. Save all your receipts and write them down. That means bills, spending money you withdrew from the bank, and anything else that was paid out in that time frame. At the end of the month, you'll have an accurate picture of what it's costing you to live for 30 days.

How to Lower Your Costs

After you get over the initial shock of your tracking experiment, you'll likely want to find ways to spend less. There are many ways to lower expenses, and they can depend somewhat on how you spend your income. Everyone is different, and not every idea will apply to each person.

Consider these ideas to decrease how much you spend each month:

- Adjust the thermostat by a few degrees to save on electricity or gas.
- Skip going out for lunch and coffee by bringing these things from home.
- Change to a less expensive cable TV, the Internet, or cell phone plan.
- Have a yard sale to get rid of unwanted items and make some quick cash.
- Carpool or use public transit and sell that second car.
- Buy groceries only during sales and stock up on often-used items.

Of course, there are plenty of other ways to save. What works for one family might not work for another. However, in all likelihood, you really don't *need* the latest gadgets, the newest car, or brand-name clothing. You may want them, but your want is not a need.

Do the Work!

Take the time and effort to track your spending for a month. Using a debit card for all your everyday purchases can make it easier to track those often-missed items. Outline your current budget exactly as you spend it.

Next, look at how much of your budget are unnecessary things. How much are these really costing you? Decide is it worth it? When you really think deeply about those questions, you'll likely find that living a little more frugally would give you a better quality of life and freedom to do more things, like travel.

HOW TO SIMPLIFY YOUR BUDGET

Finances have a knack for becoming complicated. Therefore, making your budget as simple as possible will allow you to get a better handle on your finances so that you can focus on matters that are more important. Simplifying your budget can have positive effects on all aspects of your finances by helping you keep everything under control.

Stressing out over your finances is a waste of your time, so rein them in today with a simpler, easier to manage budget.

Follow these strategies to make your budget easy, workable, and effective:

Start with a simple spreadsheet.

Keeping things in a spreadsheet can simplify your budget significantly. Set it up however you like or download a free template for Excel or Google Docs; just choose something that works for you. Free apps are available for most smartphones. If nothing else, use a piece of paper you keep in a safe place.

Devote 60% to your expenses.

The 60% Solution is a budget strategy that entails fitting your expenses into 60% of your gross income so that you can dedicate the remaining 40% to retirement, debt repayment, short-term and long-term savings, and fun or entertainment expenses.

Devote 10% to your retirement.

Put 10% of your gross income toward your retirement, such as in a 401(k)-investment plan or an annuity. Refrain from touching this money for any purpose unless the circumstances are dire. Knowing your savings are in place and growing will free you of guilt and allow you to enjoy your "fun money" stress-free.

Devote 10% to debt repayment and longer-term savings.

Invest in an index fund or stocks if these are your investment vehicles of choice. Otherwise, put the money away in a savings account and touch it only to repay debt or in financial emergencies.

Devote 10% to your short-term savings.

This money is for periodic expenses like medical expenses, auto maintenance and repairs, appliances, birthday gifts, Christmas gifts, and home maintenance costs. Spend this money when you need it because that is precisely what you're saving it for.

Devote 10% to your "fun money."

You can spend this money in any manner that pleases you. This is guilt-free money that you can spend on movies, entertainment, eating out, comic books, junk food or anything else that you wish.

Reduce the number of categories you use.

Many budget software programs instruct you to use a million different categories or subcategories. If you want to simplify your budget, use as few as you can. Rather than having a category for every entry, combine some expenses into a larger category to keep it simple.

Pay your bills online.

Automate your bill payments as much as possible so that you don't have to remember to pay your bills every month or buy stamps. Consider automatic bank withdrawals and pay bills online through automatic debit whenever you can.

Automate your savings.

Every time your paycheck is deposited into your account, have a transaction scheduled that will transfer a specific amount into your savings from your checking. Aim to find a high-yield savings account for this purpose.

Keep your fun money in cash form.

Take out your 10%, keep it in cash, and use it as you see fit. Watching the cash disappear from your wallet can actually teach you a lot about where the money goes.

Do the Work!

If you investigate, you'll find numerous techniques to simplify your budget. Make changes that work well for you and your family. Avoid struggling with a new budget plan because you think it must be better. If it isn't actually helping you budget, then it's not the "better" option for your needs. Sometimes simpler is more effective.

WHAT DID YOU FORGET TO INCLUDE IN YOUR BUDGET?

If you have a household budget, you're doing better than most! No matter how thorough we attempt to be when constructing a budget, there are usually a few things that escape our minds. It's the little surprises that can ruin well-laid plans.

Remember to consider the odd, non-monthly purchases when you are creating your budget.

Pet-related expenses.

This category includes food, boarding, health care, toys, grooming fees, bedding, and any other supplies your pet needs to be happy and comfortable.

Big-ticket items.

Is there a new car, vacation, or a new washing machine in your near future? These items often slip our minds when making financial plans. Plan for and include these expenses in your budget projections.

Non-monthly bills.

Since most bills are paid monthly, budgets are set up on the same schedule. However, some bills aren't paid twelve times a year. Depending on where you live, the water and trash bills might be quarterly.

- Automobile registration is an annual bill. This is a small amount in many states, but it can be a very large bill in others. Set aside a little each month if the expense is considerable.
- Property taxes can be built into your monthly mortgage payment, but this

isn't always the case. If you're no longer carrying a mortgage, it certainly isn't the case. Plan ahead.
- Insurance premiums are often paid annually or quarterly. Remember to budget for these.
- Subscriptions and memberships are non-monthly bills. These can include gym memberships, magazine or newspaper subscriptions, and warehouse club membership fees.
- Home and car maintenance and repair costs can vary from year to year. It's easy to plan for oil changes and furnace filters. But how is your roof looking? What about the tires on your car? These possible expenses can also be budgeted for if you remember them.
- Eye examinations, dental checkups, and annual trips to the doctor are other expenses that many of us forget when creating a budget. If you need a new pair of orthotics each year, include them, too. Consider your regular medical expenses and accommodate for them within your budget.

Clothing.

Think about your clothing costs over the course of a year and include a line item in your budget. Do you have any special occasions this year? Perhaps a wedding or other formal event will require special financial consideration. Everyone needs to buy clothes on occasion.

Gifts.

Christmas and birthdays have a way of sneaking up on us. It might be a good idea to start saving, and maybe even shopping, in January. Christmas can be a major expense, depending on your traditions and the size of your family.

School-related expenses.

School supplies, field trip fees, school lunches, physicals for sports, and numerous other expenses can add up over the school year.

When you run into trouble, remember your "Devote 60% to your expenses" category.

Remember from your original budget, the 60% Solution is a budget strategy that entails fitting your expenses into 60% of your gross income so that you can dedicate the remaining 40% to retirement, debt repayment, short-term and long-term savings, and fun or entertainment expenses.

You can further break this down into groups such as housing, monthly expenses, holiday savings, and more. If you can limit your housing expenses to 30% or lower you can create more room for things that give you a better quality of life.

Do the Work!

It's important to account for everything in your budget. A household budget isn't very effective if many of your expenses are excluded. There are many financial expenditures that are routinely forgotten when a budget is constructed. Go over your bills from last year and ensure you're including everything relevant.

SLICE UP YOUR EXPENSES USING A BUDGET CHART

Using a computer program to keep track of your budget is quite addicting. You start to feel proud and satisfied when you can add a new amount to the "earnings" section of the budget. Of course, the most satisfying part would be watching your earnings and savings increase as you cut back on spending.

But what if you need to pay an upcoming bill and you're flat broke?

Relax, there's no need to panic. Your handy budget chart will help you cut back on spending without losing the roof over your head.

Keeping track of your expenses will help you avoid spending money unnecessarily, so more funds can be allocated to saving.

This information can work for any Excel-style spreadsheet:

- Open a new spreadsheet
- In the first rows, type in the factors that you would like to track (earned, spent, saved)
- Below the label, select the formula area, and type "=sum(A2:A30)"

This is one of the simplest formulas that can be used in Excel. It adds all the of numbers that are found in column A between row 2 and 30.

You can put in the dates on the side of each row, but it's easier to just use the default row values and remove any additional rows. For example, if there are 300 rows, delete 270 so that you'll have 30 rows left, one for each day of the month.

Keeping Track of Your Saving and Spending Percentages

The formula above will add the amounts in a range of rows. But what if you want to determine a percentage difference between the two labels? For example, you want to keep track of the percent that you save on a monthly basis.

Follow this process:

- Type this formula into the formula area of the spreadsheet: "=sum(A2/B3)", assuming that you're "Total Earned" amount was on A2 and your "Total Spent" amount was on B3.
- Right click on the percentage label
- Format the cell as a percentage (from the drop-down list of formatting options)

Congratulations! You just made an incredibly simple budget chart!

Benefits of Using Your Budget Chart

When you start to use this budget chart, you'll begin to notice that each time you add an amount to the "earned" section, the spreadsheet will update, and you'll be able to see at a glance what you earn and what you spend.

Get into the habit of using the budget chart and you'll be able to easily manage your finances.

The chart will serve as a motivation to save money because no one wants to be reminded that they are spending a lot of money. Use it as a little mind game to see how high you can make that "Percent Saved" number go. When you have to spend money, that percentage will decrease, which will make you want to bump it back up.

Do the Work!

A chart adds a visual to help you see quickly what your budget and spending is doing. Using this chart will help you develop the mentality that you need to save money, which is one of the most beneficial decisions you can make. Do the work, create that budget chart, and see how much cash you can save!

QUICK FIXES FOR A BLOWN BUDGET

If you have done the steps of creating a complete budget and following your plan, you are doing much better financially within our household. However, even the best-planned budget doesn't mean that even the most responsible family doesn't have financial challenges at times.

Unfortunately, once your household budget has been blown, it gets easier and easier for additional failings to occur.

It's like being on a diet and having a piece of cake. Many people will think, "Heck, I've already blown my diet. I may as well have two pieces of cake." It would be better to admit that things get off course occasionally and then right the ship.

These four budget fixes will help you get back on target:

Ensure your budget is reasonable.

Budgets require knowing where the money is being spent, as well as how much. When first making a budget, it's easy to incorrectly estimate how much you actually spend on different items. Appearance and reality often collide.

Until you have some real data to use, build a buffer into your budget to protect against overspending. When you overspend in one area, you can use money from the buffer category to offset the difference.

Over time, your estimations will improve, and the buffer category can be phased out. You might decide to keep it in your budget permanently but keep the amount down. Later, as your buffer is not needed you can take the overflow and add it to anything you want, including your fun category!

Use the more flexible budget categories to correct spending mistakes.

Some categories are much more flexible than others. Your rent or mortgage payment isn't very flexible. But things like clothing are flexible. You can purchase a $20 pair of pants or a $300 pair of pants. That's flexibility. Eating out is similar. You don't have to eat out.

It's quite easy to cut back in these areas in the event that another category has been overspent. Eat-in instead of going out. Rent a movie instead of going to a concert.

Avoid waiting to ask for help.

When folks get behind on their bills, a good deal of them panic. Sometimes the solution is as simple as asking your creditors for a little extra time. Many are far more accommodating than you might think. Creditors know that if they're willing to work with you, you're more likely to be able to pay them.

Avoid jumping at costly solutions. Payday loans and credit card advances can be difficult debts to eliminate. These types of solutions often result in additional rounds of similar solutions. The amount of debt you owe seems to keep increasing all the while.

Negotiate with your landlord and even your utilities to see if an alternate payment arrangement can be reached. Never assume you know the answer before speaking with them.

Adjust your budget as needed.

If you're consistently coming up short, your budget likely needs to be adjusted. It might be that your income simply doesn't permit the targets you've set in the more discretionary categories, such as entertainment.

If you're still struggling, keep track of every cent that you spend for a month. This includes the spending of loose change. Track everything. Then ask yourself how this compares with the budget you've set. Where are you making an error?

Do the Work!

Living within a budget is a part of being financially responsible. Everyone overspends from time to time. The solution is to make the necessary adjustments by shifting the allocation from one category to another. If you're still having challenges, then your budget probably needs an overhaul. Get that budget under control and reap the rewards!

THE FIRST TIME MORTGAGEES BUDGET

Congratulations on buying your first home! This is surely a great achievement for you and the rewards can be very exciting. As a homeowner, you have equity that's solid. There's so much you can accomplish now that you have this asset under your belt.

What you'll now realize, however, is that your bank account has started to behave erratically! You're seeing money moving out of your account faster than ever before. Or so it seems. It's completely normal to think you've lost some control over your finances now that you're a homeowner.

What you're experiencing is a clear case of a budgeting dilemma for a first-time mortgagee. The good news is that you can learn how to budget all over again and have a positive mortgaging experience.

Make your mortgage payment first.

If you want to continue to hold on to your home, ensure you pay your mortgage on time! Remember the home is yours and you want to keep it that way. As soon as you get your paycheck, withdraw the amount you need for your mortgage.

- A great idea is to set up an automatic payment to the mortgage lender from your bank account. That way, you won't have to worry about remembering to make the payment each month.
- Sure, things come up, but defaulting on your mortgage payment could mean not having a roof over your head!
- Avoid using the equity in your home as a cash advance. Stay as far from additional debt as possible.

Prioritize other expenses.

With the mortgage payment out of the way, you now have to manage all the other expenses. Now that you have a mortgage, your priorities may likely shift.

- All expenses related to the new home are important. However, you need to ask yourself if they are necessary at this moment. Focus on the recurring monthly expenses that contribute to a comfortable dwelling.
- Social time is certainly important, especially when it comes to maintaining your sanity! But try to cut down on entertainment expenses. Instead of going to the movies 3 times per week, go out once and rent a movie twice.

Schedule home improvement.

As a new homeowner, you'll have the ongoing desire to make the home more beautiful. While your pride of place is admirable, it's important to let better senses rule!

- Make a list of all your home improvement needs and wants.
- Prioritize them, with the ones that make the home safe and livable taking precedence over the others.
- Put a schedule in place for accomplishing everything, and tie that into the associated expenses. Your aim should be to commit the same amount of money each month to home improvement.
- If there's something you aren't able to afford this month, simply leave the rest until next month.

Make saving a priority.

With all that can happen as a new homeowner, it's more important than ever to set aside money in your savings account. Major repairs sometimes need to be taken care of immediately.

Have the discipline to put aside untouchable savings. That way, there'll be something for rainy days!

Do the Work!

Mortgaging a home for the first time can leave you jaded if you aren't able to budget effectively. Pay close attention to the spending of every dollar. Once you've mastered that, you can be comfortable knowing the financial responsibilities related to your home are well taken care of!

PLAN A BUDGET THAT SETS YOU FREE

Wouldn't it be great to have enough money to live your life to its fullest, while still putting away plenty for a rainy day? You can turn this dream into your reality if you're willing to plan and stick to a budget. A well-planned budget enables you to make financial decisions that support your happiness and peace of mind.

With a budget, you see exactly where each dollar you earn is being spent. This helps you spend less on items that don't fit your life's priorities. As a result, you have more money to spend on things that really matter to you.

If you think that staying on a budget is difficult, you may be pleasantly surprised. It's easier than you think. When you plan your budget carefully, you create the right mix of spending and saving to support you in the pursuit of your dreams.

How to Plan Your Budget for Financial Solvency

Contrary to popular belief, planning a budget allows you to experience more of the fun things in life. Many believe that sticking to a budget robs them of life's adventure and spontaneity. A well-crafted budget, however, ensures that funds are available for instant adventures as well as planned expenses.

Take these steps in creating your budget:

Gather the things you'll need. Among them are your bank statements, bills, and information about how much cash you have available. It's also helpful to know how much you're spending on necessities like food and gasoline.

The budget you create can be as simple as a handwritten document or small spreadsheet on your computer.

The important thing is that the budget helps you to track what you spend and keep your financial life organized.

To plan your budget, consider:

- How much money you have right now
- What you're spending your money on
- Where you can cut back
- What you'll gain by spending less
- What you want to save for
- Your plans for the future

When you know what you want and where you're going, you can create a plan to help you get there. Don't be afraid to dream big and budget for joy.

Using a Budget to Meet Goals

With a budget, you're more likely to achieve your financial goals. Break your ultimate goal down into a series of smaller goals to keep from getting overwhelmed. The sense of accomplishment as you achieve these small goals will keep you moving forward.

Also, remember that it's okay to adjust your budget. You don't have to do everything perfectly from the beginning. The effort to get your finances under control can lead to more monetary security in the future if you stay organized and adjust your budget as you go.

Plan your budget with your significant other, if you have one. Ensure that the budget you create supports the pursuit of the things that are important to both of you. A step-by-step plan for your financial future together is more fruitful if it's a joint goal-setting effort.

Do the Work!

Track your spending, commit to a plan that supports your financial goals, and remain flexible.

Your first few budgets may need tweaks, but that budget is the first step to the financial freedom and peace of mind you deserve.

DON'T BUDGET WIPE YOUR VACATION

Do the sweet memories of your vacation tarnish a bit when you start getting the credit card bills for it the month after you return home, or as you spend a year paying off your trip from last year? Imagine how different you would feel if there were no bills to come home to!

Plan a vacation that has NO BILLS!

The best way to steer clear of anxiety and guilt is to save for your trip before ever heading out the door. This will result in a more enjoyable vacation because you'll already have the money set aside and won't have to worry. It's easy to save for a vacation if you set a goal, cut back on your spending, and save money on a regular basis. Follow these tips to budget and save for your next vacation:

Agree on a goal.

Get together with the family and agree on a vacation destination. Saving is rarely exciting, but once it's attached to an objective, it becomes tolerable.

Develop a vacation budget.

If you want to save painlessly, a budget helps. Based on your destination, create a reasonable budget. Be certain to include everything. If someone needs to care for your dog and cut your grass, include it. Take the time to be accurate.

Calculate a weekly goal.

Divide your budget by the number of weeks until your vacation. That's how much you need to save each week. Saving weekly makes it easier to get back on track if you miss a target. If you're an entire month behind, it's more challenging to catch up and meet your goal.

Find ways to "create" some excess money.

Make a detailed list of your monthly expenses and see where you can cut back. Everyone buys things that are "wants" rather than needs.

- Food is one area where most families spend too much. Avoid eating out more than necessary and make an effort to shop more economically. Packaged foods tend to be more expensive than healthier alternatives.
- Consider ditching your landline or any other service you don't really use. You, your spouse, and maybe even your children have cell phones. Do you need a landline, too? What about that gym membership? Are you using it often?
- Look at the loans you're carrying. If you haven't checked the interest rates lately, you might be able to save a significant amount by refinancing.

Put away the money you save on cutting back.

It's one thing to cut your cell phone bill or loan payment down. It's another to actually take that $50 and set it aside so it won't be spent. Create a savings account and simply transfer the money you've saved into it each week.

- Consider having some money automatically transferred into a "vacation savings account" each month.
- Try throwing all your change into a jar at the end of each day and deposit it into your vacation account whenever it gets full.

Assess your progress.

Regularly check on the status of your savings. Look at the calendar and see how you're doing in regard to your savings target. Then, make any necessary changes.

Do the Work!

Saving for a vacation can be easy and painless. It all starts with a goal and a budget. With those two items in place, you can determine how much you need to save and implement your plan. Have the best vacation ever without having to worry about spending outside your means!

ROUND OF YOUR BUDGET WITH THESE ESSENTIALS

If budgeting and preparing expense sheets sounds like a task only an accountant would do, think again. Keeping track of your personal finances -- even if you have an accountant -- is important to your financial future.

It not only gives you a keen awareness of your money situation but also increases your chances of making smart spending and investment decisions. Following these crucial tips will help you create a secure financial future for you and your family.

Spend Less Than You Earn

Although this tip sounds straightforward, you may sometimes find it daunting to actually put it into practice. However, reevaluating where you're spending money can significantly increase the scope of your earnings and help you live within your means.

- The best way to get started is to write out all of your monthly expenses and see how this compares to your monthly income. This important first step will help you determine the current state of your personal finances.
- Take a second look at this list and see if you have any expenses that can be eliminated or reduced. Be honest with yourself. Which expenses show wasting your money on things that aren't even important to you? Focus on keeping what's important and eliminating the rest. For example, while there is nothing inherently wrong with spending five dollars per day on a Cappuccino, if your income doesn't support this kind of spending, it may be in your best interest to do without this luxury for the time being.
- Invest in a good budgeting program, like Quicken or QuickBooks, or a new app for your phone to help you keep track of your spending and simplify the task.

Make Your Money Work for You

This can be as simple as taking advantage of the compound interest offered by most savings accounts.

Making sound investments can help increase your annual income over 5%. You don't need to invest aggressively to get this kind of return, either. Ask friends and family for referrals to trustworthy brokers to help you get started.

Protect Your Money

Ensure that you have a plan to protect your assets in case something unforeseen happens. There's nothing worse than working hard for your money and then losing it due to poor planning and shortsighted investments.

- Sometimes, slow and steady not only wins the race with respect to your personal investing strategies, but it can also put your money at a lower risk.
- Beware of any instant growth opportunities or investment clubs that promise overnight fortunes. These may include seminars with "self-made millionaires" that pressure you into signing up with a program that might not be a legitimate source of income. Take the time to research investment opportunities before you commit your money to them.
- Consider obtaining renter or homeowner insurance to help protect your assets.

Knowing how to manage your money is a fundamental aspect of any successful long-term personal investment strategy.

Do the Work!

If you take just a small amount of time to analyze your spending habits, you may surprise yourself with how much money you can save! You can then invest these savings in a way that will help you see returns year after year.

CHAPTER SEVEN, SUPPORT

Financial pressures can make life seem overwhelming at times. If you implement the steps and commit to maintaining a rock-solid budget for your family, you will be several steps closer to experiencing financial peace and prosperity. Every area of your life will improve as you're more relaxed and at ease with the peace of mind you've achieved.

Instead of repeating the same negative thoughts over and over replace those thoughts with some new self-talk, do the work!

Getting Started

Read through each section regarding different behaviors that can improve your life.

· First, find the ones that you are already utilizing, and pat yourself on the back. You are on the right track.

· Next, see if these behaviors you have need any tweaking based on the new knowledge you are gaining.

· After you have that done, study things you haven't included and that you may need to develop your healthy financial lifestyle.

· For the new information, spend time each day until you are comfortable with the idea of these behaviors.

· Pick the behaviors that you need the most and implement them first.

Finally, after you have all this accomplished, go back and read through your notes every three months to make sure you haven't strayed from the work you need to get done.

Peace Amidst Crisis

I remain peaceful amidst the financial crisis in my country.

Use this self-affirming language to teach your thoughts a new habit:

- Regardless of today's news about the financial state of my country, I stay calm because my future is bright. I am blessed because I make sound monetary decisions.
- Even in a down economy, I have the ability to prosper by following simple life principles such as living within my means and giving to others. The personal choices I make about my money matter more than the decisions made by my government.
- I choose to live within my means; therefore, I have peace about the financial future of my family. I also elect to believe that, in spite of challenging economic times, my job is secure because I am an indispensable worker. Each day, I work harder to prove to my employer that I am worth having.
- My mind is filled with a quiet serenity because I turn off negative media. I refuse to listen to news channels and people who revel in negativity. Instead, I turn my ear to people who have a positive outlook and are searching for ways to improve.
- I remain peaceful because, although I may not be able to control what goes on in the government, I do have power over my own thoughts and actions. I choose to think positively about the future by rejecting fearful ideas.
- Today, I embrace tranquility by crushing negative thoughts at the root. I make my mind fertile soil for positivity to grow. Peace overflows from within when I place my trust in the principles by which I live, rather than in the government.

Do the Work!

Take time for self-reflection:

1. How does living within my means ensure me a peaceful financial future?

2. Why is it necessary to shut off negative media?

3. What can I do to show my employer I am indispensable?

I Invest Wisely

I make intelligent decisions about my investments. *Use this self-affirming language to teach your thoughts a new habit:*

- I understand how the markets work, so I utilize effective ways to grow my money.
- My portfolio is filled with wise choices that continue to grow and prosper.
- My investment decisions are based on accurate information and research. I use the right data to determine if a possible investment might work well for me. I maintain a smart mix of different investments for diversity.
- I am financially independent and strong, thanks to my wise choices.
- I budget my money carefully, so I can put aside funds for investments. I make regular contributions to my portfolio. My contributions are sustainable and smart.
- I am a disciplined investor. Rather than making changes to my portfolio out of panic, or to go along with a popular trend, I diligently check the data. I consider the facts to reach my conclusions.
- I am patient with my investments. I know that the market rises and falls continuously in the short term, so I am invested for the long term. Time makes all the difference!
- Today, I intend to research some new investments. I know that taking my time to find reliable data provides me with the knowledge to make a wise decision.

Do the Work!

Take time for self-reflection:

1. Where can I learn about researching investments?

2. What is my plan for putting aside some of my income for investments?

3. What can I do to make more of my money available for investments?

Healthy Spending

I have a healthy relationship with spending.

Use this self-affirming language to teach your thoughts a new habit:

- I keep an organized spending log to see how I use my money. I analyze my statements to track my habits. I set a realistic budget based on my spending needs and regular income.
- I know how to spend intelligently at stores and online retailers. I look for the best deals to fit my needs and only spend the amount I can afford.
- I avoid shopping to fill emotional voids.
- Sales fail to tempt me to go over my budget. I know which items necessities and which ones are luxuries. My budget remains on target because I know how to tell them apart.
- I enjoy being in control of my money. I avoid debt. Instead of having to pay on debts each month, I get to choose what I do with my money.
- I include money in my budget for saving and investing. I know how important savings goals are to my financial security and future. I honor these goals. I pay me first and plan my spending accordingly.
- Today, I intend to look over my budget. I like to keep my budget flexible while supporting my spending and savings goals, and I tweak it every so often to see what works best for me.

Do the Work!

Take time for self-reflection:

1. Are my spending habits helping or hurting me?

2. How can I design a budget that works well for me?

3. How can I help my family develop healthy spending habits?

Control My Habits

I can control my spending habits.

Use this self-affirming language to teach your thoughts a new habit:

- Carefully managing my spending requires the same self-control I have in other aspects of my life.
- I anticipate days when making ends meet may be harder than usual. It is these days that give me the drive to maintain control of my spending habits and I make it a point to save for rainy days.
- How I spend is a reflection of my character. I am honest with myself, so I am honest about what I can afford. I live a worry-free life, so I ensure that my spending habits keep me from having to worry about putting meals on my table.
- I commit to spending intelligently and thoughtfully.
- Sometimes, impulse purchasing is a real challenge as the urge to give in to my desire to spend increases. But I take a moment to look at the bigger picture.
- I consider what the outcome could be if I make the purchase and refrain from buying the item if there is any possible sign of hardship to come from doing so.
- Today, I vow to work hard to control my spending habits. I know that financial situations sometimes arise which alter my plans, but I commit to handling them as good as I can.

Do the Work!

Take time for self-reflection:

1. How do I feel when a loved one asks me to purchase something for their pleasure that I know I cannot afford?

2. Do I spend the time to teach my kids how to save?

3. How do I recover after allowing myself to make an impulse purchase?

Honor as a Debtor

I honor myself by paying debts on time.

Use this self-affirming language to teach your thoughts a new habit:

- Life can be tough, so I seek out ways to build my self-respect. One strategy I use to honor me is to pay my debts on time. Although this might sound like a small thing, paying my debts before they are due is very important to me.
- I sleep well at night, knowing I do the right thing in making timely payments to whomever I owe. Being prompt with my bills helps me feel good, safe, and secure. And I feel powerful whenever I pay my debts on time. Putting in the time and effort to quickly and responsibly repay those I owe is a way to truly honor myself.
- Deep inside, I feel that paying my debts on time makes me a better person. I can go through the day knowing that I have taken care of my personal finances. I feel more financially secure. I am so proud of me for how I choose to manage my money. I honor myself by taking care of my debts as quickly as I can.
- Although I have other ways of respecting myself, I find that taking care of my debts has a big impact on how I feel from day to day. I am glad I take a stand to completely manage my money.
- Today, I feel proud of my efforts to pay bills on time. I honor myself by taking my financial debts seriously and vow to always take care of debts immediately.

Do the Work!

Take time for self-reflection:

1. Is honoring myself important to me?

2. Do I connect paying my debts in a timely fashion to how I think and feel about myself?

3. What can I do to be more diligent about paying bills on time as a way to honor myself?

Control Credit Spending

I put the credit cards down today.

Use this self-affirming language to teach your thoughts a new habit:

- When I leave the house, I leave the credit cards at home. At the start of the week, I go to the ATM and withdraw my weekly allowance. My allowance is the only cash I allow myself to spend throughout the entire week.
- I keep my credit cards in a place that I cannot access easily. Stashing my credit cards in my basement, attic, or the middle of my freezer typically curbs my spending cravings.
- My family's budget is under control because I choose to keep it under control. I am responsible for my family's financial well-being. For this reason, I am strict with my purchases.
- Before I commit to a purchase, I evaluate exactly what use I would get out of the item. If it is a necessity, I make the purchase.
- If the purchase is unnecessary, I leave the store and give myself 24 hours to think it over. If by the next day, I still want the item and have found a good use for it, I make the purchase. However, most of the time, I choose not to make a second trip to the store. In this way, I curb my impulse purchases.
- Due to my efforts, my family enjoys extra spending money each month. We can use that money as a family, by going to an event, taking a vacation, or purchasing things for our children.
- I put the credit cards down because I care about our financial security. And so far, I am doing very well.
- Today, I make conscious decisions about my purchases. I replace impulse purchases with peace of mind and financial security.

Do the Work!

Take time for self-reflection:

1. How do I spend the majority of my spending cash?

2. Have I ever fallen behind on my bills due to unnecessary shopping?

3. Am I okay with buying less expensive brands to save money?

Content with What I Have

I make do with what I have.

Use this self-affirming language to teach your thoughts a new habit:

- I am content with what I have. My personal happiness and the happiness of my family are far more important than material things.
- Each morning, I wake up to a lovely home and a vivacious family. I feel grateful for the things that I have.
- At times, I struggle financially. However, I always keep my head above water. Sometimes, that means forgoing an evening at a restaurant and having dinner at home to save some money.
- I refrain from thinking I can buy happiness with money. Luxuries are just extra icing on the cake. Sure, I enjoy luxuries when I can, but they are unnecessary for my happiness.
- I banish negative thoughts and comparing my life to others that have greater financial means. I have plenty of abundance in my life and am grateful for what I have.
- So, what if my house is smaller than the neighbors'? Does it really matter if I choose the store-brand over name-brand groceries?
- I am a humble person with a clear vision of what is important. I am thankful that I have been blessed with the necessities. Even in these tough economic times, I am surviving just fine and that is all that matters.
- Today, I allow my inner priorities to guide my life, rather than material conquests. I am content with my life and make do with what I have.

Do the Work!

Take time for self-reflection:

1. Do I try to impress others with my ability to purchase luxury items?

2. Why do I care what other people think of my economic status?

3. How can I be content with what I have?

8

INCOME

An informed stable person has a better chance of overcoming situations regarding financial stress than someone walking around in the dark.

Details exponentially increase your ability to understand financial matters. This section gives you specific details to help you save and make money. The idea that you can still vacation while living within your means is encouraging. Don't skip over the holidays, make them work for you. You are going to love all the extra tips in this section.

Getting Started

Next, let's look at saving, decreasing spending, and creating more income. The most comfortable answer isn't always spending less, sometimes you can make more.

Good luck and get started.

CONSTANTLY IMPROVE ANY AREA OF YOUR LIFE

You might not be perfect, but that doesn't mean you can't get better. While success comes rapidly at first, it slows to a crawl before too long. The key is to continue making progress over a long period of time. Becoming an expert in any field requires this understanding.

If you're motivated and patient, you can become great at anything.

Think about any skill you want to develop, or any part of your life you want to enhance. How much progress would you have made if you had started 10 years ago and worked on it each day? It boggles the mind.

Develop a philosophy of constant improvement with these strategies:

Realize that a minuscule amount of improvement each day is enough.

A tiny amount of improvement each day, or each week or month, is more than enough to achieve anything you desire.

Whether you're interested in earning more money, learning the piano, or perfecting your welding skills, slow and steady progress is enough.

Imagine 20 years of minimal progress each day. Imagine a single year of daily progress.

Become an expert.

It's not enough to read one book or to take one class. Reading one book on gardening isn't enough to turn you into a master gardener. Learning about your area of interest requires a deeper knowledge. Take the time to become a true expert. Never stop learning.

Take courses, read books, or join a community of people with similar goals and interests.

Practice daily. Regular practice is the key.

Mindless practice is insufficient. You must know what you're trying to accomplish with your practice each day. Striving to improve is critical. Remember, the intention is to be better today than you were yesterday.

Measure your progress.

You can't know if you're getting better if you don't measure your progress. Find a way to measure yourself and do so regularly. Nothing stimulates enthusiasm like success. You'll also notice when you're losing ground, which suggests that you might want a new approach.

Be patient.

Progress often comes quickly at first and then slows. Eventually, progress is barely perceptible. This is true for any field. The importance of patience can't be overemphasized. Be patient and progress will come.

Get a mentor.

A mentor is an expert with an interest in your success. Getting regular feedback from someone that knows what they're talking about can be much more effective than going at it alone. Get expert help if you can.

Celebrate progress, not perfection.

Avoid waiting until you're perfect to celebrate. That time will never come. Even if you're just a tiny bit better than you were, throw yourself a little party. Any progress is worthy of excitement and pride. Those little spurts of progress add up over time.

Set goals.

It's easier to stay motivated and on course if you have a specific goal you're working toward. Instead of just focusing on "getting better," focus on being able to play Clair de Lune by the end of the year. A goal provides direction and a time constraint. Both can be useful.

If you put in the time and remain patient, you can become amazingly good at anything. The key is increasing your knowledge and lots of practice.

Do the Work!

Avoid falling into the trap of wanting perfection. Perfection can't be obtained. Instead, put your faith in progress. A small amount of progress each day created the Grand Canyon. Achieving your goals is a piece of cake in comparison.

STRETCH YOUR VACATION DOLLARS

What if you could stretch your $5,000 budget into a $10,000 vacation? Imagine how much more you could do and enjoy: a nicer hotel, better food, or maybe you would change your plans all together. It can be done. With some research and planning, taking a nicer vacation than you think you can afford is well within your reach. Try these ideas to turn your vacation funds into more fun:

Airline Tickets.

You can save a lot of money on airline tickets if you're flexible with your travel dates. A day or two earlier or later can make a huge difference in the cost. Tuesdays - Thursdays are often the cheapest days to travel by air.

Consider alternate airports, too. Sometimes, flying into a different airport can save hundreds of dollars if you have to purchase several airline tickets. Larger cities typically have multiple airports.

Hotels.

If you're going to a popular destination, you're likely to find hotels that offer coupons or free tickets to popular attractions.

Search online for the lowest price hotel room that meets your needs. Also consider joining a hotel points program.

You can save a lot of money on food by getting a hotel room with kitchen facilities. Food is a major expense when traveling. A kitchenette can save a ton of money, especially if you have kids and are staying for a week or more.

Consider a cruise.

Cruises offer spectacular food and a lot of entertainment for a relatively small amount of money. There's always the option to sign up for off-ship excursions, which aren't free, but can be considerably less expensive when included in your trip.

You'll need to include the cost to get to the ship from your house and back again, but cruises can offer a tremendous value for the money.

Go in the off-season.

Most travel locations have a peak and off-season dependent on weather and when travelers are most available to travel there. By going in the off-season, there is much less demand and prices will be lower. This is true for air-travel, car rental, lodging, and most entertainment.

You also have the benefit of fewer crowds to deal with.

Group travel.

Traveling with a group can really cut down on expenses. Larger groups can get better rates on everything, from transportation to lodging, food, and entertainment.

Condos.

Renting a condo for a week can be much less expensive than staying in a hotel. You'll also have the benefit of kitchen facilities. Condos can be very cost effective if you're traveling with several people. A basic hotel room fills up quickly if you have several people.

Again, the off-season is when you're going to find the best deals.

Pack carry-on luggage only.

With nearly every airline charging for bags now, if you can limit yourself to carry on items, it's an easy way to save a lot of money.

All-inclusive.

All-inclusive resorts can be a great way to cut your expenses. As long as you stay at the location, all your food and entertainment are paid for.

Though they might appear expensive on the surface, if you really add up all the costs, you're likely to incur with other type of vacations, all-inclusive resorts can make a lot of sense.

Do the Work!

Stretching your vacation dollars is easy if you do your homework. Consider that your major expenses are likely to be transportation, food, and lodging. If you can do something to minimize each of those, you'll be well on your way to dramatically reducing your vacation expenses.

MONEY MANAGEMENT TIPS FOR THE HOLIDAYS

It's so easy to get carried away during the holiday season! The excitement of the season makes carefree living seems like the only way to go during the holiday.

As fun as the season is, it's important to keep an eye on your budget during Christmas time so you're not faced with a financial crisis later on.

How can you resist the urge to spend frivolously in the name of gifts and having a jolly good time?

Consider these tips to manage your holiday cash effectively:

Remember January is a long month.

Resist the urge to spend all your holiday earnings on gifts, parties and Christmas decorations. The sooner you spend it, the sooner you'll start to stress out about living through a long January on mere cents.

Always give thought to emergencies which may pop up. Leave room in your budget for spur of the moment things that could come your way in January.

Setup bill reminders.

If you have a constant reminder of the bills you need to settle during the holiday and immediately after, you'll be more inclined to manage your money effectively. As you shop for gifts, decorations, and other holiday expenses, keep your financial responsibilities in mind to ensure you can cover them when required.

Setup alarms on your phone that remind you days in advance of your bill due date.

Write due dates for your bills on your calendar.

Avoid credit cards.

There's one saying that can help you avoid credit card disasters that you'll regret for months and maybe years to come: "If you can't pay for it in cash, don't buy it on credit." As simple as it seems, it's very effective to ensure that you avoid getting in over your head with credit card expenses this holiday.

If you plan to use your credit card, ensure your bank account has at least 90 percent of the purchase total in available cash.

Aim to settle your credit card bill on time and in full.

Keep your priorities in check.

If you have your financial priorities straight for eleven months of the year, you should be more than able to keep them in check during December. Here's the perfect guide:

- At the beginning of December, make a list of your responsibilities and prioritize them.
- Determine how much of your earnings to dedicate to each priority.
- Put aside the amounts decided upon.
- Whatever you're left with after these priorities is what you can use for holiday spending.

Give yourself a gift to brighten future holiday seasons.

Open a holiday account for next year with $10. Then, starting the first week of January, add $10 each week. You'll have $500 to spend freely next holiday season. If you put in $20 per week, you'll have $1000! Take the financial stress out of your holidays with this small weekly gift to yourself.

Do the Work!

All it really takes is a little bit of discipline and a lot of focus on what's most important to you. Remember that there are many more holidays to come, so you may as well leave some of the frivolity for those! Focus on getting your priorities taken care of before you take the holiday spending plunge.

TIPS FOR LOWERING YOUR ENERGY BILL

Conserving energy is important for many reasons. Wise use of resources is important for preserving and protecting our environment. It's also important for protecting your pocketbook from skyrocketing utility bills.

A few wise choices and small changes in your daily routine can make a big difference in lowering your energy bill.

Energy Efficient Bulbs

If you replace the light bulbs in your home with energy efficient light bulbs, you can dramatically lower your electricity costs without any noticeable change in your lifestyle. In addition to lower utility bills, these light bulbs need to be replaced far less often than conventional ones.

In addition, some energy efficient light bulbs are brighter than conventional bulbs. This means that you can use only one bulb in a light fixture that requires multiple bulbs.

Turn off Appliances When Not in Use.

Develop a habit of turning off the light when you leave a room. Often, a large part of wasted utility costs is keeping all the lights in your home on at all times. Teach children and other family members to turn off the lights also.

If you're in the habit of keeping your television on for background noise, try turning it off when it's not in use. You may find that you enjoy the peace and quiet and your pocketbook will thank you for it!

Do you leave your computer on all the time? A small change like turning your computer off overnight can have a positive effect on your energy bill next month. Small changes can add up to big savings without affecting your lifestyle at all.

One or the Other

Do you like to surf the web while watching television? To save money on your energy bill, try an experiment. When you're watching television, turn the computer off. When you're surfing the web, turn the television off. When trying to do both at the same time, your focus is limited. Plus, you're wasting energy by trying to do both at the same time.

Also consider watching your favorite television shows online. Many of today's most popular sitcoms and reality shows are broadcast in their entirety online one or two days after they air on television. This will keep you from splitting your focus and save on electricity if you remember to turn the TV off while you watch your favorite program online.

Regulate the Thermostat

During the hot summer months, it's tempting to crank up the air conditioner so that you can cool off. The cooler temperature in your home is refreshing, but it's also expensive. If you want to lower your monthly electricity bill, keep the thermostat temperature closer to the outside temperature.

In the summer, keep it a few degrees warmer than normal. In the winter, keep it a few degrees cooler. This puts less stress on the air conditioner and furnace, plus it requires less power.

New Appliances

Many modern appliances are designed to use less energy than older models. It can be more expensive upfront to buy energy efficient appliances, but the monthly savings may be worth it. Eventually, your new appliances will pay for themselves in the money you save on your utility bills.

Do the Work!

If you're willing to make a few small changes, you can save money on your electric bills. All it takes is a willingness to do something different and a desire for more cash in your pocket! You can begin to experience the benefits of your efforts on your next month's bill.

TIPS TO STAY COOL AND SAVE MONEY IN THE SUMMER HEAT

In the middle of summer, temperatures outside can become scorching and unbearable. Cranking the air conditioning up as high as it'll go can certainly help you cool off, but your utility bill will skyrocket.

Thankfully, there are a number of other ways that you can cool off during the hot summer months.

Try these tips to stay cool and save money in the summertime:

Stay Hydrated.

Having an ice-cold beverage on hand at all times is a great way to stay cool. Many choose soda because it tastes great and seems to provide relief to your body. Adversely, sodas also deplete your body of the hydration it desperately needs in the intense heat of summer.

Drink as much water as you can. Sports drinks can provide a change of pace and flavor, but your body needs as much water as possible to avoid heat exhaustion and other health issues that the summer can cause.

Cool off with Water.

The intense heat of summer doesn't have to keep you shut inside your home. Swimming is a great way to beat the heat. If you don't have your own pool, find out if your community has a public pool. If not, perhaps a membership to a gym that has a pool can help you to keep cool, have fun, and get in shape at the same time.

A hose or sprinkler in the backyard can provide hours of play in cool, refreshing water. If you live near water, take advantage of the surf and sand of the beach for a cool afternoon with family and friends.

Use Fans.

Fans are an effective way to cool down a room without turning the air conditioning all the way up. Box and ceiling fans can provide extra cooling throughout your home and allow you to keep your thermostat set higher, so your air conditioner doesn't work overtime.

Keep a small personal fan in your car for times when you are out and about, and the heat is too much to bear.

Eat Nutritiously.

An often-overlooked way to beat the heat is with a healthy diet. Think of the food you eat every day as fuel for your body, and you'll begin to make better choices about the types of foods you eat.

Eat plenty of fruits and vegetables to provide your body with the vitamins it needs to stay strong during the hot summer months. In addition to fueling your body, cold fruit can be a delicious way to cool off after a workout or time playing in the hot sun.

Wear Light Clothing.

Wear breathable, lightweight clothing when you go outdoors during the summer. Heavy clothing can cause your body to overheat. Make clothing choices that keep you cool and comfortable in the summer heat.

Slow down.

Above all, remember to protect your health. If you begin to feel dizzy or lightheaded at any point, stop what you're doing and sit down. If possible, find a cool spot indoors to rest until you feel like yourself again.

Heat stroke or other serious health consequences can result if you ignore your body's plea for rest from the heat.

Do the Work!

With a little advance planning and some commonsense strategies, you can beat the heat this summer. Protect your health while you enjoy all of the recreation and fun the summer has to offer.

TAX CONSIDERATIONS FOR MARRIED COUPLES

After getting married, many things change. Among all the other changes, there are also financial changes. Your spending and saving habits affect each other and your financial plans can change. The way you handle your taxes will also change.

If you got married last year, hopefully you have considered the impact on your taxes.

If you haven't thought about it yet, there are several things to keep in mind:

You're on the hook for any discrepancies on your joint tax return.

This is the primary disadvantage with regard to taxes when married. You have to sign the tax return, even if your spouse did all the work.

You are just as liable for any mistakes or fraud as your spouse. Ensure you know what you're signing.

There are advantages for retirement planning.

For example, a non-working spouse can still contribute to an IRA. However, the other spouse must have earned money that year.

You can sell your house and keep more of your profits.

As a single person, you can deduct up to $250k in capital gains. Married couples can claim up to $500k. Both of you must have lived in the house for at least two of the previous 5 years.

It's okay if only one of you owned the home, as long as you both resided there.

The amount you can deduct for charitable donations increases.

The current limits are determined by income. By combining your incomes, the limit is raised. If you made a donation above the limit, getting married can be a good thing.

If any state considers you to be married, so does the federal government (at least for federal tax purposes).

In August 2013, the IRS ruled that all legal same-sex marriages are recognized for tax purposes. This holds true even if the couple is not physically living in a location that recognizes same-sex marriages. Feel free to get married in another state and then head back home.

Your marital status on December 31st is what matters.

For tax purposes, you were married for the whole year. Similarly, if you get divorced during the year, you're considered unmarried for that entire tax year. If your spouse dies, you can still claim to be married for that year.

You can shop for benefits.

If you're both employed, you probably have the option of picking the best combination of benefits for your family. Perhaps one spouse has a better 401(k) plan, and the other has a better medical plan.

The 401(k) plan could be used to the maximum, and any extra family money could be put towards IRAs.

Do the Work!

Marriage has a lot of perks, and that includes some tax advantages. Ensure that you and your spouse are on the same page when it comes to finances. Money is a common source of stress and disagreement among couples. Avoid letting tax season add to your financial challenges. Encourage open and honest conversation and get professional help with your taxes, if needed.

TAX-SAVING TIPS FOR SMALL BUSINESSES

Personal taxes can be complicated. Business taxes can be more difficult. If you own a small business, tax time can be challenging.

The livelihood of any company is at least partially dependent on its ability to minimize its tax liability, while meeting the requirements of the IRS.

While taxes are not an enjoyable or interesting topic, they're a part of any business owner's life. Getting a handle your business taxes can increase your income and help you avoid legal issues.

Check out these tax tips that are helpful for any small business:

Keep your tax and financial documents for at least 7 years.

If you're ever audited, you'll need those records. Any claims made at tax time require supporting documentation. Keeping good records is an excellent idea for any small business because it encourages organization. It is very difficult to reconstruct records at a later date.

Know your deadlines.

It isn't all about April 15th. While most business entities can wait until "Tax Day," C-corporations are required to file within 10 weeks after the fiscal year ends, which is traditionally December 31st.

Understand your loans.

The IRS doesn't classify most business loans as income. But the interest paid on loans is generally a deductible expense. It's important to have records regarding the use of any loans. It might be for equipment or to finance some other activity.

Know the different types of audits.

There are several types of audits and some are more intimidating than others.

Office audit: Generally, this is a simple audit. You'll be requested to report to your local IRS office to resolve some discrepancy.

Correspondence audit: You'll just be asked to send in a document via mail or fax.

Field audit: These tend to be very thorough audits and they are conducted at your place of business.

Criminal investigation audit: Consult your lawyer. You're suspected of tax evasion.

Pay your quarterly tax bill.

This is a common mistake. If you have an employer, your taxes are taken out of each paycheck. If you're self-employed, you're required to estimate your tax each quarter and pay it. Failure to pay this can result in a significant tax penalty.

You might also end up with a bigger tax bill than you can handle in a single payment. Make a habit of setting aside a portion of your profit each month in anticipation of paying your quarterly taxes.

Prepare early.

The vast number of tax filers wait until the last minute. If you're expecting a refund, this can be the worst time to file. The IRS is overwhelmed with all the tax returns that pour in. However, this can also be the best time to avoid an audit. Preparing your tax return early leaves you time to find any missing documents and answer any questions.

Get help.

Depending on the complexity of your business's finances, hiring an expert to prepare your tax return might be a good idea. In theory, the money you spend ought to result in a smaller tax burden. It's also helpful if any legal issues arise.

Avoid using taxes collected from employee payroll to pay business expenses.

This common practice upsets the IRS. When you withhold taxes, send them to the IRS!

Do the Work!

Taxes are a large expense for any business that shows a profit. It only makes sense to minimize that expense. Consult a tax professional if you have any questions or concerns regarding your business's tax situation.

DEDUCT YOUR CHILD'S ALLOWANCE: TAX ADVANTAGES OF OWNING A SMALL BUSINESS

If you're self-employed, there are many deductions available to you that the average person without a business can't take advantage of.

In fact, if you don't have a small business, you might consider the many financial benefits of starting one.

Making an honest effort to earn income from what is just your hobby can open up a lot of tax advantages, even if you keep a regular full-time job. Consider these tax deductions:

Home office.

Whatever percentage of your home is used for business can be used in deductions from your income. For example, if your rent is $1,000 / month, and you use 30% of your square footage for business, you can deduct $3,600 from your income (12 x $300).

- The catch is that the space must be used only for business. So, if your parents sleep in your office on Christmas Eve, you lose out on the entire deduction. The IRS is a real stickler on the home office deduction.
- Your computer can be deducted as well, also based on percentage. If you use your computer 50% of the time for business, you can deduct 50% of the cost.
- You can also deduct the same percentage of your utilities. That includes, heat, electricity, Internet, and more.
- A portion of repairs to your house can be taken as a deduction in the same percent. It must be a repair that affects the whole house, like a new roof, air conditioning system, or flooring.

- Of course, any money you spend on renovating your home office is also deductible from your income.
- You can deduct your child's allowance by paying them to do age-appropriate tasks around the office like sweeping, dusting, and filing.

Travel expenses.

You can deduct your business-related travel expenses, like hotel and airfare. You can also deduct 50% of the cost of your meals on your business trips or business meals in your hometown.

- It's vital to keep a journal so you can prove that your travel was business related.
- You could have a working vacation and take the family along. You won't be able to deduct their travel or food costs, but you can still deduct the cost of your hotel room. Of course, if your family members work for you, it's a moot point!
- If you are also vacationing, be sure that you're spending at least part of the time meeting with clients, going to training, or on other business-related tasks. If you only spend 2 hours out of a week on business, you're asking for trouble. Be reasonable.

Automobile.

If your vehicle is used exclusively for business purposes, you can likely deduct all your vehicle expenses. In most cases, your vehicle will be used for both business and personal use, so keep a log of your mileage, designating each trip as personal or business.

- In general, all travel between business locations is deductible. So, travel from your home office to the office supply store would be deductible. Travel from one client location to another would be tax deductible.
- However, the miles you drive to your office from your home are not tax deductible, if your office is located away from your home.
- These deductions can be used by mileage or business use percentage. If you use your car for business purposes 30% of the time, by mileage, you can deduct 30% of your vehicle expenses. Or, you can multiply your business miles by that year's designated amount from the IRS.
- Use whichever method provides the greatest deduction. Less expensive cars would use the mileage method, while more expensive cars, the percentage method provides a larger deduction. Try it both ways.

Having a small business on the side can bring many useful deductions. Just a few are mentioned in this article. With a little planning, a significant portion of your rent or mortgage, utilities, automobile, and travel expenses can be deducted. This effort can save you thousands of dollars every year.

Do the Work!

Turn that hobby into a business. You might make some money and have a lot of fun at the same time. Consider it!

MAKE YOUR CREDIT CARD WORK FOR YOU

Managing a credit card can really be rocket science for many people, and you're probably caught right in the middle of that category! However, if you apply some very simple tips and techniques for managing and monitoring your credit card, you'll find that it's a very workable tool.

In reality, you don't always have to work for your credit card. You can, instead, get your credit card to work for you based on how well you can keep track of things.

If you pay attention to the trends of credit card owners, most people end up indebted because they simply don't pay enough attention to the details!

Use these handy tips to make your credit card work for you:

Monitor your due dates.

When it comes to managing and monitoring a credit card, timing is definitely the key. The first logical thing to consider would be the importance of paying your bill on or before the due date, and most people are conscious of this. However, not many people consider the option of using the card to delay paying their other bills:

- Make a mental note of your statement generation date.
- Use the card to pay your other bills the day after the statement date.
- Those expenses won't show up on the credit card bill until the next statement.

Make lump sum payments.

A technique that many people use is putting huge payments on the credit card and then using it to make other payments. Once you make a lump sum payment before the statement is generated:

- That amount will be reflected on your statement.
- You can use the card with the newly added payment to settle other expenses and earn credit card rewards points for paying all your regular bills without incurring additional debt.

Include interest with your minimum payment.

Perhaps you're like many of us in only being able to settle the minimum payment on credit card accounts each month. But instead of paying just the minimum payment stipulated on your statement, consider paying that amount plus the figure reflected as interest for that month. With this technique, you'll:

- Be able to cut back on recurring expenses for interest although you won't be totally debt free.
- Come closer each month to completely settling your credit debt, though it'll be a bit slow.

An Additional Tip to Consider

Financial institutions are pretty competitive when it comes to the products they offer to customers. Therefore, you can easily find one that offers better rates and consider switching to that institution.

Your credit card does not always have to be viewed as the enemy! It can actually be a *very* helpful tool when unexpected financial needs arise. What matters most is how you manage the card and how well you do at repaying the debt.

Do the Work!

There's no need to be an accounting guru to get your credit card on your side. You simply need to understand the basics of debits and credits, interest, and due dates. Everything else will fall right into place!

AVOID PAYING BANKING FEES

How much did you spend on banking fees this year? Surely, you have better things to spend your money on.

There are ways to avoid banking fees! Follow these tips:

Understand the fees charged by your bank.

Some banks make understanding their fees more difficult because a charge can appear on your account without any details. You can find out more about these fees by reading the documentation you received when opening your account, calling your banker, or checking your bank's official website.

Discover how you can qualify for a free checking account.

Most banks offer free checking accounts as long as you maintain a minimum monthly balance or receive more than a certain amount via direct deposit. Find out about these requirements and look for an account that requires a minimum direct deposit that corresponds to your paycheck.

Take advantage of bank promotions.

Some of these promotions help you avoid some fees. For example:

- Some banks will give you $100 or $200 if you open an account and meet a few requirements, such as receiving a paycheck via direct deposit or depositing a certain amount. This promotional offer will cover all your fees for a year or two.
- If you are enrolled in college, most banks will offer you a free checking account. Bring your school ID when you open your account to qualify for these offers.

Watch for ATM fees.

Fees are charged every time you withdraw money from an ATM that belongs to another bank. Use these methods to avoid ATM fees:

- Always carry $20 - $60 in cash with you to avoid having to use an ATM.
- Plan your purchases in advance and drive to your bank's ATM once a week to withdraw all the cash you'll need.
- Install an app on your Smartphone to locate the nearest ATM that belongs to your bank.

Spend only the funds in your available balance.

Bounced check and overdraft fees are some of the highest bank fees you pay.

- Stop using checks. Checks can make it difficult to manage your budget because they can take days to process. Most places offer other payment options. Besides, you will no longer have to purchase checks when you run out.
- Get into the habit of checking your balance on a daily basis. This is very easy to do, thanks to mobile apps and online banking options.
- Enroll in your bank's overdraft protection plan if they offer this service for free. Keep in mind that some banks will charge a fee every time you use this service, which can end up being costly.

Be careful with automated payments.

Although automated payments are convenient for paying your bills and avoiding late fees, they might not be your best option. They can drain your account without you being aware of it. It's very easy to set up automated recurring payments for your bills and then forget when the payments are coming out of your account.

Your best option is to set up reminders on your phone to ensure you don't forget any bills and to make payments by logging in to online banking.

Do the Work!

Avoiding banking fees is easy, but it does require you to be more aware of what is going on with your bank account. Using the same bank for all your accounts and credit cards will make it easier to check all your financial information because it's all in one place. Familiarize yourself with the mobile and online banking tools offered by your bank. These tools will make managing your finances and avoiding fees a lot easier.

HOW TO BUILD PASSIVE INCOME ONLINE

When you're struggling, living paycheck to paycheck, striving towards minimizing your overall living expenses and bringing more money into the household should definitely be on your to-do list. While minimizing your expenses can be as simple as nixing fast food or moving to a smaller apartment, it's often the "making more money" part that's most daunting.

The truth is that you can stop struggling to get by. Soon, you'll be able to take your spouse out for a nice dinner and still afford to pay your bills on time. Building a passive income online is your ticket to financial security!

Building passive income online will take hard work, hours of research, and patience to surmount the learning curve. You won't earn thousands of dollars overnight; legitimate methods of building passive income aren't get rich quick schemes. But, if you're willing to work hard now, you'll earn big rewards later.

Here are five ideas that'll help you build passive income online:

Start a blog.

Throughout the startup phase, building your blogging empire will take up quite a bit of your time. You'll need to respond to reader comments, interact with other bloggers, and create daily posts just to earn dimes. But, once you've established an online presence with your blog, you can expect to earn in the range of $100 to over $1,000 per month, just for sharing your thoughts and opinions.

Bloggers earn money through several different avenues. However, some of the most common and basic methods of earning passive income through a blog are Google's Adsense program and other comparable pay-per-click systems, private advertisers, and affiliate commissions.

Write articles for ad sharing websites.

Ad sharing websites allow you to post articles to their website directory and earn ad revenue each time a visitor clicks on an advertisement next to your article.

Taking part in work at home forums is an effective way of getting leads to some of the highest paying ad revenue websites. Some examples of successful ad revenue websites are eHow.com, Bukisa.com and Suite101.com.

Flip blogs for quick cash.

Once you get the hang of it, flipping blogs can be a quick way to make money within just a few hours. Simply purchase a domain name (new or aged), find a unique WordPress theme, and post content on your new blog. After you've successfully set up the blog, place it for sale on an auction website, such as Flippa.com or Sitepoint.com.

Sell stock photography.

If you're a brilliant photographer, put your artistic skills to use and sell stock photography online. Capture images of scenes you think will sell well. Then, visually enhance the photos in Photoshop, if necessary, and place them for sale on websites like Fotolia.com or iStockPhotos.com.

Sales may be slow at first, but remember you're building passive income that treats you to nice checks month after month. Once you've built up an inventory of several dozen photos, sales will begin to pick up.

Become an affiliate marketer.

As an affiliate marketer, you'll promote other people's products online for a commission. Each time you make a sale, you'll be paid up to 75% of the sale price. Most people who succeed in this field focus on promoting products through article marketing and email marketing campaigns, but there are several strategies you can quickly learn.

Writing two articles is unlikely to result in a sale. Write 20 articles and your chances increase greatly. Write 200 articles and you'll get the ball rolling on some nice commissions.

Do the Work!

In time, you'll be able to pay costly bills and plan vacations without dipping into your paychecks. The key to ultimate success is the ability to remain focused on the end result. Allow your desires to fuel your drive toward financial security. An optimistic mindset and persistence in working to achieve your goal will see you through to online success.

BEAT LAZINESS

Everyone feels a little lazy at times. But being lazy on a regular basis can have a severe negative impact on your life. Laziness is a natural tendency. All creatures gravitate toward comfort, or at least what's perceived to be comfortable.

Laziness is indulging in short-term comfort at the expense of long-term pain. Do you know anyone with a great life that's lazy? Over time, the law of cause and effect holds true. Laziness has a long-term price.

Beat laziness and accomplish more:

Find a way to get excited.

Consider the benefits you'll receive by getting it done. It might be the end result that excites you or the fact that you're learning and growing. Maybe demonstrating self-control and discipline is something that you can get excited about. It's much harder to accomplish something if you're complaining about it.

Set a deadline.

When you have plenty of time to complete something, or no deadline at all, it's human nature to procrastinate. Setting a deadline in the near future can help to focus your attention and energy.

Create smaller tasks from the main task.

Every large task can be done in steps. Building a house has steps. First the site must be prepared. Then the foundation is created, and the framing begins. The remaining steps are followed until the house is completed.

The overall project might be big and intimidating. However, the individual tasks might be easier to handle.

Focus on taking the first step.

Once you get started, the momentum you've created can carry you far. Activity breeds further activity. Sitting on the couch tends to lead to more sitting. Instead of worrying about the mountain of work ahead of you, focus on getting one simple task completed.

Read or listen to something that motivates you.

It can be something as simple as a book of inspiring quotes or a song that energizes you. You know what inspires you. Use it to your advantage.

Consider the pain of not getting started.

We're good at imagining the pain of getting started but try the opposite. What will happen if you continue to be lazy? What will it cost you in the future? What has it cost you so far? Instead of using pain as a reason to be lazy, use pain to create action.

Remind yourself that the last few years have flown by.

Laziness is often a chronic condition. A lot of time has passed in the last 5 years, but how much have you accomplished? When one day seems to be a copy of every other day, five years goes by fast. Life is wasting away. Get up and do something!

Reward yourself for activity.

Get one thing done and celebrate. You probably haven't done enough to deserve a new car, but you have the right to get excited and be proud of yourself.

Be patient.

It's common to believe that action comes from motivation, but the opposite may be true. Action leads to results. Results lead to motivation. Be mentally tough and get busy. You'll have a reason to be motivated soon enough.

Do the Work!

Avoid allowing laziness to keep you on the sideline. It will steal your time and limit your results!

ENJOY MORE PEACE OF MIND

Living within your means has always been a wise strategy and becomes more important during uncertain economic times. Here are some of the major advantages of spending less than you earn and some painless strategies for sticking with this positive habit.

There are many advantages of living within your means.

Reduce stress. You'll feel calmer when you know you have enough set aside to keep your basic expenses covered or get you through potential emergencies like job loss or illness. By planning ahead, you can feel secure on a modest income.

Improve your finances. Some people become millionaires on remarkably low salaries. Whatever you earn, you can increase your net worth by saving, spending and smartly investing.

Reach your goals. Make frugality more pleasant by viewing it as a way to attain your goals rather than as a sacrifice. Brewing your own coffee for your morning commute can help pay for your summer vacation or the down payment on a home.

Contribute to a better society. The Occupy Wall Street movement dramatizes the impact our choices may have on other people. While predicting all future events is impossible, you can try to pay your own way without burdening others.

Use some of these strategies for living within your means.

Create a budget.

Get familiar with your monthly income and expenses. Include automatic payments like bank fees and insurance.

Pay down debt.

Contact lenders to see if you can consolidate your debts and pay them back on more favorable terms. Avoid going into debt by saving money in advance to pay for holiday gifts and weekend trips.

Manage your credit cards.

If you use credit cards, try to pay off the balance every month. If your balance has already accumulated, consolidate it onto a single card with the best rate you can find.

Save more.

Motivate yourself to save by remembering the purpose, whether it's your kid's education or your own retirement. You may be able to deduct money from every paycheck before you see it. This way, your savings are set aside before you have any temptation to spend them.

Earn more.

Of course, earnings are the other side of the equation. Consider any classes or certifications that could help you qualify for a more lucrative position. Make money off your hobby, such as giving piano lessons or selling crafts.

Remain flexible.

Life events are likely to interfere with your budget from time to time. Indulge yourself occasionally or make adjustments for unusual expenses, like if your house needs a new roof.

Tackle one habit at a time.

Be patient while you're changing your old ways. Once you get used to growing your own vegetables you can move on to learning basic home repair. For some of us, keeping a budget is a new habit. That's okay; just give yourself some time to integrate one change before you jump into the next big project.

Get outside help.

There are many sources of free or inexpensive expert financial advice. Check the website for your local government for resources or consult the National Federation for Credit Counseling.

Make your own meals.

Eating out takes a big bite out of the budget for many families. Pack your own lunch on workdays instead of buying mediocre sandwiches. Learn more recipes so you can enjoy fancy dinners at home.

Seek out cheap entertainment.

Borrow free movies and books from your local library. Play croquet in your backyard. Purchase family memberships at your local museum or zoo so you can visit often and get invited to special events.

Comparison shop for big expenses.

Researching large purchases pays off. Get the best price you can on major expenses like appliances and auto insurance.

Do the Work!

Living within your means is good for your mental and financial health. Build a better future by putting yourself on a budget that you can sustain.

COMPONENTS OF PERSONAL TRANSFORMATION

Maybe you're sick of your life, your waistline, or the person you've become. You're more flexible than you think! You can become just about anything or anyone you like. Whether you want to get fit, build wealth, or revamp your social life, you can do it!

Personal transformation is far from easy, but where there's a will, there's a way.

These strategies can help you become the person you've always wanted to be:

Identify your core values.

You won't be happy if you create a big change that puts you in conflict with your values. Most people have never really taken the time to identify their values. Take a day to consider the values that are most important to you. Write them down.

Create a vision of the future.

Think about the end result of the transformation you want to make. If you want to lose weight and become fit, think about how you would look and feel. Maybe you're more interested in becoming wealthy. What would that look like? What kind of house would you own? How would you spend your day?

Is your transformation reasonable for you? For example, you might not be able to make a trillion dollars, but you could still build great wealth.

Determine why.

Why do you want to make this change? Create a long list of reasons why you want to transform. Get excited.

Identify the qualities and skills you'll need to develop.

If you want to transform your body, you might need to learn more about exercise physiology, nutrition, and develop some discipline. Consider what it will take to accomplish your transformation.

Identify the resources you'll require.

Do you need a personal trainer, gym membership, and a blender? Maybe you need money and a mentor for your transformation. Figure out the resources you'll need.

Make a plan.

Start at the end and keep working backwards until you reach a step that you can do today. Avoid worrying about the details of step 11. You can worry about that when you're finishing up step 10. You don't need to see 10 miles down the road to back out of your driveway.

Audit your plan.

Imagine following your plan and note how you feel at each step. You're bound to feel some emotional resistance at one or more points. If you didn't, you would have made the transformation long ago.

It's important to address each of the issues that creates emotional discomfort. You're likely to quit if you don't. Either come up with a plan to work around those issues or just relax and let the negative feelings go. You'll know you're in a good place when you find yourself chomping at the bit to get started. Procrastination is a sign that something is awry.

Don't quit!

This is the most challenging part for most people. You fail if you quit. You can't fail if you don't. Keep on going no matter how bleak things seem. You can always do better tomorrow than you did today. A little bit of progress each day or week is all you need.

Do the Work!

You can transform yourself starting today. Build a vision and create a plan. Stay the course until you're satisfied with the changes you've made.

CHAPTER EIGHT, SUPPORT

Which Habits Can You Turn Around Fast?

You are stretching your mind, your understanding, and your ability to see more clearly. Continue your growth with these self-affirming thoughts.

Getting Started

Read through each section. They are designed to help you change your stinking thinking into satisfying facts.

· First, find the ones that you are utilizing, and pat yourself on the back.

· Next, see if yourself talk needs any tweaking based on the new knowledge you are gaining.

· After you have that done, study the self-talk that is new to you. Which ones are missing form your tools used to develop your healthy financial lifestyle?

· For the new self-talk concepts, spend time each day until you are comfortable with them, until you catch yourself replacing your old thoughts with your new and supportive ones.

· Pick the self-talk support that you need the most and implement them first.

Finally, after you have all this accomplished, go back and read through your notes every three months to make sure you haven't strayed from the work you need to make your life great.

Calculated Risk

Taking risks brings me fulfillment.

Use this self-affirming language to teach your thoughts a new habit:

- My most fulfilling accomplishments come when I take risks to achieve them. It is important to commit to a fearless approach. My courage ensures my successes are multiplied continually.
- The biggest risks come when making personal decisions. It is easy to back down from a decision when the thought of it makes me uncomfortable. But I ignore that discomfort.
- I remind myself that uncomfortable choices result in the most rewarding outcomes. That mindset helps me to be confident when taking personal chances. I know that my ultimate happiness comes when I decide to do what is best for me.
- At times my job can be difficult. When the finances of the company are at risk, I am hesitant to make a decision. But I remind myself to be fearlessly smart.
- My fearlessness develops the more I choose to take risks. Each time I commit to overcoming intimidation, my courage grows a little more. I buckle down and rely on my qualifications and experience to guide my decisions.
- Sometimes I wonder if weary perseverance is worth the risk. But I envision the light at the end of the tunnel instead of a roadblock to prevent me from getting there.
- Today, I commit to using risk-taking as an avenue for developing fearlessness. My focus is on living my best life with courage. I am happy with my uncertain choices when I realize they bring me the greatest satisfaction.

Do the Work!

Take time for self-reflection:

1. How am I affected when a risk I take produces an undesirable outcome?

2. When am I best served by ignoring the desire to take a risk?

3. What can I do to ensure that in the absence of risk I continue to feel fulfilled?

Grow Your Strength

Growth begins with acceptance.

Use this self-affirming language to teach your thoughts a new habit:

- Refusing to dwell on things beyond my control allows me to move on. I practice acceptance, so I can grow.
- Hardship and losses are a natural part of life. When I am sad and disappointed, I can find something in any situation that I can use to my benefit. I treat myself with compassion and take constructive action.
- I put things in perspective. Most conditions are temporary. If I experience a reversal now, I may have a happy surprise later. When I think about the challenges I have overcome in the past, I build my confidence for dealing with my current issues.
- I search for solutions. I focus on what I can do to enhance my situation. I change my attitude. I look on the bright side and count my blessings.
- I remember that struggling can make me stronger.
- When I am ill, I learn more about my condition and search for strategies that will help me to recover or manage my symptoms. I use home remedies and talk with my doctor. I engage in pleasant activities that help take my mind off my discomfort.
- When I have conflicts at work, I try to see events from my coworkers' point of view while standing up for my own values.
- Today, I accept the truth even when it is difficult. Facing facts instead of fighting them helps me to become more peaceful and productive.

Do the Work!

Take time for self-reflection:

1. What is the difference between acceptance and agreement?

2. What happens when I try to avoid uncomfortable situations and emotions?

3. How can meditation and mindfulness help me to become more accepting?

Your Focus

I focus on what matters.

Use this self-affirming language to teach your thoughts a new habit:

- Most of the things that happen in my life simply lack relevance. It is my job to determine what truly matters and give those things my attention.
- I only have so much time and energy to give each day, so I focus my attention and talents on what can make the biggest positive difference in my life.
- My values are the basis for my life.
- Knowing my values intimately makes it possible for me to make smart decisions and avoid feelings of regret. Choices are easy to make when I remember my values.
- I am free of internal conflict and confusion because I am clear on what matters in my life.
- I avoid worrying about the opinions of others. What others think about me is none of my business. If I can look at myself in the mirror, I am content. When I live for others, I make mistakes and find myself living a life that is unenjoyable.
- I know what I want to achieve. Knowing my goals, objectives, and plans allows me to identify what matters the most in my life.
- I consider my goals before deciding how to spend my time.
- Today, I dedicate my time, energy, and talents to what matters to me and my life. I avoid those things that sap my energy and will to succeed.

Do the Work!

Take time for self-reflection:

1. What do I spend too much time on that doesn't matter?

2. What matters the most to me in my life?

3. What could I accomplish if I focused my energy on what matters the most?

Meet Your Goals

I am capable of achieving my financial goals.

Use this self-affirming language to teach your thoughts a new habit:

- With open arms, I embrace the wealth that is continuously coming my way. In addition to being open to the abundance offered to me, I am also willing to work hard. For these reasons, I know that I am capable of achieving my financial goals.
- I trust that the work I do today is paying off.
- Abundance is the natural order that includes spiritual, mental, material and financial prosperity. Therefore, all I must do to receive it is to remain open to abundance and willing to put in some time and effort on my own behalf. Natural law takes care of the rest.
- My financial goals are reasonable, too. I set objectives that are worth striving for, but not so high that I feel overwhelmed just looking at them. Instead, when I think about my goals, I feel energized and enthusiastic. I know I have what it takes to meet them.
- Sometimes, I may wonder how I can get to where I wish to go. I may map out a path for myself but still feel unsure about how to connect where I am at now with where I am headed. At these times, I choose to consciously relax. Just as I have reached objectives in the past, I can achieve the ones I set for myself now.
- Today, I am confident that I can reach my financial goals. Each day, I cultivate patience, willingness, and perseverance as I watch wealth flow toward me in abundance.

Do the Work!

Take time for self-reflection:

1. What are some goals I have achieved in the past?

2. Do my financial goals seem realistic to me? Are they high enough to feel exciting without seeming overly challenging?

3. What small daily steps can I take to remind myself to trust that abundance is coming my way?

When to Spend

I spend money responsibly.

Use this self-affirming language to teach your thoughts a new habit:

- I have full appreciation of the value of money. It is easy to want to splurge when there is a surplus of money in front of me, but I am proud of my ability to show restraint.
- At times, I am tempted to make a spontaneous purchase. But my first consideration is to assess whether I need it. I also consider the impact of the purchase. If I recognize there could be a negative repercussion, I decide against it.
- Each month, I set aside money for life's necessities. I am responsible enough to first take care of the necessary expenses. I avoid spending frivolously before spending on what's important.
- I know that rainy days may come, so I am sure to save with those in mind. I put aside enough money to take care of me and my family in the event of unforeseen circumstances.
- When I make purchases for my kids, I make wholesome choices. There are times when I give in to their wants. But for the most part, I ensure I spend on things that enhance them.
- I teach my kids the value of money. I am sure to show them the wonderful ways it can be used to help others. I teach them to be responsible citizens.
- Today, I spend money reasonably. I think about the future and ensure my finances are taken care of.

Do the Work!

Take time for self-reflection:

1. Are there times I give in to impulse purchases?

2. Do I save for vacations and other activities that enhance family life?

3. Do I consistently look for ways to introduce new income streams to my household?

What to Spend Money On

I spend money wisely.

Use this self-affirming language to teach your thoughts a new habit:

- I give myself more opportunities and stability by handling money wisely. I prioritize my expenses and live within my means.
- I stick to my budget. I plan ahead for my basic needs and possible emergencies. I pay bills on time and resist overspending. I put off immediate gratification.
- I consider the true value of the items that I am considering buying. I take into account more than just the price tag when I am making a purchase. I ask myself if I really need an item and how much I expect to use it.
- I examine bargains. I shop around to compare prices. I remain firm in the face of sales pressure and make my own decisions.
- I take care of what I have. My home and car keep more of their value when I pay for their maintenance and repairs.
- I invest in myself. I buy nutritious food and high-quality health care. I add to my savings on a regular basis.
- I give generously to others. I treat my loved ones to thoughtful gifts and fun entertainment. I support charitable causes that I believe in.
- I keep material things in perspective. I know that my self-worth is based on my inner goodness rather than the brands I wear. I find fulfillment in my faith rather than my bank account.
- Today, I build up wealth by spending money responsibly. I align my spending with my values.

Do the Work!

Take time for self-reflection:

1. How do my emotions affect my spending?

2. How can I use critical thinking to help me make major purchases?

3. Where can I find help with managing my finances?

Watch Those Spending Habits

I am mindful of my spending habits.

Use this self-affirming language to teach your thoughts a new habit:

- I realize now that money does not grow on trees. The temporary financial struggles of my past have proven this to be true. For this reason, I am mindful of my spending habits.
- It is simple to swipe my card and worry about the consequences of my purchase later. However, I have an ingenious tactic to curb unnecessary spending. I directly correlate the purchase amount to the number of hours I need to work to earn the money for the desired item.
- If I earn $20 per hour and I am considering a $150 purchase, I must work 7.5 hours to earn that amount on my paycheck. This leaves me only $10 for my 8-hour time investment, not to mention the deductions, taxes, and other living expenses!
- Weighing my purchases in this manner immediately curbs my spending.
- I make purchases with a practical mindset and I avoid letting my emotions rule my money.
- I avoid the mall unless it is necessary; I refrain from purchasing sale items unless I need them; and I go food shopping after I've eaten.
- I pull in the reins on my spending for the sake of my entire family as well as for myself. I would much rather see our money sitting soundly in a savings account than draped over a sofa in the form of a throw or on my hair in the form of highlights.
- In this economy, frugality is king. A high price tag no longer generates a sense of entitlement. Now, an exorbitant price tag only produces embarrassment.
- Today, I accurately weigh my purchases. If I do not need the item, back on the shelf it goes. My money is better spent elsewhere.

Do the Work!

Take time for self-reflection:

1. Which stores generate an impulse purchase?

2. Can I shop online to minimize the temptation of impulse buying?

3. Do I shop emotionally or practically?

Healthy Control of Spending

I pave the road to financial security by controlling my spending.

Use this self-affirming language to teach your thoughts a new habit:

- In times where most families are struggling to make ends meet, I consider myself fortunate to have financial security.
- By controlling my spending habits, I minimize our bills and make a considerable contribution to our savings account every few weeks.
- I can remember a time when I found myself living paycheck to paycheck. I had to worry about how I would scramble together the money to pay my electric bill or buy food.
- Now, however, I am free from that sense of panic and financial instability! Recalling the hard times helps me put the brakes on my spending and build up our savings account!
- Do I really need HBO and Show Time in my cable package? No.
- Do I really need my Grande Caramel Macchiato from Starbucks each morning? No.
- Packing my own lunch can also save me $5 to $10 each day or up to $100 to $200 each month.
- By removing these inexpensive splurges from my budget, I can save $2,400 to $3,600 per year. That money serves a better purpose earning interest in my high-yield savings account!
- Rather than depriving myself, I am simply forgoing a few luxuries in exchange for a better tomorrow.
- When I feel like buying "just one little purse" or "just one little video game," I dissuade myself by envisioning my savings account hitting five digits. Oh, how sweet it is!
- Today, I continue to curb my spending by focusing on the end result, knowing that a small sacrifice now leads to big financial security later.

Do the Work!

Take time for self-reflection:

1. How can I minimize my living expenses?

2. What luxuries can I eliminate from my routine?

3. How much money can I manage with ease to transfer into my savings account each month?

Honor Your Circumstances

I make the most of any circumstance.

Use this self-affirming language to teach your thoughts a new habit:

- Difficult situations occur for everyone, but I know I can handle whatever fate throws my way.
- I recognize all of the different aspects of a situation - both negative and positive. I choose to focus on the positive aspects to seek an effective solution, but still learn from the negative. As a result, I can make the most of any circumstance.
- I see my struggles in a new way when I search for the positive.
- Stress and fear may try to dominate my mind during a difficult situation, but I foil their efforts when I focus on the positive.
- I concentrate on my ability to change the situation. I find the aspects that I can influence, so I can work through the situation and get back to moving forward toward my goals.
- My mind is a powerful tool in my ability to handle any type of situation.
- It allows me to avoid negativity as I determine all the aspects of a situation. Without anxiety, stress, or fear, I can see my circumstances more clearly.
- I am able to build a path toward the positive possibilities that now present themselves.
- Today, I avoid taking situations personally or allowing setbacks to destroy my positive nature. I focus on the aspects I can influence. "Keep moving forward," is my mantra as I seek an effective solution.

Do the Work!

Take time for self-reflection:

1. How can I help my family and friends learn to see the positive aspects of a difficult situation?

2. What can I do to avoid a focus on negative emotions and thoughts during troublesome times?

3. How can I maintain positive thoughts while others are being negative?

Opportunities Are Available

I create opportunities.

Use this self-affirming language to teach your thoughts a new habit:

- I am in control of my life. My choices shape my experiences. I create opportunities.
- I pay attention to my surroundings. I keep up with trends and emerging ideas. I notice the challenges that others are facing and think about what I could do to help invent solutions.
- I acquire new knowledge and skills. I value learning that increases my resources and capacity. I read extensively and take adult education classes. I ask questions.
- I leverage my strengths. I understand my capabilities and how to use them. I devote my time and energy to activities where I can have the greatest impact. I find opportunities by helping others to advance too. I provide referrals and introductions. I share my time and talents.
- I take risks. Focusing on what I have to gain motivates me to move beyond my comfort zone. I give myself credit for trying regardless of the immediate results. Some experiences pay off more down the line.
- I act promptly. I jump on opportunities while my excitement is high. I put aside doubts that could make me miss my chances.
- I collaborate with others. Networking multiplies the opportunities available to me and my contacts.
- I remain flexible. I pursue worthwhile opportunities even when they require changing my current plans. I remain true to my values while I adjust my methods. I keep my eye on my ultimate objectives.
- Today, I create conditions that bring promising opportunities. I make good things happen.

Do the Work!

Take time for self-reflection:

1. What is one new opportunity I can seize today?

2. How can I become more skillful at evaluating opportunities?

3. How can I transform setbacks into opportunities?

Control Your Finances

I control my finances instead of allowing them to control me.

Use this self-affirming language to teach your thoughts a new habit:

- I am in absolute control of my finances. I take time to prepare a budget and ensure that all bills are paid off before indulging in luxuries. Each dollar that comes out of my pocket is spent on a purchase with a purpose!
- Small financial sacrifices that I make today enable me to build a promising tomorrow for my family. Can I do without a top-of-the-line cell phone? Yes, I can! Can I live without Starbucks? I sure can!
- Millions of people live without such luxuries each day and manage to get by just fine. I can be one of those people. I know that cutting down on my spending habits puts more money in my pocket over time.
- When I was younger, I often made impulse purchases, but now I have come to realize that the little things really do add up. Now, when I am tempted to make a purchase over $50, I give myself 24 hours to think it over.
- Though conveniences are nice, I am perfectly aware that they come at a premium. For this reason, I brew my own coffee in the morning, pack my lunch for work, and chop my own vegetables. A small-time investment can result in great savings!
- Saving for a rainy day is number one on my list of priorities. If I have a dime to spare, a nickel goes to my savings account. Even insignificant contributions can make a big difference in the long run.
- Today, I laugh in the face of temptation. I am now equipped with the mindset to ward off frivolous spending.

Do the Work!

Take time for self-reflection:

1. Do I use shopping as an emotional crutch?

2. What are my financial goals and how can I work toward achieving them?

3. Can I minimize my expenses by doing things myself?

9

CREATE MONEY

Much like how a budget creates money through control, you can also create money through saving. Saving, when used as a tool, can help you eliminate unnecessary stress, bring your finances into harmony, and help you manage unforeseen challenges that always arrive at the worst time.

Getting Started

Saving and other creative forms of making money give many fun options to help you get back on track financially. Read through all the options and pick your favorites to try today.

Good luck and get started right away.

MOVE YOUR FINANCIAL LIFE: TIPS FOR SUCCESS

Does financial freedom seem like an unreachable goal for you? For some, the only goal in sight is getting that next paycheck so you can pay the bills before services get disconnected.

Even if your current situation seems dire, there are things you can do to achieve financial success.

Options that can improve your financial situation are all around you. When you want to move your financial life forward, the first step is deciding on a worthwhile goal.

What do you want to see happen? When?

As soon as you've made that determination, you can begin marching toward your success in a step-by-step fashion. A worthwhile goal ensures you know where you're going before you set out on your journey.

Long-Term and Short-Term Goals Are Both Critical

You might have a short-term goal to pay off a credit card and a long-term goal to pay off your mortgage. Those are both reachable, but one will take longer than the other. Makes sense, right?

Well, that's why it's so important to set a realistic timeframe for your goals! Stay encouraged by tracking your progress along your planned timeline. When you see a goal getting closer to achievement, you'll become more excited and motivated to keep moving forward.

If you only set long-term goals, the payoff is too far away to provide any real motivation. These goals take a while to achieve and the lack of immediate progress may make you want to quit without shorter-term goals to look forward to.

The goal is to set long-term goals and couple them with short-term goals that excite you. Or, break your long-term objectives into short-term milestones that provide encouraging feedback on your progress. That way, you remain interested in pursuing your financial success.

You Can Get There from Here!

Too many people get discouraged and stop working for their goals. Don't let this happen to you! Avoid allowing yourself to end up financially stuck and struggling because you let setbacks derail your train to financial success and prosperity.

Don't give up on your success. Live the good life you deserve.

Use these strategies to move forward:

Reap your rewards along the way.

Set *realistic* goals and reward yourself when you meet them. Divide your large goals into small steps and celebrate completing each step.

Be flexible.

Be willing to move your completion dates if you see they're too soon. If you experience a setback, learn from it, adjust your goal's completion date, and continue moving forward.

Focus.

Stay focused on what matters to you instead of getting sidetracked. Remember the reasons why your success is important to you when the going gets rough.

Make the work toward your dreams more enjoyable.

Moving forward doesn't have to be all tedious work. Include goals in your life for things you enjoy, too.

- Turn your hobby or other enjoyable activities into a profitable venture.
- Ask yourself how you can make tasks you dread more fun.
- Include a friend.
- Make it a game with yourself.
- Whatever you do, keep a spirit of playfulness in your work and success is sure to follow!

You deserve a life that's filled with rich experiences, meaningful relationships and inner peace.

Your hopes and dreams are what fuel your happiness. With a positive mindset and a determination to succeed, you can achieve all of this and more. Financial independence and the dream life you seek are within your reach.

When you reach your goals - even the small ones - you set yourself apart from most people, who dream big dreams but stay on the sidelines of life.

Do the Work!

Get in the game! Brainstorm the short-term and long-term financial objectives that matter to you. Pick the most important ones, sketch out a plan, and take the first steps toward your financial success today.

MANAGING YOUR MONEY WHEN YOU'RE BROKE

Budgeting money is rarely easy, but it's more difficult when you don't have enough of it to pay all of your bills. You might be between jobs or simply have a job that doesn't pay well enough to address all of your expenses.

It's important to change how you spend your money when you're short on funds. Follow these steps for effective money management when you're seriously broke:

Be proactive.

Don't wait until the collection agencies start calling. They are relentless and aren't known for being understanding. They only get paid when you pay them, so you can see where their priorities lie.

Call your creditors as soon as you can see that you won't be able to make a payment. You might be able to work out some sort of an extension or get reduced payments for a while.

Prioritize.

Life is all about priorities. Look at how much money you have available and then prioritize your bills in a way that supports you. A good idea is to put your mortgage, basic utilities, insurance and food first. Credit cards can be last on the list.

Consider the consequences of not paying each bill and make a decision.

Do this step after you've contacted your creditors. Your decisions might be different, depending on their responses. Now is the time to ruthlessly cut all your unnecessary expenses. Austerity has its time and place, and the time is now.

Cut back on your savings plan.

This might be the one time to stop saving part of your paycheck. The expense and ramifications of not paying your bills might be too great to cut yourself even shorter to make your savings payment.

You've always heard to pay yourself first, but sometimes that's not appropriate.

Avoid relying on credit.

When cash is short, it's a common practice to start using credit cards to replace a paycheck. The cost of this money can be incredibly high, and this debt is difficult to eliminate later on. Don't fall into the trap of viewing credit as a viable solution.

Consider how much on average you're able to save and then project how long it would take to pay off this new debt. You already have more debt than you can handle. It doesn't make sense to add even more to the equation.

Create more income.

If you don't have a job, take anything you can get for the time being. If you do have a job, consider adding a second job or getting some overtime. If you have stuff lying around the house that you don't need, it might be wise to sell it.

The less you fall behind now, the easier it will be to catch up later.

Make a new budget.

This might be the last thing you're in the mood to do, but either your financial circumstances have changed, or your current budget isn't working. Both reasons suggest that a new budget is required. Take a look at your income and bills and make some smart choices. Remember that it's all about proper prioritization.

In stressful times like these, it's easy to succumb to your anxiety and not take action but understand that this course of action will only make your challenges greater in the future.

Do the Work!

Take a deep breath and do everything you can to get yourself back on track with your finances. You'll be surprised how much you can accomplish when you really focus your intention and energy on solutions. Prioritize your bills, increase your income, and make a new budget. Things will be better before you know it.

SAVE BIG WITH A SIMPLE SAVINGS JAR

A simple glass jar can help you save a lot of money in one year. The savings jar provides motivation to stay on a plan. It's an easy way to put money aside for a vacation or home renovation.

Any glass jar will work. It's important to keep the jar see-through because seeing the money grow will encourage you to keep going.

The $5 bill plan.

This plan involves saving a $5 bill by putting it in the jar each time you receive one back as change. The plan can be modified to be a $10 bill, $20 bill, or quarters.

Instead of spending the $5 bill, you save it and slowly build up the contents of the jar.

The 52-week money challenge.

This method increases your savings gradually each week of the year.

Start with putting $1 in your jar during the first week of the year. Then, add an extra dollar each week. The savings grow until they reach $52 for the last week of the year. You can save $1,378 using this simple method.

A print or online calendar can help track the savings. Each week can be labeled at the beginning with the amount that needs to be added to the savings jar.

It may be easy to save $1 or $2 at the beginning of the plan, but how will you find an extra $52 at the end of the year? This savings method encourages you to think ahead and plan.

The traditional change method.

Saving your change by adding it to the jar is a traditional method, but it can provide results. After work or running errands, add all of your change to the jar.

The paycheck plan.

Consider adding a set amount of money to the savings jar after you cash your paycheck.

The paycheck plan also works for couples. You can cash a specific amount of money from each of your paychecks every month and add it to the jar. This works best if you have a financial goal in place.

Are you trying to save for a trip or a new electronic gadget? Figure out how much you will have to save each month from your paychecks to pay for it.

The inspiration plan.

The inspiration plan works best if you have a picture of the item or goal you are trying to achieve. It can be placed near the savings jar or attached to the lid, so you see it every day. Put money in the jar each time you're inspired to do so. Include the whole family.

Place the jar in the living room or kitchen, so it stays highly visible.

The inspiration photo depends on your goals. It can vary from pictures of vacation spots to new television sets. You can also write the goal on a piece of paper.

The photo serves as a constant reminder of why you are saving money.

The $20 weekly plan.

The $20 weekly plan is an alternative to the 52-week money challenge. Instead of slowly building savings during the year, you put a set amount of money in the jar each week.

Similar to the 52-week money challenge, you can track the savings on a calendar or chart.

At the end of the year, you can save $1,040 in the jar using the $20 weekly plan.

Do the Work!

A glass jar can help you save more than $1,000 a year. A commitment to saving money will help you achieve your goals.

INVESTING: MAKE YOUR DOLLARS WORK FOR YOU

Taxes can take away a significant chunk of your investment income. They say the only two things you can count on in life are death and taxes.

There are ways to minimize your tax burden when it comes to your investments. Let's look at the various taxes that target investments:

Capital Gains.

Anytime you sell an investment and realize a profit, you're usually going to be taxed. If you sell within 12 months of acquiring that investment, the gains are taxed as income. This could be as much as 35%, depending on your income.

If the investment is held for more than a year before being sold, the capital gains tax applies, which is 15% for most taxpayers. It can be as low as 0% if you're in the 10% or 15% tax bracket for ordinary income. Capital gains tax can be as high as 20% for those above specified income levels.

Capital gains also apply to some mutual fund distributions. This can happen even if you don't sell your shares. When your mutual fund company sells stocks it owns, those taxable gains are passed along.

Other types of investments have different tax structures. Profits from selling a primary residence are not taxed, up to $250,000 in profits ($500,000 for married couples). Futures contracts are complicated. Some of the profits are taxed as long-term investments, regardless of how long they were held.

Dividends and other income.

Not only are you taxed for selling your investments, but you also have to pay taxes on dividend and interest income: Rental income is also taxed, but at your regular tax rate. Dividends are taxed at 15%.

Interest on bonds and most other investment income gets taxed at your income tax rate.

Municipal Bonds.

This interest is tax-free for federal taxes and can be tax-free at the state-level, too. Be aware that municipal bonds and their taxation can be complicated, so be sure to consult your tax professional on the details that apply in your situation.

Strategies

Make great investments and don't sell.

Warren Buffett has relatively few investments and he seldom sells anything. Consider that every time you sell a stock and make money, those earnings are going to be taxed.

If you're making good investments, you should be able to hold on to them for a long period of time. This is another reason to invest with a long-term perspective.

Use your retirement accounts as much as possible.

Traditional IRAs offer the opportunity to invest pre-tax money. In other words, the money that you invest was not subjected to income taxes. However, there are taxes to be paid when you start taking the money back out.

A 401(k) offers advantages similar to a traditional IRA, namely pre-tax contributions. The money is also taxed when contributions are taken.

Roth IRA: the money invested is after tax, but all the gains are not taxed - even when you take the money out in retirement! There are rules to be followed regarding when you can start taking the money out without incurring penalties. But the benefit of avoiding taxes on gains is huge!

Health Savings Accounts.

These are, in essence, tax-free investment accounts for your health. Any money you put in the account is pre-tax and must be used for medical expenses.

These accounts permit setting aside up to $3,250 per year for an individual or $6,450 for a family. The money can be pre-tax in most cases, and the balance of the account can be rolled over each year.

If you have a flexible spending account with your employer, you can't also have a health savings account. You must choose one over the other.

529 Plans.

These are investment accounts for expenses related to higher education.

Contributions aren't tax deductible, but the earnings grow tax deferred. The distributions aren't taxed, provided the funds are spent on eligible expenses.

Some states also offer state-level tax advantages.

As the donor, you always maintain control of the funds. You can pull your money back out at any time. However, the earnings will be taxed. There is also an additional 10% tax penalty.

There are no income restrictions or age limits on the beneficiary of a 529 plan. If you're older and would like to go back to school, a 529 plan is an option.

You can choose a plan from any state, regardless of your residency. The funds can then be applied to any school, regardless of location.

Capital Losses.

Sooner or later, you're bound to have an investment that loses money. This loss can be subtracted from your capital gains, in most cases. If your losses are greater than your gains, you can deduct up to $3,000 from your other income, even your wages.

A common strategy is to sell off your losses at the end of the tax year. You must be careful not to buy back the stock too quickly or the deduction will be nullified. You must wait more than 30 days. This is called the "wash sale" rule.

Do the Work!

Just as there are multiple taxes to consider, there are also multiple strategies to combat them. For your best results, consult a tax professional before developing and executing a tax / investment strategy. Don't let the taxman take a bigger bite out of your bank account than absolutely necessary.

Be sure to utilize your retirement accounts as much as possible. You'll be more than a little grateful later in life.

DEBIT OR CREDIT - WHICH CARD FOR YOU?

You probably have an understanding of the basic difference between a credit card and a debit card. However, most of us are unaware of all the differences. There are advantages and disadvantages to each.

Understanding these differences will allow you to make more informed decisions about which card you'll want to use in different situations. Consider these points:

A credit card is simply access to an unsecured loan.

When you use your credit card, the card issuer is loaning you the money to pay your bill.

This means that the credit card company can't take your item from you if you fail to pay the way a bank can with a home or car. Those types of loans are secured with collateral. That's why the interest rate for home and car loans is standardly much less.

Using a debit card removes money from your account to pay your bill.

Debit cards are tied to a specific account. From a practical standpoint, it's no different than writing a check. It's just faster and easier. The effect on your account is more immediate, too.

Credit and debit cards both cost the merchant.

One method the issuer of a card uses to make money is charging the merchant a fee, typically around 2%, every time a card is used. While cards are convenient, merchants actually make more money if you pay with cash.

The appropriate use of credit cards can have a positive impact on your credit report.

Using a credit card for purchases or paying bills can help your credit score. It's important to pay your credit card bills on time and to keep your balances below 30% of your credit limit.

Likewise, the improper use of a credit card, like making late payments, has the potential to seriously damage your credit score.

The proper use of a debit card has no impact on your credit report.

Credit bureaus don't have access to your debit card information. It's not relevant to your credit report, since there's no loan involved.

The liability is similar in the long-term.

Both types of cards limit your liability to $50. Law mandates this. If you're the victim of fraud, you should be compensated for anything beyond $50.

There is a key difference, however. Credit card companies provide a 60-day window for you to notice the fraud and provide notification. With a debit card, the window is only 2 days!

The liability in the short-term is different.

If someone steals your credit card and makes purchases, you don't lose any money. It's inconvenient, but you haven't suffered a loss.

With a debit card, someone can clean out your bank account. It can take time to be compensated. You might be bouncing checks in the meantime, too.

Credit cards aren't free.

Credit cards can come with a variety of fees. Annual fees are common. There are also penalties if you're over your limit or pay your credit card bill late. If you don't pay back the full amount each month, you'll also be paying interest charges at a high interest rate on your balance.

Both can offer rewards.

While credit cards are better known for giving rewards, some debit cards are following suit. It's possible to get cash back, plane tickets, gift cards, and more.

Do the Work!

Credit and debit cards both have their place in a sensible financial plan. It's very easy to abuse credit cards, so use the necessary restraint to make wise spending decisions. Credit cards can be wonderful for your credit score and tend to provide better rewards, while debit cards, similar to cash, help you stay within your budget.

YOUR CREDIT CARDS HAVE REWARDS

Many experts predicted that most credit card companies would drop their rewards programs after the passage of the CARD Act. However, that hasn't been the case. If you're willing to put in a bit of work, you can benefit from a rewards card.

There are more ways to capitalize on credit card rewards than ever before.

There can be some confusion about which card is best for your situation. The rules can be complicated. There are point caps, minimum spending limits, blackout dates, and other restrictions that make it challenging to receive your rewards. Consider these tips on how to get the most from your credit card rewards:

Get a card with useful rewards.

A card that offers airfare rewards won't do you much good if you rarely travel by air. Find a reward card that fits your lifestyle and needs.

Watch out for limits.

Some cards place limits on your rewards. You might get 2% back on gas, but with a limit of $200. If the annual fee is high for that card, the benefit might be minimal.

Stay abreast of term changes.

Credit card companies often change their policies. If you get a notice in the mail, read it. You might find that it's time to start looking for a new card.

When you've settled on a rewards card, use it as much as you can.

The more you spend, the greater the rewards. However, avoid spending more than necessary. It's financially irresponsible to buy items just to earn rewards.

Cash back cards are a great idea.

Cash back cards are simple. Getting your rewards from other types of cards can be more challenging.

Cards that offer *only* cash rewards tend to have the best cash back rates. Pull out your calculator and do the math when choosing a card.

Some cards permit the user to turn in points toward gift cards.

Often, the amount of the gift card is greater than what you would receive from a card that offers cash back. This is because retailers are willing to subsidize the card to get you into their stores. Ensure the selected retailers are places where you shop.

Pay your bill in full every month.

Avoid making late payments or carrying a balance because interest and late fees will offset any rewards you earn.

Why do you think credit card companies are willing to offer rewards? They know that many of their customers will carry a balance or pay late, which makes it well worth their while.

Watch the expiration date on your points.

Most cards won't let you keep rewards points indefinitely. Be aware of when your points expire, so you can take full advantage of them.

Find out if there's a spending requirement.

Some cards require you to spend a minimum amount each month or year if you want to keep your reward points active.

Do the Work!

Rewards cards are a great idea. The issue isn't whether to have one, but rather, which one to get! Take the time to sit down and look at what benefits each card offers. Be realistic about your financial situation and avoid spending extra just to earn a few more rewards points.

CONSIDER A HOME EQUITY LOAN

Home equity loans are quite simple to understand. It's a loan that is secured by the equity that exists in your house or condominium. If you've ever heard the term "second mortgage," you're familiar with home equity loans.

Home equity loans can be a great way to tap into your equity and put that value to work for you.

Whether you'd like to pay off your credit card bills, invest in a rental property, or take a trip, a home equity loan can help you achieve those objectives. There are 2 types of home equity loans:

Traditional.

You receive a lump sum and make payments on the loan, just as you would on any other installment loan. The interest rate is usually fixed.

The advantages are a predictable payment and interest rate. This is a great loan for debt consolidation or any big-ticket items.

Home equity line of credit (HELOC).

This is more similar to a credit card. You can use any amount you need, up to your credit limit. The interest rate is usually variable.

A HELOC is great when flexibility is most important to you. You also only pay interest on the money you actually borrow. You can use the money whenever you need it.

Consider which type of loan is most supportive of your situation.

Each type of loan can be a viable choice, depending on the circumstances. Facts about home equity loans:

There are differences from traditional mortgages.

Home equity loans are much quicker to process than traditional mortgages. The fees are quite low, too. A traditional home equity loan can probably be secured for just a few hundred dollars. HELOCs are frequently free to acquire.

Remember that the amount of equity in your home varies.

Depending on what the market is doing, the value of your house is constantly in flux. When the value drops, the amount of equity in your home drops, too.

A HELOC can actually be cancelled if your equity drops too much. This is one advantage of the traditional-style loan. Once you have the loan, any change in home equity is irrelevant, at least from the standpoint of acquiring the loan.

Balloon payments can be part of the loan.

Many home equity loans are set up to mimic the payments of a 30-year mortgage, though the loan may only be for 10 years. This means that you'll be forced to make a balloon payment at the end of that time. Be sure to include this fact in your decision-making process.

Foreclosure is a risk.

Remember that the loan is secured against the equity in your home. If you fail to make your payment, the lender can foreclose on your home to recoup the money that was lent.

The interest rates are very good, but not as good as a first mortgage.

Since the loan is well secured, lenders are able to offer good interest rates. But the loans are junior to the primary mortgage.

If you stop making all of your payments, the primary lender will get their money back first. The home equity lender can only get its share from whatever is left over, which might not be enough. Remember that the amount of equity in your home varies.

Do the Work!

If you need to borrow money, a home equity loan might be perfect for your needs. The interest rate is very good, and home equity loans can provide a lot of flexibility for any financial purpose. Shop around for the best rates and terms.

WISE USES FOR A HOME EQUITY LOAN

The equity in your home is just sitting there. It can be tempting to put the money to good use.

As with many things in life, there are both good and poor options for home equity loans.

Use the money conscientiously and you can enhance your financial position or save yourself form disaster. Choose poorly and you're digging yourself a bigger financial hole.

There are several good uses for a home equity loan:

Home improvements.

It makes sense to use the money you take out of your home to improve your home. When you carefully choose your improvements, this can be a wise use of a home equity loan. Some add more to the resale value of your home than others. If you're planning on selling in the near future, new carpet and paint can be selling points.

Pay off high interest debt.

Why pay 19% on your credit cards when you can pay 5% on a home equity loan? This use of a home equity loan can save a lot of money and makes good financial sense.

There's one caveat: You can't use your credit cards irresponsibly and get yourself into the same situation all over again. This is a common result. Be careful.

Emergencies.

Sometimes emergencies happen. It would be much better and less risky to have an emergency fund, but a home equity line of credit can be handy when the inevitable financial disaster occurs. Again, be responsible.

A home equity loan can be useful tool when used appropriately.

Unfortunately, there are a few common uses for home equity loans that don't make good financial sense.

There are also several poor uses for a home equity loan:

Paying for a vacation.

Does it make sense to risk your home for a trip to Disney World? Borrowing money for something optional isn't a wise use of credit, especially when it can put you out in the street after a loss.

Buying consumer goods.

A new TV? A 1967 Mustang? A pool in the backyard? These aren't wise ways to spend the equity in your home. If you can't pay for these things without borrowing money, you can't afford them.

It can be tempting to use a home equity loan to pay for a trip or a few new toys, but it's not a sound financial decision. A few other options are questionable.

Some choices look great but can still have some bad outcome. Some uses for a home equity loan are questionable:

Investing.

Why not borrow money at 5% and use it to earn 12%? You can come out 7% ahead, right? The logic is sound, but you can't be certain of your return. What if you lose it all? Can you afford to keep your home? Experts consider this to be a poor choice for most investors.

Use as a student loan.

Maybe. Think about the long-term ramifications of increasing the debt-load on your home. You're postponing your retirement. If you do go this route, it might make more sense to use the equity in your home to finance an engineering degree rather than a history degree.

Do the Work!

Home equity loans can be a convenient source of funds for any purpose. It's important to objectively determine if that purpose is wise or not. Avoid the temptation to spend the money frivolously. The key to using any line of credit is responsibility. Remember that it's not an unsecured loan. Your home is at stake, so practice caution.

RENTING OUT THE EXTRA ROOM

Renting out the extra room your college-bound child leaves behind can provide you with extra income and a chance to meet new people. It's a big decision, so plan carefully and make wise choices.

Consider these tips to ensure that you create a good experience for you, your child, and your new tenant.

Help your college-bound child to adjust:

Give yourselves some transition time.

Your child is already coping with major changes while heading off to college. It will be less stressful for both of you if you wait a couple of months or so before taking on a tenant.

Involve your child in the decision.

People tend to react more positively when they're included in the decision-making process. Tell your child you're considering renting the room and want to discuss it. If they're comfortable, you can steam ahead. If they have concerns, slow down and consider your child's viewpoint.

Be sensitive to your child's needs.

Everyone will have to make some adjustments, so plan ahead to minimize any awkwardness.

Have alternative sleeping arrangements ready for when your child comes home to visit. If you don't have a guest room, you can get a futon or inflatable bed. If they'll be sleeping in the living room, ask everyone to keep out during the early morning hours.

Develop storage solutions. Store your child's prized possessions safely. This could also be a great opportunity for the whole family to get rid of some clutter.

Let your child know you appreciate their cooperation. Thank them for their flexibility and the contribution it makes to your family. Prepare their favorite meal or plan a special outing to show your gratitude.

Help yourself to adjust:

Keep it legal.

Check the local zoning ordinances in your area to get any required permits. If you're renting, consult your landlord to make sure that any arrangements are permissible according to your lease.

Play it safe in searching for a tenant.

If you live within commuting distance from any colleges or universities, their student housing agencies are an excellent resource for finding prospective tenants. Organizations like roommates.com charge a small fee but provide more security than going it alone on Craigslist. Always run a credit check and ask for references.

Sign a rental agreement.

You can get rental agreement forms from your local landlord/tenant association or housing agency. Require a deposit to protect yourself from damages.

Establish house rules for shared areas.

Discuss your expectations with your new tenant beforehand. Try to reach mutual agreement on issues like the use of kitchen and laundry areas.

Cultivate open lines of communication.

Friendly communication is fundamental. Maintain an open and respectful atmosphere so that you and your new tenant can work together to resolve any conflicts.

Do the Work!

Renting out your child's room when they leave for college can have economic and social benefits. Keep the best interests of your family and your new tenant in mind to create a pleasant home environment for everyone

HARVEST YOUR LOSSES FOR A TAX BREAK

The end of the year is nearing. You might be able to take your poor stock picks and recover some of your money by realizing a few tax breaks.

Harvesting your losses on your income taxes is an effective way to put more money in your pocket come April.

Few investors understand just how powerful it can be. Even if you want to keep a stock that has performed poorly, it can still be well worth the risk to sell it and repurchase it in a month. Tax loss harvesting has three primary tax benefits:

It can serve to defer capital gains taxes far into the future.

By offsetting your gains, you're in essence receiving a tax-free loan that you can use to invest in other securities. Until you realize any gains from that next round of investments, you're deferring your capital gains taxes.

You can deduct up to $3,000 from your income.

For many investors, the tax on personal income is higher than the tax on capital gains. If your losses are greater than your gains, you can apply the remaining loss to your personal income.

You can roll your losses over into the future.

Suppose your losses were $5,000 greater than your gains. You could write off $3,000 from your income this year and $2,000 the following year.

Consider how powerful this can be. The ability to deduct losses from your income is a huge advantage.

Harvest your losses:

Be aware of the wash-sale rule.

The IRS doesn't like it when you sell a security for the purpose of receiving a tax break. Hence, there is a law. You cannot repurchase a stock within 30 days if you chose to write off your loss. You also have to wait 31 days after purchasing a security to sell if you want to write off the loss.

Be aware that the rule applies across multiple accounts. So, you can't sell a stock in your brokerage account for a loss and purchase the same stock in your Roth IRA in less than 30 days.

Keep your transaction costs in mind.

In today's world, transaction costs are minimal. But consider the costs when deciding if harvesting your losses is worth it. If you're selling a small amount of stock, or the loss is small, it might not make financial sense.

Be tactical.

Just because your investments are down, doesn't mean that this exact moment is the best moment to sell. You might be better served by waiting. Consider what the future may hold.

Be sure to check out examples of loss-harvesting in action.

Consider this example:

Suppose that you had owned a stock for more than 30 days, and the price had fallen by 50% since you purchased it. You like the stock and would like to keep it. You also don't expect anything exciting to happen in the next 30 days.

You decide to sell the stock for a $7,000 loss. You also have capital gains of $1,000. You can avoid paying taxes on your capital gains and write $3,000 off your income. You can then rollover $3,000 of loss to the following year. After 31 days, you can repurchase the stock.

You've reestablished your position and saved a lot money in the process.

Do the Work!

Have you been taking advantage of your underperforming stocks to the best of your ability? Harvesting your losses can pay big dividends at tax time. Ensure that you're taking full advantage of the tax laws.

SOURCES FOR EMERGENCY CASH

Knowing your resources, the places you can to turn for an immediate influx of cash during emergencies, is a vital step to managing your financial stability during a crisis.

Keep these options in mind:

- **Payday Loans:** Use only as a last resort! Payday loans have high fees and interest rates
- **Savings and Checking Accounts:** If you have to drain your accounts, put a high priority on building them back up ASAP.
- **Offer Services:** Elderly neighbors & others could pay you for mowing the lawn, shoveling snow, cleaning , or professional services.
- **Credit Card and Cash Advances:** Consider the fees and interest rates.
- **Bank Loans:** You may be able to get an emergency loan from your bank.
- **Sell Belongings:** Consider garage sales, pawn shops, and online websites.
- **Personal Loans from friends or family:** You may be able to get cash from your circle of friends and family.

Do the Work!

Make sure you investigate your options before you need them. The comfort of knowing your back up plan is in place can relieve a lot of stress and give you more freedom to make better choices without the control of fear-based thinking.

GET YOUR STUDENT LOANS FORGIVEN

Debt relief is another way to create money. If you are not having to pay off debt with your limited funds, those funds can be put to work for you in other ways. Eliminating or reducing your student loan debt is a great place to start.

Lucky for you, there are a few ways to reduce, or even eliminate, your student loan debt. Consider these career strategies to shrink your student loan debt:

Join the military.

Serve Uncle Sam and you can eliminate up to 100% of your student loans. The amount of forgiveness depends on the type of student loan and where you're stationed. If you're considering joining the military, speak to a recruiter and ask for more information.

Become a nurse.

Due to the demand for more nurses, nurses are eligible to receive 100% forgiveness for Federal Perkins Loans. Nurses also enjoy high salaries, considering it only requires two years of schooling to become a registered nurse.

Work with the disabled.

Many organizations offer this student loan forgiveness program. If you provide early intervention services to the disabled, you may qualify for up to 100% forgiveness of your Federal Perkins Loans.

Become a faculty member at a Tribal university.

The government has labeled a few colleges and universities as tribal schools. These primarily serve Native Americans or Alaskan Natives. If you teach at one of these schools, you can have up to 100% of your Perkins Loan forgiven.

Join the Peace Corp as a volunteer.

You can have a great experience in a new country, help others, and reduce your student loan debt at the same time. You can earn up to 70% forgiveness of your Federal Perkins Loans.

Join AmeriCorps VISTA.

This is similar to the Peace Corp, but serves challenged areas of the U.S. Again, loan forgiveness can be up to 70%. Perhaps not exotic as the Peace Corp, but you can potentially stay close to home.

Become a teacher.

There are many places in the U.S. in desperate need of teachers. Most of these areas serve lower-income neighborhoods. Teach for five years and you can eliminate up to $17,500 worth of Federal Stafford loans. However, Plus Loans are not eligible.

Become an educator.

This program is much broader than the program aimed solely at teachers and will forgive up to 100% of Federal Perkins Loans. You can be a speech pathologist, school librarian, staff member at a pre-kindergarten program, or a teacher. Other professions can also qualify.

Depending on the position, you may have to work for a certain number of years or have an advanced degree.

Become a firefighter.

If you've considered becoming a firefighter, there's good news. You can receive up to 100% forgiveness of your Federal Perkins Loans after serving a few years.

Become a police officer or corrections officer.

The firefighter plan also applies to police officers and corrections officers.

Do the Work!

Many career options offer partial or complete student loan forgiveness. There's a common theme to these programs: you must be providing an important service to those in need. You can gain valuable experience and enjoy the knowledge that you're helping to improve the lives of others while you get rid of your student loans.

SHOP FOR THE BEST CREDIT CARD

Although it's wise to pay off all your credit card debt, it's also practical to have one or two good credit cards. When you travel or want to order something online, it makes good sense to have a credit card. Plus, being responsible while using your card will positively contribute to your credit score.

But which card is the best? The answer can be found in which one best meets your own personal needs. The best credit card for someone else may not be the best one for you. Use these strategies to help you determine which card may best meet your needs:

Choose a credit card that has no monthly fee.

Never pay a monthly fee just to have a credit card.

Avoid a variable interest rate credit card.

A variable interest rate credit card has fluctuating interest rates over which you have no control. Make an effort to get a credit card with a fixed interest rate.

Also, be leery of any cards that advertise 0% interest for the first 12 months. Find out what the interest rate will be after the initial interest-free period. You may find the interest so high that it's simply not worth it to get the first year at 0% interest. Plus, know what can trigger the end of your 0% interest - you might not even enjoy it for one year!

Read the fine print.

Even though the fine print "legalese" is difficult to decipher, it's important to be on the lookout for hidden fees and charges.

Read the terms and conditions of the card at home when you have plenty of time.

Highlight any areas of the terms that you have concerns about or need to clarify.

If you're unable to get answers to your questions or receive clarifications for a better understanding of the card issuer's policies, walk away. You're wise to say 'no' as opposed to getting stuck with extra fees.

See what's in it for you.

When you're selecting a credit card, focus on those that either give you cash back, credit toward travel awards, or reward points toward free items - whichever perk you feel you would get the most benefit or enjoyment from.

The cash back cards are, in essence, reimbursing you with "free money." Some cards issue cardholders one check per year for a percentage back on specified purchases. Receiving a check in December between $1 and $1,000 based on your credit purchases is a nice perk.

If you're a traveler, you might prefer receiving points toward your next flight, car rental, or hotel.

The third type of rewards credit card awards you points in relation to the amounts charged on the card. The points can be cashed in to purchase various items such as stereos, portable DVD players, kitchen pots and pans, dishes, and a variety of other items.

Do the Work!

Shopping for the best credit card takes time and patience. Protect yourself and your financial life by taking every precaution when selecting your credit card. Discover the freedom of using just one good credit card, paying it off monthly, and enjoying its rewards.

AVOID A PREPAID CARD UNTIL YOU READ THIS

Are you considering using a prepaid card? Before you sign up and start waiting by the mailbox for the card, learn the facts about prepaid cards and consider if these cards are the best option for you.

Prepaid cards can be useful, but it's important to understand their limitations.

Understand the data collection.

Prepaid cards may resemble credit and debit cards, but the application process is different.

Before you can get a prepaid card, you may have to provide sensitive private data that you might not want to share for just a prepaid card. You may have to provide your name, address, Social Security number, phone number, and other information.

Stay aware of the fees.

Prepaid cards can come with a variety of fees.

The fees vary from company to company, but you'll usually have to pay for ATM withdrawals.

You may also have card inactivity fees and minimum balance fees.

Fees can also include monthly usage charges, overdraft charges, late charges, and reloading fees.

It's crucial that you read the fine print so you can be aware of the fees of your card.

Consider how the cards can be loaded.

Prepaid cards can be loaded in several ways. You can add funds from your bank accounts. You can also load them at some retailers.

Prepaid cards allow direct deposits in some cases. You can directly deposit your paycheck or government benefits to the card. You may also be able to deposit your Social Security or pension benefits.

Consider FDIC insurance.

Some prepaid cards aren't protected by FDIC insurance. This means that if the bank fails, you may lose all of your money. It's important to check for this coverage.

Before you sign your agreement, read it carefully and check for statements about FDIC insurance. The terms should have this information clearly outlined.

Evaluate what happens if the card is lost or stolen.

How does the bank handle a lost or stolen prepaid card? Are you reimbursed and issued a new card without a lot of effort? Or do you lose your money on that card?

Different companies have different rules for lost and stolen prepaid cards.

You may have to pay a replacement card fee if your original card disappears. You may also have to wait for the money to be returned to the card.

Consider customer service complaints.

Does the prepaid card have terrible customer service, or do consumers praise it? Before you sign up, explore the customer service experience. Do an internet search for that card and you'll most likely find plenty of reviews.

Customer service can vary greatly among banks. You may find that the prepaid card doesn't have a call center. It's possible that customer service is limited to online and email interactions. You also have to think about the quality and speed of the service the company offers.

Compare the perks.

Prepaid cards may have additional perks for users. Before you get a prepaid card, compare the perks being offered by different companies.

These perks can include reduced fees or no fees if a balance and activity level is maintained. The perks can also include purchase protection. Cards may offer travel assistance or roadside assistance.

Prepaid cards may also have their own rewards programs. These programs may benefit loyal customers who buy or spend a certain amount of money each month. You may accumulate points in different categories that can be redeemed for prizes such as gift cards.

Do the Work!

A prepaid card can be part of your overall financial strategy. However, before you get a card, it's important to think about the fees and other aspects.

ALL ABOUT CREDIT CARD DELINQUENCY

Though credit card delinquency has become increasingly common during the past several years, most consumers' understanding of it continues to be lacking.

Too many of us don't know how to avoid or solve the personal financial challenge of being delinquent!

The good news is that once you gain a more complete knowledge of delinquency, dealing with it is fairly straightforward.

When Do You Become Delinquent?

What exactly is credit card delinquency? A credit card customer is delinquent when he fails to make at the least the minimum credit card payment. Delinquency is separated into degrees that indicate how many payments have been missed. These ranges are often referenced in terms of days.

For example, on the day after the first payment is missed, the holder is one day delinquent. After you miss a second payment, the account is deemed to be 30 days delinquent and so on.

Theoretically, a credit card holder is delinquent after just one missed monthly payment. On the other hand, delinquency is commonly not reported to the credit bureaus until after two payments in a row have been missed.

What Are the Effects of Delinquency?

Being reported delinquent to the credit bureaus most certainly has a negative impact on credit scores.

Scores could drop as much as 125 points with three consecutive missed payments. Once four payments have been missed, the impact on the credit score is more severe and the account is likely to be sent to collections. Legal action against the cardholder is a real possibility at this point.

How Do You Get Out of Delinquency?

There is a way to stop and get out of delinquency. Making a single minimum payment ends the progression of the delinquency and keeps the account at the current level of delinquency.

This is crucial, simply because being reported to the credit bureaus 120 days late is much worse than being 90 days late. Making even one minimum payment can be an effective strategy to keep things from progressing too far.

Once you start trying to make up your past due payments, be careful to avoid these damaging errors:

Making less than the minimum payment.

Unfortunately, making a payment that is less than the minimum doesn't have any effect on the delinquency. So, when you make a small payment, it really doesn't help the situation. This error can be avoided; just be sure to only make payments that are greater than or equal to the minimum payment.

Making only one minimum payment.

Consumers sometimes mistake the minimum required payment with the total amount due.

The total amount due is the amount that needs to be paid in order to bring the account current. This amount can consist of several minimum payments, so it's important to continue making extra payments until the account has been brought current.

As soon as the account is current, you can start negating the consequences of the delinquency.

The more the negative information is covered up with positive information, the less impact the delinquency will have.

Secured credit cards are especially apt for credit betterment. These cards require a deposit to open, and the cards are always approved for this reason. Since the risk is minimal for the credit card company, the fees can be less. Whenever you decide to cancel the card, the deposit is returned.

Do the Work!

While credit card delinquency cannot be recovered from overnight, it is possible to suffer no lasting effects in the long-term. Once the delinquency has been rectified, the negative history can be diluted as much as possible.

The key is to be patient and acquire a secured credit card. Using that new card carefully allows you to be trusted by lenders again. Credit card delinquency is a challenge, but it is a challenge that can be dealt with successfully.

GETTING YOURSELF OUT OF DEBT

Do you feel like your credit card debt is insurmountable? The good news is that, no matter how high the mountain appears, you can climb it.

You can pull yourself out of the metaphorical hole you find yourself in.

Here are some ways to tackle that debt and bring it down to size:

Only buy what you can afford.

The best way to keep debt from becoming a problem is to avoid the problem altogether from this point forward. Rather than splurging on a fancy piece of electronic hardware, just wait and save up for it.

By staying within budget and paying off your bills every month, you don't need to worry about debt piling up on top of you.

You can still get out of debt and feel the sweet relief of being debt free by changing your mindset from "having it now" to one of enjoying it even more when you have the money.

Pay off the lowest balance first.

Financial advisor Suze Orman often advises people in debt to take care of the higher interest debts first. In general, this is a good way to go, however, if you have a credit card with a balance of only a couple hundred dollars, it would also be beneficial to knock that off right out of the gate.

You can eliminate a whole payment, save on interest charges, and put that money towards another bill.

Prioritize bills by interest rate.

In the long run, paying off the higher interest cards first will save you the most money. It's usually the interest that keeps knocking you back. By taking out the higher interest cards, you'll feel a greater sense of progress when paying your bills every month.

Consolidate.

One of the more overwhelming aspects of being in credit card debt is being reminded of it with so many bills from different cards. One way to fight back is to consolidate your debt. You can do this by either taking out a loan from a bank or transferring the balance to another card.

If you recently got a new credit card, you can transfer a portion of the balance to that. This will save you a bit of interest since most cards will put that balance under the introductory rate.

If you take out a loan, you can pay off several of the cards and reduce the amount of mail you receive. It's less daunting psychologically to receive one big bill as opposed to a bunch of tiny ones.

Convert to cash and debit only.

One of the best ways to keep yourself in debt is to keep using your credit cards. They're convenient and it's easy to justify their occasional use by saying that it's only a soda or a tank of gas.

Those tiny charges add up quick! A dollar here, a few more there, and you'll negate the payments that you're making in a very short amount of time.

Paying with cash will help you develop new spending habits. By the time you get your debts paid down, you'll have disciplined yourself to the point where you no longer put yourself in that situation.

Debt is a problem that happens to nearly everyone at some point. Even wealthy people find themselves overextended by debt.

Do the Work!

If you're working on a shoestring budget, it's possible to pull yourself out of debt. With discipline, focus, and hard work, you can find yourself relieved of the mounting pressures.

AVOID INTEREST AND PREVENT ENDLESS DEBT

Interest can really wreak havoc on your financial position! It's so easy to end up in constant debt because of interest applied by your financial institutions and other organizations.

Interest is easy to avoid in most cases, as it essentially relies on your financial decisions and how quickly you make them.

Try these tips to avoid interest in some day-to-day scenarios:

Pay your car loan on time.

If you've acquired a car loan through a financial institution, there's bound to be fees for making late payments. In many cases, these fees are added on to your remaining balance and make your monthly payments that much higher. The best way to steer clear of scenarios like this is to pay your car loan on time.

- This bit of advice goes for any other loan you could have, including a mortgage.
- Institutions will always apply fees and charges to delinquent accounts, and you do not want to be in that position.

Avoid going over the limit on your credit card.

Having a credit card could be considered a liability to begin with if you're unaware of how to effectively manage it.

- It becomes worse when you end up going over your limit.
- The fees that the financial institutions add on once you go over your limit are exorbitant and can really push you into debt. At all costs, sidestep those expenses if you want to remain debt free.

Consider automatic deductions.

You're probably like many other people who would prefer to make monthly commitment payments on their own accord as opposed to having automatic deductions from their bank accounts. However, it makes more sense to do automatic deductions because:

- You'll eliminate the possibility of incurring fees and charges from missed or late payments.
- Automatic deductions ensure that your payments are taken from your account on a set date. As long as you have money in that account to cover the payment, you're sure to get your payments made on time without late fees or added interest for delinquency.

Avoid credit; use cash.

With credit inevitably comes interest, unless you pay the total due on your account before the first due date. It doesn't get any simpler than that! If there's any remote way you can make a purchase or complete a transaction with cash, then by all means take that route as opposed to credit to avoid paying interest.

What to Do When You're Finally Debt Free

As an added piece of advice, your intention should be to remain debt free once you've gotten to that point. It will take some keen attention, but it's undoubtedly attainable. These strategies will help keep you from incurring debt and additional interest:

- Return all but a couple of your credit cards. Keeping some open and active will enable you to build a higher credit score for future loans, like a mortgage loan.
- Use your cards from time to time but have the cash available to pay off the total amount charged before the first payment is due.
- Settle any interest or debt you do incur at the soonest possible time.
- Build up your savings to handle emergency cash needs.

Do the Work!

Adhering to these simple tips will make it easier to prevent debt and interest and maintain control of any debt you do incur. Use these easy ways and avoid interest being applied to your day-to-day expenditures. By using these tips, you'll significantly lessen the chance of being exposed to the burdens brought about by debt.

ELIMINATE DEBT WITH A CONSOLIDATION LOAN

Household debt in the United States totals over $2 trillion; even more shocking, that total doesn't include the money we owe on our homes. Consumer debt has become a way of life in our country. How can you get a handle on your household debts?

For many, the answer is debt consolidation. Is debt consolidation a good option for you? Read on to learn the pros and cons.

Debt consolidation fundamentally involves taking all of your debts and consolidating them into a single loan. This often includes home-equity loans, car payments, credit card balances, personal loans and mortgage debt.

Most banks and other lending institutions have a variety of debt consolidation options. When used properly, debt consolidation should result in an overall lower interest rate and a lower monthly payment. Ideally, this new, lower payment will free up enough money each month to enable you to make the payment on your loan and still live within your income.

Why Debt Consolidation Might Not Be Your Answer

While there are a number of financially wise individuals that utilize debt consolidation as an effective means to manage their finances, this is often not the case. For many consumers, the need to engage in debt consolidation is a sign that they may need to learn how to handle their money differently.

It is a fact that many individuals that avail themselves of consolidation loans will go out and continue using their credit cards, which now have a $0 balance due to the consolidation.

If you give in to the temptation to continue to use your credit cards, you're likely to acquire so much additional debt that, before you know it, you're once again in financial straits. You'll find that you cannot make both the consolidation loan payment and the payments on your new debt.

Debt consolidation is the very first step in getting your debt under control, but transforming your habits is a critical part of the process, too.

For debt consolidation to have a meaningful and lasting impact on your economic circumstances, you must break the debt habit. It's important to refrain from spending funds that you haven't acquired yet.

If You Don't Have It, Don't Spend It

One of the easiest ways to minimize your spending is to put away your credit cards. Credit card abuse is one of the leading causes of consumer debt. If you don't have your cards with you, you can't use them to add to your debt!

Another easy action is to refuse to take on any new loans. Your debt consolidation loan was obtained to make your debts manageable, so taking additional loans is counterproductive. Remember that "loans" also include anything that will require payment in the future, such as any no payment / no interest deals that come your way.

Your Debt-to-Income Ratio

Continuing to reduce your debt is critical to the long-term success of debt consolidation. Financial experts state that your total debt, including credit cards and mortgage obligations, should not be more than 36% of your gross monthly income. This number is also referred to as your debt-to-income ratio.

The ratio is calculated by simply dividing your total debt payments each month by your gross monthly income. When you pull out the calculator, you may be shocked to find out that your ratio is much higher than the recommendation.

As you pay down your debts, however, you'll see your ratio get closer and closer to the recommended level, enabling you to enjoy feeling more financially secure.

Successful Debt Management

Debt consolidation can be a powerful debt elimination technique, if used properly. Used unwisely, it can only add to your financial challenges. Use debt consolidation as a tool to get your financial life back on track. Then, live within your means to make your consolidation a great success.

Do the Work!

Before you take on debt to eliminate debt, be sure to do the work and determine that this is your best course of action.

TIPS TO CREATE A BRIGHT FINANCIAL FUTURE

Regardless of the type of work you do, it's possible to take action now to start creating a bright financial future for you and your family.

When you start now, then things like a raise or better-paying job will become the icing on the tasty cake you've already made, and add to your pleasure, rather than having to bail you out of a financial jam.

Try these strategies to ensure your financial outlook is bright:

Save at least 15% of your paycheck.

This amount will give you something to fall back on when times are especially lean or funds to invest so your money can be working for you.

For example, if you clear $500 a week, ensure you put back at least $75 dollars for your future.

Find a stockbroker you trust.

As you save your dollars, it's wise to have an overall investment plan to earn the most interest over the long haul. However, look at the facts and listen to your gut when it comes to making the final decision on making a particular investment.

Have just one major credit card and use it sparingly.

Charging a small amount on it each month and paying that amount back before the end of the month builds your credit and keeps you out of debt at the same time.

Keep the major part of your credit allowance open for emergencies.

Vow to never pay finance charges again.

Of course, you'll likely be paying a mortgage and perhaps a car loan that include finance charges you may be unable to avoid. However, outside of those two payments, paying finance charges is like setting fire to your dollar bills. Take steps to insure you pay as few finance fees as possible.

Pay all your bills on time.

There are a few good reasons to do so:

- You build a positive credit record.
- You keep money in your pocket instead of wasting it on late fees.
- You build confidence that you can manage your money on your own.

Find a competent tax preparer and accept his financial advice.

A great tax accountant will tell you how you can pay fewer taxes and how to rack up some helpful deductions. He may offer helpful guidance about how much money to put into your Individual Retirement Account (IRA), Roth IRA, or a 401(k).

Set limits with your kids about money.

Teach them from the time they're young that they must earn their own money and save at least 25% of it. They'll gain an understanding of money management that will serve them well the rest of their lives.

Apply $500 to $1,000 yearly extra toward your mortgage principal.

If you prefer, pay an additional mortgage payment each year. It will save you thousands in interest. Plus, you'll pay your home off years earlier, freeing up your funds for whatever you want.

Keep your resume up to date.

You never know when you'll want to apply for a promotion, change careers, or develop side projects for extra streams of income.

Consistently accept part-time, short-term, or temporary second jobs.

Bringing in extra money in addition to your full-time work pads your bottom line.

Hone your computer skills.

Those who know their way around a computer are more likely to be successful at work. Broaden your horizons further by learning about new software in your industry.

Do the Work!

Put the above strategies to work to strengthen your money situation. Care for your finances and nurture your financial situation today and every day. When you do, you'll live the incredible life you've always wanted!

* * *

Complete the *Create a Bright Financial Future* questionnaire in the Tools Section.

FIVE STEPS TO SAVE $4,000 IN A YEAR

Are you ready to dig into the details of creating more money? The rest of this section details how you can change your habit and begin saving with a goal.

Stop living from paycheck to paycheck. Instead of using credit cards to keep up with your bills, use this information to regain your control.

Feeling that you don't make enough money to save anything is a sign that you would benefit from taking a pro-active approach to saving.

Having a savings account will bring you peace of mind and help you manage your finances more efficiently. It will also help you spend less money on your living expenses because, when a financial emergency arises, you won't have to borrow the funds to cover the crisis and then pay them back with interest.

Saving money could also allow you to take a well-deserved vacation, put together a down payment for your dream home, or buy a new car. Regardless of what you need money for, you can save up enough if you make a few changes to the way you handle your finances.

You might think that the only way to save up money is to make sacrifices. Not even close! Saving money doesn't have to be hard. You can still have an enjoyable lifestyle when you're putting money away.

The key to saving money is to be smart about your finances.

You'll discover how to save a few dollars each day. The changes may look insignificant, but small savings add up! Following these tips will help you save $4,000 in a year. Sooner than you think, you'll have a hefty savings account and find more ways to save money as you get the hang of it!

Five Steps to Save $4,000 in a Year

Step #1: Take Control!

Budgeting and money management don't have to be complicated. You just have to find a system that works for you, and these tools will make managing your finances a lot easier.

Tracking your spending habits can take a while because you'll want to see where your money goes for at least a month.

The immediate benefit of tracking your spending is to identify the recurring expenses that you could avoid.

You could save from $3 to $15 a day depending on your habits:

Do you pick up a cup of coffee on the way to work?

Make coffee at home and buy a travel mug. This effort could save you $3 or $4 a day.

Do you only read a few articles from each daily newspaper or magazine you purchase?

Look up the free versions of these publications online and save $4 or $5 a day.

Do you buy fast food every day for lunch or to feed your family?

Feeding a family of four at McDonald's costs at least $10 to $15 if you choose the most affordable menu items. You could save this money by buying groceries and cooking meals in advance.

Try an App

These free tools will help you get an idea where your money goes and to readily identify expenses that you can avoid:

Mint **is a free app that tracks what you earn and spend.** This app organizes your expenses in different categories so you can get an idea of how much you spend on groceries, clothes, entertainment, and more.

BudgetSimple **is another free tool that tracks your expenses.** This tool is especially useful because it generates suggestions to show you where you could cut down on spending.

Establish a Budget

Once you've tracked your spending to see where your money goes, you can create a customized budget that works well for you.

The key to creating a budget that works for you is to find a method you like using. There are many online tools designed to create a budget that corresponds to your needs.

These apps require you to enter your income and link your bank accounts so they can track your expenses for you:

You Need A Budget, also known as YNAB, is one of the most popular budgeting apps. This free tool organizes your expenses by categories, helps you put money aside, and generates a budget based on your current expenses. The *You Need A Budget* website reports that people using this tool started saving an additional $200 a month on average.

Pocket Expense and BudgetSimple are tools similar to YNAB. The main features are the same, but you might find that the interfaces of these tools are more convenient.

If you're not a fan of tools that create budgets for you, there are some apps you can use to manually allocate where your money goes.

This approach is inspired by the old practice of placing cash in different envelopes. GoodBudget and Mvelopes are two good online apps that make it easy to create a budget in this way. Budgeting is worth it, and these 21st century tools make budgeting easier than it has ever been.

Sticking to Your Budget

Establishing a budget is the easy part. Spending accordingly can be more difficult. Following these three rules will help you stick to your budget and save $200 a month or more:

Assess how much you need to cover all your recurring expenses.

Put enough money aside as soon as you receive your paycheck. An app like Mvelopes or other online tools can help you allocate these funds. Your bank may provide a tool in their online banking app.

The money that is left after you cover all your expenses is not for splurging!

Spend a reasonable amount on things you love because you worked hard and deserve a reward, but it's important to make saving some of this money a priority.

Use Level Money or a similar app to keep your spending under control on a daily basis.

This app shows you how much money you can spend over the month, week, or day. Get into the habit of checking this app whenever you feel like buying something you don't really need to decide whether or not you can afford to splurge.

You must gain control over your money or the lack of it will forever control you.

Sticking to a budget requires discipline, but you can still live comfortably while living frugally. Follow these rules to ensure you pay important bills and avoid spending too much on impulse purchases.

Establishing a budget that works for you and sticking to it could help you save $200 a month, or $2,400 a year!

Five Steps to Save $4,000 in a Year

Step #2: Find Financial Support with Free Services

Beware of small expenses; even a small leak can sink a great ship.

How much do you spend on banking fees? Banking fees can seem trivial, but these expenses add up over time. There is no need to pay for these fees when free options are available.

If your bank is currently charging a monthly fee for their services, find out why. In most cases, banks will charge you a monthly fee only if your average balance is under a certain number, if you do not make enough transactions, or do not receive enough via direct deposit to qualify for a free account.

The average monthly cost of a checking account is $7 at a bank and $2 at a credit union. Opting for a free alternative could help you save $84 or $24 a year.

If you cannot avoid a monthly fee at your bank, get a free checking account elsewhere.

Some banks will even offer a signup bonus when you open a new account!

If you cannot find a free account that corresponds to your needs or would rather not open a new bank account, a good option is a service offered by American Express called Bluebird. Bluebird gives you the possibility to receive direct deposits and use the money to pay bills, withdraw money from an ATM, or write checks without paying any fees.

Overdraft protection is the only service you should be paying for if your bank does not offer free overdraft protection.

Did you know that the average American spends an average of $225 a year in overdraft fees? This money could be easily saved by taking a few minutes to sign up for this service.

Avoiding Payment Processing Fees

How do you pay your utilities and other bills? Depending on the payment method you use, you might be wasting money on payment processing fees. Even if these fees are only $2 or $3 for each transaction, this is money you could be saving. On a yearly basis, you could be paying around $100 a year in such fees.

Follow these tips to avoid payment processing fees:

Use online banking to schedule automated payments directly from your bank account.

This way, you can avoid paying the fee most utility and insurance companies charge you when you pay with a card. Automated payments are also a good way to avoid paying late fees.

Always compare your payment options and ask about fees.

Scheduling automated payments from your bank might not be the best solution for all your bills. For example, insurance companies often charge a monthly fee to process your payment regardless of how you pay your premiums. Consider paying your insurance premiums in one lump sum on a yearly basis to avoid paying this fee.

Avoiding Credit Card Interest and Late Fees

Do you use credit cards for bills or daily expenses? Take a look at your account to get an idea of how much you spend on interest and other fees. If you feel that your credit cards are costing you too much, contact the company and ask them to reduce your fees, or shop around for a better option.

Transferring your balance to a different card can be a good option if you qualify for a lower APR or for a card that doesn't compound your interest on a daily basis.

It's important to understand how interest is calculated on your credit card accounts. Most cards compound interest daily and use your average daily balance. This means carrying a higher balance will result in higher fees. You can easily avoid this by making a higher payment than usual if you make a large purchase with your credit card.

Use these strategies to reduce the amount of money you spend on credit card fees:

Always pay more than the minimum monthly payment.

Each payment goes towards the interest first, then towards the balance on the account. If you only make the minimum payment, your payment will cover the interest, but will not lower your balance by much. Making larger payments will help you pay off your balance more quickly and eliminate having to pay interest. The best method to avoid interest is to pay your entire balance each month. So, whatever you charge in a month, pay it off that same month.

Schedule automated monthly payments to avoid late fees.

Most credit card providers also provide you with an online tool you can use to check your balance and make payments.

You could save roughly $350 a year by avoiding banking fees, overdraft fees, and payment processing fees!

Five Steps to Save $4,000 in a Year

Five Steps to Save $4,000 in a Year

Step #3: Become a Smart Shopper

The best approach to smart shopping depends on how you and your family live, how much time you can spend on shopping and cooking, and on what you enjoy. Try different strategies to figure out what works for you and your family.

Adopt these simple habits to save on groceries and other household expenses:

Use coupons and discounts to save on items you buy.

You've probably seen couponing TV shows or websites where people save hundreds of dollars each week with coupons. The truth is that this type of extreme couponing is incredibly time-consuming and tedious.

Follow these tips to save money with coupons without any hard work:

- The golden rule of couponing is to never purchase an item just because you have a coupon. Rather than saving a few dollars or cents, you're spending to buy an item you would otherwise not buy.
- Subscribe to the newsletter, mailing list, or download the app of the grocery stores where you shop. Check these sources on a weekly basis to look for items on sale and clip coupons for your usual items.
- Avoid spending hours looking for online coupons or going through hundreds of paper ads. Download apps to look for coupons instead.
- *Grocery IQ* is an excellent choice if you use a grocery list, since this app will automatically look for coupons for the items you intend to buy anyway.
- You can also use *The Coupons App* to scan barcodes on products and look for coupons or to find all the deals offered at any nearby stores.

Plan your meals ahead of time and make grocery lists.

These simple habits will help you stick to a budget every time you go to the grocery store and could also help you adopt a healthier lifestyle.

- Apps like Pepperplate, Ziplist or Plan to Eat help you find new recipes, save the ones you like, plan your meals for the entire week, and the app creates the grocery lists for you.
- Use Supercook.com to find simple recipes based on the ingredients you have at home. This could become your go-to solution whenever you're about to take your family to a fast food restaurant because you're low on groceries.
- If you're short on time to cook during the week, set aside some time during the weekends to make large quantities of your family's favorite foods and freeze meal-size portions. This works great for chili, casseroles, and other dishes. You'll have easy lunches and dinners to just heat and eat throughout the week.
- Eating out is fun! You don't have to completely eliminate this expense.

Determine a reasonable budget for taking your family to their favorite restaurant once a week.

Shop at several locations.

Try different grocery stores to determine which one has the best prices or selection. Find several alternatives for your regular household items.

- **Go to the grocery store once a week to buy items such as fresh produce, dairy products, meat, and non-perishable items.** Look at the per-unit price or check the quantities or weight to determine which products are the best values. Stock up on discounted items only if you will use them in your meal plans.
- **Visit the dollar store once a month.** Stock up on dish soap, cleaning products, sponges, shampoo, soap, toothbrushes, toothpaste, glassware, school supplies, and wrapping paper. You would **on average** pay between $2 and $4 for these different items at a grocery store, so going to a dollar store for some bulk shopping is worth it.
- **Shop online for household items and non-perishable items.** You will get access to a wider selection and have the option of buying large quantities at discounted prices. Consider getting an Amazon Prime membership to get free shipping and lower prices on some household items.

Buy used items from online auctions, online consignment stores, or local thrift shops.

This is a great way to save on clothes, toys, electronics, and décor items for your home. You can find used furniture on sites like Craigslist and OfferUp.

Shopping for clothes on eBay, Goodwill, or online consignment stores could help you cut your clothing budget in half! If you have children, this strategy could save you a lot of money.

Plan in advance before making big purchases.

Things such as a new TV, computer, or video game console. This will give you time to put money aside and compare your options. You might want to wait for Black Friday or Cyber Monday to get low prices on these items if you don't want to buy them used.

Gas is another recurring expense.

Gas prices vary a lot and it's difficult to determine the best time to gas up. Try using an app called GasBuddy to track and compare gas prices at different gas stations in your area.

The amount you can save by being a smart shopper depends on your needs, how many people you're shopping for, and how much time you can afford to spend on comparison shopping.

Five Steps to Save $4,000 in a Year

Step #4: End Unnecessary Expenses and Spend More on Things That Matter

You could save a lot by eliminating some unnecessary expenses.

Consider these examples:

Reduce your cell phone bill.

Try these tips:

- Shop for a family plan if you need more than one line.
- Cancel your contract and switch to a service that will bill you only for what you use. This could help you cut down your phone bill to $20 or $30 a month if you don't use it a lot.
- You may have a landline bundled with your internet service. Use this line, instead of your cell phone, whenever you're at home.
- Wait until you are home and can use your own Wifi network if you need to go online and don't have unlimited data on your phone.
- Shop around for an affordable Smartphone. Your own provider might not have the best price.

Cut down your cable bill.

There are more affordable options to watch TV. The downside is that you'll get fewer channels or shows to choose from. Buy an antenna to watch TV for free over VHF and UHF signals and try different online streaming services to determine if these could be a good alternative for you.

Exploring alternatives is worth it since the average monthly cable bill is $64.

Save on your entertainment costs.

You can save a lot by taking your family for a bike ride or by organizing a football game in the backyard instead of taking them to the movies or the arcade. There are plenty of free things to do that will help everyone get more exercise and have a great time!

Avoid anything that is individually packaged.

Buy food items in bulk and make your own snacks and to-go meals instead of stopping at a fast food restaurant, gas station, or coffee shop.

Think twice about buying a name brand.

Spending more to get a name brand product is worth it if the product meets high quality standards and will last longer or work better. However, spending more to get name brand items that are not any different from cheaper options is a waste of money.

On the other hand, there might be some things you are not spending enough on, which results in more expenses on the long-term. Consider these examples:

Health insurance.

Purchasing more coverage could help you save in the long-term. Raising your premiums to get a lower deductible and co-pay is worth it if your family visits the doctor a lot.

Car maintenance.

Repairs and preventative maintenance can go a long way towards lengthening the longevity of your vehicle. Learn how to do an oil change and perform other simple maintenance and repair tasks to save money.

Home maintenance.

Investing in new windowpanes, better insulation panels, and newer appliances could lower what you spend on utilities. If you're renting, talk to your landlord about making a few improvements to help lower your bills.

Quality products.

Some products such as tools, razors, cookware, or furniture will last longer if you purchase slightly more expensive products from well-known brands.

Organization products.

Keeping your pantry and household supplies organized will prevent you from purchasing items you already have. Spending money on items that will help you get rid of an expensive bad habit or that will help you track your finances can save you lots of money.

You could save $64 a month by ditching cable and at least $20 a month by looking for a more affordable phone service provider, which roughly translates into $1,000 a year!

Before you make any purchase, ask yourself if you really need it. In most cases your life won't be any less full or rich without it, and every dollar you save will reduce your ecological footprint.

Five Steps to Save $4,000 in a Year

Step #5: Learn to Save First and Spend Afterwards

All the tips you have read so far will help you reduce expenses. However, you will not actually save money until you transfer it into a savings account.

Saving is a lot easier if you make it a habit and set up automatic savings systems.

Follow these tips to put money aside without any stress:

Try an app like *Digit*.

This tool automatically takes money from your bank account and puts it aside. You choose the amount you would like to save each week. This is perfect if you're busy and don't want to think about putting money in a savings account.

Schedule automated transfers from your bank account to a savings account.

If you would rather not trust a tool like *Digit* with your information, you can always use your bank's online platform to schedule an automated weekly transfer to your savings account.

Identify your two or three most expensive habits and get rid of them.

This could be smoking, going to Starbucks, buying some snacks, or spending money to get extra lives in Candy Crush Saga. Put the money you would normally spend on these things into a savings account.

Make saving money a game!

Set some weekly or monthly goals and reward yourself when you reach these goals.

Using Digit or another system to put $5 aside every week means you would end up with $260 in a savings account by the end of the year!

Five Steps to Save $4,000 in a Year

Do the Work!

All these tips are easy to follow. Saving should not be hard because you already work hard to earn a paycheck. All the tips you just read can be easily incorporated into your daily life and will help you save money one dollar at a time.

The key to saving money is to find something that works for you. Make a step-by-step plan, focus on adopting one new habit at a time, and reward yourself when you save. You'll soon have a hefty savings account for emergencies, a down payment on a home, or for your next family vacation!

CHAPTER NINE, SUPPORT

Which Habits Can You Turn Around Fast?

You are ready to dig even deeper into your personal financial growth. Continue your growth with these self-affirming thoughts.

Getting Started

Read through each section. They are designed to help you change your stinking thinking into satisfying facts.

· First, find the ones that you are already utilizing, and pat yourself on the back.

· Next, see if yourself talk needs any tweaking based on the new knowledge you are gaining.

· After you have that done, study the self-talk that is new to you. Which ones are missing form your tools used to develop your healthy financial lifestyle?

· For the new self-talk concepts, spend time each day until you are comfortable with them, until you catch yourself replacing your old thoughts with your new and supportive ones.

· Pick the self-talk support that you need the most and implement them first.

Finally, after you have all this accomplished, go back and read through your notes every three months to make sure you haven't strayed from the work you need to make your life great.

Be Responsible

My success is my responsibility.

Use this self-affirming language to teach your thoughts a new habit:

- I know that I hold the key to success in my heart, mind and soul. I embrace my inner drive and determination, and it is this drive that converts my efforts into achievements.
- I view obstacles as only temporary pauses in obtaining the success I am destined for.
- When I am confronted with a challenge, I stare it square in the eye. I wield my power over the challenge, and it is unable to conquer me.
- The bravery with which I approach challenges is the tool which helps to erase any fears I may have at the onset. Winning is inevitable once I overcome those fears.
- I embrace my responsibility to ensure that each project I embark on yields positive results. I relish my role as the master of my efforts. I believe in my ability to persevere because I often experience successful outcomes after consistent effort.
- Today, my success is the focal point of my day-to-day exploits. Each situation I encounter reminds me of my part in reaching my goals. I happily go after every goal with the mindset that I deserve only the best and have what it takes to get it.

Do the Work!

Take time for self-reflection:

1. How do I empower others to rely on their own abilities to turn situations around?

2. Do I remain positive if I am unable to achieve success with something?

3. When challenges seem difficult to bear, how can I allow others to help?

Abundance Is Everywhere

I steer toward abundance.

Use this self-affirming language to teach your thoughts a new habit:

- I open myself up to the fact that abundance is everywhere, and it is for everyone to enjoy.
- I view myself as strong and prosperous. When I wake each morning, I take stock of what I plan to accomplish throughout the day. This helps me steer toward my long-term goals.
- When things get tough, I remind myself that the peaks and valleys of life come and go, but I still have what I need.
- As I navigate life's inevitable challenges, I focus on my long-term goals. By keeping the end point in mind, I plant a seed that blossoms into awesome abundance down the road.
- The future takes care of itself if I focus on today.
- My desires are powerful, and they motivate me to take action. But I understand how important it is to prioritize. I focus on the desires that benefit me today and tomorrow. And I support myself by staying away from distractions that can slow me down.
- As I get closer to what I desire, I remain even keel. Although my excitement fuels me, I keep my eyes on the horizon.
- Each day presents me with another opportunity to focus my attention on what I truly want by noticing the abundance that is around me, I remember that success is within my grasp.
- Today, I notice the riches that surround me. I am cognizant of how I perceive things. When I feel my focus fading, I think about my long-term goals.

Do the Work!

Take time for self-reflection:

1. When have I allowed myself to focus on negativity?

2. What have I done to show that I am grateful for the little things?

3. Why do I believe that I can be successful?

Experience Success

I deserve to experience success.

Use this self-affirming language to teach your thoughts a new habit:

- A part of living life to its fullest means there are times when I am struggling to keep my head above water and other times when I am flying high with the thrill of meeting a goal.
- I know that when I reach high to achieve my goals, then I have a decent chance to accomplish at least some of them. I am sure that I deserve to enjoy the successes of my labors.
- Occasionally, I reflect on the connection between how I live my life and my right to success. Knowing that my way of living is tethered to my ultimate success keeps me striving forward and working toward my goals.
- Noticing some of my other character traits also helps me to see that I have the right to experience success.
- I strive to be strong physically and emotionally. I am a diligent worker. And I take the time to be kind to others, lifting them up when they need it. These attributes assure me I am deserving of any riches, accolades, and blessings I receive.
- Today, I know I can reach for the stars to experience success. I am worthy. I deserve to know and enjoy many successes in my life.

Do the Work!

Take time for self-reflection:

1. Do I believe that I deserve to experience success? Why or why not?

2. In what ways can I remind myself each day that I am worthy to live a beautiful life?

3. Which life goals have I achieved? Did I let myself savor the success of reaching each of those goals?

Increasing Income

My income is constantly increasing.

Use this self-affirming language to teach your thoughts a new habit:

- Each month, my income increases. I have a seemingly endless number of options to earn more money. I know I can always find or create more income with a minimal amount of effort.
- My subconscious is constantly scanning for new moneymaking opportunities. These new opportunities seem to just pop-up spontaneously. I am grateful that my mind is so in tune with creating wealth.
- My bills are becoming easier and easier to pay. Every month, I am able to save more money. My investments and net worth are increasing nicely. I smile when I think about how soon I can retire.
- I consider myself to be a wealth magnet. Money and moneymaking assets are drawn to me like moths to a flame. I can feel abundance flowing to me.
- I track my monthly income and find it increases regularly. When I notice an increase in my income, I congratulate myself. I am thankful for all I have and all that is coming to me.
- I am responsible with my new level of income. I invest wisely and only make necessary purchases. My investments provide ever-increasing streams of income. I want to be able to live using only these passive income streams.
- Today, I scan my surroundings for new income opportunities. I am committed to finding at least one new source of easy income to maintain this joyful trend of ever-increasing income.

Do the Work!

Take time for self-reflection:

1. How much income do I wish to eventually create?

2. How many sources of income do I currently have?

3. How can I create a new source of income or generate more income from a current source?

10

GIVING

If giving makes you feel good, why not give in a way that also gives back to you? In these units, you will learn how giving can also give back to your financial health and wealth while creating a wonderful set of circumstances for those that are receiving your gift.

Getting Started

It is important to understand the significance of your gift and how it can help your financial picture and even allow you to give more. Start with these concepts:

·Everything starts with a giving mind-set. When you truly understand and feel how giving to others supports your life you will find a freedom you have never known.

·Giving to the planet is just as important as giving to yourself. The health of the planet nurtures you while you grow your health and wealth so you can nurture others.

·When you can set your children off on the right foot for their financial future you can free yourself from the financial burden of rescuing them from their mistakes.

THE POWER OF GIVING

Household budgets are strained and giving is more difficult than ever. Everyone is working with reduced resources and most of us feel as though we don't have enough to enjoy our own lives. The idea of giving may seem unreasonable. But maybe now, more than ever, is the best time to give. There is a power in giving.

Most of us have already been blessed with so much. Our parents, teachers, relatives, friends, and others have given us a lot. But many others are not so fortunate. Consider this:

- 25% of the world's population is starving.
- 15% of the world's population cannot read or write.
- 25 children die every minute from a preventable disease.
- 1.5 billion people don't have access to clean water.

You can stay close to home and find real need.

The United States has many homeless people. Many people not receiving proper nutrition and health care. There are children that aren't getting the attention they need to flourish. In giving, you'll discover many personal benefits:

- A sense of pride
- Happiness
- Health
- Love
- Peace
- Opportunity to make new relationships
- The realization that you have much more than you think

One of the more profound benefits to the giver is the reduction in fear.

With everything going on in the world, many people live in fear of economic collapse, natural disasters, crime, paying their bills, caring for their children and their parents, and numerous other things. This is a function of real events and the overly sensationalistic coverage by the media.

What's insidious is the effect it has on many people. People become more isolated and less connected with society and their community. Many don't even know their neighbors. By giving your time, you open yourself up to others and your community.

Giving helps you reach your full potential.

Mahatma Gandhi said, "To find yourself, lose yourself in the service of others."

Reaching your full potential is much more likely when you give. No one can fully realize what they're capable of without being passionate about their day-to-day activities.

A person that can't move beyond the more superficial aspects of life can never do anything spectacular, because he will never be exposed to anything that will generate that kind of prerequisite passion.

Even if you've forgotten, human nature is to give.

Witness most children: sure, some of them are all "mine, mine, and mine" but most kids are really quite giving and share readily. They want to take their friends everywhere with them. They want to feed the baby ducks. They want to take care of their dolls.

However, somewhere along the way, have you developed the belief that you must keep what you've gotten for yourself? If so, you're punishing yourself. You're giving in to a scarcity mindset which, in itself, will limit your personal success.

Do the Work!

Make a plan to give what you have. You may have time, money, or both to share with those less fortunate, but give something and witness the impact it has on your life. You'll be pleasantly surprised in the power of giving and the benefits it brings into your life.

GO GREEN TO SAVE GREEN

Long before the green movement, efforts to halt the progression of pollution were solitary and far between. However, since the media has placed the spotlight on the green movement, both companies and individuals alike are doing their part.

Take advantage of incentives and make a conscious effort to save the planet from pollution.

By following the tips below, you can also save some cash while living green:

Go shopping.

Continuing to use dated appliances without an Energy Star seal costs more money each month. Substantially reduce your yearly utility bill by purchasing energy efficient appliances. Even though you may spend more money upfront, you'll make back your investment many times over the long run.

The United States government offers tax incentives to homeowners that purchase appliances equipped with the Energy Star seal. Take advantage of this tax break to offset the cost of the appliances.

You can also minimize the upfront costs by selling your old appliances. You may be able to pocket $1,000 to $4,000 depending on the condition of your used appliances and how many you have.

Start paperless billing.

Many companies, such as cable television providers and insurance companies, offer discounts for paperless billing. The reward can be as little as a $1credit on your bill each month, or as much as 5% of your auto insurance policy.

Although a $1 deduction may seem worthless, it certainly adds up. If 12 of your service providers grant you a $1 deduction on your bills each month, you can save up to $144 each year and up to $720 within five years.

Bring your own bag.

By bringing your own reusable shopping tote, you can save green while going green. Some chain grocery stores now encourage you to go green by charging a fee per paper or plastic bag used to bag your groceries. The fee ranges from $0.04 to $0.10 per bag.

If you forgo 15 plastic bags in one shopping trip, you can save up to $1.50 per order. Assuming you shop for groceries every week, you're able to save $78 per year, or $390 over five years.

You'll also save yourself from forming an ever-growing pile of plastic bags in your kitchen's broom closet.

Recycle.

Some retailers offer freebies and discounts to customers that recycle used containers. For example, Mac Cosmetic offers a free lipstick for every six containers returned to the company. Staples and other office supply stores offer a store credit for ink cartridges that are returned to the store.

Switch to CFL.

Did you know that most of the energy emitted by incandescent light bulbs is heat? Only a small portion of the energy used actually goes into lighting your home. Switching to CFL (Compact Fluorescent Light) bulbs saves both energy and money.

CFLs last up to ten times longer than incandescent bulbs. They produce significantly less heat and use only a third of the energy.

CFL bulbs can cost more money upfront than incandescent bulbs. But in a matter of a couple months, you'll recoup your initial investment and then some with the money you save on your energy bill.

Do the Work!

By following these small steps, you can do your part to preserve and protect the health of our planet while saving money at the same time. Many of the small things you can do require little to no decrease in your quality of life. Choose one or more of these ideas to implement today, and you'll save green while going green

SEND KIDS TO COLLEGE AND SAVE ON TAXES

Paying for a child's education is certainly one of the greatest gifts you can give. But the costs of higher education have been rising at a shocking rate. With in-state expenses at a public school averaging just below $20,000 per year, you may be wondering what you can do.

One excellent solution to ease the financial challenge of paying for college is the 529 College Savings Plan.

These are state sponsored savings plans that allow for tax-free earnings. Contributions are not deductible for federal income tax purposes but are deductible in many instances for state tax purposes.

To open a plan, here are some basics you'll need to know:

Tax write offs can be huge.

Every five years, account holders can write off up to $55,000 from their estate per beneficiary without having to pay federal gift tax. For married couples, the limit is $110,000.

As an example, a wealthy couple with 5 grandchildren could deposit $550,000 ($110,000 x 5) towards their grandchildren's education and eliminate that amount from their estate. They could do that every 5 years until the maximum is reached ($300,000+ per beneficiary in many instances).

You maintain control of the assets.

If you decided to close the account, you would have to pay a 10% penalty and income tax on any earnings. The balance is yours to do with as you wish.

The beneficiary can be changed.

If your son decides that he's not going to college, the account can be reassigned to someone else. The account must be transferred to an eligible individual within the same family.

Different states, different plans.

Each state has its own plan(s), and some are much better than others. But you can invest in nearly every other state's plans.

In theory, you could be an Arizona resident, invest in a Connecticut 529 plan, and send your child to school in Florida. A lot of flexibility is available, so be sure to shop around before you open an account.

The fees associated with the various plans are also important to consider. Some will be much higher than others. In fact, many experts consider the extra charges to be the most important criteria when choosing a plan. Some fees are incurred when opening the account; there are also annual maintenance charges.

If you know for certain where you want to send your child to school, many universities offer prepaid 529 plans. This would allow you to lock in the cost of future credit hours at the current rate. Unfortunately, there are penalties should you decide to later send your child somewhere else. So, if you choose this option, be very sure where you'll be sending your kid to college.

On the downside, investment options are rather narrow, and the ability to switch between available investment options is also limited. The tax code currently curtails changes to once per calendar year.

Do the Work!

Like any investment, 529 plans may or not be right for you. Consider the numerous other options to finance a college education, each with their own benefits and limitations.

However, if you've evaluated your investment options thoroughly, you may find that a 529 plan is an excellent option to ease the burden of paying for a college education. The tax benefits are considerable, and you always maintain control of your account. With the rising cost of college, your kids will thank you for investing in their futures.

PASS FINANCIAL HABITS ON TO YOUR CHILDREN

You might be concerned that your children never listen to you. The good news (and the bad news) is that your children are always watching. Kids quickly assimilate your habits and attitudes regarding money. Are you demonstrating habits that will help or harm their financial future?

When faced with uncertainty, it is common to rely on experience.

When your children grow up and face financial situations, they're going to mimic what they know. You can set an example that will enhance their financial future.

Consider these financial habits that make life more challenging:

Using credit cards unwisely.

This may be the most devastating financial habit to acquire. Credit cards are convenient and can be an effective way to take yourself out of a financial jam, but the use of credit to purchase unnecessary items is one of the leading causes of financial stress and bankruptcy.

Giving in to impulse purchases.

Children already have impulse issues. Witnessing a lack of financial control by a parent makes self-control even more elusive in the future. Show your children that purchases should be decided ahead of a shopping trip.

Not sticking to the budget.

Sticking to your budget is another demonstration of financial self-control. Allow your children to know that a budget exists and that certain purchases can't be made because of the budget.

Not making a clear distinction between needs and wants.

Demonstrate to your kids that needs are to be taken care of first. Wants are only considered after the critical items have been addressed.

Avoid demonstrating these financial habits to your children. Remember that they're always watching you!

Help your children to develop positive financial habits by setting a good example.

Not all habits are negative. Are you sharing these positive financial habits?

Consistent saving.

Make a big deal out of saving money from each paycheck. Encourage your child to do the same with a portion of any money they earn or receive as a gift. If you had saved 15% of each paycheck since you started working, how much would you have today?

A robust savings account is an effective solution to many of life's financial challenges.

Paying bills on time.

Your children notice those bills with the words "Past Due." They are also aware of when you avoid the bill collectors that call day and night. Pay your bills and avoid the late fees. You'll also be setting a great example for your child.

Sacrifice.

Making great financial strides requires sacrifice. Let your children know that you're not buying a new car because you believe to save for college or retirement is more important. Give them the option of making a small purchase at the sacrifice of something else. All financial decisions have positive and negative consequences.

Enjoying the rewards of financial responsibility.

No one wants to sacrifice all the time. The whole point of sacrificing is to enjoy the end result. Show your children that regularly saving money results in a vacation or a new television. Let your kids witness the positive outcome of good financial habits.

Do the Work!

Are you demonstrating good financial habits to your children? Are you demonstrating poor habits? You have a tremendous amount of influence over your child's financial future. They're likely to behave in a fashion similar that which they observe. Consider what you're teaching your child each day with your money habits.

TAX TIPS FOR YOUR CHARITABLE DONATIONS

Giving to charity feels good and there's even a financial benefit. You can deduct any charitable donations from your taxable income. However, many rules govern these donations. Cash gifts are handled differently than non-cash gifts, and different rules apply depending upon the amount of the donation.

Tax laws can be complicated, but you can easily find out the details for everything you need to know with some online research or from your local tax professional.

Check out these 8 tips to ensure you're getting the most out of your charitable donations:

Ensure the organization qualifies before claiming a tax deduction.

For example, contributions made to political candidates or to a specific person are non-deductible. An organization goes through a process to acquire the proper status with the IRS and become qualified.

Any organization you contribute to financially can provide information about their status regarding tax deductions.

If you're donating anything other than cash, the value is claimed at the fair-market value.

These values would be similar to what you would pay if you bought something at a thrift store or yard sale.

You can look at the prices on social media selling platforms and apps to help you determine value of your donated items. Those are typically fair-market values.

There are also special rules when you're donating a vehicle.

Maintain accurate records.

A receipt is an excellent way to keep track of your donations. In lieu of a receipt, your own banking records are also sufficient. For any amounts over $250, it's best to have both a receipt and a banking record.

Reduce your deduction by any value you receive.

If you're receiving any benefit from your donation, like tickets to sporting events, you're required to subtract that amount from your donation when claiming a deduction on your taxes.

For example, if you donate $500, but benefit by receiving "free" carpet cleaning worth $200, your tax deduction would be $300.

Contributions above certain amounts have different rules.

A single donation of $250 or more has certain reporting rules. Another set of rules, primarily an appraisal by an expert, comes into play when the amount is $5,000 or more. If you're making non-cash donations that total $500 or more, be sure to follow the additional rules. Go to www.irs.gov for more information.

Consider giving assets that have appreciated.

Gifts of stock, for example, that have appreciated in value have an added benefit. You can deduct the full value, and you're not taxed on the capital gains, since you didn't benefit from it.

The extra money comes off of your taxes and goes directly to the charity. Everyone wins, except the IRS.

You can deduct your costs for helping the charity, too.

You can deduct mileage and any other out-of-pocket expenses related to any direct service you provide to a charity. This can include parking, tolls, travel expenses, lodging, and food.

Proceed with caution when you're claiming these types of deductions. The IRS tends to scrutinize anyone who takes advantage of this opportunity. Honesty is the best policy!

The limit is 20%.

You can certainly give away every last cent to the charitable organization of your choice. However, your charitable tax deductions are limited to 20% of your adjusted gross income. You might be able to carry over excessive contributions to the following tax year. Visit a tax expert if your contributions exceed this limit.

Do the Work!

Many great causes could use your support, and it feels wonderful to be able to help them! Even better, you can reduce your tax burden in the process! Use these tips to claim the tax deductions you deserve.

LEAVING YOUR 401(K) TO CHARITY

Many of us wish to leave the majority of our assets to our loved ones, but we also want to offer some to charitable organizations. This is where some smart tax planning can really pay off.

One of the most important parts of setting up your 401(k) is naming a beneficiary. This ensures that your 401(k) can pass to someone without going through probate. However, the beneficiary will have to pay income tax on the 401(k) balance. The tax rate in this circumstance can be very steep, depending on circumstances.

There are other assets that can be passed to your heirs that are not taxed as aggressively. For example, if you pass stocks held outside of a qualified account to your heirs, your beneficiaries are not responsible for any capital gains that were achieved while you held the stock. The current price becomes their new price-point.

Leaving your 401(k) to your favorite charity and leaving the more tax-advantaged assets to your heirs makes a lot of sense. A greater percentage of your wealth will pass to where you choose, instead of to the government. Charities, since they are non-profit organizations, are tax exempt. So, they pay no income tax on assets they receive.

Planning ahead now will help you avoid common mistakes.

These are the three primary issues that can create significant challenges when passing on your 401(k) to a charity:

Imprecisely or inaccurately naming the beneficiary.

Listing "Greyhound Rescue" as the beneficiary is likely to result in your money going through the probate process. Instead, you'll want to write in something more along the lines of "Southern Florida Greyhound Rescue Society."

Also, be sure to list the Tax ID number for the organization. Many Tax ID numbers can be tracked down at www.guidestar.com.

Possession of the account.

To avoid unnecessary taxation, it is imperative that the account passes directly to the charitable organization of your choice. If your heirs or your estate were to take possession of the account and then attempt to transfer the account to the charity, your heirs would be liable for income and estate taxes.

Your spouse.

If you wish to give your 401(k) to a charity, your spouse must sign a form agreeing to give up all rights to the account. Interestingly, this requirement is not necessary for IRAs.

Remember that you have options. Managing your estate is not necessarily all-or-nothing. You could name multiple beneficiaries and assign a percentage to each. You could also leave your 401(k) to your heirs, and your 401(k) would only pass to the charity if all the other listed beneficiaries were deceased.

Also, keep in mind that the Pension Protection Act of 2006 allows IRA holders to transfer up to $100,000 to charity without paying income tax on the withdrawal. You do have to be over 70 ½ years of age to qualify, however. So, using your IRA for charitable contributions is also an option.

Do the Work!

Leaving your 401(k) to charity can be a really smart move. The tax burden on passing your 401(k) to your heirs is considerable, while charities do not have to pay income tax. Be sure to realize the total tax burden created by your choices and plan accordingly.

Estate planning is one area where the services of a professional can really pay off. Whatever you choose to do with your 401(k), good luck, and happy planning!

BEWARE OF TAX PENALTIES BEFORE GIVING GIFTS

Are you planning to give family members gifts of money this year? Before you start wrapping the presents, you may want to consider the tax penalties.

Consider these important tips about tax penalties:

- **Gift Tax Rules:** The gift tax states that you must report all gifts from family members if they're $14,000 or more. The person who receives the gift will have to pay taxes on it.
- **Annual Rule:** The $14,000 refers to an annual amount. If you give less than this amount in one year, then they won't have to pay taxes.
- **Exclusions:** Paying a family member's tuition for education doesn't count as a gift. In addition, health expenses don't count as a gift.
- **Rules for spouses:** If you're both citizens, then you can give each other any amount without tax penalties. However, if one partner is not a citizen the tax penalty applies.

Do the Work!

Tax penalties can reduce the amount of the money you give as a gift. Consider the tax implications before making monetary gifts. Speaking to a tax professional can help you set up your gifts in such a way that you avoid these penalties.

CHARITABLE DONATIONS AND TAXES

It's nice to be able give back to your community or to those less fortunate. The federal government has been kind enough to permit you to reduce your taxable income by an amount equivalent to your charitable donations, to a point. In order for a contribution to qualify for a tax deduction, follow the rules.

Receive the most for your charitable contributions with these strategies:

- **Property can only be deducted at the market rate.** If you donate a car to a charity, the current value of the car is deductible, not the original price. The same goes for real estate, stock, or any other personal property.
- **You must file an itemized tax return to claim deductions for charitable donations.** Use Schedule A to make your claims.
- **Know the limits.** You can't contribute and deduct an unlimited amount. You can only reduce your gross adjusted income by a certain percentage. For most public charities, the limit is 50%. It's 30% for many private foundations.
- **The organization must have an IRS designation as a charitable organization.** A contribution to an individual isn't deductible. Political contributions aren't deductible either. Most organizations eagerly advertise their charitable status. Just ask.
- **Any compensation you receive for your donation must be taken into account.** For example, if you donated $1,000 and received a free diner in return, your deduction would be reduced by the fair value of the dinner.
- **Keep records.** You can be required to show a receipt, cancelled check, or bank record to support your claim. A letter from the organization can also suffice. Ask for a receipt.
- **Your time is not deductible.** Even if you're a brain surgeon and you volunteer your time to a charity, you cannot take a deduction.

Do the Work!

It's wonderful to be able to share your good fortune with others. Charities provide a means to share while also providing a tax-break for you. A little research and planning can help to avoid headaches in April.

GET A TAX BREAK WHEN DONATING YOUR TIMESHARE

Do you have a timeshare that you're desperate to eliminate? You may qualify for a tax break if you decide to donate it. Even if you do not own a timeshare, this concept of giving could help you in other areas.

Consider these important tips about how to take a tax break:

- **Find a qualified charity.** The first step is to find a legitimate charity willing to accept your timeshare. The charity must have a 501(c)(3) designation from the IRS in order for you to get a tax deduction.
- **Research the charity.** You shouldn't have to pay upfront fees to get rid of your timeshare. However, you may have to pay transfer fees once it's accepted.
- **Be careful about middlemen or brokers.** They may promise to help you donate to the charity, but they can charge high fees and take months to get rid of the timeshare.
- **Get your timeshare appraised.** If you want to claim a tax deduction of $5,000 or more, then you need an official appraisal of the value of your timeshare. You can only get a deduction for the fair market value of the timeshare.
- **Transfer the title to the charity.** Keep copies of all your paperwork related to the transaction and claim your deduction when you file your taxes.

Do the Work!

If you're ready to rid yourself of your timeshare, consider donating it while getting a nice tax break.

CHAPTER TEN, SUPPORT

Sometimes the gifts you can give to yourself and your loved ones are the support of financial freedom and excellent financial health and wealth. When you give the gift of your heart and your love you are repaid twenty-fold.

Getting Started

Read through each section. They are designed to help you change your stinking thinking into satisfying facts.

· First, find the ones that you are already utilizing, and pat yourself on the back.

· Next, check if yourself talk needs any tweaking based on the new knowledge you are gaining.

· After you have that done, study the self-talk that is new to you. Which ones are missing form your tools used to develop your healthy financial lifestyle?

· For the new self-talk concepts, spend time each day until you are comfortable with them, until you catch yourself replacing your old thoughts with your new and supportive ones.

· Pick the self-talk support that you need the most and implement them first.

Finally, after you have all this accomplished, go back and read through your notes every three months to make sure you haven't strayed from the work you need to make your life great.

Giving Makes Me Rich

I enjoy giving because giving is the gift that gives back in more ways than I can know.

Use this self-affirming language to teach your thoughts a new habit:

- I am blessed because I love to bless others. Rather than give because I am rich; I am rich because I give.
- Having money and being rich are two very different ideas. The grandness of my wealth cannot be measured by standard measurements. My wealth is of substance and value because it is everlasting.
- A large home, an expensive vehicle, and all the luxuries in the world pale in comparison to how I feel when I meet a need. The things money can buy are temporary, but the joy of giving lasts a lifetime.
- Seeing the expression of gratitude and relief in the eyes of a person I have helped is worth more than anything money could buy. By helping others, I become rich in love and relationships.
- I give extravagantly, expecting nothing in return. I give to people in need and to people who I simply want to bless. When I purchase gifts for friends, I give thoughtful gifts of high quality. Doing something kind for someone else energizes me.
- My heart is full, and my household lacks nothing when I share what I have. I look for organizations and individuals whom I can help. From local schools, classrooms, and churches to national non-profit organizations, I do my part to support the noble work of others.
- Today, I choose to open my eyes and my wallet to help someone else. I enrich my own life by giving to others.

Do the Work!

Take time for self-reflection:

1. How does giving enrich my life?

2. Who can I give to today?

3. Why is giving better than taking?

Joy of Giving

I rejoice in giving.

Use this self-affirming language to teach your thoughts a new habit:

- Giving to others is a pleasure because it reminds me that I am blessed. I count it a privilege to be able to give. Every day, I am showered with blessings, which I look forward to sharing with others.
- When I give to others, I am the one who benefits. Seeing the look of joy on someone's face after receiving my gift makes it all worthwhile. My giving comes from the heart, therefore I never feel empty.
- I give freely, with no strings attached. I refrain from competition, comparison, and boasting because I give based on what I can give, regardless of what others may give.
- I choose to give free from pressure. I put a lot of time and thought into my giving. Before I offer a gift, I am filled with joy and excitement in anticipation of the reaction of the recipient.
- Giving is more satisfying than receiving. Knowing that I have helped a person in their time of need is priceless. Just as I would want others to be there for me in my time of need, I am available to help others.
- My giving is not limited to financial or material things; I give of myself, too.
- When I am around my loved ones, I make it a point to be present at the moment and to give all of my attention to them. I volunteer for worthy causes because giving of my time and strength makes a difference.
- Today, I choose to make an impact on the lives of those around me by lovingly opening my arms. After all, the more I give away, the more I gain!

Do the Work!

Take time for self-reflection:

1. Why do I give?

2. Which non-material gift can I share with my loved ones?

3. What can I give today?

11

LIVING

Life can lose some of its flare and fun when all you do is concentrate on budgets, saving, and working hard. It is time you were exposed to ideas that can help you live life. Stretch your imagination and grow the miracle you need. Live your life fully.

Getting Started

Dive right in. The only limits to creating an excellent life are the ones you choose to control your experience. Start with these concepts and expand on them to change every limiting factor of your matrix.

STICK TO YOUR BUDGET WHILE EATING OUT

Eating out is one of life's great pleasures. You can enjoy a great meal with your loved ones without any cooking or clean up.

When you learn to eat out for less, you can even visit restaurants more often!

Here are some ideas to start saving money today. Begin by picking the Right Restaurant for Your Budget.

Take advantage of restaurant week.

Many communities offer a special restaurant week when some of the most expensive eateries drop their prices to attract new business. They'll probably limit the menu, but you'll get sample creations from great chefs and enjoy the ambiance.

Search for places where kids eat free.

Look online for places where your kids can eat for free or at big discounts. Plan ahead for family vacations when you may be eating out for most meals. That way, you'll have a variety of options.

Make the most of your birthday.

You can browse online to find free meals or at least a free dessert or drink for your birthday. Even if the restaurant has no official program, tell them you're celebrating a birthday when you make your reservations and ask if they'll throw in something special.

Use coupons.

Sign up for daily deal notices. Pay attention to the details like one coupon per table or a drink minimum.

Negotiate your own discounts.

Many restaurants will offer discounts to nearby businesses to attract repeat customers. Ask your employer if they've got any deals in place or ask a restaurant owner if they'd consider making some kind of arrangement for customers at a nearby movie theater or gym.

Enjoy ethnic restaurants.

Ethnic restaurants are often a treasure trove of low prices and great food. Pick your favorite cuisine or tantalize your palate by trying something new.

When you order wisely, everything else is easy. Try these tips:

Spend less on water.

To avoid surprise charges on your bill, let your server know if you want tap water only. Even in expensive restaurants, it is up to you whether you want to pay for water.

Evaluate the specials.

Some restaurants promote deals that make the most profits for them. Ask for clarification on the price even if the server fails to mention it.

Practice portion control.

The servings in many restaurants are far more than one person needs for a single meal. Share a dish or put some aside to take home for lunch the next day.

Approach small plates strategically.

Small plates are a great way to dine. However, you can easily wind up with too much food that will just end up assorted into individual tablespoon-sized dollops of mismatched leftovers. Try ordering a few dishes at a time and ask the server to let you keep the menu. That way you can order more if you really want it.

Consider the mark up on wine.

Wine is another big profit center for restaurants. The mark up can easily be 400% or more compared to retail prices. A great wine can be worth it but consider the investment before you splurge.

Meals can be fabulous without wine, too, so remember that you can always elect to save this pricey treat for only the most special occasions.

Go as a group.

Restaurants may be willing to design a limited fixed price menu if you let them know in advance that you're bringing a group. Depending on your guests, be sure to have options for vegetarians and for medical needs such as diabetes and allergies.

Visit at lunchtime.

You can often order the same dish at lunchtime for around 20% less than the price on the dinner menu. If the restaurant is slow, they may even be willing to make your favorite dinner dish at lunch, regardless of whether it's on the menu.

Do the Work!

Dine well and pay less for the same great experience. If you pick the right restaurants and order wisely, you can have a great time and sample fine cuisine while you stick to your budget.

ENJOY LIFELONG LEARNING ON A SHOESTRING BUDGET

Lifelong learning enables you to enrich your mind and expand your career opportunities even if you completed your formal education a long time ago.

If you're on a limited budget, there are still many ways, both in your community and online, to build your knowledge and skills.

Educational Opportunities in Your Community:

Visit your local library.

Borrowing books is a good enough reason to make a trip to your local library, but they now offer much more. Search the downloadable media for audio books and test-preparation guides for graduate school exams and civil service tests. Browse the event calendar for free lectures and courses.

Give yourself a museum membership.

Museum memberships are a great bargain compared to the ticket prices for sporting events or movies. Being a member will usually give you access to special events and classes for the whole family.

Take advantage of education benefits at work.

Check your employee manual for tuition discounts and other benefits your employer may offer. Ask if you can organize a lunchtime speaker series. Many local professionals will welcome the opportunity to share their expertise on financial management or vegetarian cooking.

Do an internship.

In a tough job market, internships are one way to get the training you need to succeed. Target organizations where you can make a contribution while learning new skills.

Volunteer your services.

Volunteer work goes far beyond stuffing envelopes. Sign up to assist with a project outside your usual line of work. Most communities have nonprofit clearinghouses with a wide variety of choices or contact a favorite charity you already support.

Let your kids instruct you.

Ask your kids to teach you what they're learning in school. It's a great way to help them master their coursework while you pick up a new language or review geometry.

Teach a class.

Try teaching a class on a subject where you have some expertise at your local church or community center. Preparing for classes and interacting with students is an effective way to deepen your own knowledge.

Retire to a university town.

University towns are becoming increasingly attractive to those who are retiring with smaller savings than they expected. You receive access to all kinds of educational resources with a lower cost of living than many major cities.

Search for financial aid.

If your goals require that you go back to school, there are options for defraying the costs. Talk with the financial aid office at the university you select about scholarships, loans, grants, and veteran benefits that may be available to you.

Educational Opportunities in the Digital World:

Take free university courses.

Hundreds of respected universities and colleges offer free online courses. You can download audio and video courses from Oxford or Ivy League schools on every subject imaginable, from poetry to physics.

Switch to smarter YouTube channels.

Tear yourself away from the videos of kittens petting puppies to visit organizations like the Aspen Institute that airs nonpartisan seminars on critical world issues or the Nobel Prize where past and current Nobel Laureates talk about cultural and scientific advances.

Turn on the subtitles.

Foreign movies are a fun way to help you learn a new language or brush up if you're getting rusty. Use the subtitles while you watch to learn correct pronunciation and expand your vocabulary. Some television stations also air subtitled foreign news programs where you can learn about world events while you improve your language skills.

Do the Work!

Enjoy the thrills of new discoveries and the satisfaction of improving your mind. Many educational opportunities cost little or nothing, so all you need is a commitment to lifelong learning.

HOW TO BUDGET FOR A GREAT SUMMER

Summer is a wonderful time of year. The kids are out of school, the weather is nice, and there's a grand feeling of fun that comes with the season. With so many choices for recreation, however, you may find it challenging to fit everything you want to do within your budget.

If you plan ahead, you can enjoy all the advantages of summer without breaking your bank!

Take in a Matinee

Many of the most exciting film releases of the year occur in summer. Many summers, you can catch a new movie every week for the entire season. Seeing an afternoon showing offers a way to beat the heat and relax. You can enjoy the latest releases and often pay half-price compared with an evening showing!

For even more savings at the movie theater, cut back at the snack bar. Your waistline will thank you, and so will your pocketbook. Your afternoon at the movies will be just as satisfying.

You can save even more with a movie rental subscription. That way, you can sit back and relax in the comfort of your own home and still enjoy an inexpensive evening of entertainment.

Take Advantage of Group Rates

Many theme parks and attractions offer a family package or discounts for groups of a certain size. Sometimes, you have to ask for the group rate. But if you're planning an outing with friends, you can stretch the money you save on a group rate and enjoy more of the activities that the summer has to offer.

Airlines and hotels frequently offer family or group rates for travel during the summer. If you're planning to travel this summer, shop around for the best bargains and save yourself some cash.

Think Local

In the summer months, many of you travel far away in search of adventure. In many cases, you can experience a similar adventure without venturing too far from your home. Save money on hotels, plane tickets, and baggage fees by exploring all that your local area has to offer this summer.

If you're not sure about what fun things are available in your area, try searching the Internet for your city's name and "tourism." You might be surprised to find that the adventure you seek is right in your own backyard!

Browse for Deals

Shopping around for the best deal is important when traveling this summer, but it can also save you money close to home. Stiff competition in your neighborhood could cause restaurants, diners, and attractions to offer great specials to steer you away from the competition.

Bowling alleys, golf courses, zoos, and many other fun summer activities often have summer deals for customers. If you invest a little time to search for these deals, your friends and family can often enjoy an outing together for much less than you would expect.

Know Your Limits

Summer offers many recreational choices. Sometimes, however, the best option is to say no. Your body needs rest, and so does your mind. Choose the activities that best fit your interests and say no to the others. You'll experience more energy and peace within yourself while saving money at the same time.

Do the Work!

Summer can be an expensive time of year, but it doesn't have to break your budget. By making wise choices with your money and slowing down a little, you can enjoy summer recreation and save money at the same time.

A WEEKEND WITHOUT TELEVISION

How much time do you spend watching television? According to recent research, adults between the ages of 35 and 50 watch over 33 hours of TV per week. That's almost 5 hours per day. It's fair to say that most people watch more television on the weekends than they do during the week. Think of all the things you could do with that time!

How much different would your life be if you spent those 5 hours each day working on something else?

Consider the changes you could make to your health, social life, family life, and personal development. Spend one weekend without TV and see what might happen.

You'll be forced to investigate other interests.

Watching television is often a default action. You do it when you can't find anything else to do. Invention is the mother of necessity. Without your default distraction, you'll find other ways to entertain yourself.

Maybe you'll find something even more enjoyable. You'll certainly find something more productive.

You can spend more time with your family.

Instead of watching the ball game or Rocky for the 12th time, take your family to the park. Have a cookout in the backyard. Go camping. Take a weekend road trip. Or just sit together and talk.

You can improve your health.

How would your health change if you dropped just 4 hours of television per week and spent that time exercising? This weekend is a great chance to start on a new exercise program.

You can connect with other people.

Instead of ordering a pizza and sitting in front of the TV on Saturday night, pick up the phone and call an old friend. Leave the house and be around others. You might make a new friend or find the love of your life.

If you have a family, take them out for a night on the town.

You could read a book.

Most people fail to read even one book per year. Imagine the advantage you'd have if you became a regular reader. If you don't have the time or funds to visit India, you can read about it. Nearly every bit of information in the world can be found in a book.

It's a great time to tackle a major project.

Big projects are challenging when you first start. It's a little easier to gravitate to the TV and stay there until there's not enough time left to do any real work. Maybe next weekend. Turn off the television and you'll have plenty of time to tackle a major project and get a great start. Your significant other will be thrilled, too.

You can spend time with yourself.

Can you stand to sit with yourself for an hour? Most people can't. Television is a great distraction. TV has sound, moving pictures, and a compelling story. It's a perfect way to distract yourself from your thoughts. If you're stressed, your TV is one of your first stops.

You'll have time to address your challenges.

You could use your extra time to address the aspects of your life that make you unhappy. Watching TV solves nothing. Spend that time enhancing your life by facing your challenges head-on.

With effective action, you can change your life quickly.

Do the Work!

If you usually spend your weekend watching television, consider unplugging for just one weekend. When you realize how much more you can accomplish, you'll be hooked. Your TV habit is limiting your life. Spend more time with your family this weekend. Leave the house and enjoy your life.

MAKE LIFE EASIER AND MORE FULFILLING

Is your life unfulfilling and overly full of challenges? If so, you'll be happy to know that you can make changes, starting today, to turn your life around!

Creating a wonderful life is the result of consistently doing things that support your happiness and fulfillment.

Avoid stressful challenges and enjoy your life more with these behaviors:

Be proactive.

Avoid waiting until you're forced to take action. Plan ahead. Many of life's challenges are easily managed if you deal with them quickly. Most of life's difficulties are preventable.

For example, you know that your car needs regular oil changes. A natural result of *not* changing the oil is a ruined car. You can prevent this challenge simply by changing your oil on time. If you can't afford to have the oil changed, learn how to do it yourself. This is one task anyone can learn.

Being proactive also applies to any task that you're aware of ahead of time, such as projects and reports at your job. Waiting until the last minute to do something ensures that when you finally do it, you'll be full of stress and won't do your best work, both of which can cause further challenges.

Set goals, write them down, and take action to achieve them. Do something each day to bring you a little closer to the life you desire.

Pay attention to your diet and fitness.

It's easy to gain 50 pounds one pound at a time. A poor diet can ruin your health with imperceptible changes, a little at a time.

Keep an eye on your weight and set a hard limit. Once you've reached that limit, it is time for serious action. You can't weigh 250 pounds if you never allow yourself to weigh over 150.

Start feeding your body the nutrition it craves for peak performance. Make changes a little at a time. For example, add a vegetable or fruit to each meal. Make something homemade with organic ingredients instead of buying processed food. Do this often enough, and you'll develop a taste preference for delicious, healthy food.

Minimize time watching TV or surfing the internet.

TV, the internet, and your smart phone are all great ways of wasting your precious time. Consider all the other, more productive, things you could be doing instead.

Imagine if you spend three hours each day split between exercising, learning a musical instrument, and running an online business instead of watching YouTube videos. How would your life be different after five years? You can determine today how your life will be in the future.

Save money consistently.

Having secure finances is crucial. One unfortunate incident, such as blown transmission in your car, can be catastrophic if you don't have any money in the bank. Keep in mind that you can't work forever. Sooner or later you'll be forced to live off your savings and social security.

Start a savings account today and add to it each week. You can start small and, once you form the habit of saving consistently, begin a program of increasing your savings.

Start investing. A great start is an index fund. Find one that you can join with small payments and add to your investment each month. Start with as little as $25.

Consider the actual value to you of your purchases.

Buy things you need, rather than things you want due to the impulse of the moment. It's difficult to save money if you routinely make unnecessary purchases. These items rarely bring true enjoyment anyway.

Make decisions.

Making decisions can be scary and feel restrictive. You might not want to take that much responsibility for your life. But even a poor decision is often better than no decision at all. Without decisions, your fate is determined by luck.

Maintain friendships.

Friends drift away unless you make an effort to maintain your friendships. As you age, you may think you have fewer opportunities to make new friends. Keeping a friendship alive takes effort, but it's less work than finding and nurturing a new friendship. Few things in life are better than an old friend.

Do the Work!

A few bad habits can create a very hard life. A few effective habits can reward you greatly. Strive to develop habits that support your happiness. Be proactive, make your health a priority, use your time wisely, and be responsible with your finances. An exciting life with minimal distress can be yours.

BE MORE OPEN AND SHARE YOUR FEELINGS

Some people have no trouble sharing their feelings. They are devoid of the fear and anxiety that most of us feel about sharing something personal or potentially controversial. Down deep, you're jealous of these people. Openness provides a level of freedom that eludes those that are more private. It's important to be able to share your feelings and concerns openly.

Your concerns can't be addressed if you're unwilling to share them. You have to face your challenges alone if you keep them to yourself.

Share your feelings and enjoy the resulting freedom it provides:

Be more accepting of others.

It sounds counterintuitive, but if you're afraid to share your feelings, you may be judgmental of others. Naturally, you would expect others to judge you, too. It's impossible to accurately judge others. There's always more going on than you realize. Be accepting of others and you'll expect others to be accepting of you.

Start small.

Share something small, but relevant. Once you can share your feelings without negative repercussions, you'll be more likely to share them again.

Determine the source of your fear.

You may fear judging, rejection, ridicule, or embarrassment. Perhaps attacking that fear is the first logical step to lessening your anxiety around sharing and openness.

Be brave.

It is impossible to be 100% comfortable about sharing your feelings until you've done it several times. A certain amount of courage is required at the beginning. Be brave enough to share your feelings. It becomes easier over time.

Encourage others to share their feelings with you.

You might feel more comfortable if your conversation partner goes first.

Stay in the present moment.

You generate feelings of fear by worrying about the possible outcomes. Stay at the moment, and your fear will dissipate. Avoid imagining the worst possible outcome.

Calibrate the other person.

Others are often careless when they believe something doesn't matter. You'll find that others are more empathetic and understanding if you let them know that something is important to you. It can be as simple as, "I want to tell you about something that's important to me." Put others in the proper state of mind before you share.

Be honest.

The willingness to make yourself vulnerable will enhance your results. If you're sharing something that displeases you about the other person, it's important to empathize first. Sharing your feelings requires consideration of the other person's feelings, too.

Take a deep breath and just do it.

The anticipation is usually worse than the actual event. Sometimes, you just have to go for it. You can do it. Focus on how much better you'll be after you share.

Do the Work!

Change isn't easy. Sharing can be scary, but the benefits outweigh the anxiety experienced. In time, you'll learn to share your feelings and worries more easily. It just takes practice. Focus on the benefits you'll receive and let the words flow. The other person will appreciate your effort and you'll find that you receive what you want more often.

HOW TO LIVE CONSCIOUSLY

Have you ever seen ants marching in search of food? They just follow one another in an almost endless game that seems to drone on and on. Does your life resemble an ant's life--as if you're going from day to day, doing the same thing, the same way, and nothing ever changes?

If so, then there's a very good probability you're not living consciously.

Conscious living is being aware of your life and the things you're doing. It's about taking the time to stop and smell the roses so you can enjoy where you fit into the whole picture.

Living consciously is a vital component in enjoying the fleeting moments we have on Earth.

Take note of what's going on around you and be aware of what you're doing. Living consciously brings us an understanding of what we're capable of doing and paves the way for us to get where we want to go.

Benefits of Conscious Living

Perhaps you're wondering, "What's in it for me?" Conscious living brings with it many benefits, which you may already be seeking in your life. Here are just a few of these benefits:

Relieve stress.

Conscious living can be a great stress reliever. Not only does it make life more enjoyable when you alleviate your stress, but it also makes you healthier. Stress affects every process in our bodies and can cause serious disease if it builds up within us.

Expand your horizons.

As you become more aware of your surroundings, you'll find that you can better understand the world and your place in it.

Live at the moment.

Throughout the day, you'll be more focused on your work because you're consciously acting on a specific task at the moment.

Enjoy more passion in your relationships.

While living consciously, your relationships will become more meaningful because you'll be appreciative of them as well as the other person. You'll be more in tune with your partner and aware of every want and need.

Know your importance.

Your job will become more fulfilling because you're more conscious of your role in the grand scheme of things. You no longer just answer a phone or hand someone a photocopy, but you are consciously making a difference.

Bring color into your world.

Your surroundings will become more vibrant because you'll notice things like the subtle differences between the shades of the trees and the direction of the soft breeze.

Being conscious of life makes life more fun.

When you're living consciously, bad days are few and far between.

Action Steps to Living Consciously

Luckily, transforming your humdrum life into one filled with vibrant joy is easier than you may think! You can make some simple adjustments to your everyday routines to live consciously and more fully enjoy your life. Here are some action steps you can take to bring conscious living to your life:

Stop.

Take some time to stop throughout the day and look around. Be aware of where you are and what's around you. Become conscious of your surroundings and be aware of how you fit into them.

Notice the details such as the green on the trees, or the condensation dripping down the side of the cup. Become in tune with what your body experiences and search out the sensations of your fingers and toes while feeling your chest rise and fall with each breath.

Breathe.

Take deep breaths and be at the moment. Don't think about what you've done or what you still have to do, just take a minute or two to just breathe!

Learn.

Take a few minutes each day to try something new. Pick up a book you've wanted to read or learn a new skill. By doing this, you're starting to become conscious of your life and the things you can do with it.

Do the Work!

Living consciously is one of the easiest changes to make on a day-to-day basis. Take a few of these ideas, integrate them into your routine and begin enjoying the benefits of living consciously!

CHAPTER ELEVEN, SUPPORT

Which Habits Can You Turn Around Fast?

Have you been able to lock in your success? Keep going. Use this next section to help you change the way you think of yourself and what you can accomplish. Change your way of thinking, develop habits that create your success patterns, and give yourself the mental support for your success.

Getting Started

Read through each section. They are designed to help you change your stinking thinking into satisfying facts. See who you can be, who you are becoming, and who you truly are.

My Success

I define success on my terms.

Use this self-affirming language to teach your thoughts a new habit:

- My success is unique, and I am the only one who can characterize it.
- I appreciate the successes of those around me. I can learn from them and enjoy their achievements. I appreciate my own success, even if it is not the same as others. My success is determined and defined by me. That is what matters most. I can see the progress I make and only I will know where it came from.
- It doesn't matter what other people think about my progress because I build momentum on my terms. Others have their own ideas of what success means to them, but I have my own mind to create goals unique to me. I let go of worrying about what others think and I embrace my goals with passion.
- My success is perfect for me! I am proud of my progress and I celebrate each success, whether big or small.
- Today, I choose to focus on my own progress and celebrate each success on my journey. And when I do, I feel satisfied knowing that I can surpass any goal I have set for myself.

Do the Work!

Take time for self-reflection:

1. What areas have I defined as successful?

2. How does my success make me feel?

3. How have I celebrated my success?

Consistency and Success

Consistency is a key to my success.

Use this self-affirming language to teach your thoughts a new habit:

- Thankfully, I enjoy successes in my everyday life. I realize that my behaviors, choices, and emotions play a large role in my being successful.
- Although I have many personality characteristics that compel me to do my best and achieve my goals, I find that my consistency is an important key to my success.
- Reflecting occasionally on my capacity to be consistent is integral to my accomplishments. In striving to be consistent, I apply logical thinking. I endeavor to be orderly in my efforts. And I put all my energy into what I am doing at the time.
- Striving for consistency also gives me persistence. I stick with a task until it is completed to the best of my ability.
- Consistency comes with a guarantee: if I continue diligently in focusing on a task, apply organization, and use logical thinking, I succeed. I firmly believe that my success is largely due to my ability to be consistent.
- Another positive aspect of consistency is that I set an excellent example to others to be logical, orderly, and focused.
- Today, I am pleased when I reflect about how consistency pays off for me in my daily life. I know I can continue to be consistent at home, with friends, and at work. I am successful because I am consistent.

Do the Work!

Take time for self-reflection:

1. How important is consistency to me?

2. Would people who know me describe me as a consistent person?

3. Do I want to improve my level of consistency? If so, how can I do it?

Success and Good Fortune

I am a magnet for success and good fortune.

Use this self-affirming language to teach your thoughts a new habit:

- I am drawn to success and success is drawn to me. We coexist in the world. I have a knack for choosing the best path to any success. My natural instincts pull me to my goals.
- I am fortunate. Many people consider me to be very lucky. When I need something, it appears in my life. I have a strong connection to the universe. I am given what I require. However, I find that I receive the most when I am diligent and proactive. Good luck, good fortune, and good timing go hand in hand.
- I am grateful for all that I am receiving each day. The more grateful I feel, the more I receive. I rejoice in the good fortune of others, too. This generates good will and strengthens my relationships.
- I work hard for success and good fortune. The harder I work, the more fortune and success I experience. I am willing to take responsibility for my life. There are numerous small advantages that I make the most of each day.
- I have strong relationships with others. This creates many opportunities in my life. Good opportunities are presented to me on a regular basis.
- Today, I am opening myself to greater success. I draw success and good fortune to me like a magnet. I deserve success. I am aware of my objectives and work toward achieving them each day.

Do the Work!

Take time for self-reflection:

1. What are the greatest opportunities in my life right now?

2. When have I been the luckiest?

3. Who and what am I fortunate to have in my life?

Love and Success

When my open arms give love, I gain success.

Use this self-affirming language to teach your thoughts a new habit:

- Each morning, I recommit to living with a higher purpose. My open arms give love to others and gain success in return.
- I open my arms to others by serving as a listening ear or a shoulder to cry on. Letting others know that I am here for them teaches me to live life selflessly.
- When I take in the heartache and difficulty being faced by someone else, it eases their pain. It is my brotherly responsibility to ensure that those around me are comforted. Their well-being is just as important as my own, and I vow to take care of it.
- I also open my arms to those who feel unloved. Each chance I get, I tell others how important they are. I encourage them by showing them their value.
- When I choose to live for others more than myself, success comes my way. My choice to sacrifice my own comfort for that of someone else is rewarding. Gratitude is poured into my life, and I am positively overwhelmed.
- Although the future is sometimes unclear, I avoid feeling doubtful. When I keep my mind and heart open to possibility, I often receive it.
- Today, my arms are a vessel for receiving and giving goodness. I love what they symbolize in my life and the lives of others. Love and blessings abound when I choose to share myself with others.

Do the Work!

Take time for self-reflection:

1. In what ways do I share myself with those around me?

2. When is it enough to just listen to someone express themselves?

3. How eager am I to dive into the unknown?

Supportive Decisions

I trust my ability to make the right decisions.

Use this self-affirming language to teach your thoughts a new habit:

- I trust my ability to make the right decisions because I have taken the time and effort to think clearly and surround myself with wise people.
- I let go of the idea that I should automatically know the answer to everything. While I am unafraid of tackling a problem on my own, I am also aware that I am strongest as part of a community.
- I am fully willing to assist those younger and less experienced than I, and so I am confident that my older and wiser peers are equally eager to help me. I take advantage of that, knowing that I can only be my best if I make use of the many resources at my disposal.
- However, I may not always have access to guidance. In this case, I advise myself by recalling my experiences.
- I think about my goals and whether the situation at hand will assist me in reaching them or whether it will hinder me in some way.
- I think about my energy level and skills and assess honestly whether I am capable of taking on the task. If I do decide to take it, I make it a point to be aware of my strengths and weaknesses and where I may need help.
- Because I pay attention to the lessons I have learned from my past, and because I have a clear picture of where I am headed in the future, I know that I can make wise choices.

Do the Work!

Take time for self-reflection:

1. Who can I consult when I need advice?

2. Do I keep a clear picture of my goals in mind when making decisions?

3. What have I learned from experiences that I can apply to current decisions?

12

THE LOOKING GLASS

Wouldn't it be great to have a magic looking glass to help you see into your financial future? How much stress would this relieve in your life? How many things would you do differently if you knew the results of your actions?

Even though every life journey is unique, financially everyone follows the same general patterns. These patterns affect life in similar ways for each of you, no matter the order you go through them.

To help you make the best decisions you can at each step of your journey, all you need is a little insight into what is possible. Imagine what can happen when you are educated and prepared to make the best decisions possible during the different stages of your life's financial journey.

Getting Started

Your financial knowledge is a process. Each age group has knowledge and information that is needed for the next. These financial success steppingstones will help you create a successful life path. A lack of knowledge for any step can set you up for mistakes in your later years.

Take time to go over each stage. This will help you realize impact possibilities for your entire financial future. For instance, even if you do not have small children, the information you needed to know in your youth is here. The more complete your picture is of lifetime financial choices, the more likely you are to make better and accurate choices all along your journey.

START THEM YOUNG

Children can benefit from finance education at an early age. A study from the University of Cambridge, *"Habit Formation and Learning in Young Children,"* found that money habits are formed by age 7.

This may surprise you:

Researchers share it's important to start basic finance education by age 3.

Luckily for us all, children pick up money habits quickly. Start them as soon as you can. Give them the right tools and direction.

Your support is crucial to their success.

Start children with basic currency literacy.

A study from Yale University found that children can recognize and remember coins by the age of 3.

- Educate your children about the different coins and dollar bills.
- Consider teaching them about foreign currencies during vacations. This will expand their minds and help them learn more about the countries you're visiting.

Create money jars.

This fun project has a visual impact. The jar's hands-on aspect allows for a fun and easy way to educate your child.

- You can create three types of money jars. Jars for spending, saving, and giving. These three categories cover the basic lessons of understanding how to use money.

- You will need to teach your children how to use the three jars and why they're important.
- Trust that children have the desire to learn. You can use the jars to separate money after holiday gifts or allowance payments. When you start them young, your children will learn how to save for the future with less effort and no stress. It will simply be normal for them.
- Use the giving jar for charities. Children will learn about giving and understand how they can help others with their money. They can donate the money to local animal shelters, food pantries, their school, or other organization of their choice. They can also create a savings fund that earns money for later charitable creation such as a business or grant fund.

Use coupons.

Coupons can provide an important lesson on saving.

- Cut out coupons with help from your children and leave them in charge of handling the papers at the store.
- According to the Children's Financial Network, kids as young as 5 can benefit from learning how to use coupons in a store. They will begin to understand how to save money and make wiser shopping decisions.
- Teach them to search online for the best discount and coupon codes for every purchase.

Set a money goal.

Children can set a money goal to purchase a favorite toy or other items.

- Money goals are an easy way to teach children financial patience. They also provide a lesson on how to save money.
- Set realistic goals, so children will be motivated to stay on a savings plan. If the toy they want is expensive, it can take a while to reach their goals. Will they stay interested? Picking smaller and less expensive targets is better.

Go shopping.

Let your children use their spend jars at the store to make purchases.

- Shopping provides an easy lesson setting. How will your children spend their money? Will they use their entire jars at one store or spread them out over many shopping trips?
- An outing to the local toy store also gives you the chance to discuss comparison shopping. Point out different prices on similar items and teach your children about finding inexpensive options.
- Additional online searches and purchasing opportunities can help them understand that not all shops have the same price or shopping opportunities.
- Evaluating the results of the shopping trip will help them understand their

choices. How will they restock their spending jars for their next transaction?

Use yard sales.

Yard sales offer another way to educate children about finances.

- Yard sales can help you clean out your children's rooms and teach them about money at the same time.
- Ask your children if they want to participate in the yard sale by selling their old toys or clothes. Help them select items they no longer use and find appropriate prices for them. They can use the experience to refill their money jars.
- Older children can help sell items at the sale. They can keep track of change and watch customers. This is also a valuable opportunity to learn about price negotiations with customers.
- Items that do not sell can be sold online or saved for a future sale. Things that do not move can be donated to create room for change in your child's life.

Finance education can begin before your children are in school. They can understand basic money rules and form healthy financial habits.

Do the Work!

If you didn't have this kind of support as a child, take some time to go back through your experiences. Consider what you could have done differently had you had this knowledge at an early age.

START SUCCESS HABITS EARLY

As your children age, you can graduate them to bigger and larger concepts. Giving your children the gift of financial wisdom is priceless.

Consider discussing these ideas with your children:

The real cost of what you're buying.

Understanding the cost of spending money versus saving money can be a real eye-opener for children and adults alike.

If you spend your money on something, that money isn't available for anything else, like investing.

Example: A $500 stereo doesn't just cost $500. Invested at 10%, $500 could grow to almost $27,000. This is commonly referred to as opportunity cost.

Show your child how to use a simple savings calculator.

These free calculators are available all over the internet and are a great way to show what can be accomplished by consistently saving a little money each month.

If you save $50 a month at a return of 8% for 30 years, you would end up with almost $68,000.

Teach them about debt.

The average household has over $7,000 in credit card debt. When kids go to college, they're inundated with credit card offers from the first day on campus. Credit with no means to pay it off can be a terrible habit. Teach your child not to fall into the debt trap.

If you never piled on debt, imagine how much better your lifestyle would be.

Start building their credit.

Consider co-signing for a credit card that gets paid off every month, if they aren't old enough or experienced enough to obtain one by themselves. Look for a card with a low rate and no annual fee. Teach them how to use the card wisely.

An alternative is to take out a loan together. Banks will loan money to anyone if the loan is fully secured. With a small deposit in a savings account, a comparable amount can be borrowed easily.

Most young adults are unable to purchase a home for several years, often due to a lack of credit history. Start early.

Pull their credit report.

After some credit building activities, teach your child how to view their credit report and check for errors. The majority of credit reports have errors, typically not in your favor.

Clean and clear credit creates a clean and clear financial consciousness.

Teach them how to save.

Most of us pay our bills, have a little fun, and then plan to save whatever is left. With that approach, there's rarely ever anything left. Teach your child to immediately save 10-20% (or more) of every dollar earned.

Think about the wealth you would have accumulated if you saved first and then spent second since you were 18. The money you would have!

Teach them to be giving.

Allow your child to choose a charity and contribute to it. For a young child, it might be just a few dollars. Your child will ultimately come to understand that giving affects them as much as it does the person or organization receiving the money.

Create change by creating hope in things that have value to you.

Encourage them to work during the summer.

All teenagers want more money. Give them the chance to earn it. Their perspective will change.

If you work for it, you can better understand the value of a dollar.

Money is an important part of life. Money provides security, opportunity, and a greater ability to help others. You have a lot of control over the financial habits your children develop. Help them to have a financially successful life.

Do the Work!

If you didn't have this kind of support as a child, take some time to go back through your experiences. How can you use this information to turn your credit debt around, increase your savings today, and become responsible with your finances?

TAILORED TEEN EMERGES

As your teen begins to move out into the world, they will need more knowledge. Help your teen enjoy a bright future by teaching them financial responsibility. Knowing the basics of money management will help your child to plan ahead and achieve their life goals.

Teach your teen to save, budget, and shop wisely.

These steps can make it easy to explain budgeting, shopping, saving, and using credit wisely:

To save more, establish goals.

Help your teen to set short and long-term goals that will motivate them to build up some savings. They may want to buy a car or put away money for college.

Savings and the power of interest.

Provide an introduction to the power of interest. Your child may want to save more if they realize how much money they can earn by starting a savings account when they're young. You can help them leverage money through guaranteed investment savings.

Develop a savings strategy.

Help your teen find a plan that works for them. They may want to set aside a small percentage of their allowance or half the money gifted to them for their birthday. If possible, you can provide an extra incentive by offering to match whatever amount they save.

Learn the basics of budgeting.

Explain budgeting in simple terms as a plan for income and expenses. Discuss examples of trade-offs and the concept of needing to earn more or spend less in order to remain financially secure.

Get familiar with ordinary household expenses.

Give your teen an early start on knowing the cost of typical goods and services. Let them see the cable TV bill and your monthly car payment.

Monitor your spending.

Ask your teen to keep track of their spending for a month or more. Your kids may be surprised by how much they really spend on something like eating out or clothing.

Manage your income.

As long as their school remains the top priority, encourage your teen to have some income of their own to manage. You can provide an allowance or support their efforts to find a summer job. They can use a hobby to generate income with your encouragement.

Shop together.

Go shopping together to demonstrate how to find the best value. Compare prices for generic and brand name products at the grocery store. Look for special sales at the local mall.

Research major purchases.

Assign your teen some research when they want to make a major purchase such as a cell phone. Let them compare plans and help decide what features they really need.

Analyze materialism.

Advertising bombards people with messages to consume more. Discuss the importance of moderation and basing your happiness on sources other than your possessions.

Use credit wisely by selecting the right instrument for you.

There are many kinds of cards to choose from now so you can find the level of parental control that's comfortable for you. Debit cards give you the peace of mind of enforcing a pre-established spending limit, and many cards give you the option to review all statements.

Pay your entire balance monthly.

Let your teen know that interest works against them when borrowing. Show them how paying off a credit card balance each month protects them from paying much more than the original price for the goods and services you charged.

Know the significance of good credit.

Talk with your teens about the importance of good credit. Explain how being responsible for paying off bills helps people to qualify for financing when they need student loans or want to buy a house.

With a little information and guidance, your teen can master the basics of money management. By encouraging them to be responsible, you'll protect your family's financial security while you help your child pursue their dreams for college and beyond.

Do the Work!

If you didn't have this kind of support as a child, what steps do you need to take today to create a budget you can live with, shop and spend money without going into debt, and save for your future?

CREDIT USE DURING COLLEGE

Sending kids off to college isn't easy. Even though you think your child is ready to experience life on their own, you know they'll still depend on you for some financial support. One of the biggest questions you'll struggle with is the whole credit card dilemma.

Should you turn your teen into a credit-card-carrying adult with no strings attached?

Not so long ago, new college students were inundated with credit card applications and could easily apply for and receive a card without their parents even knowing about it.

However, this situation changed dramatically after the passage of the Credit Card Accountability, Responsibility and Disclosure Act of 2009. This act made it more difficult for a student under 21 to open a credit card account without his parents' approval.

Making the decision to bring credit card debt into a child's life when they have no means to pay that debt is a big choice. Consider their level of responsibility and knowledge before moving forward.

Has he had any money management experience?

Perhaps you've let him use one of your cards in the past. Maybe he received an allowance or worked at a part-time job during high school. These things teach your child about money--how to consider it, save it, and use it as he's maturing.

By the time he's ready for college, you'll know how he's handled money in the past. Use that info when deciding whether he should go off to school with his own credit card.

How does your college student handle their earning, budgeting, and spending of money?

If you have started him young, you have a decent idea about how your child approaches the whole money thing. Does he spend every cent right away or carefully save a certain percentage? Knowing this can help you both decide if a card spending limit needs to be set to help control the process until the experience is present to make good decisions.

What are the college's arrangements for payments of dorm and meal costs?

These facts can play a major role in the credit card decision.

If your kid will be living in a dorm, room and board are usually required to be paid in a lump sum beforehand, which you could do.

Most colleges now have a meal card arrangement, which means each dorm dweller is provided with a meal card that's scanned to "pay for" meals. So, no credit card is really necessary.

Think about making your college student an authorized user on your credit card account.

A card is issued on your account in the student's name. Your monthly statement will show your child's purchases.

Designating your college student as an authorized user on your card account is great because you can set the monthly limit on his card. Some credit-card-issuing institutions even allow you to change your student's monthly limits as you like.

For example, if you know next semester's dorm charges are due in December, you can bump up the monthly limit for December to $2,000 or whatever's required. Otherwise, select a lower monthly limit.

Handling the credit card dilemma by making your child an authorized user on your account gives your student a chance to show his financial choices while you monitor and control the amount available for his spending.

Consider a secured credit card.

Especially good for college students, a secured credit card account requires a certain amount of collateral be placed on the account, like $300 to $500. This deposit is placed in a low-interest-bearing bond or money market where it will be held up to one year.

If your student shows he can pay monthly credit card bills on time consistently, he'll eventually receive back the initial deposit. In essence, your kid is rewarded for responsible, consistent money management skills when using a secured credit card.

If the card is through a bank, you kid can also develop and grow their credit score while learning to be responsible.

After you consider all these important points, you'll likely arrive at the best decision regarding credit cards for him and for you!

Do the Work!

If you didn't have this kind of support as a student, what steps can you take today to strengthen your healthy use of credit? If you have damaged your credit, can you put aside $500 to open a secure credit card and start building your fresh start? Look into which option works best with the time you have to move you closer to your dream financial situation.

PITFALLS OF COLLEGE CREDIT

Credit card companies used to market aggressively to college students. Laws now prohibit this type of activity. Still, getting a credit card can be an important step for college students to build their credit score for future purchases.

Using a credit card irresponsibly can create a huge financial challenge.

As you move forward with your decision to help your college student own a credit card, for best results, avoid these credit card mistakes:

Not getting a credit card at all.

Now is the perfect time to establish credit and build a good credit score. You might think you're being responsible by not getting a credit card, but you'll face a significant challenge when you want to buy a house or automobile with the support of credit.

To resolve this issue, get a card or two and use them responsibly. That means the occasional, small purchase that you can afford. Buying gas or paying your cell phone bill are two examples of how you can use a card to create credit without creating unnecessary debt.

Getting too many credit cards.

Two cards are plenty when starting out. Imagine the damage you can do with five or more credit cards. Give yourself a chance to become familiar with the responsible use of credit.

Carrying a balance.

Pay the entire balance each month. Once a small balance becomes comfortable, a moderate balance isn't far behind. Use self-control and avoid ever carrying a balance to the following month.

Getting a credit card before you're ready.

Some teenagers are more mature than others. If you don't have a bank account, have never held a job, or don't know how to save, it might be better to wait. Another option is to obtain a card with a very low credit limit.

Failing to track purchases.

You can easily jump from store to store and spend a lot of money quickly. Keep track of your receipts and keep a running total. Post it where you can see it. Everyone with a credit card has been surprised at least once by the size of the monthly bill. Avoid any unpleasant surprises.

Not paying the bill on time.

Being late with your payments will kill your credit score. Know when the bill should arrive and keep your eyes open. College dorms are notorious for losing mail.

Set a bank alert or an automatic minimum payment to avoid ever paying your credit card bill late. Remember that you can see your bill online and pay it instantly whether you receive your paper bill or not.

Making purchases you can't afford until you get that big job.

Many college students have used credit cards irresponsibly by telling themselves they'll pay it all off in a few years when they're raking in the big bucks. It can be tough to find a job after graduation. You'll also have the expenses of moving, buying furniture, possibly paying back student loans, and more.

Remember, your responsible choice is to make a small purchase each month and pay the bill in full. If you can't pay the entire bill at the end of the month, you're outspending your income.

It would be a shame to waste the great opportunity college students have to begin building their credit scores. But using a credit card irresponsibly can haunt your finances for years. Give credit the respect it deserves. Use it as a powerful tool, one that can either help or hurt you. Use it wisely.

Do the Work!

If you have already damaged your credit with some of these behaviors, it is never too late to turn things around. Take the time to clean up your credit, reverse the damage, and build a strong base that will help you achieve your financial goals.

RIGHTS OF A STUDENT BORROWER

Student loan debt has risen sharply over the last several years. The average borrower currently owes approximately $25,000. This debt can be extremely challenging, especially if you struggle to find a job after graduation.

Many students fail to understand the magnitude of the debt and the amount of time it requires to pay it back.

But there is good news if you have federal student loans. You have several, powerful rights that can make paying back your loan easier. These same rights are generally not available to those with private student loans. All debt can be cumbersome. It only makes sense to understand your rights.

As a federal student loan borrower, you have the following rights:

You have the right to accept or refuse the loans offered to you.

You even have the right to accept part of the loans. You can change your mind and simply refuse to accept the loan.

You have the right to defer you loan payments.

Check out the variety of ways to qualify for a forbearance or deferment with your federal student loans. This can be helpful if your financial situation makes it impossible to make your loan payments. There's no reason to go into default. It is quite easy to take advantage of these options.

You have the right to repay early.

Most people just assume that all loans can be repaid early, but that's not always true. Those with federal student loans can pay off their loans early without penalty. If you have the extra income available, it's nice to have the option to eliminate your debt without penalty.

You have the right to a full copy of your promissory note.

A promissory note spells out all the terms of your loan. You can insist on seeing it prior to receiving your loan.

You have the right to make payments based on your income.

There are a variety of loan payment options that are dependent on your discretionary income. The remainder of the debt is forgiven after a period of 20 to 25 years.

You have the right to consolidate your student loans.

Consolidating your loans can make billing easier, reduce your payments, and even possibly reduce your interest rate. Consolidation has many advantages, especially if you have several loans or need to extend your payment period.

You have the right to see a Loan Approval Disclosure when your student loan is approved.

This will include the interest rate and the repayment schedule. You must be provided 30 days to shop around for other loans without fear of losing access to this loan.

You have the right to change your payment schedule.

While the normal repayment period is 10 years, you can extend your payment schedule out to as long as 25 years. This will decrease your monthly payment but increase the total cost of the loan. Still, if your income can support paying back your loan in 10 years, you can decrease your payments this way.

Do the Work!

Federal student loan delinquency has been rising rapidly. Use these rights to ensure that you make your loan payments on time. If you're unable to pay each month, make the appropriate arrangements to keep your loan out of default. Your student loan debt doesn't have to be a tremendous burden. By using these rights, you can make your debt manageable.

COLLEGE CREDIT BUILDING YEARS

One of the great things about being a young adult is you probably do not have any negative marks on your credit. Having a great credit score is the result of having positive credit items, a good payment history, and time. A good credit score requires some credit history -- the longer, the better.

Building credit is quite easy and there's never a good reason to put it off. The sooner you start, the better your credit score will be.

Just like you need tools to build a house, you'll need tools to build your credit.

Credit cards.

This is the most common way to start. Credit card companies usually consider you to be a good risk, primarily because they believe your parents will jump in and help save you from trouble.

Since you do have a lot of options, be choosy. Look for the best card. The primary things to look at are the interest rate and the annual fee, if any. Be sure to read the fine print. A card might give you a rate of 8.0%, but then revert to 21.0% after 90 days. Or the rate might rise dramatically if you are even one day late with a payment.

Use your card wisely. That means that you *pay it off, in full, every month*. It also means that you don't buy things you don't need. Books, gas for your car, plane tickets, food, and more are all reasonable. Just be sure that you have the cash on hand to pay the bill when it arrives.

Your credit score will be influenced by your payment history and the percentage of your available credit that you use. If your limit is $1,000 and your balance is $500, then your utilization rate is 50%. The goal is to keep it below 30%. Higher than 30% lowers your credit score.

Get a loan.

Any kind of loan will do, as long as the payments are reported to the major credit bureaus. So, you could obtain a car loan or even a loan against your savings account. In the case of the latter, the bank would freeze enough funds in your account to cover the amount of the loan. As you pay off the loan, the corresponding funds are released.

The nice thing is that you don't even have to come up with the money to pay back the loan. Use can use the loan itself. Just deposit the loan proceeds into another account and then pay back the loan with that money. You could even take out another loan with that money. Remember, this is about building your credit and not about spending money you do not have.

Secured loans are very easy to get since they're 100% backed by your own money. If you have to, borrow the money from your parents to start. Just be sure to make the payments on time. Then, when your loan is paid off, open another one, and repeat the process.

Creating great credit is quite easy; it just takes a little discipline and planning. If you can open 2 credit cards and use them appropriately, you'll be well on your way. If you can also get and pay off a couple of loans, you'll be shocked at how great your credit score is by the time you graduate.

Do the Work!

Remember, use your credit wisely. Don't let credit become a burden. If you realize you are digging yourself a credit pit, immediately turn around a clear it up as fast as you can.

NOW THAT YOU'RE A GRADUATE

Many people who graduated years ago probably wish they could go back and do a few things over. Most financial challenges can be avoided by doing things carefully.

Adopting healthy finance habits can make your future a lot easier and more enjoyable.

Keep in mind that unhealthy financial habits can create challenges that take years of work to fully recover. So, start your adulthood on a positive financial path from the beginning.

Consider incorporating these tips into your financial life as an adult:

Read a basic book on personal finance.

Good personal finance habits aren't complicated, but they're very important. They're also most effective when started early. Do your research either on the internet or by getting a good book on this topic and read all about it. Then actually follow the advice.

Create a simple budget.

Consider your salary and then put together a budget that makes sense for your income and expenses. Remember to set aside some money for savings and investing each month.

Avoid debt.

Poor spending habits can cause challenging situations quickly. Avoid saddling yourself with debt. A possible exception is taking out a loan to buy a home—own over rent. Debt, in general, is a dream killer because it takes years to resolve.

Reduce your current debt.

Few things feel better than being debt-free. Your debt is a barrier to fully enjoying your future. Set up a plan to end your debt. You'll be glad you did!

Create an emergency fund.

Start with the goal of setting aside three months of living expenses. If you should ever require it, you'll be prepared and grateful to have it.

Begin investing as soon as possible.

The greatest financial leverage young adults have is time. Even small investments can grow into incredible sums given enough time. Educate yourself about stocks, bonds, mutual funds, insurance products, and start today.

Take full advantage of tax-deferred retirement accounts.

It's hard to find a better deal than a 401(k) available through your employer. Between the matching, tax deductions and tax-deferred growth, you won't find a better investing deal around. Remember to investigate the different IRA offerings, too.

Leave your 401(k) alone.

Many young adults come up with a reason to dip into their retirement accounts, under the guise of having enough time to make up for it later. This is a huge mistake. You're better off doing without than having to raid your retirement funds.

Secure health insurance.

No country has higher medical costs than the US. Because of this, many bankruptcies are due to medical expenses. Illnesses and accidents happen, so be prepared. Everyone requires health insurance to mitigate this substantial risk.

Spend your money on worthwhile experiences.

You can't just save like a miser. Life is short, enjoy it. It's okay to spend some money on enjoyable experiences without being afraid. This is a big part of the reason you earn money in the first place. Make sure your budget includes money to play.

Avoid the many pitfalls of developing poor personal finance habits. Mistakes made at this point in your life are recoverable, but the entire experience can still be extremely challenging.

Do the Work!

Good habits ensure good outcomes. Your financial future can be great if you're willing to put a smart plan into action right now. There's no reason to repeat the mistakes of others.

Plan to implement the tips that apply to your life within 15-30 days and you'll find your financial life will have a minimal amount of drama and challenges. Avoiding mistakes is a huge part of being successful.

CONQUER YOUR STUDENT LOAN DEBT

College is expensive! Sixty percent of those who graduate from college with a bachelor's degree also graduate with around $26,000 worth of student loans. For those who go on to pursue a postgraduate degree, the debt can be significantly higher.

Luckily, there are some ways to reduce, and in some cases eliminate this debt.

Loan Forgiveness Programs

There are several programs you may want to consider that can eliminate part or all of those loans:

Volunteer for community service.

If you apply to the AmeriCorps program, you can help people in your community while also reducing your debt. The program will repay part of your loans based on your service.

The Peace Corps and Volunteers in Service to America also offer loan forgiveness programs.

Military service can help you pay for school.

If you enlist in the military before you start college, they can help you pay for your schooling.

There are some loan forgiveness programs available if you enlist after you've graduated. Speak to a military recruiter about a plan that could work for you.

The profession you choose may help you pay down your debt.

If you pursue a career in teaching or the healthcare field, speak to your employer or Human Resources Department about programs to reduce or pay off your debt from student loans.

Financial Hardship Programs

If you don't have a job, earn very little, or your loans are a large percentage of your earnings, one of these plans may be able to help:

Income Contingent Repayment Plan (ICRP).

This program applies specifically to Federal Direct loans that aren't PLUS loans.

ICRP bases the number of your monthly loan payments on how much money you earn. The payments can be as little as a few dollars per month. Even better, once you've made these small payments for twenty-five years, any debt remaining on the loan is forgiven.

Income Sensitive Repayment Plan (ISRP) for your FFEL loan.

The amount of the loan, your income, and the size of your family all determine how much you will need to pay each month.

The payments you make have to be at least enough to cover any interest that accrues, and the loan must be paid off within 10 years.

Income-Based Repayment Plan (IBRP).

This plan is available on both FFELs and Federal Direct loans. IBRP offers flexible payment options for twenty-five years. After this time, the rest of the loan is forgiven.

In order to qualify for this plan, you can't be in default on your loan payments.

Hardship Repayment Plan on Perkins Loans.

This plan has a minimum payment of $40/month. There are also extensions under certain circumstances, such as if you've been without work for a while or if you have a long illness.

More Programs -- No Financial Hardship

These options can also help you, even if you're not having hard times financially:

Loan consolidation.

Combine several high-interest loans into just one, lower-interest loan. This option allows you to utilize a lower interest rate and cut down on multiple payments.

Defer your student loans.

If you're experiencing economic hardship, a period of unemployment, or if you're going back to school, you may be allowed to defer your student loan payments until a later time.

Get a loan forbearance to give yourself more time to pay off the loan.

A forbearance is a temporary reduction in payments.

A lender may grant you a forbearance if you're unable to pay off your loan after a certain number of years. They may also grant a forbearance if your payments on your student loan are greater than 20% of the money you earn each month or if you run into a number of other unforeseen problems.

These tips and payment plans can help you manage and pay off your student loans. Consulting with a financial expert can bring to light additional ideas that can help, too.

A 5-STEP PLAN FOR DEALING WITH STUDENT LOANS

The nation's student loan debt is over $1 trillion and is not only larger than the country's collective credit card debt, but there are also 5 million ex-students that are delinquent with their payments.

Student loans are unique in that they're one of the few debts not discharged with bankruptcy. Only a federal judge can let you out of your obligation to pay, and they don't do that often.

The only reliable way to eliminate your student loans is to pay them off.

People frequently get into trouble with their student loans, and it makes getting a mortgage or a car loan much more difficult. While credit repair agencies can do a lot to help remove bad credit history attached to debts that are paid off, current debts are another story. A slip can haunt you for a long time. This process makes it easier to handle your student loans effectively:

Assess your situation.

Student loans can be confusing. You're likely to have more than one loan and those loans were probably made by different financial organizations. The company servicing the loan might be completely different from the one that provided the loan.

A great central source of information is the National Student Loan Data System www.nslds.ed.gov. This resource may provide all the important dates and other information about your loans, including the services.

However, private student loans are not covered in that data system. Your credit report can be a good way of tracking down the information regarding your private loans. Your college should also have the information you require.

Ensure your information is current.

For example, the address listed probably belongs to your parents. When you have your own address, you should change your information accordingly.

Update all the applicable information, including your email address and phone number. You want to know when there is an issue with your account.

Create a strategy for repayment.

Your options depend on whether your loans are federal or private.

Federal loans have very flexible repayment options. You can extend your payments out as far as 25 years. You can establish a plan with lower payments now and higher payments later on. Payments can even be a function of your income.

There can be other options for private loans, but they will vary, depending on who made the loan. Be sure to give them a call and see what other options are available.

Consider automatic payments.

Federal loan interest rates are reduced by 0.25% if you have your payments taken automatically out of your bank account. Similar deals are usually available with private loans. Either way, you'll never be late if the payments are taken out of your account automatically.

Be focused.

It would be wiser to put any extra funds towards higher interest rate debt. But if your student loans are your only real debt, then put some extra money toward the principal when possible. Debt is like a slow leak that keeps draining money away from you.

Consider a second job to rid yourself of those loans quicker. The interest rates are relatively low on student loans, but the payback period is long. The interest adds up over 10 years or more. Pull out a calculator and look at the cost.

Create a goal of making all of your payments on time. Create a second goal of paying your loan back early.

Do the Work!

Dealing with student debt is a big responsibility. It might even be a newly graduated student's first big responsibility. While making loan payments is never fun, it is a fact of life for most adults at one time or another. Get on top of the situation now, and the future will be much brighter.

HEALTHY CREDIT HABITS FOR BEGINNERS

You know that establishing and maintaining a solid credit rating is vital to your future financial success. The challenging thing about credit, though, is that it often seems impossible to increase and use credit unless you've already established good credit.

For young people who want to start on the right foot, beginning from scratch with no credit history can seem like an impossible task. But with the right strategies and responsible use of the tools available to you, you can establish solid credit in the early years of your adult life.

These strategies can help you get yourself off on the right foot and establish a solid credit rating, right off the bat.

Check your credit report.

In order to know where you're going, first, assess where you are. When you're first starting out, your credit file is probably sparse. However, with identity theft on the rise and other credit dangers lurking, be sure and check your credit first to make sure you are indeed starting from scratch.

Check your credit report often.

Check your credit file as often as possible. Federal law allows you to obtain a free copy of your credit report from each of the three major credit reporting bureaus once per year.

Monitor your credit report.

To continuously monitor your credit throughout the year, stagger your requests for these reports. That way, you'll quickly be alerted if something improper has been added to your credit file. Instead of requesting all reports at once, request one from a different bureau every four months. This will give you time to take action without a lot of undue pressure.

Pay your bills on time every month.

One of the most important factors that influence your credit score is your history of paying your bills on time. When you pay your bills by the due date every month, in the eyes of creditors, you're living within your means.

Get a recurring bill in your name.

Often, students will have regular monthly bills listed in a parent's name. However, if you receive a cell phone bill or other monthly recurring bills in your name and pay them in full every month, you'll establish yourself as a person who is responsible for handling financial matters.

Have someone you know put in a good name for you.

You can actually use someone else's good credit to establish your own solid reputation. You can do this by having that person cosign a loan for you or by becoming an authorized user on that person's credit cards.

Get a student credit card.

Often, college students can open credit cards more easily than others can. In fact, on many college campuses, you can find booths at student events that promote credit card sign-ups with cash prizes or other incentives.

Use these cards sparingly but regularly.

If you're obtaining credit cards mainly to increase your credit rating, you need to use the cards to experience the boost in your score. Make small monthly purchases with the cards and pay the balance in full each month.

Remember, though, that a credit card is not cash. Borrowing from a credit card means agreeing to pay much more than the purchase price if you don't pay it back on time. Avoid credit bondage. Be smart and make only small purchases that you can cover in full when the bill comes due each month.

Set up a monthly budget.

One of the most important factors in maintaining a solid credit rating for life is a lifestyle of wise financial decisions. When you list all of your income and expenses, you know the financial resources you have available to you. When you do, you're less likely to get yourself into a credit bind.

Do the Work!

Setting yourself up on solid financial footing early on in life sets the stage for a lifetime of fulfillment. Misuse of credit, however, can set the stage for a lifetime of bondage. Choose fulfillment by applying these strategies to establish a solid credit rating right off the bat. If you fall behind quickly make a plan to get back on track.

FINANCING OPTIONS FOR NEW VEHICLES

Most people look to purchase a new car in their twenties. Check out your financing options.

Paying upfront for a new vehicle is usually not an option. This is why most buyers use financing, including financing offered by car lots, banks, credit unions or online lenders. The financing option you choose will impact what kind of vehicle you can afford and how much you end up paying for the vehicle.

Shop around to find a financing option that's right for you.

Compare loans and different lenders to find one that is affordable and that will provide you with a good experience.

Typically, having a good credit score will make finding affordable financing easier. Consider applying for a loan via a bank, credit union, or online lender instead of choosing the financing option offered by the car dealership, as these institutions are usually more affordable as long as you have good credit.

Finding an affordable loan is also easier if you have a trade-in or a down payment so that you don't have to finance the entire cost.

Ideally, your trade-in or down payment should cover 15% to 20% of the cost of the new vehicle.

The main thing to look at when comparing financing options is the total amount of the loan. You can use online tools to compare rates offered in your area and get an idea of how much a loan will cost you.

Look at these items when comparing auto loans:

The APR or Annual Percentage Rate.

The APR will impact the total amount you end up paying for the loan and for your vehicle.

The duration of the loan.

A shorter loan means you can build up equity in the vehicle faster and end up spending less on fees and interest. A loan with a longer duration means your monthly payments will be lower.

Late payment fees.

Ideally, you shouldn't miss any loan payments, but you need to know how your balance will be affected if you do.

Monthly payments

Monthly payments are important because you want to find a loan that's a good fit for your budget.

Insurance premiums.

You should purchase enough insurance to cover the amount of the loan. Ensure you can afford the insurance premiums.

The reputation of the lender.

You'll have a more enjoyable loan experience if you borrow from a company that has a good reputation, offers good customer service, provides you with an easy way to make your payments, and doesn't make mistakes when processing payments.

The terms of the loan.

Read the terms of the loan carefully and look for additional fees, variable interest rates, and other details that weren't mentioned by the lender.

Even if the dealership encourages you to take the vehicle, avoid taking it off the car lot until you have financing figured out.

Some car lots will let you drive the vehicle and offer conditional financing, which means the terms of the loan, interest, and payments can change once you have the vehicle. Securing financing before you drive the vehicle allows you to be in control of what you end up paying.

Do the Work!

Following these tips will give you a more pleasing loan experience so you can spend your time enjoying your new car.

BUYING VS. LEASING A CAR

Leasing a car has tempted all of us from time to time. You see the TV commercial for a car that's normally out of reach, but with a lease, the payments seem pretty reasonable. It seems too good to be true, but, is it? Does it make good financial sense to lease a vehicle that you can't afford to buy?

Consider these points:

Qualification: Not only do leases have lower payments, they are also easier to obtain than an automobile loan. Leases frequently have low or even no down payment. If you're short on cash and your credit is a little shaky, a lease might make sense.

Best Lease Term: most experts believe that a 3-year leases are the best leases for the lessee.

Extra Expenses: Insurance rates can be higher for leased vehicles. There are also additional fees that can accumulate that come due when you turn in the vehicle.

Mileage Limits: You will pay a cost per mile charge above and beyond your mileage allotment. If you drive a lot, a lease might not be the best choice. Be sure to negotiate the mileage you need before you sign the lease.

How long do you want to keep your car?

- If you only plan to keep a car for 5 years or less, leasing is generally a better alternative.
- If you prefer keeping a car longer than 5 years, purchasing is generally the best option. Consider that the insurance gets lower over the age of the car.

Eventually the car is paid off. And while you might not have a lot of equity, you can sell the car and get something for it.
- A lease potentially has a down payment every 3 years (assuming a 3-year lease). You also have a monthly payment that never ends.
- Over a 10-ear period, leasing will cost about 50% more than buying a car, assuming the same model cars are leased or owned. Purchasing also results in having some equity, further lowering the cost of ownership.

Do the Work!

As a general rule, if you want to drive a new car and get a new car every few years, leasing makes the most sense. If you're going to keep a car for a longer period of time, buying is much less expensive.

BEFORE YOU COSIGN ON A LOAN - READ THIS!

Have your adult children asked you to cosign a loan with them? Especially if this is their first loan, the financial institution is likely to ask them for a cosigner, such as their parents. However, cosigning a loan with anyone carries responsibilities.

It's crucial for your own financial health to understand what your part in the loan could amount to.

If you're thinking about becoming a cosigner, consider these tips:

Evaluate why you want to cosign.

If you're cosigning a loan out of guilt or an obligation, then these aren't the best circumstances for serious financial decisions.

You may be tempted to help a family member or friend, but cosigning a loan is a big responsibility. If this person defaults on the loan, then you may be responsible for the entire amount.

You're putting the relationship at risk by signing a loan because things may not turn out the way you expect.

Understand the default consequences.

If the person who is asking you to cosign can't make the payments, then you become responsible. The lender can go after you and demand the payments plus interest and fees.

In addition to being responsible for the payments, your credit scores will be affected by the default.

You may have trouble getting future loans because of cosigning on a loan that defaults.

Understand the issues of release.

Although many loans have the option of releasing the cosigner after a period, the reality is different.

You may find that you can't be released from the loan, and you may be stuck as a cosigner for the entire term. Lenders don't like to release cosigners because it increases their risk.

Get alerts about the loan.

As a cosigner, you have the right to receive alerts about the loan. You can sign up for alerts that go to your email or phone. These loan alerts will notify you of any changes and issues.

Consider a separate account with automatic payments.

You should have access to this account, so you can monitor payments.

Set up guidelines.

How will you handle a default on the loan you cosigned?

Before a tragedy occurs, you may want to discuss guidelines for defaulting. Your relationship is at stake, so be careful with your discussion.

You may want to set up a rule that the person who is getting the loan notifies you before he or she can't make a payment. This keeps you involved and prevents your credit from being hurt.

You may also want to discuss the consequences of defaulting before it occurs.

Understand the collateral clause.

If the loan requires collateral, are you prepared to handle a default?

If the loan goes into default, then you may lose your collateral. You could permanently lose the home, property, car, or other items you listed as collateral.

Get copies of all the documents.

The lender is responsible for giving the borrower all the paperwork. However, as a cosigner, you may not get a copy. It's crucial to ask the borrower to share the documents with you.

Inspect the documents yourself before you sign anything.

Understand the collection process.

Did you know that the lender could go after you *before* going after the borrower in a collection process? If you cosign on a loan, this is one reason that you want to ensure the payments are always current.

Do the Work!

Cosigning a loan is a large financial responsibility with serious consequences. Ensure you understand all the terms of the loan -- and your responsibilities -- before getting involved.

MARRIAGE AND MONEY GOALS

Getting married is an important step in your life. Money and financial matters might be the furthest things from your mind right now, but this topic is crucial to a bright and secure future together. As newlyweds, you need to address your financial life together and make a plan that works for you both.

Talking about money early in a marriage is important because it allows you to start on the right track and it will help you avoid conflicts and stress in the years to come. Making money talks a habit will make your family stronger and help you prepare for any kind of crisis that could arise in the future.

If you are hoping to start a family or buy a house, you will need to talk about finances with your partner.

Your goals and priorities probably changed when you got married. Discussing long-term goals is important because these goals will help you pick a general direction for your life and finances. You might set some long-term goals such as buying a home, having children, or maybe launching a family business.

A lot of young couples create some clear long-term goals but fail to talk about short-term goals. The larger picture, which probably includes buying a home and starting a family, is important, but there are some priorities you can set for the more immediate future that support your long-term goals and help make them possible.

You will need to consider your important short-term goals and priorities.

Save money for emergencies.

An emergency fund will ensure that you have money to cover insurance deductibles and other emergencies. Create a joint savings account and put a portion of your paychecks aside every month.

Think about upgrading your insurance.

You might find that you need more extensive health insurance coverage before you have a baby. Getting married also changes your needs for auto or home insurance.

Buy a life insurance policy.

This is especially important if one spouse provides for the other. A lot of young couples feel that life insurance is not a priority, but now is the perfect time to secure a low rate.

Manage your debt.

Do you have student loans or other debts? Getting married means that your debts are now combined. Discuss how much money you owe and how the payments will be made.

Talk about living arrangements.

If you've been living together for a while, discussing living arrangements isn't necessary. However, if you're moving in together for the first time, finding an affordable place will definitely be a priority.

Discuss your career goals.

Talking about your career goals early in your marriage will give you an idea of the kind of income you can expect to earn. You can make plans together for both of you to further your careers or take career breaks as needed.

Your credit is another crucial matter.

Check your credit reports and plan how you can raise your credit scores together.

Do the Work!

It may be tempting to skip these serious topics, especially as you realize you and your new partner do not have the same thoughts or beliefs. Take it slow. Schedule time to address at least one topic each week. Most important, do not give up and think things will just work out on their own.

MERGING YOUR FINANCES AFTER MARRIAGE

How do you and your spouse want to combine your finances? Do you want to maintain some separate accounts? Even though you're married now, there are many variations of combined and separate accounts that you could choose from.

Consider together where your independence ends, and your interdependence begins.

Open a joint checking and savings account.

This will make managing your finances easier and having joint bank accounts is a good way to start communicating more about money matters. You can still have separate accounts, too, but the joint accounts will provide an opportune way to handle joint expenses.

Figure out how getting married will affect your taxes.

You have the option of filing jointly or separately. Filing separately sometimes makes sense, for example, when a spouse's tax return can be confiscated to cover child support payments or other obligations.

Add your spouse's name to your insurance policies or purchase new coverage together.

You should be able to get a better rate as a married couple.

Talk about your debt.

Getting married means that you become responsible for some of your spouse's debt, such as student loans. Using your joint account to make payments makes sense once you both become responsible for this type of debt.

Consider getting a joint credit card.

You can also add your spouse to an existing credit line.

Add your spouse as a beneficiary.

If you have a will, life insurance, or any other similar financial product, you may want to change your beneficiary designations or add your spouse as a beneficiary.

Talk about your lifestyle.

Now that your finances are merged, figure out a budget, and adopt a lifestyle that corresponds to what you can afford.

Do the Work!

If both of you do not already have a healthy financial lifestyle, it may take time to set the goals, guidelines, and boundaries for how you will handle your finances moving forward. It is important to give each person the freedom they need while still working together with short and long-term goals.

WHAT ABOUT YOUR MARRIAGE CREDIT?

Most young couples haven't had the time to work on raising their credit scores, might have a limited credit history, or might have adopted some bad habits when it comes to using credit cards or paying bills on time. Raising your credit score will make obtaining financing for your big projects, like getting a house, easier.

Getting married doesn't mean that your credit histories merge.

Since a credit score is tied to an individual's social security number, you and your spouse will have separate scores and credit histories. The best way to raise both credit scores is to open a joint credit account.

However, joint credit accounts are not always easy to obtain, since most credit card companies will not approve you unless you meet some requirements. Opening a joint credit line could be a goal for the long-term.

Meanwhile, you can add your spouse to an existing credit line as an authorized user. The spouse who is added as an authorized user isn't legally responsible for the debt, but the history on this credit line will impact their credit score. So, a credit line with a history of late payments could have a negative impact on the credit score of the authorized user.

Some couples make the mistake of opening all their credit lines in one spouse's name. These credit lines will help only one spouse build their credit history and improve their credit score as long as they make payments on time and carry a reasonable balance from one month to the next.

It might be best to open two different credit lines so that both spouses can build a positive credit history.

Having two strong credit scores will definitely make things easier for you once you need to finance a large purchase like a new car or a home.

Do the Work!

Communication is crucial when it comes to managing credit and debt. Talk to your spouse about any credit lines and debts that exist prior to the marriage, be upfront about how much you charge to your credit cards, and agree on how the monthly payments will be made.

CREATE A NEW-LYWED BUDGET

Newlyweds often face the same issues regarding budgeting. For starters, a lot of couples spend too much on their wedding, which can lead to some difficulties as they begin their life together while having to pay for these expenses.

The other common issue is that talking about money and budgeting without fighting is not always easy.

You may find as you begin this process that one of you might be spending too much or not taking responsibility for helping out with paying bills.

Regardless of your situation, remember that communication is very important and follow these steps to create a budget that works for you:

Figure out how much you're earning as a couple and list your sources of income.

Ask yourselves how your income is likely to change in the near future and plan accordingly.

Assess your recurring and flexible expenses.

Make a list of all the bills you have to pay on a monthly basis and calculate how much you usually spend on flexible expenses such as groceries and entertainment.

Establish financial priorities.

Putting some money aside for an emergency fund or making your student loan payments are examples of priorities you might want to set.

Talk about impulse spending.

It's very easy to find yourself carried away and to overspend on fun activities and entertainment. Establish a weekly budget for your activities and look for inexpensive things to do together to save money.

Review your budget regularly.

Schedule weekly or monthly money talks to go over your budget and make improvements.

Set some goals as a couple and some individual goals as well.

For instance, one spouse might want to work on reducing their impulse spending while another might have a challenge with paying bills on time.

Find ways to cut down on your expenses.

You might want to think about switching to a vehicle that is more affordable in terms of insurance and gas, transferring your credit card balance to a more affordable one, cooking more meals at home, or making other changes to your lifestyle.

Saving should be an important part of your budget.

Both an emergency fund and long-term savings are important.

Do the Work!

Sticking to your budget will be easier if you put it in writing or use an app or another tool to track your spending and set reminders to pay bills. Find a way to stay on the right track and remember that you'll usually enjoy better results when both spouses are involved in the budget creation process and in keeping track of expenses.

ESSENTIAL MARRIAGE MONEY DISCUSSIONS

Getting married is the first of many important steps you will take together. When you plan together, it makes it easier to be financially stable in the future and able to achieve your goals together.

When you are about to be newly married, there are more issues than just making sure you have a balanced budget.

Establish a budget for your wedding and honeymoon.

Ask for help from your families, avoid overspending on things you don't really need, and ask for gifts that will help you save money if you decide to create a registry.

Which items will you purchase for your new place if you're just moving in together?

Establish a budget for appliances, furniture, and other items you might need.

Are you thinking about having children soon?

Raising a baby is easier if you already have some money put aside for medical bills, diapers, baby clothes, and other baby supplies.

Credit cards.

Agree on what credit cards will be used for and where the money for credit card payments will come from.

Do you wish to purchase a house soon?

Make a plan to save for your down payment.

Make plans for retirement.

Talking about retiring can seem premature, but making plans now makes sense since you will have plenty of time to save and make your money work for you.

Investments.

Investing your money means taking risks, but this is the best way to improve your financial situation over time. Agree on the kind of investments you're both comfortable with and plan a workable investing schedule.

Borrowing money is another important topic.

Ask yourselves under which circumstances you would consider borrowing money and how you would manage this debt.

Do the Work!

These topics can be scary, especially when you start finding differences. It is critical that you are honest and share openly your thoughts, beliefs, and needs.

COMMON COUPLE MISTAKES TO AVOID

You might feel that you know enough about money and how to manage it as a couple, but this doesn't mean you won't make mistakes. In fact, young couples tend to make the same mistakes.

Being aware of the most common mistakes will help you avoid stress and achieve your goals.

Avoiding money discussions before you get married.

It's important to know about each other's spending and saving habits if you're planning a life together. Equally as important are discussions about your financial goals, both individually and as a couple.

Not talking about money once you're married.

A lot of couples avoid the topic altogether because they cannot talk about money without arguing, which makes adopting good financial habits difficult.

Expecting things to remain the same after you get married.

Among other things, getting married also means you might become responsible for some of your spouse's debts or that you'll have a common budget to plan together.

A lot of young couples feel that the next milestone in their lives is still far away.

The next milestone, such as having a child or buying a home, will come a lot faster than you think, and making plans for the future will help you prepare for these milestones.

Hiding financial information, especially about debt.

Talking openly about your finances will enable you to find solutions together for any challenges and make concrete plans to deal wisely and effectively with any situation.

Overspending on your wedding.

Many want to celebrate this event in a grand way but sticking to a budget will help you enjoy a more secure start together.

Failing to acknowledge money challenges.

You might be tempted to avoid bringing up an issue such as your spouse's overspending in order to avoid a fight. However, challenges like debt or overspending only become worse if you ignore them.

Not understanding or acknowledging your differences.

Money is perceived differently from one culture or background to another. There might be some differences in how you spend money, how you feel about handling financial issues, and expectations for your lifestyle.

Trying too hard to share responsibilities equally.

Each couple has his or her strengths and weaknesses. Find between you a way to manage your finances that works for you, even if the result isn't a 50/50 partnership.

Assuming that you can manage all your financial challenges yourself.

If you are in over your head, seek help from relatives, friends, or a financial advisor.

Do the Work!

Starting a life together is a very exciting time! Don't let bad financial habits or a lack of knowledge regarding money rob you of your dreams. Be proactive! Adopt positive financial habits and take responsibility as a couple for your financial situation. Planning for a bright financial future together will benefit you for the rest of your life.

HELPFUL MONEY TIPS TO HEED FOR NEWLYWEDS

Getting married is a happy and exciting time. One of the issues that can quickly put a damper on the positive energy, though, is money. Financial issues can create a lot of stress and even animosity. Ideally, you've already had a lot of communication regarding your finances. If you haven't, a little prevention isn't a bad idea.

It can be much nicer to discuss the topic of money before it becomes necessary and tensions are high. Be proactive.

Agree on a set of financial rules and goals.

Work together to establish a few rules around your finances. Will you pay your own, previously established debts? Will bills be split evenly, or will the person with the greater salary pay more?

Often, when you share a vision of the future, you can easily see eye to eye.

Create two wills.

You'll both need a will. If you already have one, speak with an attorney and have it modified. Ensure that you're taking care of each other.

Put all your financial cards on the table.

Do you have a credit card with a $20,000 balance you've kept from your significant other? Will it take 20 years to pay off your student loans? Let your spouse know what's going on and expect them to do the same.

Control your expenses.

Just because you're splitting the rent and the utilities it doesn't mean you should spend your excess funds foolishly.

It is time to take advantage of your extra cash and maximize your contributions to your retirement accounts. Invest rather than spend whenever you can. You might even consider saving one salary and living on the other.

Talk about extended family financial issues.

If your brother wants to borrow $1,000, how will you handle that as a couple? If your spouse's mom needs a new roof, will you chip in? Your respective families may handle these matters very differently. Have a conversation.

Update your beneficiaries.

You'll probably want to list your spouse on your life insurance, retirement accounts, and several other accounts and policies.

Create a budget together.

You'll find out a lot about your partner's spending habits by creating a budget together. A budget sets limits and expectations. An effective budget is an important part of a bright financial future.

Decide on a banking structure.

One joint account or two separate accounts? Maybe you prefer a mixture of joint and separate accounts. There is no right answer, just be sure you're both on the same page.

Choose one person to pay the bills and schedule regular meetings to go over bills.

Choose one person to be responsible for paying all the bills. Have a weekly meeting to go over the bills and ensure they're all being paid on time.

Decide on a limit for purchases that don't require collaboration.

Your spouse probably won't mind if you stop on the way home from work and purchase a candy bar without a family meeting. But stop and buy a $20,000 bass boat and you might create a little friction.

Do the Work!

Discussing your finances together while you're still newlyweds can be an excellent way to avoid unnecessary drama. It might not be romantic, but it is important. You can talk about it now or wait until later. Doing it now will be more enjoyable.

EXPECTING THE STORK

A new baby on the way is always an exciting and celebratory time. However, a baby can also be a huge financial challenge, especially if you don't take the appropriate steps to prepare yourself. Keep these tips in mind when preparing your finances for the new arrival.

You can plan for New Baby Expenses as easily as you can plan for every great adventure in your life.

Medical bills

Find out in advance what medical bills you're likely to incur. This would include prenatal, delivery, and postnatal expenses. Do you have insurance? How much will it pay? If you don't have insurance and have low income, your state has programs that will minimize the expense.

Depending on your insurance situation, you may want to have additional funds set aside for unforeseen medical issues.

Baby items

Here we're talking about things like car seats, strollers, changing tables, cribs, bottles, clothes, diapers (2,700 just the first year!), rocking chair, swing, dresser, baby monitor, and more. Go out to your local store and price these items.

If you are going to breast-feed, you may need a breast pump if you plan on ever leaving the house without the baby. If you're not breastfeeding, you'll need bottles, nipples, and formula.

Do you need daycare or a babysitter? Call around to compare costs or ask a neighbor or friend what the going rate is for daycare in your area.

Borrow and buy used

You can lower your cost by borrowing items or buying used. Babies outgrow things long before they wear them out. You shouldn't have any problem finding quality used baby clothes, toys, and furniture. There are even stores that specialize in used baby items. You can also check on resale platforms like Craig's List, Offer-Up, and FaceBook Market. These used items can be much less expensive than the new stuff.

Tell everyone you know about your happy news. You'll almost certainly be offered plenty of baby-related items that people have hung on to for this very reason, to share with someone they love.

Wait for gifts

People can go crazy giving gifts when a baby is involved. You never know what you surprises you have in store. Wait until the dust settles before you start making purchases. The gifts you receive can be a real financial boon. Be patient so you don't end up with two of the same things.

Remember that you don't need everything

Your baby doesn't require every gadget under the sun to be safe and happy. Ask the mothers you know what they consider to be the most important items.

Start saving now

You can never start saving too soon. Now is the time to eliminate all those things and services that you don't really need. Sit down and look at your monthly bills and find ways you can cut back. Reduce your expenses as much as you need to so you can save enough money to be as comfortable as possible when the baby arrives.

Review your life insurance and will

Sit down with the appropriate expert to ensure you have the proper insurance coverage when the baby arrives. Also, be certain that your will is up to date.

Do the Work!

Financial preparations are just as important as picking out the perfect name. Pacing yourself and addressing all of these issues prior to the birth of your bundle of joy can make the first year after childbirth less challenging.

PREPARE FOR YOUR ROARING 20'S AND 30'S

There are many advantages to being in your 20s and early 30s. The decisions you make now have a tremendous amount of influence over your future. Make the effort to ensure that you're making wise choices.

You can build a foundation to ensure your financial success for a lifetime. The earlier you can take advantage of these strategies, the better!

Create an emergency fund.

It only takes one minor financial catastrophe to affect your finances for many years. A $1,000 car repair can cause more challenges than you think. You might have to max out your credit card, which negatively affects your credit score. The additional monthly payment can make you late for other payments.

Save a few months of living expenses, and you'll be able to handle nearly anything.

Begin saving for retirement.

Time really is on your side. You don't have to save much each month to retire in style if you start early enough.

Waiting 7 years will cut your eventual nest egg in half. Waiting 14 years will cut it by 75%. Start right way!

Build a positive credit history.

If you ever want to purchase a car, home, or receive any other type of conventional financing, your credit history is important. Your credit score can affect many things, including purchasing a cell phone plan or getting a job.

Responsible use of a credit card or two is the easiest way to accomplish this. A small loan from your bank is another simple option.

Avoid debt.

Dealing with debt is akin to climbing a mountain with rocks in your backpack. Avoid purchasing items you can't afford. Few stresses match the feeling of being heavily in debt. Even very wealthy people have accumulated more debt than they could manage.

Consider a used car.

A new car may seem like a mandatory purchase, but new cars are considerably more expensive than those just a few years old. Remember to avoid taking on too much debt.

Examine your online presence.

Your employment can be affected by your online presence. Look at all of your social media accounts and determine if your employer would be impressed.

Make sure what you share gives the impression that you're an intelligent, mature adult.

Start a second income.

One of the best ways to ensure that you always have an income is to have more than one income stream. It could be a second job or a small online business. This is a great opportunity to increase your savings while being prepared for job challenges.

Get insured.

Protect yourself and your possessions. At the very least, have renter's insurance to cover your possessions and health insurance to protect against catastrophic medical bills. Other types of insurance may also apply. It can worthwhile to contact an insurance professional.

Take advantage of your employer.

Many employers offer many benefits. Ensure you're getting all you can out of them. These can include life insurance, savings plans, 401(k) matching, and a host of other benefits. Read your employee handbook and talk to your HR department.

Consider waiting to start a family until you're financially stable.

Getting married is easy but staying married can be difficult. The failure to stay married can create many financial challenges, especially if you have kids. Even in secure marriages, children are expensive. When you're 30, you won't recognize your 22-year old self. There's no hurry. Make a wise decision that is right for you.

Do the Work!

This age group is perhaps the most influential period of your financial life. Any mistakes can potentially affect your financial future for decades. Getting off to a good start is the best way to ensure a positive financial future. You also have tremendous financial freedom. Use that freedom to build a strong financial foundation.

CHALLENGES FOR YOUR ROARING 20'S AND 30'S

Millennials have unique challenges, including a soft economy with no end in sight. Entry-level jobs are also of much lower quality today. It's more likely that a recent graduate will be forced to endure a minimum wage internship than start at a healthy salary. Being a young adult is not easy.

Consider these financial issues and see how you can resolve them.

A lack of preparation for financial emergencies.

Everyone needs to have an emergency fund. While the lack of an emergency fund is common within every age group, millennials are especially likely to not have any money set aside for emergencies.

Strive to set aside 3 months of living expenses and you'll be okay. Set aside 6 months and you will be prepared for most financial emergencies. Six months gives you enough time to formulate a new, effective plan.

Failing to take advantage of 401(k) matching.

If your employer offers 401(k) matching, take advantage of it. Not only will your money work for you, but your employer is giving you the same amount as what you're investing. Considering future growth, your employer could be handing you a fortune -- for free!

Becoming a homeowner.

The rate of homeownership by younger adults continues to decline with each passing year. Before signing that expensive lease in the fancy apartment complex, think about the future. Downsizing today can mean homeownership in the future.

Becoming debt-free.

Younger adults have more issues with debt than any other generation. The high cost of a college education and medical care are two of the primary culprits. Irresponsible use of credit cards plagues every age group. You can easily accumulate debt quickly.

Eliminating debt can take years. Make a plan to deal aggressively with your debt. Get started today for a brighter tomorrow.

A failure to plan ahead.

Your 20's and 30's are an expensive time. This is when most young adults marry, go on a honeymoon, and have children.

Few can accommodate these expenses without a significant amount of planning and preparation. Avoid waiting until the last minute to prepare for your upcoming expenses.

Not choosing a college major with employment in mind.

College has never been more expensive. While majoring in art history or the trombone might sound intriguing, there are few employment opportunities within these fields. Consider the future when planning your college years.

A lack of health insurance.

You may be at the healthiest point in your life, but serious illnesses and accidents can happen to anyone. It may be expensive, but health insurance is necessary. Even a plan with a high deductible is better than nothing and will protect your wallet from a major health issue that has a cost of $100K or more.

A failure to save for retirement.

The common thought is you have plenty of time in the future to save for retirement. All those 65+ year-old's you see working in fast food and retail thought the same thing.

Get in the saving habit early in your career. Over time, your investments will grow to fund an enjoyable retirement. Start early enough and you might be able to retire years early, too!

Failing to create and follow a budget.

Whether you earn minimum wage or $1 million per year, you need a budget. A budget is a great way to limit your spending and make yourself aware of your financial situation on a monthly basis.

A lack of education.

It would be difficult to find a topic covered more thoroughly than personal finance. Buy a popular finance book or two. Try books on budgeting, saving money on taxes, or making the most of your investments. All the information you need is readily available.

Do the Work!

Millennials face many financial hurdles that grow taller each year. Now is the time to create a budget, plan for the future, and embrace a little austerity. Suffering a little today can result in a bright future. Taking it easy today ensures a challenging future. The choice is yours.

ARE YOU READY FOR YOUR BLAZING 40'S?

Your 40s can be a challenging financial time. However, you can take steps to avoid the common money mistakes that create challenges with your personal finances.

It's time to set your site on retirement while still working hard.

Plan with liquidity in mind.

How much of your portfolio is accessible in liquid assets? Liquid assets refer to cash or investments that can be easily turned into cash.

During an emergency, you may need fast access to cash. In your 40s, emergencies can include a family member's unexpected trip to a doctor that isn't covered by insurance. They can also include an unexpected breakdown at home or at work. How will you pay for these items?

You want to avoid being in a financial situation that forces you to sell your belongings or take out loans because you need cash. Evaluate your portfolio and ensure you have enough cash to handle a variety of emergencies.

Balance your payments.

You need to have a balance of payments, so you're not spending too much in one area. Trying to pay off the entire mortgage too soon is a common money mistake. It's tempting to put extra payments toward the house, but other areas may need to be examined.

Are you trying to pay off your mortgage while a pile of credit card bills sits on your desk? Although it feels good to own your home, paying off the mortgage shouldn't be the only goal.

Extra mortgage payments can wait in many instances, so you can focus on higher interest debt such as credit cards, student loans, and other types of loans. In addition, it's important to be contributing to your retirement during your 40s so you give your money time to grow. Also, consider your children's college savings funds.

Focus on retirement.

In your 40s, it's easy to expect that you can continue to work for several more decades before retirement. However, your retirement savings need to be a priority.

Retirement savings work best as a long-term goal. Your 40s are an ideal time to build your investments.

You may want to avoid the common money mistake of taking out cash from your retirement savings. In addition to penalties and fees, you're reducing the portfolio's ability to grow.

If you take money out of your retirement funds, you may also face large penalties from both the federal and state government during tax time.

Consider your job security.

During your 40s, it's easy to become complacent about your job.

Pay attention to your company's culture and consider job security. Are you watching older workers being pushed out for the younger generation? Are older workers in the same field struggling to find replacement jobs?

Job security can affect every aspect of your financial life. It's important to consider your income. Do you expect it to rise, or is it at a stable level? In your 40s, you may expect income to continue to rise, but experts share that this may not always be the case. Be wise and avoid the money mistake of spending too much because of hopes for a raise.

Do the Work!

If you're in your 40s, be aware of these common money mistakes and protect your financial future. This is a perfect time to strengthen your financial foundation at home and at work.

HELP YOUR CHILDREN BUILD THEIR CREDIT

It's never too early to start building credit. If your child is in college, now is a perfect time. Your child can land a dream job, have saved several thousand dollars, but still, be unable to obtain a loan for a car or a house without a solid credit history.

There are many ways to help your child build credit.

A few options cost a little money, at least in the short-term. Other options are free but carry more risk. Regardless of your situation, there are things you can do to help your child.

Assist your child to create a good credit history:

Get your child a secured credit card.

A secured credit card appears to be just like any other credit card with one key difference: A deposit has been paid to open the account. The available credit limit is no more than the amount of the deposit.

- While normal payments still have to be made, the bank offering the card is 100% covered. If your child fails to make the payment, the money is taken from the deposit.
- In time, many banks will allow a secured credit card to be converted to a conventional credit card.
- The deposit is returned when the card is canceled. Keep in mind that these cards are often loaded with fees, making them expensive to use.

Cosign a loan.

Allow your child to take out a small loan with your support. The amount doesn't have to be large, even a few hundred dollars is enough to start building a solid credit history. Just ensure that the loan is getting paid. It's not a bad idea to keep the proceeds from the loan in your own account and make the payments yourself.

Use a secured loan.

Your child can use a savings account as collateral for a loan. Banks love this type of loan because they're 100% covered whether the borrower makes the payments or not. The funds in the savings account are released as the loan is paid off.

These loans are easy to acquire and work as well as any other means of building your child's credit.

Add your child as an authorized user on your credit card account.

This is easy to do, too. A quick call to the issuing company is all you need to do. Your child will receive their own card with their name on it. Any charges they make will appear on your bill. This is good news since you'll be aware of their spending habits.

Remember that the account is still your responsibility. If your college student flies off to Cabo for a wild weekend, you're still as legally as responsible as your child for the bill.

Co-sign a credit card.

Your child will have their own card, and you won't receive the bills. How much do you trust your kid? Be careful.

As a co-signer, any failure on the part of your child will affect you, too. You can be held responsible for the bill, and your credit rating can be harmed, too. This is the riskiest option for a parent.

Do the Work!

It's important to build a credit history before you need it. If you've ever had poor credit, you know how challenging it can be. It can limit your options. Naturally, you want to give your child a solid financial start by beginning the process of establishing credit before they complete high school. Investigate all the available options and put a plan in place.

GETTING MARRIED...FINALLY

As a mature couple, are you considering marriage? There are over 1,000 tax breaks available to married couples that are unavailable to those simply living together. However, it's not just about the tax breaks. There are many financial advantages and disadvantages to both marriage and cohabitation. This issue requires a tremendous amount of research and expert advice.

There are several areas to consider:

- Taxes: You could pay less or more.
- Benefits especially benefit acquired through a previous marriage: In most cases, these benefits are lost.
- College financial aid for any children: you could be in better or worse shape after a new marriage.
- Estate issues: Complicated.

Be sure to weigh the advantages and disadvantages before taking this step at this stage of your life.

Consider these ADVANTAGES of getting married:

Married couples often pay less in taxes.

Unless your income is significant, you'll pay less in taxes if you're married. However, if your income is at the upper end you can actually pay more in taxes.

Marriage may help your child qualify for financial aid.

Getting married increases your household size by at least one. If the increase in household income is minimal, it can help your child qualify for additional aid.

Your estate can be affected, positively or negatively, depending on your location.

In a few states, your spouse is entitled to a portion of your estate, regardless of any will or agreement you have with your spouse.

Your state of mind and comfort can be affected, positively or negatively, depending on your beliefs.

Of course, there are emotional and religious advantages to marriage, too. Depending on your community and support, marriage could change your social standing and how much support your community gives your family.

These are just a few of the many advantages of marriage. Further research is necessary to understand all the implications.

Now, consider these financial DISADVANTAGES of getting married:

Social security benefits can be negatively impacted.

If you're divorced, your social security benefits may be dependent on your ex's past earnings. This most often affects women who stayed home to raise children. Remarrying could result in the loss of those benefits.

If you're a widow or widower and remarry before the age of 60, you lose any social security survivor benefits. You can, however, reinstate those benefits if your second spouse dies or the marriage ends in divorce.

Alimony payments usually stop after remarriage.

Are either of you on the receiving end of a lucrative alimony agreement? In most cases, alimony payments are eliminated in the event of a new marriage unless a prior arrangement addressed this issue specifically.

Pension benefits and annuity payments can also be impacted.

Spouses of police officers and firefighters are often paid through annuities. These benefits can be lost due to remarriage. Most pension benefits are lost when the surviving spouse remarries.

Your child's ability to receive financial aid can be affected.

The household income is used to determine eligibility for financial aid. The non-parent spouse's income is included in that calculation.

Costs related to health care can be a burden on the healthy spouse.

Remember that both spouses are responsible for any medical bills, including long-term care. Your spouse's bills could wreak havoc on your personal finances, including assets you intended to gift to your children.

You can easily see that the issue isn't simple. Getting married can have both positive and negative implications.

Do the Work!

The decision between marriage and cohabitation is very complicated. Examine all the potential changes in your finances so you can make the decision that works best for you. Consulting a tax expert is a smart step. An attorney may also be needed, especially if there was a prior divorce for either partner.

From a purely financial perspective, a marriage later in life can have far-reaching consequences. Ensure that you're making a wise decision. Do your research and seek the professional advice you need.

THE END IS IN SIGHT

Eventually, you will be ready for your retirement. Whether you can pull it off in your 40's or you decide to wait until your 70's, a good plan makes all the difference.

What do you imagine when you think of your retirement? Perhaps you picture retirement like a long vacation: you'll play golf, travel, or enjoy leisurely days by the pool. With good financial health, such a picture is entirely possible -- as long as you take action to turn those pleasant dreams into reality!

However, a picturesque, happy retirement can be cut short if you run out of money. Taxes, market fluctuations, inflation, and unexpected living expenses can erode your nest egg faster than you ever thought possible.

And what if you live to be 107? Will your retirement funds last that long?

Insurance Companies Don't Just Sell Insurance

Even though you plan for retirement mentally, you will have to find hands-on vehicles that can carry you to that dream and further. You can incorporate into your plan Financial Vehicles like:

- Insurance Strategies
- Ways to protect your assets from the tax man
- Creating a Tax-Advantaged Retirement Income You Can't Outlive
- Set up an income plan that ensures you'll never run out of money no matter how long you live!

Among your options, you can now enjoy the higher yields of a variety of stock market investments along with tax-free or tax-deferred gains. Plus, you can find these perks all within venues that carry the added security of guaranteed death benefits or income for life -- benefits that are lacking in traditional retirement plans.

Whether you're just getting started in the workforce or preparing to retire, there are tactics you can use now to make strategic investments in life insurance, annuities, or both.

Do the Work!

Let's break these down and give you some details for each so you can start making strong financial decisions. Pull out your pencil and paper and make notes about each product's pros and cons.

LIFE INSURANCE INVESTING

When you think of life insurance, you might not think about it as an investment because, with many policies, you are given insurance. If you die while the policy is in force, your beneficiary gets the death benefit. This type of insurance is called term insurance. It provides security for your family if you should die.

However, there are also various permanent policies that build up cash value. This is money you can take out and spend while you're alive. You don't have to wait until you die to receive money from the insurance company.

It can be a good strategy to buy life insurance and save for the future with the same contract.

There are several types of permanent life insurance policies for different investment goals:

Whole Life. The oldest one is called whole life insurance. This is what originally started the trend of permanent policies. Part of your premium is used to pay for your life insurance and the rest of it builds cash value.

- With whole life insurance you build up cash as you pay your monthly premium, and it's kind of like a bank account. Each month the life insurance company will pay a fixed interest rate on your money, and it will grow over time.
- With whole life, your premium stays the same over the life of the policy.

Universal life. Similar to whole life, universal life pays a guaranteed interest rate, but it changes based on the market rates.

Can be riskier, because some months you'll make more than whole life and some months you'll make less, but it still grows over time and you don't have to manage it. · The other thing with universal life is you can change the amount you pay each month, so there's more flexibility.

Variable life. This type of insurance is like combining a brokerage account with your life insurance.

- When you put money in variable life, you can use it to buy stocks, bonds, and other investments within the policy. You also have a choice in how to manage your investments.
- That means you can make more money, but it also means you can lose money, so it can be a bigger risk.

Guarantees

All of these policies have a death benefit, which is guaranteed to a point. You'll find these additional guarantees:

Whole life. Besides a set, guaranteed death benefit, with the whole life policy, the rate of return is also guaranteed. So, you also know what you're going to gain when you retire.

That means the insurance company can tell you, "If you put X much money in per month, you're going to have $300,000 when you're 65." Since both the death benefit and the cash value are guaranteed, you'll know from the quote what the contract will provide.

Universal life. With universal life, the interest rate can change over time. What the insurance company will do is give you a range, telling you what they think you're going to hit when you retire but it could be less or more.

Variable life. With variable life, there typically aren't guarantees. Similar to investing in the stock market, they can make an estimate based on past market trends, but it really depends on how well you invest your money.

Tax Strategy -- How to Get Tax-Free Gains

With life insurance, there's a tax loophole that, if you use it correctly, your gains are tax-free.

The money in your life insurance account grows tax-deferred, which means as long as you leave money in the account you don't owe taxes on it.

If at some point you decide to cancel your life insurance policy and cash out all your investment gains, you'll owe taxes on those gains, which isn't what you want to do. So, don't cancel your policy!

Instead, follow this process:

- **Get a policy loan.** Say you reach retirement and you have a big pile of money in there. You can take a *policy loan*, which means you're borrowing

money from yourself to take it out. Luckily, the government doesn't tax loans.
- **Keep the policy in force.** Because it's a permanent policy, at some point you're going to die, and the death benefit will pay off your loan. The government doesn't tax life insurance death benefits.

Basically, you take your money out tax-free, and then the death benefit pays off your loan and what's left over to your heirs tax-free as well.

Downsides

What could be an issue in using a life insurance policy as a tax-free investment?

Consider these points:

- You'll have to be healthy enough to qualify for life insurance to set this up. It might not be an option if you have serious health issues. There's a required medical exam.
- Your investment gains will be lower than if you had just invested in a stock account because each month a little of your money goes towards paying for your life insurance.

If you need life insurance for a time, but then want to switch to other tactics as your needs change, you'll see how to accomplish that change as well as we delve further into our strategies.

Do the Work!

Determine if Life insurance investing will work for you. It is especially advantageous if you can't qualify for a regular retirement plan. Unlike IRAs, life insurance doesn't really have any income restrictions, so anyone can set up a plan like this as long as they're fairly healthy. Also, if you don't have a 401(k) at work, that doesn't leave you with many options for tax-advantaged investments.

If you want life insurance to protect your family, it's an added benefit to be able to save for tax-free income later on all within the same contract. And if you forget to invest regularly, permanent life insurance offers automatic, forced savings, ensuring that you provide for your future, even when you're not thinking about it.

ANNUITY INVESTING

Annuities are more of just a pure investment contract than life insurance. When you buy an annuity, it's split into two different stages:

- The first stage is called the *accumulation phase*, which means you're putting money into your contract and the annuity company is investing it for you. You're saving up money in an investment account.
- When you're ready to retire, you convert your annuity into the *payout stage*. You'll have options to choose from, like, "Do I want guaranteed payments for the rest of my life? Do I want guaranteed payments for 20 years?" The company will tell you the payment amounts for your various options so you can get a clear picture.

Plan for the risks and benefits with a guaranteed income you can't outlive.

The risk involved depends on what type of annuity you buy. Like life insurance, there are different types.

There are two types of annuities, fixed and variable:

- Fixed annuities pay a fixed rate of return that's guaranteed. Like whole life, you know exactly what your account value will be when you retire. They're very safe. However, like all investments, lower risks usually provide lower returns.
- With variable annuities, you're investing in the stock market, so how well you do is dependent on the market and there are no guarantees as to your account value when you're ready to retire.

The one thing about the annuity that life insurance doesn't offer is you can guarantee income with it for the rest of your life. For example, if you have $300,000 in your annuity and you're ready to start the payout phase, you can choose to receive set, guaranteed payments for the rest of your life, and they'll turn it into a lifetime pension for you.

So, no matter how long you live, you'll keep getting those payments. Plus, the amount of the payments will never go down, even if your total payments surpass that $300,000.

Do the Work!

In comparison to life insurance, you'll likely make more money with an annuity because you're not paying for any life insurance with your premiums. Do your research? See which product offers you more protection for the needs and goals you have for yourself and your family.

LIFE INSURANCE OR ANNUITY?

Which investment would work better for your situation?

You might prefer life insurance:

- If you have children and need a life insurance policy, that's usually enough to swing you to investing in life insurance, because then you're hitting two goals at the same time.
- If you want to retire early, life insurance might be a better choice because there are no restrictions as to when you can take money out with a loan. With the annuity, you're supposed to keep money in there until you're at least 59 ½, according to the IRS. If you take out money earlier, it can lead to a tax penalty.

You might prefer an annuity:

- If your goal is to get to retirement as soon as possible with the most money, an annuity will generally have a higher account value. · If you're not healthy enough to qualify for life insurance, then an annuity is your option because there's no health exam for an annuity. It's open to everyone.
- If you're single, don't have children, and don't need life insurance, that would push you towards investing in an annuity.

Do the Work!

These are very important decisions you need to make early. Consult a professional, do your research, and make sure the product you choose has the flexibility to change as your life changes.

TAX-FREE AND TAX-DEFERRED INCOME STRATEGIES

Now that you understand the basics of investing in life insurance and annuities, let's delve further into using specific strategies to achieve tax-advantaged income. Read through these four strategies several times and make sure you understand the differences and financial implications. It can be a good idea after you have a strong understanding to consult a professional with your questions.

Tax-Free and Tax-Deferred Income Strategy #1

Using Life Insurance Cash Value for Tax-Free Income

The big question is how to get guaranteed income in retirement that's tax-free. That's the dream for everyone. It's not always easy or possible, but that's obviously the goal you want to approach.

What would happen if you only used your life insurance cash value to fund your retirement? All your income in retirement would be tax-free.

For this strategy to work, remember you don't want to cancel your life insurance policy, because the minute you do, all your investment gains are taxable. However, as long as you keep your insurance policy in force, you can borrow money from it.

When you borrow money, since it's a loan, it doesn't count as income, so you don't have to pay any taxes on it.

So, each year, maybe you borrow $30,000 from your life insurance.

When you eventually die, the death benefit from your policy will pay off your loans so nobody else has to pay it. Life insurance death benefits are tax-free, so your heirs never have to pay tax on your investment gains or on the rest of the money they receive.

Important Considerations

Keep these facts in mind when considering this strategy:

Tax-free, but not guaranteed.

The downside of using life insurance for your retirement income is that it only achieves the tax-free goal. It doesn't meet the guaranteed goal.

It's up to you to figure out how much money you can take out each year, so it doesn't run out. So, there's a chance you can outlive your money.

How much do you want to leave for your heirs?

The one thing you need to balance out is your income requirements versus if you want to leave an inheritance.

· When you borrow money from your policy, you also deduct against your future death benefit for your heirs. For example, if you want to leave $300,000 to your grand kids but you spend $200,000 of your $300,000 life insurance policy, they're only going to receive the $100,000 balance.

· Just be aware the more you spend from your policy, the less you'll leave to your heirs.

Tax-Free and Tax-Deferred Income Strategy #2

Using an Annuity to Guarantee Income for Life

When you invest in an annuity, you already know that the main benefit is guaranteed income.

So, if you have $300,000 in your annuity, you can ask the company to turn it into guaranteed payments for the rest of your life.

That way, no matter how long you live, you'll receive the same amount of money per month. If you live to 120, you know you're still going to be collecting checks. That's a good tool, especially since we're living longer than ever.

Tax Treatment of Annuity Payouts

Another benefit of annuities is that they're tax-deferred, which means the government doesn't tax your gains while they're in the account, but when you start collecting payments, your investment gains are taxable.

When your taxes are deferred, your money grows faster because there's more money to work for you throughout your accumulation phase.

When you start receiving payments, part of those payments is considered to be the money you put in and the other part comes from gains. Only the part that comes from your gains is taxable since you already paid income taxes on the money you used to fund your policy.

The payments are divided into taxable and non-taxable portions based on the same proportions they make up in your account. For example, if half of your

Tax-Free and Tax-Deferred Income Strategies

account is what you put in and half is from your gains, then your payouts reflect that same 50/50 split. Half of a payout check is taxable, and half isn't.

Important Considerations

Annuities work really well, as long as you plan properly and reserve it for your retirement savings.

Keep these points in mind when using annuities to fund your retirement:

Choose carefully when you decide how long you want payouts.

If you're choosing the guaranteed life option, it works great if you're going to live a long, long time, but it can be an issue if you die early.

Say you're 65 and you choose payments for the rest of your life, but you only live one more year. You've probably only collected $4,000 of your $300,000 annuity, using our same example as before. · Fortunately, you don't have to choose *only* the guaranteed life option. Many annuities let you set it up where you say, "I want it for the rest of my life, but I want a minimum of 10 years' worth of payments." Or you might choose a minimum of 15 or 20 years. · That means if you die in one year, at least your heirs will receive payments for the rest of the term you chose (9, 14, or 19 more years based on your option).

Wait as long as possible before you start payouts.

If you start receiving guaranteed payments when you turn 60, you'll receive less money per month than someone that waited until 70.

The longer you can stretch out your accumulation phase, the more money you'll get per month in your payout phase, regardless of which option you choose.

Avoid withdrawals before age 59 ½.

If you are stuck in a money jam and you need to take money out when you're 50, like just a lump sum withdrawal, the IRS charges a 10 percent early withdrawal penalty, which really hurts your investment gains.

So, if you're putting money into an annuity, plan to lock it in until you're at least 59 ½.

Tax-Free and Tax-Deferred Income Strategy #3

1035 Exchange: Life Insurance Cash Value into an Annuity

Just because you use one product, doesn't mean you can't use the other. Perhaps you no longer have a need for life insurance and now you want those guaranteed payments of an annuity because you're retiring.

It's a really easy switch to turn your life insurance into an annuity!

You simply perform a transaction called a 1035 exchange. Your insurance company will have the forms to fill out. This will take all the money from your life insurance and deposit it into an annuity.

This transfer doesn't count as a withdrawal, so you won't owe any taxes on this move. It will just be like you had saved in an annuity all along.

From there, with your new contract, you can set up the guaranteed payments for retirement.

Change Your Plan as Your Needs Change with No Tax Consequences

Your financial needs change over time. When you're in your 30s with children, you need life insurance, but once you're in your 60s and the kids are gone, you might not.

So, this is an exit strategy. Taxes are eliminated.

Maybe you don't have quite as much money as if you had just used an annuity your whole life, but you may have needed life insurance, so that wasn't an option anyway.

Important Considerations

This is a one-way street.

You can turn life insurance into an annuity tax-free, with a 1035 exchange, but you can't go the other way. You can't turn your annuity into a life insurance policy.

It's a permanent decision.

You need to know that once you make this move, you've lost your insurance. You can't change your mind a couple of years later and get it back.

As you age, your health may change, and it will be harder to qualify for life insurance. So, you may be giving up that opportunity for the rest of your life.

Tax-Free and Tax-Deferred Income Strategy #4

Using an Annuity + Life Insurance

Use this strategy to maximize your benefits by using both life insurance and annuities.

If you're married and own an annuity and you want guaranteed payments for retirement, you have two options:

- You can base the annuity on both your lives, which means as long as one of you is alive, you're going to be collecting payments, or
- You can base payments based on one person, for example, just basing it on the husband. However, if the husband dies, the payments stop, so the wife wouldn't have any more income.

When you base an annuity on one person the risk is higher, but you get significantly more money. Depending on age, you gain 20 or 30 percent more per month.

If you base it on two people, you get less money, but at least you have a safer retirement.

The Solution:

As an example, a husband could open life insurance on himself and then do the annuity based on his life, because as long as he's alive, they're collecting that larger income.

If he dies first, the annuity payouts would stop, but his wife would collect the death benefit from the life insurance (tax-free), which she could use to fund the rest of her retirement. Hopefully, they both live very long and collect that higher income for the rest of their lives, but then they're also protected in case the annuity spouse dies.

If the wife dies first, the husband keeps getting the higher annuity payments he has been getting all along.

For this strategy, because it is a bit more complicated, it's important to sit down with a life insurance agent or financial planner to make a plan that works for your situation.

You can always get free annuity and life insurance quotes online, but when you're doing a more complicated strategy like this, it helps to sit down with a professional. You don't want to make a mistake here.

Younger vs. Older Investors

It's better to plan sooner with this strategy.

If you're in your 30s or 40s, that's the time to buy the life insurance policy because you'll likely be healthy enough to qualify for an affordable rate. If you wait until you're in your 60s or 70s, you can't really do this anymore, because you won't be able to buy a large enough policy, and you might not be able to qualify at all.

You can get the annuity at any time, but if you get it when you're young and add funds to it on a regular basis, you have the advantage of letting your money work for you for many years of tax-deferred growth before you switch it to the payout phase.

Comparing Tax Advantages of the 4 Strategies

The only strategy that is completely tax-free is just using life insurance (strategy number one).

Anytime you use an annuity, you're going to end up paying some taxes on your investment income. Unfortunately, there is not really a way to guarantee income for life without an annuity, which means paying at least some tax.

Strategies two, three, and four do delay taxes until retirement, which gives your investment more momentum to grow. Plus, with annuity income, only part of each payout is taxable.

You'll pay less tax with strategy number four, where you use life insurance and an annuity because the life insurance death benefit will be tax-free.

How can you start?

Typically, both these products are offered by insurance companies.

If you would like to invest in an annuity or life insurance, it's best to get a few quotes from different companies to see which ones look best. For your security, you'll want to use an insurance company that will most likely be around many years from now when it's time to get payouts, so choose one with A+ ratings from the A.M. Best Company.

You usually need to see an agent and sit down for a meeting before they'll prepare a quote for you.

However, you can find companies online that specialize in putting together rate quotes. For example, AnnuityQuotes.com will send you a few quotes from major companies if you enter your information.

Do the Work!

It's really something to consider, this match up with life insurance and annuities. We're at a time when most of us don't have pensions, so it's hard to find a way to guarantee income in retirement. Setting up an annuity with guaranteed income is really the only way now for most people to get income for the rest of their life. The tax advantages are just icing on the cake!

Make sure you have your long and short-term goals established before making these decisions.

* * *

Complete the *Tax-Advantaged Retirement Income You Can't Outlive, Questionnaire* found in the Tools Section

MAKE YOUR HOBBY YOUR MONEY-MAKER

There's no doubt that a moneymaking hobby can dramatically reduce the amount of time until retirement. Not only can you sock away more money, but you can also use that income during your retirement. This reduces the amount that you need to save prior to retirement. Since hobbies are enjoyable, it's a win-win situation.

But like most other income, income from your hobby is also taxable.

Taxes are a considerable expense, so they should be minimized, when possible.

For tax purposes, understand what "hobby" means.

This is a touchy issue for the IRS. Many people try to deduct losses for activities that are primarily conducted for enjoyment. It's easy to get yourself into trouble.

The IRS considers a hobby to be an activity that is done primarily for enjoyment, not for making a profit. If your activity is considered to be a hobby, you can't use the tax deductions available to a legitimate business. However, you will be taxed for profit and can deduct your expenses in the same year.

For example, if you bought $1,000 in rare coins and didn't earn any income, you couldn't deduct the $1,000 from your other income. However, if you sold the coins for $1,200, you would be taxed on the $200 profit, provided you sold the coins in the same tax year they were purchased.

Hobbies are terrible for tax purposes.

It's important to create a business for your hobby. Think business, not hobby. If you expect to make a profit, and your expectation is considered to be reasonable, then you can consider your hobby to be a business. There is more information available from the IRS by searching, "Hobby or Business, IRS offers tips to decide."

There is no advantage to not declaring your hobby a business if your intention is to earn income. When it comes to the IRS, remove the word hobby from your vocabulary.

Consider hiring your non-working family members.

Remember that no income tax has to be paid below a certain income threshold. Paying your children or non-working spouse a salary to help you with your business is a great way to avoid income taxes.

Paying your spouse keeps the money in your collective pockets. Paying your children can provide a great way to save money for college, tax-free. Ideally, you would be in the position to pay both.

If your goal really is early retirement, consider investing the profits in tax-deferred retirement accounts.

Depending on how much income you earn, your options will vary. But at the very least, an IRA makes a lot of sense. You can shield your income from taxes, at least temporarily.

A Roth-IRA requires after-tax income, but the earnings are tax-free. A traditional IRA uses pre-tax income, but the earnings are taxed.

IRAs are great but remember the money is out of your hands until the standard retirement age. If you want to retire early and need that money, be sure to invest the money wisely. Avoid spending the extra income on other things.

Learn how to run a business wisely. There are a plethora of books and other sources that will provide the information needed to run a business effectively. Maximize your income for the amount of time you want to dedicate to your hobby. Don't hesitate to get expert tax advice, too.

Do the Work!

A moneymaking hobby can be an important part of any early retirement plan. Think about the things you like to do and make a list of ways you can make money from those activities. But take the steps to avoid paying more taxes than necessary.

DON'T WRECK THE FINISH LINE

Even if you've made the perfect financial decisions all the way up to retirement, it's still possible to make mistakes that can make your retirement far less enjoyable than it could have been. Making smart decisions is just as important during your retirement years. The need to make sound financial decisions lasts throughout adulthood.

As the rules change, your perspective and decision-making process should change, too. Retirement is a time to change gears and adjust your financial decisions.

Poor decisions can significantly detract from your retirement wealth. Consider the following poor decisions and avoid them:

Listening to the wrong people.

It seems that we all have a family member or friend that claims to be a financial guru. While your friend may have made great decisions regarding his retirement, it doesn't mean he will have all the answers for your unique situation. Get professional advice.

Failing to educate yourself.

The laws and rules around retirement accounts, taxes, investing, and social security regularly change. Retirement might be a long way off, but that doesn't mean you shouldn't be learning continuously.

Not having a budget or not creating a new budget.

Are you still using the same budget from your working days? As your income and expenses change, it's important to create a new budget.

Not understanding distributions.

Not everyone understands the tax consequences of removing funds from retirement accounts. Simple mistakes can impact the rest of your retirement. Educating yourself or hiring a professional to create a distribution strategy makes good sense.

Not including your family in your finances.

You might want to consider having a conversation with your children about your finances. Will your kids know what to do if you become incapacitated or pass away? It might be easier if you let them know your financial situation and provide advice now.

Not diversifying risk.

Many retirees operate with the belief that a savings account, Social Security benefits, and an IRA will be sufficient. However, there are additional steps that you can take to protect yourself against market fluctuations.

Spread your risk over a wider range of investments. That probably doesn't mean eliminating all risk from your investments. While your level of risk should change, having too little can mean running out of money before you run out of years.

Failing to maintain an emergency fund.

Many retirees figure it's time to spend the emergency fund. This might seem logical since the threat of losing a job is no longer an issue. But there are other emergencies to consider. Unforeseen medical expenses are one example.

Failing to do any estate planning.

Estate planning is about taking care of your spouse, children, and any other heirs. It's about considering tax implications so your wealth transfers to the people and charitable organizations that you cherish instead of the government.

Arbitrarily choosing your retirement age.

While you could be forced into retirement by layoffs or health issues, you may still have a choice. Begin your retirement planning early and work as long as needed. Let your finances be your guide.

Underestimating medical expenses.

While medical expenses seem to always be significant, they tend to be more frequent and expensive as we age.

Keep making good financial decisions into your retirement years. Hire a professional as needed to help you navigate the significant complexities of taxes and distributions. Avoid undoing all your hard work by using the above information wisely. Your retirement can be every bit as great as you always wanted.

Do the Work!

It's time to really dig in and see if what you planned up to this point will give you the fruits of you labor as planned. Don't be complacent. Look at all your needs and verify you are positioned to meet them with grace and ease during your golden years.

AFTER YOUR LOVED ONE HAS DEPARTED

The loss of a spouse is challenging emotionally and financially. For many, death is an uncomfortable subject and few of us have prepared sufficiently to deal with the aftermath.

My condolences when you find yourself in this situation. I hope these steps can help you minimize the negative financial aspects of this life change.

Consider these steps after the loss of a spouse.

Keep a digital copy of the death certificate for easy access.

You'll need to print out some hard copies as well. It's necessary to send a copy to the Social Security Administration, credit card companies, insurance companies, and many other financial institutions. While some will accept your digital copy others will not. The death certificate is necessary to verify your spouse's death.

A death certificate is also necessary to change or remove names from accounts. This can also include changing beneficiaries.

Contact the necessary professionals first.

Ideally, you'll speak with a tax accountant and an estate-planning attorney before taking any significant action. These experts are knowledgeable on the financial ramifications of your situation. Before receiving an insurance payout, or taking any other major financial step, speak with an expert.

Avoid taking the advice of well-meaning friends and family. Unless you know someone that works in an applicable field, you have to consider that their advice could be missing some important steps. It might not be the best course of action available to you based on unknown and unforeseen variables.

Update your will.

It's likely that your spouse was the primary beneficiary of your will. In most states, your will becomes invalid when your spouse dies. This means the state will determine how your assets are distributed until a new will is created.

You may also reorganize your assets after a loved one passes. Consider which assets are used now that were previously set aside for later distribution. Reorganize your beneficiary information accordingly.

Contact the social security administration.

You are probably eligible for a death benefit and a survivor's benefit. This can be a huge help with funeral expenses.

Ensure that you're paying your bills on time.

It's common during times of grief and stress to ignore day-to-day activities. Remember to take care of yourself and pay your bills on time. The additional stress of late fees and phone calls from creditors is the last thing you want or need.

Collect all insurance policies and contact the companies.

This includes life insurance, automobile insurance, any insurance provided by your spouse's employer, mortgage insurance, and any other insurance.

In some cases, you'll receive a benefit. In others, you may receive a refund when you cancel a policy that has become unnecessary. There are instances where you may keep a policy but wish to change the beneficiaries. Companies can help you sort it all out, but you must contact them and let them know of the change in your life.

Contact the Department of Veteran's Affairs if your spouse was in the military.

There are funds available for funeral expenses. It's also possible to receive monthly payments if your spouse was receiving disability benefits.

These are just a few of the necessary steps to secure your finances if your spouse passes away. It's very important to work with the appropriate financial experts.

Do the Work!

Take time to speak with your spouse before this circumstance occurs. Discuss how these financial issues will be handled and get your papers in order. Take the initiative to get as much organized beforehand to make the transition easier for the survivor.

Taking care of your financial duties may be the hardest thing you have to do after the loss of a loved one. If you find yourself unable to move forward and get things done, reach out for support from a trusted friend, family member, or a community support group.

GIVE THE GIFT OF LIVING INHERITANCES

Have you thought about the timing and tax issues of when your children will receive their inheritance from you?

Financial experts are saying that due to steadily rising life expectancy, many of us will live into our 80s and 90s, and your kids are likely to be in their 60s or 70s before receiving their inheritances.

You can easily pass along some assets during the prime ages of your children.

Fortunately, you don't have to die to be able to give them portions of their inheritance.

Consider these suggestions for some tax-advantaged strategies for passing along assets while you're alive:

Talk with your children about starting education savings for each of their kids.

Many states offer savings plans that grow tax-free. Some of these plans even allow kids to use their education dollars at a university in another state.

- The sooner in your grand kids' lives that you set up the education accounts, the more money those accounts will accumulate because they'll have a longer period of growth.
- In the event you wish to give the money directly to a university, you don't have to pay a single bit of taxes to do it.

Give your kids "gift" dollars each year.

Whether it's for their birthdays, Christmas, or May Day, you can give each of your children up to $14,000 yearly (as of 2013) tax-free. In fact, you can give up to that amount to as many people (related or not) as you like without you or them being taxed on that money.

- Consider how your children in their 30s could use the money when they're working so hard to raise young families.
- Can you imagine the joy, pleasure, and perhaps stress-relief you can give to each of your kids by making some generous gifts now, without anyone paying any taxes on the gifts?

Pay for expected medical costs.

If you have children or grandchildren that will always need a special type of medical care, give some money to the medical facility. This way, you'll avoid having to pay any taxes on the money you give, no matter how large the amount.

Use your life insurance cash value.

You can borrow money, tax-free, against your life insurance cash value and give it to your children. The government doesn't tax those borrowed funds, regardless of the amount you take out of your policy.

- Your kids will also receive the funds tax-free as long as each gift is below the IRS limits ($14,000 in 2013).
- As long as your policy stays in force, those funds remain tax-free to you. You don't need to ever pay them back if you don't want to. Upon your death, your heirs don't have to pay those dollars back to the life insurance company, either. The policy will cover the loans.
- Keep in mind, though, that the loans will reduce the death benefit to your beneficiaries. So, taking out the loans is giving your children some funds now *instead* of later.

When you give now to your heirs, you'll also reduce your overall assets that may be taxed upon your death.

Everybody wins:

- You get to see the looks on their faces when you gift a large amount of money.
- Your heirs get to use the money now, when they might really need it.
- Your heirs will pay fewer taxes and retain more of the assets upon your death.

Do the Work!

With a little planning, you can surprise your children by gifting some of their inheritance tax-free now, when you can all enjoy the special time together!

TAXES AND YOUR INHERITANCE

As if taxes and death weren't bad enough, the government has managed to combine the two into a single, miserable experience. In many cases, you don't have just a single tax to pay. There can be multiple taxes due at various points in the inheritance process. Little, if anything, can be done to reduce taxes after death.

Proper estate planning before death can make a huge difference.

A skilled estate planner can utilize trusts, properly timed gifts, insurance policies, and donations to minimize the taxes owed.

Look into the idea of Estate Tax versus Inheritance Tax

First, estate tax and inheritance tax are not the same thing, even though you'll find many experts that use the terms interchangeably.

An estate tax is imposed before the heirs receive any property or monies.

The executor pays the remaining debts from money or property in the estate. Any funeral or legal expenses are also paid. The federal government taxes whatever remains, if it's a large estate. Much like income taxes, the rate varies with the value of the estate. A few states also have an estate tax.

In a nutshell, all the bills are paid using proceeds from the estate. What remains is subject to a federal tax if the amount is larger than the current exemptions, and possibly, a state tax.

The heirs then pay inheritance taxes after receiving their inheritances.

This tax is a state-level tax. It's not just the home and the funds in the bank account that are subject to inheritance tax. It's just about everything:

- Cash, stock, bonds
- Real estate
- Business interests
- Boats
- Cars
- Art
- Anything else of value -- The value of the estate is determined by the fair market value of all the assets.

Exemptions

There are a few tricks that can be used to pass more to your heirs and less to Uncle Sam:

There is a spousal exemption.

The surviving spouse is not subject to any estate taxes at the federal or state level. This exemption does not apply to children or siblings.

There is a limit exemption.

Any estate worth less than $5.43 million is exempt from estate taxes. This is for an individual. Unless you're quite well off, estate taxes are a non-issue. However, the amount of tax can be significant for a large estate, up to 40% at the highest rate.

Even if you're over this limit, a good estate planner may be able to structure your assets in such a way that you're below the threshold.

Remember that this is an estate exemption. There's only one estate, regardless of the number of heirs. The exemption can only be used once.

At the state level, there are no hard and fast rules.

Remember that many states don't have a tax at all. Those that do offer exemptions to certain family members, but not to others. The tax rates can also vary based on the relationship to the deceased.

As of 2014, 31 states do not have either an estate or an inheritance tax.

Most estates fall well under the exemption limit. In addition, many of those above the limit can be organized in a way to bring them under the limit. If you've been worrying about the government taking a bite out of your estate, you're probably in the clear.

Do the Work!

The average person doesn't have to worry about federal estate taxes, and most states don't tax the estate or the heirs. Large estates, however, are well-served by knowledgeable and aggressive estate planning. Certainly, this area requires expertise. If your family has a large estate, an estate attorney can save you a lot of money.

EFFECTIVE STRATEGIES TO REDUCE ESTATE TAXES

Even if you're not wealthy, an estate plan can ensure that your assets pass on to those whom you want to receive them.

Estate taxes are imposed on the heir of an estate and include any real estate, stock, cash, or other assets transferred to heirs at the time of death. There are both federal estate taxes and, in some states, state estate taxes.

Wouldn't you rather see these items stay in your family instead of being eaten by Uncle Sam? Laws can vary from state to state, so be sure to find the details that apply to your situation.

Use these tips to reduce your estate tax burden:

Give the money to your children while you're still alive.

You can give up to $14,000 per year to any of your children or grandchildren. If you're married, you and your spouse can each give a total of $28,000 per child each year. This can add up.

Be charitable.

Charitable gifts and lifetime transfers are a way to reduce your estate taxes and get your money to the organizations that mean the most to you.

There are several ways to gift money and assets to charitable groups. Not surprisingly, charities are well versed in gift giving and taxes. Their help is also free!

Set up a trust.

An irrevocable life insurance trust permits the transfer of assets up to the value of the life insurance premium. The real benefit comes from the value of the policy.

Life insurance proceeds are normally free from taxes. This is quite simple to set up, but a trust attorney can ensure that it's done properly.

Transfer assets to your spouse.

Gifts given during your lifetime or left to your spouse in your will are not subject to income taxes, up to approximately $10 million.

However, your spouse will eventually have to pay taxes upon their death. But this extra time can be put to good use to further reduce the tax liability.

Enjoy it.

Any money spent won't be part of your estate come tax-time. If you've focused on saving in the past, maybe it's time to enjoy some of your money.

Move.

Not all states collect an estate or inheritance tax. Moving to a different state could save your estate a lot of money. A little over half the states don't collect these taxes, and one of them may appeal to you. Do some calculations and see how much you would save if you moved.

Set up a family partnership or family LLC.

These business entities are another way to potentially reduce estate taxes.

Do the Work!

Estate planning isn't just about protecting your assets. It's also about meeting your financial goals. If you don't have an estate plan, it's never too soon to start. An attorney is a great place to begin. Just be sure that they have expertise in estate planning. For example, most attorneys don't have the slightest idea how to set up a trust.

If you have significant assets, estate taxes can approach 40% of the value of your estate. It only makes sense to reduce this burden as much as possible. Your heirs will thank you.

CHAPTER TWELVE, SUPPORT

Which Habits Can You Turn Around Fast?

You are at a place where you are starting to manage your own financial expectations. Use this section to reinforce your goals and dreams for you and your loved ones.

Getting Started

Read through each section. They are designed to help you change your stinking thinking into satisfying facts. See who you can be, who you are becoming, and who you truly are.

Path to Enlightenment

I see a clear path to enlightenment.

Use this self-affirming language to teach your thoughts a new habit:

- I see my journey to peaceful, joyful, and purposeful living in front of me and cherish it. It is my way of reaching complete happiness. The path has challenges, but I have the ability to move past them.
- I know the path is gradual.
- I know I must take small steps along the way. However, the payoff is tremendous. I see how to obtain happiness and peace that lasts, one step at a time.
- I purify my mind and body as I walk the path.
- I eliminate my suffering. This is why I stay on the path to enlightenment and continue to move ahead. I free my mind and body from pain, negativity, and harm.
- I understand that my own mind can spring me forward or cause challenges -- both mental and physical. I work to make my mind a clean slate that avoids negative thoughts.
- I develop my mind, so it is strong and smart. I take advantage of meditation and yoga to reduce stress and bring me clarity, calm, and focus. I use my network of friends and family to stay strong. I train my mind on the path to enlightenment. I make my mind pliable and amazing. I listen, reflect, and examine my path.
- Today, I stay on the path to enlightenment. I remain positive, focus on each tiny step forward, and use my resources wisely.

Do the Work!

Take time for self-reflection:

1. What can I do to stay focused on the path to enlightenment?

2. How can I avoid or overcome the obstacles in my path?

3. How can I maintain my path to enlightenment during busy times?

I Listen to My Heart

My heart drives decisions that are tied to emotion.

Use this self-affirming language to teach your thoughts a new habit:

- I know that deciding with emotion sometimes results in undesirable outcomes. But I give my heart great credit for keeping me connected with the softer side of people.
- I rely on my heart to tell me when I am making the right choices for my happiness. I am careful with my definition of true happiness. I know I can rely on my heart to help me find it.
- My family and friends are special to me. I like to make them happy by my words and actions.
- I am also very honest with them. They deserve to know the sometimes-undesirable realities of life. But at times, their emotional well-being takes precedence. I often find it necessary to overlook practical decisions to keep them happy.
- Listening to my heart helps me be sympathetic to people in pain. Even when I am personally unaffected by an incident, I avoid appearing disconnected.
- Emotional maturity means I am able to empathize when others need my support. I am careful to listen to their cues and do my best to cater to their emotional desires. My family members have a shoulder to lean on when their heart is aching.
- Today, I am committed to achieving balance between emotional and practical thinking. Such equilibrium helps me to effectively handle situations. It also helps me to remain connected to those I care about.

Do the Work!

Take time for self-reflection:

1. In what scenarios does my heart unwisely cloud my judgment?

2. What is the best mental state to be in before making a decision tied to emotion?

3. How helpful is dialogue in helping others make wise decisions?

Providing for My Family

I feel confident in my ability to provide for myself and my family.

Use this self-affirming language to teach your thoughts a new habit:

- I know that I am capable of providing for myself and my family. After all, my family and I have all of our needs met at this very moment.
- Each day, as I get ready for bed, I take notice of my possessions and how well they serve me. I feel the plushness of my bed as I get in it. I think about what a luxury it is to have running water and heating when so many in the world do not have these things. And I have had a hand in bringing all of these possessions into my life.
- Perhaps I provide the money needed to obtain all the material goods that my family and I have at home. Or maybe I take care of the kids instead so that my partner can work. Either way, my time and energy are invested in all that we have at home.
- When I see the results of my labor all around me, my confidence in my ability as a provider grows.
- Aside from just the material objects that make our lives easier, I offer many things to my family.
- I provide my family with a sympathetic ear when they feel troubled. I give them companionship when they want a friend or playmate. And if anyone ever needs a hug, they know they can come to me. These are all gifts beyond measure.
- Today, I cultivate gratitude for all the ways in which I can be of value to my family. I notice my family's needs and tend to them, and I feel confident in my ability to do so.

Do the Work!

Take time for self-reflection:

1. What are some non-material ways I provide for my family?

2. At what times do I feel a sense of abundance?

3. How can I increase my ability to provide well for my family?

Money Making Opportunities

I clearly see opportunities to effortlessly make money.

Use this self-affirming language to teach your thoughts a new habit:

- Opportunities to make money are obvious to me. The world is full of money, and I am deserving of my fair share. I can see the possibilities for abundance everywhere I look.
- The financial abundance in my life is continuously growing. I realize there are unlimited ways to create wealth while being ethical and responsible. I am a highly capable person when it comes to money.
- I am rapidly becoming the richest person I know. I may have struggled with money in the past, but my future looks abundant. I handle money easily and with great skill. Everyone is amazed by my ability to attract money.
- I cease to worry about money because I know that wealth is always available to me. My bank account is at an all-time high.
- Every day, I look for new possibilities to generate income. My income grows greater each week. My income opportunities are limitless. The means of dramatically increasing my income are all around me. I just need to keep my eyes open to the possibilities.
- Though financial challenges may happen, I am free from fear because there is an abundance of ways to make money quickly and effortlessly. I am confident in my ability to make money.
- Today, I see many opportunities to increase my income. The more opportunities I see, the more money I make.

Do the Work!

Take time for self-reflection:

1. What are the three ways I could easily increase my income?

2. What has stopped me from making more money?

3. Am I comfortable with the idea of being wealthy?

Financial Hope

I am hopeful about my financial future.

Use this self-affirming language to teach your thoughts a new habit:

- My financial future is secure. I am more than able to fully provide for the needs of my family. When I think about my financial future, I am filled with joy because I see myself in a better place than I am today.
- I am hopeful about my financial future because I make better choices today than I made in the past. Armed with new knowledge, I am taking control of my financial situation and working toward my goals.
- I am unmoved by the fear that surrounds me. I stand steadfast on the values that hard work and responsible spending will secure my financial future. I refuse to sulk about where I am. Instead, I use my current state as motivation to press on.
- When I am faced with adversity, I stop and think about how to improve my situation. The loss of a job is simply a bump on the road. Unexpected expenses are temporary setbacks, which I am fully capable of overcoming.
- The necessary tools to rewrite the story of my finances are within my reach. I may have made mistakes in the past, but I have learned from those mistakes. I am savvy when it comes to my finances.
- My financial future is bright because I use my creativity to increase my income. By rejecting excuses and embracing hard work, I am positioning myself on the path to success.
- Today, I choose to look at my financial future with positivity. Regardless of where I find myself today, I know what lies ahead is better than what I leave behind.

Do the Work!

Take time for self-reflection:

1. What have I learned from the mistakes of my past?

2. Where do I want my finances to be 5 years from now?

3. What small change can I make today to improve my financial situation?

13

ADVANTAGE

Not everything in life is solely about work, sacrifice, and limiting your spending. Sometimes, you need to look towards the advantage that things and situations can give you.

Getting Started

Some challenges can be shifted to your advantage. Check out what you can do with the information in these units.

BENEFITS OF BEING ALONE

Perhaps you find yourself spending a lot of time alone. Do you struggle with how to spend that time? Although you have plenty of things you'd like to accomplish, getting focused, and staying that way seems to be a challenge when you're alone.

Are you wasting precious, solitary hours that you could be spending more productively?

Consider these benefits of being alone:

Do whatever you want.

Being alone means you're completely in charge of your decisions. How often does that happen? You can select what you want to do each hour that you're without some company. Think of it as being rich with time.

Need to clean the garage? Want to learn how to speak Spanish or German? Never finished that sewing or wood-carving project?

Having alone time means you can accomplish all those things you've been putting off.

Set a goal and achieve it.

Now, that you have no distractions, take some time and set one or two goals. Write them down. List the steps you'll need to follow to achieve each goal and check off each step as they're completed.

You have the power and time to make even your wildest dreams come true.

Take up a hobby you've been considering.

Maybe you've had a secret desire to participate in a certain pastime that appeals to you. What's stopping you? At least, make a call of inquiry about getting involved or observe people engaging in the activity.

Read more.

Reading will broaden your horizons and make you a more interesting person. Read what you love or try a new genre.

If reading has been less than appealing in the past, go to the library and pick out a book on a subject that interests you. Select a classic novel, a biography of a celebrity who piques your interest, or a how-to book.

Exercise.

If you're alone a lot, then you have plenty of time to improve your physical shape. Design your own exercise plan. Include a schedule for when you'll exercise and the type of exercise you'll do. Then follow through. You can even change it up to keep it interesting.

You can be proactive and overcome any physical fitness or health issues you may have.

Becoming the healthy, vibrant person you've yearned to be is completely within your reach.

Start some soul-searching.

What do you want out of life? When you've thought about the life you want to live, you'll be more likely to obtain it. Spend some time considering what's important to you and what you hope to accomplish in your lifetime. Having extra alone time means you can create the very life you desire.

Become excellent at something.

Nothing makes us feel better than to know that we can do at least one thing really well.

Maybe mastering playing the guitar, doing yoga, or writing a children's book is exactly what you want to do. Whatever it is, spend some of your solitary time practicing becoming the best you can be at something. It'll be a great confidence-builder.

Do the Work!

When you're alone, you have an abundance of time to spend in ways that bring you the opportunity to learn, achieve, and enjoy your life. Relish the time you spend alone. It gives you the power to do anything you want. Your time is now!

ADVANTAGES AND DISADVANTAGES OF AUTOMATIC BILL PAYING

If you struggle to pay your bills on time or can't find the time to deal with your finances, auto bill paying is one possible solution. One of the great benefits of online banking is auto bill paying. Your bills are paid without effort by you on the date you set for each month. A checking account or credit card can be used as the payment source.

Comfort exists when you know your bills will be handled each month with a minimal amount of effort on your part.

Auto bill paying has several advantages:

Your credit score might improve.

Many people find that their credit scores improve after a few months of paying bills automatically. Late payments should be a thing of the past, provided you keep your checking account funded adequately. Late payments are a primary cause of lowered credit scores.

You'll save money.

Paying your bills on time means few late charges. It also results in less money spent on checks, envelopes, and stamps. How many times have you been unable to find a stamp at home?

Auto bill-pay saves time.

Though auto pay is not an excuse to put your bills out of your mind completely, you'll spend less time and energy worrying about paying your bills. You won't need to sit down and make time for bill paying activities.

It benefits the environment.

No more paper bills, checks, or envelopes. You'll have less impact on the environment and save a few trees. The mail carrier won't be burning gas to deliver your payments, either.

There's a lower risk of identity theft.

Identity theft continues to be a significant issue nationwide. Sending snail mail with your account numbers and credit card numbers available to credit thieves is always a risk. While taking care of business online isn't foolproof, there is far more effort made to keep your financial information safe.

There are many advantages to setting up auto payments for your bills. Unfortunately, there are also a few disadvantages, too. Consider both before making a final decision. Consider these disadvantages:

It can be challenging stopping payments.

Automatic payments set up with your bank are usually easy to stop. However, automatic payments set up with a credit card or with the merchant can be very challenging to stop. Be sure to investigate the process for ceasing payments. In many cases, written notification is required.

Excessive credit card debt.

If you're using a credit card as your auto payment vehicle, you can rack up a lot of debt quickly. Be sure to keep your eye on your balance and pay it in full each month.

The costs can be higher.

Most auto bill paying services are free or very inexpensive. However, some do charge high fees. Be sure the costs are reasonable.

A lack of awareness.

Do you know how much your bills are each month? Can you be certain that you have enough money in your account to cover the bill? When your bills are paid without any attention from you, there is the potential to lose awareness. Review your bills and your bank account balance regularly.

There are a few disadvantages with auto bill paying, but the benefits outweigh the risks for most. The time and money savings are a significant advantage overpaying your bills manually.

Do the Work!

Maintaining awareness of your bills and the balance of your payment vehicle is important. Spend a couple of minutes each week monitoring the situation. Auto bill paying can save time, money, and improve your credit score. Consider adding this useful tool to your financial tool belt.

ARE YOU FINANCIALLY PREPARED TO RELOCATE?

Most people relocate because the move will increase their quality of life in some way or another. But, if your finances aren't quite prepared to carry you through the move and beyond, the negatives of relocating can more than outweigh the good.

Take some time to consider the financial responsibilities of moving before you give the go-ahead.

Use these strategies to financially prepare yourself for your move ahead of time:

Create an emergency fund.

In households that are about to undergo an expensive relocation, a well-stocked emergency fund is a requirement.

When you move, surprise fees and expenses will spring up at every corner. You might need to stay at a hotel for a night. You'll be charged activation fees for every service you start. Or, you may not land a job as soon as anticipated.

Sell big-ticket items you own, like televisions, computers, cars, antique furniture, and the like. In this way, you may be able to quickly create an emergency fund that will support you through a few months in your new home.

Have job offers before you move.

Ideally, you'll want to have a job lined up in your new location. This saves you from the emotional and financial pressure you'll endure once your savings begin to dwindle.

Set up interviews with companies you'd like to work for before relocating. In doing so, you'll have a higher likelihood of landing a job sooner than if you were to start sending applications once you arrive at your new home.

If you're relocating because your spouse has a job offer, be prepared to adjust your expenses to be within budget based on a single income at first. Once you land a job, you'll be able to add luxuries, like expensive cable packages and dining out.

Research and plan for the cost of living increase.

If you're going to take on a higher cost of living, you need to have the financial backing to do so, especially if you don't have a job lined up in your new location.

At the bare minimum, you should have at least three months' worth of living expenses saved up if you don't have a job in-hand. Include approximately one to two months' worth of expenses for emergencies even if you do have a job.

Visit the area beforehand.

With services, such as rent.com and Craigslist.org, it can be tempting to simply view the listing's pictures online and feel as if you know enough to rent the apartment but resist the urge.

Landlords display only the most flattering photos of their rental properties. Therefore, what is shown online isn't always the whole story.

You need to visit the property in person to discern whether the neighborhood is safe, whether the apartment truly is of high quality, or whether the neighbors seem to be trustworthy people.

Determine a plan.

If you're moving to an area where you know very few people, you need a plan. Sure, it may be tempting to take the higher paying job offer, or to greatly slash your expenses, but how much of it will you really enjoy if you have no friends or loved ones in the area?

Moving to a new state is an emotionally taxing process. Create a list of your favorite hobbies and the qualities you like in your current circle of friends. Then, think of places (book shop, coffee shop, sports teams, church, and volunteer work) where you may be able to meet friends that fit your criteria.

Do the Work!

Even if you feel that you aren't prepared to move at this moment, by simply delaying your goal a few months and drastically minimizing your expenses at your current location, you can still pursue the life you desire by edging towards your relocation one step at a time.

FINANCIAL CONCERNS WHEN STARTING A NEW JOB

Getting a job offer is always an exciting time. Whether you're getting your first job, a promotion, or changing careers, there's a lot to be happy about. Be sure to consider the financial aspect of any decision; starting a new job is no exception.

Before You Accept the Job:

Negotiate your pay.

It never hurts to ask for a little more money. Keep in mind that any increase in salary you earn now will only compound your future raises. Respectfully asking for more money doesn't cause any harm.

Negotiating is the highest paying activity you're likely ever to take part in. Consider that just a minute or two could result in thousands of dollars in additional income for many years. When was the last time you made that much money for a couple of minutes of work?

Ask about the benefits.

Typically, you'll be told the general aspects of the company benefits. Don't be afraid to ask for details. For example, some medical insurance plans are much more expensive than others. A job with a little lower salary might be much better when you have all the details.

After You Start Your New Job:

Deal with your previous 401(k).

Either roll the money into an IRA or move it into your new 401(k). Resist the temptation to withdraw the money; the tax penalties are significant. Ask your new human resources department about your options and then make the smart choice.

Keep your lifestyle in check.

Just because you receive a raise doesn't mean you have to buy a more expensive house or car. If you can maintain your spending level for even one year, you can save a lot of money. If you do increase your lifestyle, then be sure to bank at least part of your raise.

Getting a raise is a great opportunity to save a lot of money or aggressively pay down your debt.

Start paying yourself first.

Set up your bank account with automatic savings of part of your increased income so you start saving money immediately. It will be easier to start saving now than later because you won't miss the money that you've never seen.

Ensure you're withholding enough for taxes.

It is not financially smart to get a huge refund every year. On the other hand, it can be pretty challenging both financially and psychologically to have to pay more at tax time. Be confident your withholding is enough to guarantee a small refund each year.

Make benefit choices wisely.

Set up your life, health, and disability insurance, and other benefits intelligently for your own unique needs. For example, the most expensive medical plan might not be the option you want if you're young and in perfect health. Your life insurance needs will vary depending on your family situation.

Have your paycheck deposited into an interest-earning account.

Interest rates are so low right now that it might not matter a lot, but it makes sense to deposit your paycheck into an account that pays interest. You can always transfer what you need into your checking account later.

Do the Work!

Being financially healthy is the result of making smart decisions consistently. A job opportunity is a time for celebration; just ensure you're making positive financial moves to take your best advantage of this occasion.

GET THE MOST FROM MEMBERSHIP SERVICES

Membership services can help you save money on many common items that you purchase. You can find membership services at stores and boutiques. Hotels, airlines, theme parks, and other businesses also offer them. Roadside assistance programs are another type of membership service.

Although these memberships can include many delightful benefits, some of them cost you more than you would ordinarily spend.

Learn to find the membership opportunities that you'll use the most and that will bring you the best savings.

These tips will help you determine the most advantageous membership services for you and your family:

Read the benefits.

Before you spend money to become a member, examine the benefits of joining. The fine print is an important part of the evaluation process.

Membership services commonly go beyond standard benefits and features. For example, a roadside assistance program can also include benefits for travel and insurance. You can save money in multiple ways by becoming a member.

Compare membership plans and calculate costs.

If a program has several membership levels, it is important to compare the costs and benefits of each one.

The lowest-priced membership plan may not always be the best one for you. By comparing the price of each plan and figuring out how much you'll save, you can better understand the value of a program.

Keep the benefits in mind.

One of the common issues with these memberships is that you might forget the scope of the benefits after you join.

For example, did you know that a roadside assistance program could help you with discounts for passport photos? This type of program can also help you with free travel guides and vacation planning services.

Consider printing out the benefits of the ones you join and keep the list where it will be handy.

Ask questions before spending money.

Before you spend money on a repair or vacation, check the membership services for discounts and savings.

You may want to make a phone call or check the latest benefit statements before spending money. Services change. Be sure to have the latest information.

Keep track of your savings for renewal.

Before you automatically renew your membership service, check how much you saved with that membership in the past year.

You may want to avoid setting up automatic renewals from your bank or credit accounts. This will allow you to renew it or not -- whatever you decide.

Keep track of every penny you save with membership services. Did you get a discount at a restaurant because you're a member? Did you save money on movie tickets because you're a member? You can create a spreadsheet and list the amount you save. By making a spreadsheet on your phone, you can update it easily.

Pay attention to the small details.

Membership services often offer coupons to a variety of stores and other businesses. However, you have to take advantage of them before they expire.

Benefits can vary widely from program to program. You may be required to sign up separately for affiliated services or download benefits before you can use them. For example, maybe you need to download or print out coupons to receive your discounts.

The small details can include taking additional steps to access the full benefits. Assumptions about automatic benefits can cost you money.

Do the Work!

Before you walk away from a potential money-saving opportunity, spend time to examine the benefits of membership services. They offer discounts and savings on a variety of items.

FIND THE PERFECT BANK FOR YOUR SMALL BUSINESS

It can be challenging and frustrating to find the perfect bank and suitable account for your small business. Choosing the perfect bank is an important decision that requires time and attention. You want to avoid a bank that charges you an arm and a leg in fees.

Simplify your life by finding a great bank for your business.

Follow these tips to find a bank that suits your small business needs:

Get online.

You can find out more online in a few minutes than in a few hours driving around to different banks. Make an initial list of banks to check out further. Before long, you'll have a list of fitting candidates.

Realize that all banks are different.

Many people erroneously believe all banks are the same. Although the banking industry is one of the most heavily regulated, there is still enough wiggle room for differences to emerge.

Banks are free to create their own policies around account minimums, interest rates, fees, extra charges, services provided, and loan qualification criteria.

Ensure you're choosing a bank with the services you require minus the exorbitant fees.

Know the requirements of your business.

Consider all the services you want your bank to provide for you and your business. Will you be taking out a loan or are you just looking for a place to stash your cash? What is your monthly cash flow?

Can your bank of choice meet those requirements? It might be worthwhile to make a list of your requirements and research how they mesh with the bank's offerings.

Consider the types of accounts, deposit frequency, credit cards, wire transfers, loan availability, minimum balance requirements, payroll services, and any other services you're interested in.

Watch the fees!

The fees are interesting. They don't seem significant until you add up how much they are costing you over time. Always keep the fees in mind.

In the long run, the difference between 2% vs. 1% can be costly.

You might find that one bank provides free wire transfers and other charges $15. Also, investigate whether a bank charges ATM fees.

Hit the road.

Drive around and check out all the banks meeting your requirements. Stop in and ask to speak to an account manager. Let them know what you're looking for, and they'll tell you all about their accounts and services.

How much do you like the bank and the employees?

The customer service department and the compatibility you feel with the people in your branch can make a huge difference. A good relationship with those at your bank is important.

While you might be inclined to work with a large bank, you might want to give the smaller, local banks a look.

Ask other small business owners about their experiences with banks.

Never totally stop shopping for a bank.

Even after you find a bank, occasionally look around at what other banks are offering. Your new bank might be the best one for you at this moment, but maybe not in nine months.

Do the Work!

Finding a great bank is an important part of your business success. Take the time to do your research. Figure out what you're looking for and go visit the banks that meet your criteria. No one enjoys shopping for banks, but the success of your business demands it. A supportive and reliable bank makes life so much easier.

ELIMINATE OVERDRAFT CHARGES

Likely, if you are receiving overdraft fees, already have some financial challenges to get into that situation in the first place. To add insult to injury, you're charged a considerable amount of money as a penalty.

Banks are growing more reliant on these fees. These fees account for over $32 billion in income for banks each year.

Overdraft fees can be real killers.

Banks even have software that maximizes your overdraft charges. Imagine that you have $100 in the bank and two outstanding checks for $200 and $50. If both of those checks become payable around the same time, the software will ensure that the $200 check gets paid first. That way, you're overdrawn twice rather than just once.

While many banks offer overdraft protection, this is rarely the answer. It has been shown that those that overdraft habitually would actually save money by paying the overdraft fees rather than opting for overdraft protection. Try these strategies to eliminate or reduce your overdraft charges:

Use a credit card instead of a debit card or checks.

This method is not without risk. It requires you to keep careful track of your spending and to have the necessary discipline to avoid overspending. This method can be dangerous if you're unwilling or unable to control your spending.

With this method, you only need to write one check each month. That makes it tough to be overdrawn.

You can enter all of your credit card purchases into your checkbook, just as if you had written a check. This will help to control your spending.

Keep some extra money in your checking account.

This is similar to keeping an extra $20 in your car for emergencies. It might sound silly, but many people avoid overdraft problems by keeping extra money in their checking account. This can also help to stay above the minimum balance required to avoid unnecessary fees.

Use online banking systems to stay on top of your balance.

Most banks today offer many types of alerts to keep you up to date with your account balance information. You can check on your pending payments at the end of each day and make the necessary corrections.

Many accounts will allow you to set up low-balance alerts.

Only use cash.

If you never use a check or debit card, it is difficult to overdraw an account. You also can't be overdrawn by withdrawing too much cash. The bank simply won't let you have it.

Use cash for your day-to-day expenses. You can pay your bills with online banking, but a better alternative might be to pay your bills with money orders. Your bank can provide you with a money order, but so can your local post office. These generally aren't free, but it's a sure way to avoid being overdrawn on your account again.

Overdraft fees can create a tremendous amount of financial challenges if you're already struggling. Those with at least one overdraft pay an average of over $250 in overdraft fees each year. You can certainly find something better to do with that money other than giving it to your bank!

Do the Work!

Follow one of these strategies or come up with your own. Responsible banking is simple, yet many people struggle to manage it responsibly and effectively. Always be aware of how much is in your account and track your spending. You may need to review your balance and spending on a daily basis. Develop a plan that works for you.

FIND OUT YOUR CREDIT SCORE

With all the commercials on television and the Internet, everyone seems to know how to view their credit report. But what about your credit score? Seeing the information on the report is great, but what most of us want to know is the actual credit score that banks and other institutions are using to determine if we deserve the credit we desire.

Keep in mind is that the true, 'official' credit score is only available through Fair Isaacs, the originator of the FICO score (Fair Isaac and Company).

All other scores are estimations meant to simulate your FICO score. Fair Isaacs won't release their formula, so everything else is merely a good guess. At this time, the FICO score is used by 96% of banks. You can obtain credit scores through these venues:

CreditKarma.com.

Credit Karma will allow you to view your Trans Union score. Trans Union is one of the 3 major credit bureaus. The score only reflects your Trans Union credit report, however, and is not your true FICO score. On the plus side, Credit Karma is free and allows you to track your score over time.

There are other similar sites that provide free scores. Some of them include:

- QuizzleCredit
- SesameEquifax
- Credit Score Card

Quizzle and Credit Sesame provide your Experian score. Experian is another one of the 3 major credit bureaus.

Credit monitoring services.

These services typically provide all 3 credit scores and either all 3 credit reports or an all-inclusive credit report that compiles all the credit reports into a single report.

These services are about $20 a month, but most come with a free trial, usually 7 days. Again, these are not the FICO scores that most banks use, but the individual scores of each of the credit bureaus.

Some examples of these services would be www.creditreport.com and www.gofreecredit.com.

Apply for a loan.

If you apply for a loan, you can request that the lender show you your scores. Applying for credit will slightly hurt your credit score. This is not the preferred way to view your scores, but you're likely to see your real FICO scores. There are less damaging ways to receive your scores for free.

FICO scores.

If you want to view the real thing and don't want to apply for a loan, go to www.myfico.com. You can sign up for a credit monitoring service that's $15/month with a 7-day free trial. You also have the option of purchasing individual scores and credit reports at the same website.

A smart solution is to follow your free scores and track them over time.

Periodically, check your FICO scores and see how well the estimated values are tracking with the 'real' scores. Your credit scores are no laughing matter. Keep track of your credit scores and be diligent in raising them when you can.

Many employers check credit scores to determine whether to even give you a job! A difference of 100 points in your credit score can also mean a difference of many thousands of dollars in additional interest charges over the years.

Do the Work!

Be wise: check your credit scores today and monitor them regularly.

CREDIT SCORE DESTROYERS

Your credit score not only determines whether you can get a credit card, mortgage, or auto loan, it's also a critical factor in determining the interest rate you have attached to those items. A low credit score can cost a lot of money over your lifetime.

Not everyone is aware of the many factors that determine a credit score. It's easy to make assumptions that seem logical but are actually false. Acting on incorrect beliefs is a sure way to make a critical mistake.

Save money and make your financial life easier by avoiding these seven credit destroyers:

Carrying a big balance on your credit cards.

While having a lot of debt is never a good idea, using more than 30% of the available credit on your credit cards hurts your credit score.

For example, if your credit limit is $10,000, your score drops if your balance is over $3,000. This is referred to as the "utilization ratio." Keep yours under 30%.

Paying late is a huge factor in your credit score.

Experts estimate that 35% of your credit score is determined by your payment history. Any late payments will lower your score.

Closing credit cards is a credit score killer.

This is related to your utilization ratio. By closing a credit card, you lower the amount of credit that's available to you. Your credit score is also sensitive to the length of your credit history.

Defaulting is an obvious credit score mistake.

When you fail to pay back a loan you owe to a lender, you can lose as much as 100 points from your credit score. Make every effort to pay back your loans.

If you're struggling, contact the lender and attempt to make other arrangements. They can be very flexible if failing to do so means not getting their payments.

Applying for too much credit.

Everyone needs to have some credit but applying for too much has a negative effect on your score.

Each time you apply for more credit, your potential lender makes an inquiry about your credit history.

Each of those inquiries lowers your credit score.

Avoid sending in every credit card offer that shows up in your mailbox.

Not having a credit card at all.

Many people are getting rid of their credit cards in an effort to avoid debt. Still, this does nothing to help your credit score.

Experts believe that the ideal credit score includes 2-3 credit cards. Credit diversity can account for as much as 10% of your credit score.

Credit cards help to keep your credit history current.

Co-signing for someone else can be a mistake.

Putting your credit on the line by co-signing for someone else is a huge risk. Their failure to stay current with the payments can destroy your credit score.

You're equally responsible for that debt, so any late payments or defaults will show up on your own credit report.

You can even be subject to collections and lawsuits. If a lender won't do business with them, you might want to reconsider before co-signing.

Do the Work!

Avoiding these common mistakes can help give you a great score that will guarantee you the lowest interest rates, even if your credit score is poor now. It may take time to boost your credit score, but it's definitely possible.

Give your credit score the amount of attention it deserves. It makes life a lot easier!

DISPUTING CREDIT REPORT INFORMATION

The information in your credit report can affect many areas of your life, so it's important to keep track of what's in it. If you find information that is incorrect for any reason, it's your job to dispute that information in order to have it removed from the report.

Only you are looking out for your own credit rating, so it's to your advantage to pay attention to your report.

There are actually three credit reports: from Experian, Equifax, and Trans Union. Monitoring all three of these credit reports is essential because the information can differ from report to report.

Follow this process to ensure your credit reports are accurate:

Request your credit report.

The fastest way to get a copy of your credit report is to visit AnnualCreditReport.com, where you're entitled to receive a copy of each of your three reports for free once per year.

- If you haven't been following what's in your credit reports, start out by requesting all three reports at once, because the information they contain can actually vary quite significantly, depending on who has reported what to them. The differences from one report to the next can amount to a significant credit score difference.
- Once you've obtained and corrected past information in your reports, you can stay updated by spreading out your credit report requests every 4 months. Simply request your report from *one* of the credit reporting agencies every 4 months, and over the course of a year, you'll have received all three.

- Of course, correct important mistakes in all 3 of them if you find an error.

Verifying information accuracy.

Comb over all three credit reports thoroughly in search of incorrect or inaccurate information. Any detail that isn't right should be changed, even if it's just a wrong address because these pieces of information can have an impact on how lenders view you.

Contact the credit reporting agency.

If you find information that needs to be changed in your credit report, the next step is to contact the agency in charge of that specific report. It can take some time to dispute incorrect information, so the sooner you begin, the better.

Writing a dispute letter.

You can find sample dispute letters online that will give you a good starting point for writing this letter. Be professional and include all the necessary proof that the information is incorrect so the credit agency can make the change.

Include copies of any documents that support your position. Do not include the originals.

Disputing an item.

Typically, the credit agency (Experian, Equifax, or Trans Union) will contact the company that reported the false information, and an investigation will follow to determine whether the information is inaccurate.

Add accounts to your file.

If not all of your credit accounts are being reflected on your credit file, then you may want to ensure that missing information is added. You can achieve this by contacting the companies that aren't reporting your credit history and asking them to begin reporting for you.

Not every company is going to want to report this information for you, so it can take some time for you to have this information added to your account. However, if you're diligent, you should be able to have the information added.

Following up.

Follow up on your requests if you don't hear anything from the credit reporting company within 30 days, as this is the normal length of time for an investigation.

Do the Work!

The power is in your hands to keep your credit report in good standing. If there is inaccurate information in your credit report, or if important information is missing, then take the steps to get the information corrected. Your next job, home, or loan may depend on it.

ERRORS ON YOUR CREDIT REPORT

It's important to monitor your credit reports at least yearly.

That way, you'll be able to spot and handle any mistake that occurs on your credit report that could adversely affect you.

Using this process will help you find errors on your credit report and correct them:

Go through the report with a fine-tooth comb.

When you receive a copy of your credit report, sit down and take the time to review it. Consider it an important part of your financial goals to find out what your creditors are "saying" about your financial life.

Look at each item.

Thoroughly check each entry to spot any listings that don't look familiar. If you don't remember an item, make a note out in the margin, like "What's this?" or "I didn't apply for this loan."

Notice the names of companies and financial institutions.

Are there any you haven't heard of? If so, put an "X" by them so you can look up the names on the internet. An unfamiliar name may well be the name of a company that is known by various names.

Consult your own financial records.

If the company still sounds unfamiliar, pull your own financial records for the year in question. Perhaps you'll see some record of what you did that will refresh your memory regarding that part of your report.

Call the credit bureau where the report originated.

If you can't resolve or figure out a particular listing on your report, contact the bureau who issued the report. Experian, Equifax, and Trans Union each offer customer service and might be able to assist you.

Contact the company that you believe has made false claims against you.

Try to resolve the situation with the entity directly and insist they make the proper changes to the credit bureau to correct your information.

Dispute the claim.

In the event you are unsuccessful in resolving a credit issue with a creditor, you can formally dispute the claim. You do this by phoning the credit bureau that produced the report. You can also contact the credit bureau online to fight the claim there. State you want to dispute the claim. You'll likely have to explain why.

Place a fraud alert on your credit report.

If your identity was stolen or any of your banking accounts or credit cards were inappropriately used by others, you should contact the agency where you received your credit report and follow their steps to place a fraud alert on your credit report.

This way, the agency will monitor your account extra close to ensure your privacy and security and might even inform you of any action as it occurs on your account under your name.

Do your homework.

Learn more about credit reporting from the Federal Trade Commission's website at http://www.ftc.gov/bcp/menus/consumer/credit.shtm.

Do the Work!

Your credit report should be an accurate reflection of your financial life. Go through your credit report and examine each entry thoroughly. Take notes of entities issuing information about you and then peruse your own financial records to support any claims you may use as you go through this process.

Stay on top of your credit reports so you can correct errors right away. Protect your credit and identity by obtaining your credit report at least yearly and following up on questionable data.

REMOVE CREDIT REPORT ERRORS

Checking your credit reports on an annual basis can be a great idea. A study done by the Federal Trade Commission found that 25% of all consumers have an error on their credit report that negatively impacts their credit score.

There's a good chance that your reports have one or more errors.

The study also showed that 80% of those that challenge items on their credit report are able to get at least some negative information altered or removed. That's great news!

Follow this process to get these errors corrected:

Get copies of your credit report from the three major bureaus.

You can get a free copy of each report each year from AnnualCreditReport.com. If you've recently been rejected for credit, you're also entitled to a free copy of the report containing derogatory information.

Get your official credit scores.

It would be a shame to do all this work and not know how much of an effect your efforts had on the metric that matters the most.

Find and record all the errors that are harming your credit score.

Some people decide to simply challenge all the negative information, whether it's accurate or not.

Write a dispute.

Your dispute can be very simple. Provide enough information that the credit bureau can identify you and the item you're disputing. In general, it's most effective to declare that you were never late or that the account isn't yours.

Mail your disputes and request a return receipt.

The credit bureau is on the clock from the time they receive your complaint. If they can't complete their investigation within 30 days, they basically have to make the changes you requested. Include only one dispute per letter.

The credit bureaus would love for you to file your dispute online. It saves them money and helps to automate the process. Receiving your letter is much more cumbersome for them. So, send your complaints via snail-mail.

Watch the calendar.

Their response should be postmarked within 30 days of receiving your letters.

Evaluate the responses you receive back.

It's likely that some of your disputes will be found in your favor. It's also likely that some will not. One credit bureau has been known to simply give you what you want without investigating at all!

Continue disputing all the negative items.

At the end of the day, the credit bureaus exist to make money. They make money by selling credit reports, not by dealing with consumers. Your disputes cost them money. With a little diligence, you're likely to get your way, so be persistent.

Consumers have historically done well when suing the credit bureaus. It's difficult for them to truly verify the information in your credit reports. If you're not satisfied with the results, consider filing a claim in small claims court. Credit bureaus get fined $1,000 per infraction. You'll likely settle out of court and get your credit report cleaned up.

Stay organized.

Maintain records of all your correspondence. Make copies and keep those copies filed in an organized manner. Be sure to keep track of dates.

Do the Work!

Fixing the errors on your credit reports is simple, but it does take time. It's important to check your reports every year. The cost of credit reporting errors can be staggering, as they can dramatically increase your interest rates on any loans you receive.

Request your credit reports today and spend the time to examine them carefully. Consider making it a part of your annual financial housekeeping.

HIDDEN BENEFITS OF USING A CREDIT CARD

Credit cards come with several hidden benefits. Companies offer multiple perks to help you get the most out of your card. Are you aware of some perks of using your card?

Check the terms of your credit cards for these benefits:

Roadside assistance.

Did you know credit cards often offer roadside assistance that is similar to AAA?

This perk varies largely based on your credit card provider. Companies either offer free service or a paid service. You'll have to check the policies as you sign up for this perk.

If you're stranded and need help, roadside assistance can come to rescue you.

Longer warranties.

Did you purchase an appliance or electronic device with your favorite credit card? Your credit card may extend your warranties.

Protection from cancellations.

Did you miss your concert or play? Credit card companies can refund the money you spent on tickets. However, you have to use the card to make the initial purchase.

Even if it's your fault you missed an event, you might still get a refund. This service is only provided by some carriers, so check your card before you claim this benefit.

Exclusive access while you travel.

The fancy airport lounges can be yours if you have the right card.

Credit cards can offer you the chance to stay in the best airport lounges and hotels, at no extra charge. These exclusive offers vary greatly based on your card, but many of them will grant you special access. Enjoy a unique cocktail or appetizer while you wait for your next flight.

Extra help while you travel.

The lounges are not the only travel benefit. If you have an emergency while you're traveling, credit cards can help you. They offer services such as insurance to help you if your luggage disappears or your phone is lost.

Companies can offer assistance in several ways. They may replace the luggage or send you money so you can replace it yourself. They may also help you track down the luggage.

Replacing stolen items.

Was an item you purchased stolen?

If one of your purchases is stolen, credit cards can help you. As long as you paid for the item with a credit card, you can report it to them. This will vary by provider, so check your card.

Items that can be replaced vary from electronics to furniture. However, not everything is covered. For example, stolen food isn't covered by most cards.

Return items.

The sweater you purchased is too pink, and the shoes are too tight. Your credit card can help you return these items.

If the person or business refuses to take back the items, then the credit card will refund it anyway. This is done within 90 days of the purchase.

You'll need to save the receipt and tags to ensure everything is covered.

Credit cards limit the total amount of money that can be refunded, so extremely expensive items are usually not covered. In addition, some items like food may not be a category that falls into the help section.

Do the Work!

Credit card perks are often hidden in the fine print. However, you can benefit greatly by being aware of these benefits.

WIN BIG WITH CREDIT CARD REWARDS

If you have good credit and you're not using rewards credit cards, you may want to reconsider. Using rewards credit cards will allow you to access all kinds of discounts and freebies without spending any more money than normal.

Let's take a look at some rewards cards that are available, and the goodies you can get when you use them:

Cash Back Rewards Cards.

Cashback rewards credit cards are one of the most common types, and they're simple to understand. Each time you spend money, you'll earn points. Then you can use those points to get cashback or credits on your statements.

Gas Rewards Credit Cards.

Gas rewards work **similarly** to the cashback rewards cards. This type of card allows you to earn cashback whenever you buy gas.

If you do a lot of driving or if you have to pay for your own fuel when you're on the job, you can earn a lot of points with this type of card.

The best cards available offer up to 5% cashback on gas purchases with a cap of $1500 per quarter.

Sky Miles Credit Cards.

Rather than offering cashback, some credit cards allow you to earn Sky Miles when you spend money using your credit card. This is a way to achieve largely discounted or even free trips anywhere in the world. You can also use your points to upgrade from coach to first class.

If you do a lot of traveling, you may also want to sign up for rewards programs that airlines, hotels, and rental car companies offer. These are separate from the credit card rewards programs, but when you combine the two, the savings can really add up.

Find out how to get the most out of rewards credit cards:

Use a rewards credit card for everyday purchases.

Get the most out of your rewards card by buying groceries, gas, clothes, and even paying your bills with your credit card.

The more you spend, the more points you'll earn, and the closer you'll be to the rewards.

Avoid spending money just to earn points.

It isn't a good idea to buy things you wouldn't normally buy just to earn points. There are plenty of necessities that you're already buying, and those will earn you plenty of points.

Try not to carry a balance on a rewards credit card.

Since these types of cards tend to have higher interest rates, it's a good idea to pay off your rewards cards every month.

Although rewards cards can have many benefits, it's important to be aware of these possible drawbacks:

On the surface, rewards credit cards may sound too good to be true.

You can absolutely get some great deals, but ensure you read the fine print. It's important to know all the rules that go along with any type of rewards program.

Some rewards credit cards have hefty annual fees.

Some cards don't offer their best rewards until you've spent a certain amount of money in a given period.

There may also be restrictions that make it difficult to claim your rewards.

The rewards you earn may also have an expiration date, which puts you in a "use it or lose it" situation.

Do the Work!

Find out all the rules and avoid the issues that are buried in the fine print when you're looking into getting a rewards credit card. You want to make the most out of these types of credit cards and reap all the benefits. With a little effort, you can use these cards to enjoy some tremendous rewards.

SAVE YOUR ESTATE: AVOID PROBATE ISSUES

All estates must go through the probate process. Probate is the legal process of determining if a will is valid, paying any qualifying debt and estate taxes, and distributing whatever assets remain.

It is potentially a very complicated legal process, and an attorney should be involved in any estate planning activities.

Using these strategies will help you design your estate to avoid some common challenges of the probate process and save you money:

Have a valid will.

Probate can last up to a year in many cases; typically, this is due to a protracted process of validating the will. Probate is a legal process, so the longer it takes, the more money the attorneys make. Be sure to draw up your will with an attorney and review it annually for anything that needs to be addressed.

Avoid having your assets pass through probate.

- **Create one or more trusts.** Assets and property within a viable trust avoid the probate process. They are simply transferred to the beneficiaries of the trust. This also has the effect of providing greater protection of the assets from creditors.
- **Name beneficiaries for your 401(k) account.** This will allow the account to avoid having to pass through the probate process. Again, this can provide protection from creditors.
- **Name beneficiaries for your IRA.** As with the 401(k), naming at least one beneficiary will avoid probate and can shield the assets from creditors. Just call your IRA firm, and they can help you out.

- **Name beneficiaries on your life insurance policies.** This is the same situation as above. If you don't name a beneficiary, then the proceeds are simply paid to your estate and must pass through probate, increasing the attorney's fees. Be sure to name your beneficiaries!
- **Own Assets Jointly.** This can include almost anything: real estate, vehicles, stocks, and more. A jointly owned asset is passed onto the survivor automatically. Your bank account can have a paid-on-death designation (P.O.D.), and brokerage accounts can have a transfer-on-death (T.O.D.) designation, allowing ownership of the accounts to pass directly to the beneficiaries upon your death.
- **Give it away:** You can gift your assets to anyone you choose, each year, up to a specific amount, tax-free. As of 2011, you can give as many people as you want a gift up to $13,000 without having to worry about paying taxes on the gift. Also, the tax only kicks in after you have gifted a total of $1 million over your lifetime. Any gifts that do not exceed $13,000 do not count towards the $1 million limit. Interestingly, it is the gift-giver that is responsible for paying the tax, if any. This reduces the amount of your estate and will lower the probate costs since they are based upon the total value of the estate. See your tax advisor for more information.

Except for certain circumstances, assets that avoid probate are still subject to federal estate taxes, including those assets held in living trusts. A good estate tax attorney can guide you through this maze so that probate expenses will impact your family as little as possible.

The real enemies in the probate process are lack of planning and failure to utilize all the available options. Having your will prepared properly will eliminate the amount of time your estate spends in the probate process. In the legal world, time is very expensive. You don't want the attorneys to get your money instead of your heirs.

Do the Work!

By planning your estate with the appropriate financial and legal professionals, you can maximize the amount of your estate that passes to your family, friends, and charitable organizations. The unfortunate alternative is that more of your estate will pass to your creditors, various attorneys, and the legal system.

TAX TIPS FOR HOMEOWNERS

You may already know that you can deduct the mortgage interest you pay on your home, but what other tax advantages are lurking in that house?

One of the biggest challenges of owning a home is dealing with the tax laws, especially those around points and cost basis.

Just a little knowledge can really clear up these frequently confusing terms. Here's the scoop on mortgage basis points and how they're used in your home's value, cost basis, and tax burden.

What are Points?

Points are fees that you pay in order to enter into a mortgage. Points are considered to be prepaid interest, and as such, you can deduct them. The issue is, can you deduct the full amount upfront, or must you divide your deductions out over the life of the loan?

- You can deduct all the points the first year if all the following are true:
- The loan is used to purchase or build your primary home.
- Paying points is customary in your area.
- The points aren't paid for appraisal fees, title fees, property taxes, or similar fees.
- You didn't borrow the money to pay the points.
- The points were based on a percentage of the loan and that fact is easy to see.

Cost Basis

Cost basis is the original value of an asset for tax purposes. The cost basis is quite easy to calculate; it is simply the price you paid for the home plus any capital improvements that have been made. Then you would subtract any seller-paid points, depreciation, and losses.

Capital improvements would be anything that increases the home's value. Capital improvements would include such things as swimming pools and adding a room.

Understanding the Tax Burden When You Sell

If you owned the home (and lived in it) for at least two out of the last 5 years, you most likely don't owe any tax at all. A single person doesn't pay tax on capital gains of less than $250,000; for married couples, the limit is $500,000. So, as a married couple, you could purchase a home for $100,000 and sell it for $600,000 and not owe any tax on the proceeds.

There are circumstances under which the two-year requirement is waived, such as health issues, divorce, change of employment, and more.

In these cases, the amount of the exemption is based on the number of months the home was lived in. So, if you were single and lived there for 12 months, you would be entitled to an exemption of $125,000, or half of the deduction allowed if you had lived there the required two years.

Inherited Property

The cost basis on inherited property is the market value *at the time of the owner's death*.

This is great because it doesn't matter how much your grandmother paid for her home back in 1960. If you inherited the home, she paid $20,000 for, and it's now worth $175,000 (when she died), you would not owe any tax on the proceeds even if you were to sell the home immediately.

Do the Work!

While it's likely that the related tax laws will change again (they always do), it's always a good idea to understand your home's cost basis and your potential tax liability. Sooner or later the information may be pertinent to your tax situation, so keep abreast of the tax implications and deductions for your home.

TAX BREAKS FOR HOMEOWNERS

Some of the biggest benefits of owning your home are income tax deductions. While you may be familiar with the more common deductions, there are a few that might surprise you. Let's examine a few ways to get more of your money back from the government as a homeowner.

Mortgage Interest:

- All of your mortgage interest is tax deductible, provided your home loan is less than $1 million.
- The interest on home equity loan payments is generally tax deductible as well. The equity loan must be less than $100,000 to be able to deduct all the interest.
- There are some limitations, but you can also deduct the interest on loans for second homes. These can also include boats and recreational vehicles, provided they have sleeping, cooking, and bathroom facilities.

Mortgage Points:

- Mortgage points are also tax deductible. The only real question is when you can take the deduction.
- In general, if the loan is to purchase or renovate your main residence, you can take the full deduction that year.
- If the loan is a refinance or home equity loan that is not used for renovation purposes, then the points can only be deducted equally over the lifetime of the loan.
- Any points paid on loans for a second residence can also only be deducted over the life of the loan.

Property Taxes:

- You can deduct what you pay for property taxes for as long as you own your home.
- Property taxes are an itemized tax deduction on Schedule A.

Sales Gains:

- Provided that you owned the home for at least two years and lived there at least 2 out of the last 5 years, you don't have to pay taxes on up to $250,000 of profit you may realize when you sell. The amount rises to $5000,000 for joint filers.
- If you're forced to sell before meeting these requirements, you may still be eligible for some tax relief. The IRS has a list of exceptions that can help, which includes death, divorce, job loss, and some other events.

Do the Work!

Keep track of your information and use it to your advantage.

GET THE FACTS: COMPARE TAX-ADVANTAGED INVESTMENTS

Missing two page chart

CHAPTER THIRTEEN, SUPPORT

Which advantages can be used to create your financial health and wealth?

You are ready to take advantage of your new thoughts, beliefs, and understanding. Use this section to reinforce your ability to create change.

Getting Started

Read through each section. They are designed to help you change your thoughts into reality.

Create My Reality

I create my own reality with my thoughts, focus, goals, and effort.

Use this self-affirming language to teach your thoughts a new habit:

- I am the creator of my reality. I choose to be the creator of my life. I refuse to leave my life up to chance and circumstance.
- I have a direction for my life and take full responsibility for fulfilling it.
- I have the power to choose how I view the world. By holding positive thoughts, I have a positive outlook on life. I am always looking for opportunities to move my life in the direction of my dreams. The way I choose to look at the world helps to create my reality.
- My goals are clear to me. My goals are my destination. I create my life by choosing my future and then moving toward it. I focus on my goals each day. In this way, I design and create a future that I can love.
- I have the ability to choose how I spend my time. This is the most important tool for creating my life.
- My time and effort have the power to shape my world and my life. Continuous effort created the Grand Canyon with the simple flow of water. I can accomplish equally impressive things in my own life.
- Today, I accept responsibility for creating my life. I choose to see the world from a healthy perspective and use my time intelligently. I know I can accomplish great things today.

Do the Work!

Take time for self-reflection:

1. Does the way I view life help or hinder me?

2. What do I want from life?

3. How can I spend today in order to create positive change in my life?

Engage My Mind

I sharpen my mind by keeping it engaged.

Use this self-affirming language to teach your thoughts a new habit:

- I am aware that the easiest way to reduce mental sharpness is to fail to fully use my mind. I believe that keeping my mind engaged helps me to be smart, creative, and capable of anything.
- I regularly participate in activities that keep my mind sharp. This approach helps me to come up with great business ideas at work. My contribution to my job is obvious because I provide original concepts and solutions.
- It is important for me to engage in a regular exercise regimen. When I am physically active, my brain works much better.
- I recognize the opportunities in front of me and am able to process ideas more quickly when my mind is engaged.
- I am also a better parent when I keep my mind sharp. I am able to help my kids with their homework and stay active when they want to play.
- I am conscious of the roles I play in life. I am aware that my mental capacity is necessary to be effective in each role. I do what is necessary to ensure I remain effective because I take my responsibilities seriously.
- I strive to be the best parent, spouse, friend, and employee possible.
- Today, I commit to including time in each day for sharpening my mind. I acknowledge that it is a precious resource worth preserving. My quality of life benefits when my mind remains sharp.

Do the Work!

Take time for self-reflection:

1. What games can I play to keep my mind quick and sharp?

2. How do I ensure I get enough rest each night, so my brain is fresh in the morning?

3. In what ways can a sharp mind help me with my daily responsibilities?

Moving Forward Daily

I move my financial life forward each day.

Use this self-affirming language to teach your thoughts a new habit:

- I see the importance of having financial security and I work to attain it. Being financially secure is worthwhile to me. Each day, I work to advance the quality of my financial life and future.
- When I see financial challenges, I tackle them right away. There is always something to learn from a challenge. My life is improved because of the financial obstacles I overcome.
- I ensure a sound financial life by paying my bills on time, keeping my debt under control, and saving for the future. I earn more than I spend.
- By improving my financial life, I can also help others. My family, friends, and community all benefit from my financial prowess.
- It is much easier for me to think about my purchases and make good choices than to waste money on impulse purchases that I may later regret. My frugality keeps me from having too many bills. Having enough money is important to me.
- Because I have enough financially, I am able to focus on my future. Saving, investing, and giving to others are all things that I enjoy. I can do those things because I take care of the money that is entrusted to me. It is very important to me to help others financially, and I do it readily and happily each day.
- Today, I actively work to improve and advance my financial life.

Do the Work!

Take time for self-reflection:

1. What can I do to ensure I'm making the right financial choices for my future?

2. How can I help my family make good financial choices?

3. What is the best way to improve my financial future right now?

The Economy and My Strength

I strengthen my financial situation regardless of the economy.

Use this self-affirming language to teach your thoughts a new habit:

- My business transactions are thriving. My money management principles prevent me from being affected by the economic crisis. Despite the reports and warnings about a wavering economy, my finances are improving.
- I buy only what I can afford. I meet my needs and those of my family first. I use my leftover money to build my savings, make investments, and purchase things I desire. I stay away from buying items just to keep up with the others who appear to have more.
- My finances are flourishing because I am a giver, not a borrower. I give to others freely. When I am in need, I devise a plan to save enough money for the purchases I need to make, instead of buying things I cannot afford.
- Giving myself time to establish savings prevents me from falling into the cycle of borrowing and staying in debt. Living by the principle of only buying what I can pay for frees me from the bonds of debt and causes my finances to thrive.
- I look ahead with positivity, trusting that any economic setback is simply a temporary stage. My finances are on the rise regardless of what I see around me. I free myself from fear and financial stress, so I can think clearly and make sound decisions.
- My finances are improving one step at a time. I am patient with the process. In the meantime, I look for ways to reduce my debt and increase my sources of income.
- Today I choose to rest on the arms of peace knowing that I am steadily strengthening my financial situation regardless of the economy.

Do the Work!

Take time for self-reflection:

1. Why is it necessary to be patient when building my savings?

2. Am I living within my means?

3. How can I improve my finances further in the next six months?

Business Opportunities

I am open to new business opportunities.

Use this self-affirming language to teach your thoughts a new habit:

- Because I strive to be financially fit and responsible, I am willing to try different kinds of work to earn money.
- Sometimes I fall into the lull of continuity. Being content with the sameness of my existence can be a good thing. Even so, I keep my eyes open to any new business prospects that might come along. I want to be prepared to benefit from golden opportunities to increase my income whenever they arrive.
- One of my goals is to be financially secure. Therefore, I strive to be ready for any chance to do business with others. Whether the new proposal is related to my life's work or just a novel business opportunity that comes along, I am ready and willing to consider all prospects.
- When an occasion to earn extra dollars presents itself, I examine it and ensure I fully understand all aspects of it. I weigh the pros and cons. Then, I make a decision. If I decide to accept the offer, I follow through with whatever I must do to make it profitable.
- Any venture might lead to bigger business possibilities in the future. I never know who I might meet or what skills I might gain that can benefit me. So, I stay aware and open to all prospects.
- Today, I am willing to invest some time into looking at new business opportunities and considering them with an open mind, adventurous spirit, and an optimistic attitude.

Do the Work!

Take time for self-reflection:

1. Am I open to new business opportunities?

2. What are my concerns or fears about taking a chance on a possible venture?

3. How much time or money am I willing to invest in new opportunities?

14

PLANNING

You are at the detailed planning stage of your financial health and wellness. This section goes into great detail about how to:

- Turn Your Passion to Profit
- Write an Effective Business Plan
- Financial Therapy
- And more!

The more support you have to plan for a successful financial future, the more prepared you will be.

Getting Started

It is great to have the opportunity laid out before you. Take every advantage you can and plan for your constant success. Put the action in and you will have the privilege of being financially satisfied as you enjoy reaping the rewards of your labor.

TURN YOUR PASSION TO PROFIT

Everyone has things they absolutely love to do. Maybe you love to write. Maybe taking photos makes you feel like a million dollars. Or maybe you love crafting hand-made signs. Your passion is the thing that makes you come alive.

But you don't think you could ever make money from your passion. Nobody would pay you to do that. It's too much fun and you love it too much. No way could you make money doing it.

That's where you're wrong. Thanks to the internet, almost any passion can be turned into a profitable side hustle.

You can make money doing the things you love the most.

Yep. You can turn your passion project into a profitable project. Let's be honest. You all could use some extra cash in your lives. You've got bills to pay, kids to send to school, car repairs to make, and a dozen other expenses. Some extra cash could be useful and go a long way toward making your lives easier.

How would it change your life to make an extra $1,000 per month? You can easily make money if you know how to create a profitable side hustle. In fact, if you know what you're doing, you may be able to turn your passion project into your full-time job.

Can you imagine how rewarding it would be to do what you love for your job? Your quality of life would drastically improve, and your overall life satisfaction would go through the roof.

How Do You Start?

A side hustle isn't just about money in the bank, as helpful as that can be. A side hustle changes your life. When you build something for yourself, even as you continue to work your day job, you become empowered. You gain confidence. You create security, both in the form of extra cash and also in the fact that you're opening up future opportunities for yourself.

Of course, all this raises the critical question: how do you start a side hustle? Because a lot of questions come with starting a side hustle.

- What products or services should you sell?
- Where should you sell them?
- How much should you charge?
- How do you market yourself?
- How do you determine if your side hustle will ever make money?

In this unit, *Turn Your Passion to Profit*, you will follow a road map for making your passion into a profitable side hustle. You will be guided step-by-step to making money doing what you love. By the end, you'll know everything you need to know to start making money on your side hustle right away.

Ready? Let's get started!

Prepare Yourself

If you're interested in get-rich-quick schemes, then this idea isn't for you. Because here's the reality: creating a profitable side hustle takes a lot of time, diligence, hard work, blood, sweat, and tears (well, hopefully not tears!).

If you want to succeed with your side hustle, prepare to put in some work. You shouldn't expect to start working and immediately have boatloads of cash pouring in. You need to be ready to put in many hours of work over the long haul.

How do you create the motivation needed to put in the necessary hard work?

Take a look at your life as it currently is. Are you living your best life now? Are you deeply fulfilled with your day job? Are there other things you would love to do to make money? Do you see others doing what you want to do?

If you're not living your best life now, let that serve as a motivator for your side hustle. You can make money doing what you absolutely LOVE. You can generate significant income by doing something that brings great satisfaction to your life.

How would it change your life if the work you were doing made you happy? How would it revolutionize things for you if you actually enjoyed the work you do every day?

To increase your motivation for your side hustle, envision what a successful outcome would look like for your side hustle. Paint a picture in your mind of what your best life will look like.

Get very clear on:

- How badly you want to succeed in your side hustle
- The benefits you'll experience
- How the extra cash will help you
- The joy you'll experience in doing what you love

If you're not highly motivated to make your side hustle a reality, it won't happen. Because here's the truth: your side hustle is going to take you away from other good things you could be doing.

You may need to give up:

- Television
- Hobbies
- Some time with friends

You may even need to sacrifice some time with your family, although we obviously don't recommend doing this over the long haul.

The point is simply that you're going to have to make sacrifices to make your side hustle a reality.

You're going to need to do the hard work necessary. You have to be willing to give up some good things in order to achieve a great thing. What most people don't realize is it usually takes a significant amount of time and work before you start making good money from your side hustle. Success happens over the long haul, not overnight. If you want your side hustle to be profitable, you need to be willing to make sacrifices again and again until you've finally reached your objective.

Success is no accident.

It is hard work, perseverance, learning, studying, sacrifice, and most of all, love of what you are doing or learning to do. If you want to succeed, you must be willing to work hard and persevere. The good news is if you persevere, you will succeed.

You must be confident in your ability to do it. If you continuously doubt yourself, you'll have a hard time getting traction. But if you have faith in yourself and believe firmly in your abilities, you truly can achieve great things. The best time to start a side hustle is right now. Don't wait any longer. There will never be a perfect time to start. Start working on your project today and simply adjust as time goes on.

Identify Your Passions and Interests

So how do you identify what your side hustle should be? How do you know what you should give your time to? How can you determine the best activities to focus on?

Start by identifying the things you are most passionate about and interested in.

See, a side hustle is the intersection of passion and profit. In other words, success is all about taking the things you love and are good at and turning them into a profitable gig.

The first step is to identify what you love to do AND are good at doing. Both elements, what you LOVE and what you are GOOD at, are required.

If you want your side hustle to be sustainable, you must love doing it. If you don't, you'll burn out fast. When hard work and sacrifices are needed, you won't want to. A successful side hustle involves an activity that you love doing.

You must also be good at your side hustle. In other words, you must have the necessary skill set to make it a reality. If you're not good at creating your product or performing your service, others simply won't want to pay you for it.

These next questions will help you find the intersection of passion and profit. Ask yourself:

- What do you absolutely love doing?
- What have people said you are good at?
- What do you lose track of time doing?
- What valuable skills do you have that people would pay for?
- What needs can you meet?

They'll help you determine both your skillset and what you love. When these two things combine, you have a viable side hustle.

There is a psychological concept called "flow." You find yourself so immersed in an activity that you lose all track of time and are simply focused on what's in front of you. Your mind isn't distracted at all. Rather, you simply "flow" with your activity.

When do you find yourself in the "flow" of things? Pay attention to these moments. These activities could turn into viable side hustles.

Validate Your Side Hustle

Once you've determined what you think your side hustle should be, you need to validate it. In other words, be able to demonstrate that people will really pay you for what you offer them. Determine if there is a "market need" for the product or services that you will offer.

After all, it won't do you any good to start your side hustle, only to discover that no one wants what you're offering. You'll end up spending hours and hours on things that won't generate any extra income. You'll also become discouraged and eventually want to give up.

It is essential to ensure that people will want what you have to offer, even if it's just a few people. So how can you do that? Where can you find an audience on which to test out your idea?

Some simple ideas include:

- Ask your friends on social media if they would be interested in what you have to offer.
- If you have an email list, send out a poll to them, asking who would be interested in what you're going to offer.
- Create a sign-up list where people can get more information. If numerous people sign up, it's a sign that your idea has legs.
- Offer to let people pre-purchase your offer. If a number of people purchase from you, you know that you're onto something good.

Your goal is to avoid wasting time on ideas that won't gain any traction. If your polls, emails, and sign-up list aren't getting much of a response, it may be time to move on to a different side hustle.

It is really important that you not become discouraged at this point. If you can't obtain any traction on your side hustle, that doesn't mean you have to give it up altogether. It means you may not be able to make a sustainable income from it. Or, you may simply need to adjust your approach to your product.

There are dozens of ways to make money, and you can certainly find a side hustle that allows you to do what you love.

What Sets You Apart from Competitors

Unless you're building something completely new and revolutionary, you're going to be competing against others. Whether you're selling a widget or offering coaching services, there are going to be others against whom you're competing for business.

If you're going to succeed with your side hustle, you need to find a way to differentiate yourself from your competitors.

In other words, figure out how you're going to stand out from the crowd. How you're going to attract customers. How your offer is different from what others are offering.

How can you differentiate yourself from your competitors? There are numerous ways, including:

- Better quality products or services
- Better customer service
- Faster delivery
- Less expensive products or services
- Aggressive sales tactics
- Higher or lower profit margins
- A noble cause that you support with profits from your product

Sell Some Soap

Think about this example: Let's say you're selling soap online. You could create a unique soap that is of better quality than most other soap out there. Because your soap is of better quality, you can sell it for a higher price and make higher profit margins.

Or you could sell your soap at a discount and sell a higher volume of soap. Or you could create an aggressive online marketing campaign where you're trying to put your soap in front of more eyeballs than anyone else.

If you don't find a way to differentiate yourself from your competitors, there's no reason that customers should purchase from you. You must find a way to stand out in the crowd.

Define Your Goals

Once you've determined what your side hustle will be, have validated that idea, and determined how you'll stand out from the crowd, it's time to define your overall goals. Defining clear goals will help you know what steps you need to take to turn your hustle into a reality.

Consider laying out a set of goals that sequentially follow one another.

For example, if you're going to sell products on eBay, your first goal may be to create an eBay account. Your second goal may be to research the products that sell best on eBay. Your third goal may be to source the products to sell and your fourth goal may be to list those products.

When setting your goals, ensure that they are realistic. Your goal is to start some traction, not reach your end goal right off the bat. Setting a goal of selling 1,000 bars of soap is a great goal, but there are a dozen smaller goals that need to be achieved before you can reach your final goal.

Each goal should be realistic and achievable.

If your goals aren't realistic, you'll again find yourself getting discouraged when you don't meet those goals. The more discouraged you become, the more inclined you'll be to give up your side hustle.

So, what are some small goals you can set that will give you traction on your hustle? These small goals should all contribute to your big, overall goal.

Do you need to...

- Research your market?
- Research the desires of your ideal customer?
- Create a website?
- Send out an email to your list, letting them know about your offer?

Start taking small steps that will lead you to your overall goal. Try to set goals that will move you forward on a daily, weekly, and monthly basis.

Create Milestones

One of the great temptations with a side hustle is to put off the launch. You can be so caught up in trying to make things perfect that you never actually get your side hustle off the ground.

You just need to start. Yes, you need to reach the small goals that will lead you to your big goal, but eventually, you just need to place your idea out into the wild and evaluate the response.

Side hustles are iterative. In other words, you launch, refine, fix problems, and then keep going. With each iteration, your side hustle gets better and better. The more iterations you do, the more refined your hustle becomes and the more revenue you generate.

In order to launch, set milestones that will force you to take action. Setting milestones for yourself will ensure that you take action and don't delay.

Each milestone should be tied to a date.

For example, let's say you're launching a coaching program. Your first milestone might be to create your website within the next month. Your next milestone might be to send out an email to all the potential clients you know. Your third milestone might be to advertise your coaching practice on Facebook.

Think of it this way: Milestones equal movement. When you set milestones for yourself, it forces you to move forward and prevents you from trying to make everything perfect.

Like your goals, your milestones should also be realistic and achievable. For example, it's not realistic to think that you can design a website in a day (unless you're an amazing web designer). Give yourself a reasonable amount of time to achieve your milestone.

The more you reach your milestones, the more encouraged you'll be about your side hustle. The more encouraged you are, the more you'll want to reach more milestones, which will keep your project moving at a rapid pace. Avoid making excuses when it comes to meeting your milestones. Hold yourself to deadlines, and if you need to ask friends to hold you accountable, don't hesitate to do that.

Determine How You Will Sell

Before you can launch your side hustle, you'll need to determine how you're going to sell your product or service.

Thankfully, there are dozens of ways to sell products and services.

You can always sell in person.

- If you're selling a product, you can take it to trade shows and markets.
- You could even go from door to door if you have the courage.
- You can sell directly to your friends or host parties where you show off your product.
- You can meet one-on-one with potential customers and tell them about the benefits of the service you offer.

You can also sell just about any product or service online as well.

- If your product is crafty (like soap), artisan, or vintage you can sell on Etsy.
- If you're getting products from thrift shops, you can sell them on eBay or Poshmark.
- If you're trying to break into the freelance world, you can find jobs in dozens of industries on websites like Upwork, Fiverr, or Thumbtack.
- If you're selling eBooks, you can list them on Amazon.
- If you're promoting a course you've created, you can sell it through Kajabi, Teachable, Udemy, or Thinkific.
- If you're a handyman, you can find hundreds of jobs on TaskRabbit.
- If you're a coach, you can use Tailored.coach to connect with your clients.
- And, of course, you can build your own website -- your business home on the web.

No matter what you're selling, there is an online platform to sell it. A simple way to find the platform that's best for you is to Google "Sell [PRODUCT/SERVICE] online". This will bring up dozens of results and allow you to find the best place to sell your product or service.

Start Selling

This point is short and sweet. Once you've done the initial work, you must start your new business and product launch.

Your side hustle will not be perfect when you first launch it. You'll make mistakes. You may have trouble landing your first customers. Regardless, at some point, you must launch your side hustle if you want to make any money from it.

As noted above, building a successful side hustle involves a lot of tweaking, refining, and making changes on the fly. If you try to get everything perfect before you launch, you'll never start.

In the initial launch phase, it may take some time for you to gain significant traction.

You'll have to work hard to promote yourself. But it is worth the work. If your side hustle is valuable, people will eventually buy into it.

Avoid getting discouraged if you don't have massive success right off the bat. Keep working, refining, promoting and selling. You'll hit on the right combination and the customers will start coming.

Market Yourself

To make your side hustle as successful as possible, it's essential to consistently market yourself. You'll need to promote your hustle, so it gets in front of as many people as possible.

If you believe in what you're doing, then go for it with all your might.

Don't be modest on this point. Market yourself hard and relentlessly. What are some effective ways to market your side hustle?

- Ask your friends and family to spread the word.
- Hand out fliers telling others about what you offer.
- Give out free samples (if you're selling a product).
- Tell others about it on social media.
- Build an email list and regularly promote your product or service to the list.
- Start a blog and talk about pain points your customers' experience.
- Create a YouTube channel dedicated to giving loads of value to potential customers.
- Start a podcast in which you talk about elements of your industry and business.
- Appear as a guest on other's podcasts.
- Do webinars where you teach valuable lessons and then promote your product or service at the end.
- Use paid advertising to drive people to your website.
- Apply for jobs on the platforms mentioned above.

Generally speaking, the more value you can give potential customers for free, the more likely they are to pay for your product or services.

For example, let's say you're a health and fitness coach. You could create a YouTube channel in which you teach people exercises and workout routines. This is giving free value to people. The more you do this the more people will see that you're an expert in your field and the more they'll want to hire you as their health and fitness coach.

Again, don't be afraid to market yourself. You've put in hours of hard work at this point. You've created a product or service that you truly believe in. So, get yourself in front of as many people as possible. Don't worry about what others will think. If you want to succeed with your side hustle, you must market yourself constantly.

Get Feedback from Your Customers

After you've launched, keep improving. If you want to achieve the kind of success that will change your life, you need to constantly better the product or service that you're offering. Even so, some people will buy an okay product or service. A LOT of people will buy an outstanding product or service.

Your customers can honestly tell you what is and what isn't working.

This is where customer feedback is invaluable. They can help you see past your blind spots and identify areas for change that you never would have seen on your own.

Ask your customers these important questions:

- What do they like about your product or service?
- What features do they find most valuable and which ones could use improvement?
- How has your product or service benefited them and what benefits would they still like to see?
- Which pain points could you more effectively solve?
- What features could you add that would make your offer even more valuable to your customers?
- How can you create the absolute best experience for those who have bought into what you're selling?

Asking customers for feedback is a way of being transparent and authentic with your customers. It shows them that you really care about them and their opinion and that you want to offer them the best possible product or service possible.

The more authentic you are with your customers, the more they'll support you in the long run. As they see how dedicated you are to constant improvement, they'll want to continue working with you and using your product or service.

Provide Amazing Experiences

One of the best ways to find new customers and keep your existing customers is to create amazing experiences for them. These experiences don't need to be anything crazy. Your goal is to show them that you care deeply about them and want them to be amazed and happy with what you have to offer.

How can you create incredible experiences for your customers?

There are literally dozens of simple ways:

- Provide amazing customer support
- Send a handwritten thank you note with every product
- Include an extra surprise with your product
- Dedicate extended time to helping your clients work through their challenges
- Send a card on the anniversary of their first purchase
- Create short, custom videos thanking each one of your clients or customers
- Call each customer just to say thank you

The list goes on and on. The goal is to make your customers know they are special. You want them to know they really matter to you and aren't just a way for you to make money.

The more you can delight and surprise your customers, the more likely it is that they'll tell their friends and colleagues about you, which will generate a referral business.

If you really go over the top with the way you treat your customers, you may even get exposure to prominent publications.

But ultimately, it is not about getting referral business or big exposure, although those things are valuable. Treat your customers like real people who you care about.

Build Sustainable Cash Flow

Eventually, if all things go well (and they will!), there will come a point where you have to decide whether you want to quit your day job and make your side hustle your full-time job.

You can turn your passion project into a full-time, income-producing job!

The final step is to achieve sustainable cash flow. In other words, you need to have a stable amount of money coming in every month. If you have consistent cash flow, this gives you the option of quitting your day job.

How much sustainable cash flow should you have? Ideally, you want your side hustle to be generating at least 75% of your income. This will give you the flexibility to decide whether you want to quit your day job.

When thinking about your income, remember to take into account expenses. You'll have to pay a self-employment tax at the end of the year. You also have expenses involved in keeping your side hustle up and running. Take all these things into account when deciding whether to take the plunge.

One important thing to note when it comes to quitting your day job. There will be a sense of fear and apprehension around quitting your job. After all, your job offers you stability.

Avoid allowing fear to keep you from following your dreams.

Fear is a big dream killer. If you've got your side hustle to the point where you're generating significant income, then it's time to seriously consider whether you should focus on doing it full time.

And consider this. If you're only doing your side hustle part-time and you're making enough money to consider quitting your day job, think about how much more you could make if you were doing it full-time! Going full-time with your side hustle could actually produce significantly more income for you.

When that time comes, ask yourself, "What is keeping me from taking the leap? What is keeping me from pursuing my dream full-time?"

If the answer is fear, that might be a signal that the time has come to go all-in on your side hustle.

Side Hustle Your Way to Freedom

The beauty of the side hustle is that, when done properly, it can create freedom for you. If you're working a day job, it can give you additional income that can set you up for financial freedom. If you're not working a full-time job (like a stay-at-home mom), a side hustle can provide valuable income to your family.

And eventually, you may be able to take your passion and turn it into a full-time job. That's the real power of the side hustle!

You've learned a lot! We talked about:

- Preparing yourself for the hard work of the side hustle
- Identifying your passions, desires, and skills
- Validating your side hustle
- Defining the goals that you want to achieve
- Creating milestones that will keep your side hustle moving
- Determining how you'll sell your side hustle products or services
- Starting the actual process of selling
- Marketing yourself effectively
- Getting feedback from your customers
- Providing amazing customer experiences
- Building sustainable cash flow

You now know what you need to do to start making money with your side hustle. You even know what you need to do in order to transform your side hustle into a full-time job.

The only question now is, "What's stopping you?" Nothing is holding you back from getting your side hustle up and running.

So, don't wait any longer. Get hustling!

* * *

Complete the *Turn Your Passion to Profit Worksheet* in the Tools Section

WRITE A HIGHLY EFFECTIVE BUSINESS PLAN

After you have identified your Passion, a detailed business plan can help you grow your income and success.

A business plan will help you build a business that will support you financially, have an impact on those around you, and leave a lasting legacy you can be proud of. But can't you just get things up and running and make adjustments on the fly? Can't you learn as you go? Yes, you can do those things, but the odds that your business will fail are much higher.

Ready? Let's get started!

Why Do You Need a Business Plan?

A business plan functions as a "crystal ball" of sorts. It helps you to peer into the future and predict different outcomes. Though it is certainly not perfect, it helps you map out where you currently are and where you're headed.

Specifically, a business plan helps you to:

Estimate total startup costs.

Once you know the approximate costs, you can determine whether you'll need to raise funds from investors.

Project revenues and profits.

By forcing you to define both your market and how much of that market you expect to reach, a business plan helps you estimate potential revenues and profits.

Convince investors.

A business plan shows investors that you have a clear and defined strategy for achieving success. If this strategy isn't present, investors won't want to finance your business.

Compete from the start.

As part of your business plan, you'll identify key gaps in the marketplace which your company will fill. This allows you to hit the ground running.

Anticipate challenges.

When you create your business plan, you'll look ahead and try to identify any potential problems you might encounter. This prepares you to address these issues if they do arise.

Are you starting to see the value of a business plan?

It may be helpful to think of it in construction terms. If you were building a new house, you would use a plan, right? If you didn't use a plan, you'd encounter all sorts of issues. Wires and pipes and even walls could end up in the wrong places. A building plan keeps you on track.

In the same way, a business plan helps keep you on track.

A business plan ensures that you focus your attention on the right things and helps you avoid mistakes that could sink you.

So how do you write a business plan? What things need to be included?

That's what this unit is all about. We're going to walk you step-by-step through the process of creating a solid business plan. By the end, you'll know exactly what to do to create your own plan.

Before You Start Your Plan

You're itching to start creating your business plan, and that's a good thing. But before you start there are a few things to consider.

Many business plans are wildly unrealistic.

Excitement surrounds the start of a new business. You've got big dreams, big goals, and huge amounts of ambition. You want to make a serious impact.

The problem is that this excitement often causes entrepreneurs to massively overestimate how successful they'll be and underestimate the problems they'll encounter.

In order to be effective, a business plan needs to be realistic.

Remember, ultimately, you're the one who's going to be pouring time and money into your venture. Before you launch, you want to be relatively confident that you have a good chance of succeeding.

So, in many ways, a business plan should help you decide whether your idea will pan out. This doesn't mean that you need to anticipate every risk. There's no way you can do that. However, be thoughtful, methodical, and careful as you put together your plan.

It's possible that you may put together your business plan and then realize that the potential outcome isn't as bright as you initially thought. You might realize that the competition is much tougher than you realized or that the market is smaller than you anticipated.

That's okay. In fact, it's a good thing. It forces you to go back to the drawing board and reevaluate. Realizing these things before you launch your business is better than after you spend tens of thousands of dollars.

At a minimum, your business plan should convince you that you'll succeed. When you logically evaluate all the data you've assembled in your plan, your confidence increases and you can trust that you're going to achieve your goals. When you're confident, you're more likely to convince potential investors to back you too.

So, with all that said, be patient as you assemble your plan. Take the necessary time to do the market research, analyze your financial needs, and map out your strategy for the future.

Is it a pain?

It all depends on how you look at it. If you see it as the thing that's preventing you from getting started, then creating a business plan will seem like a necessary evil. But if you view it as building a foundation for a successful, lasting business, it changes your perspective.

As you see, a business plan is vitally important to your success.

Next, let's look at what all you'll want to put into your business plan.

Create Your Executive Summary

The first part of any business plan will be the executive summary. Think of it as a high-level snapshot of your business. It gives a general sense of what your business is all about, what products or services you provide, where you've been, and where you're headed.

This section shouldn't be more than two pages long.

However, just because your executive summary is short doesn't mean it is less important. Some investors might only want to read your executive summary at first. If the summary doesn't capture their attention, they might not read the rest of the business plan.

The Small Business Administration recommends that your plan contain at least these six things:

1. Mission statement. A short (one paragraph) summation of your business and the big picture goals that you're pursuing.

2. General information. This includes the founding date of your business, names, and roles of founders, how many employees you have, as well as the number of locations (if you have more than one).

3. Company highlights. Draw attention to important growth highlights in your company. This may include financial highlights or other important things your business has achieved. If possible, include hard numbers as well as charts and graphs. If you're just getting started, be sure to include information from past ventures.

4. Products and services. A short description of what you sell and who your customers are. If you haven't yet developed your product or service, lay out the plans you have for developing one.

5. Financial information. If you desire funding, you'll need to spell out both your financing goals and any sources of funding that you may already have.

6. Future plans. A quick glimpse of where you're headed with your business.

The executive summary is the introduction to the rest of your business plan. It helps readers quickly understand your business, goals, and needs. Think of the executive summary like a detailed elevator pitch. It highlights the most important points of your business plan without going into all the details. It helps you focus on the things that will most contribute to the success of your business.

It is important to carefully craft your executive summary. If your work is sloppy, readers might simply ignore the rest. If it's not engaging or unclear, they may assume that you don't really know what you're doing. The summary should be crisp, concise, and compelling.

You may want to consider writing your executive summary after you've written the rest of your business plan. Why? Because you'll be much more familiar with all the information in the plan and be in a better place to summarize that data for readers.

Company Overview

Next, sketch out a quick overview of your company. This provides others with more detail regarding the specifics of what your business does and how it's structured. Like the executive summary, this section should be relatively short.

In this section, explain exactly what your business does. This should include:

- The industry you're in
- Your primary customer base
- The big problem that you solve for customers
- How you solve that big problem

Essentially, you're explaining the reason for your business's existence. You're identifying a specific customer need in a specific market and then clarifying exactly how you'll meet that need. It should be clear how your business will be different from the competition in the eyes of the customer.

The overview section functions as your Unique Value Proposition.

It clearly and concisely explains the unique value that your business offers. Additionally, it should highlight any particular competitive advantages you have, such as expertise or the physical location of your business.

If you're struggling with this section, try to answer the following questions:

- Who do you serve? Working moms? Hiking enthusiasts? The CEO of Fortune 500 companies? As much as possible, try to clarify who your ideal customer is.
- How do you serve them? Do you offer a superior product? Better services? Lower prices? A better location? In other words, what do you offer that other companies don't?

Avoid over complicating things. Ultimately, your business exists to solve a particular problem. The more clarity you have on the nature of this problem and the solution you provide, the better your company overview will be.

Market Analysis

Now is the time to get into more detail. The market analysis section of your business plan provides in-depth information about your industry, your specific market, and the competition.

If this section is done properly, it assures readers that you know what you're getting into. That you understand how the industry works, who the big players are, and what you need to do to thrive in such an environment.

In your market analysis, seek to include the following information:

1. Key industry information. What is the current size of the industry? How much has it grown in the past and what sort of future growth is projected? What sort of trends are occurring in the industry and how do they affect businesses in the industry?

2. Target market data. Within the industry, which customers are you targeting? What are their specific needs and how are they currently trying to address those needs? What demographic information characterizes your target market (age, gender, income, employment, and more)?

3. Target market size. How much does your target market spend each year on purchases? How often do they purchase? When do they tend to purchase? What is the projected growth of your target market? The Small Business Administration offers helpful resources regarding this specific information.

4. Market share potential. What percentage of your target market can you acquire?

5. Barriers to entry. What things might make it difficult for you to enter into and succeed in your target market? High technology costs? Strict regulations? Difficulty finding qualified personnel?

6. Competition. Who are the top competitors within your target market? What is their current market share? What are their key strengths and weaknesses? In what ways might they make it difficult for you to succeed?

This section will take a significant amount of research, but it's time well spent. First and foremost, it prepares you to succeed. The more you know about the market you're entering and the competition you'll be facing, the more you can customize your approach.

Second, it helps investors know that you've done your due diligence. They can be sure that you're not just diving into the deep end without knowing what's involved. They know that you know what's required to succeed.

Organization and Management

Next, describe how your business will be organized and structured. The objective is to explain the role of each team member and the experience that each member brings with them.

Spell out the general structure of your business, both in organizational terms and in legal terms.

Where does each key stakeholder fit into the big picture of your business? Include an organizational chart that shows the roles of stakeholders, who reports to whom, and other pertinent details.

In terms of legal setup, are you:

- LLC?
- S-Corp?
- C-Corp?
- General partnership?
- Sole proprietor?

As you discuss the legal setup of your business, it should be clear who the owners are and what percentage each person owns.

Next, describe the background of key members of your team, including:

- Owners
- Board of Directors
- Managers
- Partners
- Any other essential people

This part is especially important if you're seeking funding. Investors want to know that you have experienced, successful individuals who can help ensure that your business succeeds. You may want to include resumes of the key members as proof of their experience.

Finally, describe any key hires that will be necessary.

This may not be immediately relevant, especially if you're just getting started, but it will matter much more during your growth and expansion.

Products and Services

Now it's time to explain in detail exactly what products or services your business will provide to customers. Your goal in this section is to show how your product or service is uniquely positioned to make a splash within your target market.

Start by describing your particular product or service and the specific need it will meet. As much as possible, try to avoid using industry jargon or buzzwords. Speak in clear, simple terms that the reader is sure to understand.

Clarify exactly how your product or service will stand apart from the competition.

If you're selling a well-known item (mobile phone cases, books) you don't need to spend much time focusing on the details of the product itself. Rather, focus on what makes your offering unique (price? quality?).

However, if you're creating something entirely new, spend enough time explaining exactly how your product or service functions and why it's valuable. If you don't do this, readers and investors won't have sufficient information to make a clear evaluation regarding your business.

Within this section, you should also discuss:

1. **Product/service status.** Do you have a product or service ready to take to market, or are you just in the idea stage? Make it clear how far along you are with your core product or service.

2. **Development objectives.** If your product or service isn't ready to go, map out the steps you'll take to finish it. Specifically, spell out the research and development actions you'll take to ready your product or service for the market. Also, note any future products or services you plan on developing.

3. **Proprietary information.** Do you have any intellectual property, patents, or proprietary information that is essential to the success of your business? Clarify that information in this section.

4. **Supply chain.** If you depend on suppliers or vendors for any aspect of your business, list the details. Make it clear who supplies what, how often you receive those supplies, and the method by which you receive them.

Your product or service should really shine through in this section. It should be abundantly clear both to you and the reader that you have something unique to offer and that you're in a prime position to attract customers.

Marketing and Sales

You've discussed the critical details about your product or service. Now it's time to talk about how you're going to move your product or service into the hands of customers. You may have the greatest product or service in the world, but if you don't have a specific plan for selling it, you'll struggle to succeed.

Your objective in this section is to make clear both how you will make customers aware of your product or service and how you'll convince them to buy from you.

Let's talk about marketing first.

The first element in your marketing plan needs to be positioning. In other words, how will you position yourself in relation to your competitors? Why should customers come to you? Will you position yourself by offering:

- Lower price?
- Superior quality?
- Superior service?

Next, discuss the specific promotional methods you'll use to circulate the word out about your product or service. Will you use online advertising? Do you have a content marketing plan? Will you hire a public relations firm?

Additionally, clarify the metrics you'll use to evaluate whether your marketing efforts are working (leads generated, social media reach, website visitors, and more).

After laying out your marketing plan, discuss your sales plan:

1. **First, explain your specific sales strategy.** What method will you use to convince customers to buy from you?

    - Cold calling?
    - In-person meetings?
    - Webinars?

2. **Next, talk about who will be doing the selling.** If you need a sales force, who will train them and how big will the team be?

3. **Lastly, lay out the budget you have for both sales and marketing.** This will help readers gauge the scope of your efforts and possibly estimate results.

Financial Projections

This is a critical section of your business plan. In it, you paint a clear picture of your business's current financial status, while also mapping out where you hope to be in the future.

Investors will closely examine this section to determine whether they want to give you funding. They want to be confident that your business will generate a profit, and solid financial projections can give them the necessary confidence.

Additionally, this section will help you understand how viable your business really is.

If you've been in business for a while, include as much past financial data as possible, including:

- Income statements
- Balance sheets
- Cash flow statements
- Operating budget
- Accounts receivable and payable statements (if appropriate)
- Documentation of any debt you're carrying

Your financial projections for the future will either be based on your past data or industry and competitor research (if you don't have past data).

The Small Business Administration says:

Provide a prospective financial outlook for the next five years. Include projected income statements, balance sheets, cash flow statements, and capital expenditure budgets. For the first year, be even more specific and use quarterly -- or even monthly -- projections. Make sure to clearly explain your projections and match them to your funding requests.

If you're not sure how to create these projections, consider hiring an accountant or financial advisor to help you. They can guide you in building accurate financial projections. Wherever possible, use graphs and charts to provide a visual representation of your financial history. They make it easy for readers to quickly grasp your financial situation.

Funding Request

If you need funding to achieve your business goals, be very clear in what you're asking for. In this section, lay out exactly how much funding you'll need over the coming five years. Explain how you'll use the funding to achieve your goals.

Include the following details in this section:

- The amount of funding you need
- The type of funding you desire (loan, investment, etc.)
- The terms you're requesting for the funding

If you're offering some sort of collateral in order to secure a loan, include detailed information about that collateral.

Additionally, make it clear how you will be using the funds. Will you be acquiring inventory? Paying down debt? Hiring employees? If you'll be using the funding for multiple things, clarify how much will be used for each.

It's also critical to lay out your future financial plans so that investors have a good idea of what they're getting into. If you're getting a loan, show how you will repay it. If your goal is to eventually sell your business, make that clear as well.

As much as possible, try to customize your funding request based on the person you are talking to.

Banks want to know that you'll repay a loan, while investors want to know what sort of return they'll receive from their investment. If you're asking a bank, provide them with a repayment plan. If you're asking an investor, give them an estimated ROI.

In terms of how much funding you should request, that will depend on both your needs and your financial projections. You want to secure enough funding to ensure you're a success, without asking for so much that it becomes burdensome.

Appendix

You're almost done with your business plan. The last section you need to include is the appendix. This final part matters just as much as all the other sections.

In the appendix, include supporting information and documents that substantiate what you've written in the previous sections.

You may want to include:

- Credit histories
- Permits
- Product pictures
- Legal documents
- Licenses
- Patents
- Contracts

This is also the place to include key information about yourself and your team, such as resumes.

Think of it this way. In all the previous sections, you're trying to paint a compelling picture of what your business is like and where it's headed. You want to provide the reader with enough data to help them grasp your vision but not so much that you bog them down.

The appendix allows you to give extra details to the reader without disrupting the overall experience. If the reader wants to look at these details, they can simply refer to the appendix. At the beginning of your appendix, include a table of contents that corresponds to each section in the business plan. This allows readers to quickly see which pieces of information go with which section.

Build Your Dream

Yes, creating a business plan is a lot of work. It takes many hours to create a compelling plan that will convince others to support your vision. But they are hours well spent.

Creating a business plan will give you incredible clarity about and unique insights into what it will take for your business to succeed.

Your business plan will push you to differentiate yourself from your competitors. It will compel you to create a powerful marketing and sales plan. And it will force you to know your financial numbers inside and out.

If you're overwhelmed at the thought of trying to get everything done, just focus on getting one section done at a time:

Step #1: Executive Summary

Step #2: Company Overview

Step #3: Market Analysis

Step #4: Organization and Management

Step #5: Products and Services

Step #6: Marketing and Sales

Step #7: Financial Projections

Step #8: Funding Request

Step #9: Appendix

Do one step, then the next, then the next. Before you know it, you'll have completed your entire business plan.

As you work on your business plan, keep the big picture in mind. The reason you're doing all this work is so you can build your dream business. The time you invest upfront on creating a thorough business plan will be repaid in full, and then some, when your business is fantastically successful.

Don't wait any longer to create your business plan. Your dream business is just around the corner!

* * *

Complete the *Write a Highly Effective Business Plan Worksheet* in the Tools Section.

HAPPY NEW YOU! IT'S A BRAND-NEW YEAR!

The beginning of a new year is a time of hope and enthusiasm. Even if you just completed a challenging year, it's natural to entertain the possibility of something better. It's common to start the year with several lofty resolutions, and it can be exciting to contemplate a life with more money, more love, and fewer pounds. A Paris vacation sounds nice, too!

Sadly, few resolutions are ever realized. Health clubs are packed with new members for a couple of weeks. Half of those new members are never seen again after two weeks, and 95% are gone within a month.

We quickly forget our resolutions.

This year can be different! A systematic approach can make all the difference. If you've failed to make meaningful changes to your life, you're in luck! In this report, you can discover a process that's guaranteed to work if you're diligent. Where will you start?

Take time to go through the next six sections. These will help you make the most of your new year, new opportunity, and the new you.

Ready? Let's get started!

#1 Evaluate Your Life

A very famous golf coach once said that it's impossible to create a good golf swing without evaluating a client's current situation. Likewise, how will you know where to go if you don't know where you are? It is not possible to develop an intelligent and effective plan of attack without evaluating your current situation.

Determine the Low-Rated Areas of Your Life

The deficiencies in your life limit your happiness.

You're not unhappy because:

- You live in a 3-bedroom ranch instead of a 7,000 square foot mansion.
- You're not married to a supermodel.
- You don't own a $200-pair of shoes.
- You drive a Honda Civic instead of Mercedes.
- You don't have a million dollars in the bank.
- You don't have the body of a Greek God or Goddess.
- You only have five friends instead of 20.

You can certainly be unhappy because:

- You live in an unsafe part of town.
- You're alone.
- You can't afford appropriate clothing for yourself or your children.
- You drive a car that might not survive the drive to work.
- You don't have enough in savings to cover any emergencies.
- You're 50 pounds overweight.

That's not to say you can't make any part of your life spectacular. However, dealing with the most challenging aspects of your life first will result in the greatest return on your time. Focus on these low-rated parts of your life. Finding a few friends can do more to enhance your life than buying a sailboat if your social life disappoints you.

Try this 3-step process to determine the parts of your life that would make the biggest difference for you if you were to change them:

Think about your average day and record your thoughts.

A few examples might include:

- "My alarm is going off, and I can't stand the thought of getting out of bed."
- "I'm afraid I won't make it to work because I can't afford gas until payday."
- "I have to sit alone at night because I don't have anyone to spend time with."
- "I only have two pairs of pants that fit because I've gained so much weight."
- "I hate my job."

- "I wish I could go back to school."
- "I'm tired of my girlfriend/boyfriend."

Complete this exercise with a weekday, weekend day, and holiday.

Try to cover all the bases. Your dissatisfaction during the week might be different from those you face over the weekend.

On a scale of 1 to 10, rank each item.

A "10" is perfect. It couldn't be better. A "1" is as bad as you can imagine.

You don't need a personal jet to be happy and fulfilled. The low-rated areas of your life are weighing you down.

Do the Work!

Examine your life and rate the various aspects on a 1-10 scale.

#2 Choosing Areas to Enhance

Focus on the low-rated areas of your life. Improving a "5" to a "10" will mean less to you than improving a "2" to a "10." We're all limited by the amount of time we have available to us. Focus your time and energy on the aspects of your life that will provide the greatest benefit. Spend your time wisely.

Determine which area of improvement will provide the greatest benefit:

Create the "10" version for each item rated less than five.

Design a version that you'd be excited to add to your life. Once it feels right, see if you can make it any better. A few examples from the previous list:

- "I wake up refreshed. I can't wait to start my day."
- "My car is reliable, comfortable, and I am proud to own it."
- "I have plenty of good friends and an active social life that brings me joy."

Put your revisions in order of preference.

Consider which of your new 10's would add the most to your life. Imagine your life with the corresponding changes and trust your gut. Which would have the biggest impact? Put your list in order.

Where do you feel the most pain in your life? What causes you the most stress? Many psychologists believe that we're naturally happy. It's only the negative parts of our lives that make us unhappy. So, you don't need anything in order to be happy other than to be free of the bad stuff!

It is human nature to turn to our strengths and avoid our weaknesses, but this is a mistake in certain circumstances. The weakest parts of your life limit your happiness and sense of well-being. Ensure you're prioritizing your focus.

Do the Work!

Address the low-rated parts of your life first. When these have been conquered, you can turn your attention to other areas.

#3 The Process of Change

Changing your life is unlike repairing a broken fence. It's not a single event. Changing your life requires ongoing effort. Your habits create your life. The little things you do on a consistent basis determine your outcomes.

Changing your habits is a priority, but there are several other components to creating a new life.

Successful change requires several steps:

Decide what you want.

The previous activity accomplishes this requirement. You now know which area of your life you want to change.

Create a goal.

Your goal is a target. An effective goal is:

- *Measurable:* How will you know you attained it if you can't measure it?
- *Time-bound:* Without a time-limit, you'll take your sweet time and never reach your goal. A time limit creates a sense of urgency and focus.
- *Specific:* "Losing weight" isn't an effective goal. "15 pounds" is specific and effective.
- *Reasonable:* You won't even start on a goal you don't believe you can reach. Only push slightly beyond your comfort zone.
- *Desirable:* All goals should be desirable. Why waste your time on anything less?

Now create a goal based on your number one priority. An effective goal might be, "On or before March 31st, 2016, I will have lost 20 lbs."

Prioritize the goal. Read and write your goal each day.

Twice is ideal. Review your goal once in the morning and once before bed. How many times have you started on a new goal only to realize you'd completely forgotten all about it? Reviewing it daily will prevent that from happening again.

Develop habits that will result in success.

You don't become rich, poor, fat, skinny, lonely, popular, unpopular, or an expert overnight. Your daily habits have a huge impact on your results in life.

Deal with discomfort.

Any change is uncomfortable. Actually, any significant change is uncomfortable. And that's the key. Keep the amount of change in your life relatively small. A series of small changes are as effective as a significant change, but the small changes are much easier and comfortable to implement.

There are many ways to decrease the amount of discomfort felt when altering your life. We'll explore several later.

Measure your progress.

It would be difficult to reach a weight loss goal if you never stepped on the scale. Regular evaluation of your progress ensures that you're on the right track.

Adjust your approach.

If you're not making sufficient progress, that's a sign that you need to improve your approach. Consider that most people either continue with the same actions or give up. Both guarantee failure. Steer your ship.

Do the Work!

It looks simpler when you list the steps, and it is simple. However, it's easy to lose focus, become uncomfortable, or give up. If change were easy, we'd all be living the life of our dreams. There are several steps to making lasting change. Be sure to follow them.

#4 Habits

The importance of your habits cannot be overstated. Your income, fitness, relationships, clutter, and just about everything else in your life are the result of your current habits. New results will require new habits.

New habits can be developed with less effort if you're patient.

How to use the power of habits to create a new you:

Habits take time to develop.

The common belief is that a new habit takes 30 days to become ingrained. It actually depends on the person and the habit! Studies have shown that it can take as long as 7 months to develop a habit. Be patient.

Willpower isn't what it seems.

You might admire the willpower of someone that works out every single day. But it doesn't require any willpower to hit the gym if you have the habit of working out.

Willpower is great for developing new habits. It's insufficient for consistently taking an action you don't enjoy. Use your willpower for habit development.

Willpower is limited. If you find that you're struggling too much, more willpower isn't the answer. The solution is to reduce the demand on your willpower.

Focus on the habit of getting started.

If you want to go for a walk each day, the first step might be to put on your walking shoes. Let that action be your focus.

Getting started really is the hardest part. If you can put on your walking shoes and head out the door, you're walking.

Have a trigger.

Think about the habits you already have. You wash your hands after using the bathroom. You turn on the nightly news after putting the kids to bed. A preceding action or event triggers most habits.

An effective trigger happens on a regular basis. Using the restroom, starting your car, going to bed, and eating a meal can all be effective triggers. Find something that happens every day and makes sense for the habit you're seeking to develop.

Start small.

If you want to write a novel, creating a habit of writing 1,000 words per day might be too much. Set a goal to write for at least five minutes after putting the kids to bed. Are five minutes too much? Then set a goal of writing a single word! Interestingly, if you write a single word, you'll probably end up doing much more.

A very small goal might not appear important to accomplish much, but you're creating the habit of getting started with the activity. When you're consistently taking that small step, you can begin increasing the demands you make upon yourself.

Reward yourself.

It seems silly to reward yourself for writing one word, doing one push-up, or saying "hi" to a stranger. However, it's a wonderful start. Reward yourself for even the smallest accomplishment! Tell yourself that you're doing a great job or do a little dance.

Ensure that your reward is intelligent. Giving yourself a cookie for taking a long walk might be counter-productive!

Work on one new habit at a time.

Starting a diet, sticking to a new exercise routine, learning French, and beginning a meditation practice is too much all at once. You'll end up right where you started. Wait until you've shown some success with one habit before introducing another. Define success as performing the new habit at least 90% of the time that the trigger occurs.

A 90% success rate is excellent. The difference in results between 90% and 100% is quite minimal. A 70% success rate provides little in the way of results. Strive for at least 90%. Try following a diet 70% of the time and notice the results!

Do the Work!

Anyone could look in your home and accurately determine your housekeeping habits. One glance at your body reveals your daily eating and exercise habits. Your habits are evident for all to see. Create new habits and your life will change.

#5 Dealing with Discomfort

Whether you're starting a new diet, increasing your social circle, or going back to school, you're bound to experience at least a little discomfort along the way. This is natural!

Discomfort is a part of your change.

Deal with discomfort effectively:

Understand that discomfort is a misguided defense mechanism.

Scientists believe that the discomfort experienced during change serves to keep us alive. Your brain is worried about life and death. Your happiness is secondary. It views any change as potentially life-threatening. Imagine that 10,000 years ago:

You're hiding under a bush from a tiger and consider making a run for it. Under the bush, you're still alive. Running out in the open could be hazardous. Most of us would freeze and stay under the bush where it's safe.

You decide to stroll up to the beautiful woman in the next tribe for a little flirtatious fun. You might take a rock to the head from a foreign tribesman. Many social psychologists believe this to be the reason why men are uncomfortable approaching beautiful women. Your discomfort protected you 10,000 years ago. Now the same discomfort harms you.

If your life isn't at risk, your discomfort may be misleading you. Take discomfort as a sign to evaluate the situation. Respond in a reasonable manner.

Welcome discomfort.

If you're uncomfortable, there's a chance that something meaningful will happen. Where are you most comfortable? On the couch watching television? Has anything great ever happened when you were doing the same things you always do?

When you're uncomfortable, things have a chance of changing for the better.

Be mindful.

If you're uncomfortable, you're thinking about negative outcomes. But if you'll just stay focused on how delicious your grilled-cheese sandwich tastes, you can't be worried about the future.

A good rule of thumb: Your mind should be focused on your surroundings, your breathing, or your current activity. If your mind is focused on anything else, you're not really living. Life can only be lived in the present.

Learn to meditate.

Meditation is simple, but not always easy. There are many books and videos on the subject. Spend some time learning how to control your mind.

Exercise.

A good workout can rid you of nervous energy. If you're stressed, go for a run, hit the gym, or pull out the tennis racket. Notice how much better you feel afterward.

Toughen up.

If you're used to giving into uncomfortable feelings, you can do better. Try sticking with your discomfort for as long as you can. Notice that you're still fine. In time, you'll be able to handle discomfort much more effectively.

It's just a few chemicals.

A few stress hormones and neurotransmitters don't have to dictate your actions. These compounds can alter your pulse, blood pressure, and feelings of anxiety. But the effects are harmless. Remember that your brain is trying to keep you alive. Anxiety is just a sensation in your body. You've survived much worse.

Focus on the result rather than the process.

Thinking about your diet might make you miserable but thinking about the results is exciting. Keep your mind on the prize when you're down.

This is true for anything you don't like doing. Avoid thinking about how awful it will be to clean the garage. Think about how great you'll feel when you are done.

Do the Work!

Discomfort can be embraced as a positive sign. It means that you're changing your life. The only way to eliminate discomfort completely from your life is to never try. Discomfort can be managed and minimized, but it's a part of being human. You can choose to make progress in spite of your discomfort.

#6 Develop a 12-Month Schedule

It's challenging going from writing one word each day to completing a novel, losing 30 pounds, finding a romantic partner, and financing a trip to Egypt. The first step is simple, but creating a cohesive plan is a little more challenging! How can you do it?

Remember that you prioritized the list of changes you'd like to make.

That's the first step. You simply work your way down through the list. When you're successfully working toward one goal consistently, it's time to add in the next priority.

As a rule, you can add a new priority each month.

If a habit takes longer than a month to become automatic, that's okay! Continue to focus on that one habit until it becomes automatic. Even 3-5 changes over the course of a year would be very significant. Imagine if you:

Found your perfect partner, found your perfect job, got in great shape, and had one great adventure.

When was the last time you had a year this good?

Create a rough schedule.

Find a calendar and make some notes on it. Avoid tying yourself down, as it's impossible to predict your progress. But get a rough idea of what you can accomplish in a year.

Set priorities.

You've already prioritized your list. Do it again. Choose the few items you're absolutely committed to accomplishing this year. Four items equal one per quarter. What will you have accomplished by March 31st, June 30th, September 30th, and December 31st?

Maybe you have a goal that will require 12 months, but what milestones will you have reached by these target dates?

Stay focused on your habits.

Getting in shape is little more than 2 habits: eating and exercising effectively. Learning to speak Russian requires studying the language often. Many successes aren't complicated if you focus on the proper habits.

What have you accomplished in the last year?

If you're like most people, not much. A few changes are a huge improvement over your past results. Avoid overwhelming yourself.

Visualize the new you.

Imagine how you'll look and think at the end of the year. Keep coming back to this picture when you're struggling.

If you think about how much you hate eating oatmeal every morning, you'll never make it. If you're focused on how great you'll feel at the beach this summer, the year will fly by.

Reward yourself handsomely for significant results.

If you make your quarterly goals, do something nice for yourself. You've earned it!

Be patient.

A year can seem like a long time to wait. Focus on today. Tomorrow will come. Stringing together enough good days is the key to success.

Do the Work!

Achieving your goals is not as important as what you become by achieving your goals. Put in the work.

Summary

When the New Year is upon you, take the steps to make this one your best yet. If you find yourself in the middle of the year, start anyway. Make yourself a 12-month plan and dive in.

This can be the year you create a new you, even if you've failed to create meaningful change in the past. If nothing in your life seems to be working, there's good news. It doesn't take as much to enhance your life as you might think. Just a few changes in your daily habits can bring about incredible results.

Prioritize the changes you'd like to make. Only so much that can be accomplished in a year. Why waste your time fooling around? Determine the most important changes and get busy!

Develop the habits necessary to reach your goals. Many of your current habits have shown themselves to be inadequate. New habits provide new results. The real work is in developing those habits. Running isn't hard. Putting on your shoes and getting out the front door is hard.

Be patient with yourself but start today.

This could be the year of a new you!

FINANCIAL THERAPY: CHANGE YOUR MONEY BELIEFS AND CHANGE YOUR LIFE

If your life is one financial challenge after another, financial therapy might be just what the doctor ordered. Over 75% of Americans list money as their primary source of stress. Financial therapy is a growing field and focuses on the emotional and psychological roots of financial behaviors that create financial stress.

For example, someone that grew up in poor surroundings might hoard money and be excessively frugal. Overspending can be caused by stress or anxiety.

While some issues may be better left to the professionals, there are many financial issues amenable to self-therapy. After all, many overweight people are able to lose weight without a psychologist, dietitian, and personal trainer.

By addressing the beliefs, thoughts, and habits related to your financial life, you can bring about real changes.

If you're not following through on the actions that you know would increase your financial stability, your beliefs are likely to blame. Beliefs that inhibit financial results can come from many sources:

- Parents
- Teachers
- News
- Erroneous personal observation
- Childhood trauma related to family finances
- Books
- Personal experience throughout life

The source of the ineffective belief doesn't matter. But recognizing and addressing harmful money beliefs is very important to your financial progress. Beliefs create and limit your reality. It might only be a few faulty habits that are holding you back from the financial security that you desire. How exciting is that?

Let's look at how your beliefs create and limit your financial reality.

Beliefs Create Your Financial Reality

Your beliefs are the seeds that create your reality. Your beliefs affect your thoughts, which affect your actions, which ultimately create your life circumstances.

Changing your beliefs can be the most powerful way to alter your life. Altering your beliefs changes the entire cycle.

There are several ways that beliefs ultimately alter your financial behavior:

Beliefs influence your self-confidence.

The set of beliefs you have about yourself and your capabilities determines your level of self-confidence. In turn, your confidence affects your ability to learn and apply new financial habits.

Confidence also impacts your ability to pursue financial goals. If you're not confident in your ability to achieve results, you won't persevere.

Beliefs alter how you process information.

Scientists have found that people use new information to support beliefs they already possess, rather than to form new beliefs. If you believe that you can't save money, you'll look for evidence to support that belief.

Information that is contrary to your beliefs is quickly discarded and ignored, which makes change challenging.

Beliefs create limits.

If you believe that you'll never be wealthy, you're right. If you believe you can't stick to a budget, you're right again. This is why it's so important to change your beliefs to viewpoints that support, rather than limit, you.

Beliefs affect results.

If you don't think you can have a pleasant retirement, you're unlikely to save or learn about the various types of retirement accounts.

If you believe that money changes people for the worse, you won't take the steps to accumulate a significant amount.

Beliefs are the core of financial challenges. Enhanced beliefs lead to enhanced thoughts, actions, and results. Attacking your negative behaviors is a less effective route to success. Instead, focus on your beliefs and you're more likely to enjoy positive benefits from your efforts.

There are many ways to change the course of your financial life. Addressing your beliefs is the most effective way to create the financial future you desire. With more supportive beliefs, it will be much easier to create the habits necessary to earn, save, and accumulate wealth.

Do the Work!

What are your beliefs about money? Make a comprehensive list of your beliefs regarding money, both positive and negative.

Here are a few examples:

- I'll have to work really hard to make a lot of money.
- Making a lot of money will cut into my free time.
- I already have enough money.
- I don't need a budget.
- Money equals freedom.
- If I make too much money, my ex-spouse will take most of it.
- I wouldn't know what to do with a lot of money.
- Money makes the world go around.
- Good people don't care about having a lot of money.
- More money would solve my problems.

Take the time to make a complete list. You'll need it later.

Achieve a State of Financial Health

Financial health isn't just how much money you make. There are multiple components to financial prosperity and stability. There are people earning over a million dollars each year with desperate financial challenges. The belief that income is all that matters is a limiting belief.

Do you have all of these financial components under control?

Budget.

Whether you're earning minimum wage or running the most successful hedge fund the world has ever seen, a budget is important.

Know how much you're spending and where the money is being spent. The information is valuable to you and provides boundaries that ensure your financial success.

An income that surpasses your bills.

If your bills outpace your income, you're going to have financial woes. The most likely long-term outcome is bankruptcy. Everyone would be wise to increase their income and lower their bills.

An emergency fund.

Life is neither perfect nor predictable. Sooner or later, an unexpected expense will occur. Many families are only a few weeks away from being homeless if sudden unemployment or a major expense occurs.

A minimal amount of debt.

No matter how much money you have or make, it's very easy to create more debt than you can handle.

Avoid debt whenever possible. Especially avoid debt to purchase items that are consumable or lose value.

Controlled spending.

It's also easy to spend more than you make. Are you an impulsive shopper? Do you like to purchase items that are out of your income bracket?

Saving regularly.

Are you saving a percentage of each and every paycheck? With a regular savings plan, anyone can retire in style.

Investing your savings appropriately.

Saving is great but leaving your money in a savings account is less than ideal. Do your investing activities address your needs? Are you saving for retirement?

The necessary insurance to prevent financial catastrophe.

A serious illness, fire, or death can derail the best-laid plans.

Do the Work!

Look back at your list of beliefs and note which of the above items are influenced by your beliefs. You'll probably have several additional beliefs to add to your list now. Remember, earning a lot of money is a great advantage, but it's not sufficient on its own to ensure financial security.

Negative Money Beliefs

Consider the list of your money beliefs. Recognize which beliefs are negative and which are positive.

Positive beliefs are those that allow you to positively affect the 8 components necessary for financial health. Negative beliefs get in the way of addressing the 8 components.

Examples of beliefs that keep you poor:

Rich people are greedy.

Some rich people are indeed greedy. But some poor people are greedy, too. Many rich people became rich through kindness and helping others. Whether you are greedy is up to you.

I don't deserve to be wealthy.

Everyone that creates value deserves to be wealthy. If you're content with a minimum wage job or spend the day sitting on the couch, you can change your financial circumstances by creating value and charging the world for it.

I'll have to do a lot of things I don't like to become wealthy.

While doing things that others don't like to do can be a faster way to wealth, there are numerous ways to accumulate wealth. At least one of them would be enjoyable for you.

My friends won't like me if I'm rich.

It's common to find new friends as your life situation evolves. Some of your friends might not like the fact that you're rich. But your true friends will be happy for you. Every change in life has the potential to influence everything else.

Many wealthy folks still have the same friends from elementary school. You can choose to do the same.

Money is the root of all evil.

The actual quote is "The love of money is the root of all evil." Money doesn't create negative situations. Money is just a piece of paper or a number attached to a bank account.

Money provides opportunities. You choose whether the actions you take are positive or negative.

I can't be spiritual and have a lot of money.

Many religions espouse the belief that being poor is somehow looked upon kindlier by the great powers that be. But if you were looking to convert a population that was 99.9% dirt-poor, you'd probably say the same thing.

Having money gives you more opportunities to be good to yourself and others. It can also free up your time to engage in more spiritual activities.

I'm disrespecting my parents if I make more money than they do.

Most parents would be thrilled to see their children doing so well.

It's hard to make a lot of money.

It can be hard to make any amount of money. Most people with moderate incomes complain about work. If you're going to work, why not make a lot of money while you're at it?

With the appropriate habits in place, it's not too difficult to enhance your career, save more, spend less, and invest more wisely.

If I had a lot of money, I'd just lose it anyway.

Keeping money is as much of a skill as earning and saving it. There are plenty of resources that can help you learn how to handle money wisely.

The belief that you'll end up where you started will prevent you from taking any meaningful action.

I shouldn't have more money than I need.

Everything is life is easier with a buffer. Imagine having more time and love than you need. Having more money than you "need" is comforting and opens up many possibilities that simply don't exist without a surplus of funds.

It is much easier to make a career change or go back to school. You can afford to send your child to Harvard instead of the local community college. You're better prepared for any financial catastrophe. The belief that you shouldn't have more money than you need to survive will lead to surviving instead of thriving.

Do the Work!

Do you have any of these common beliefs about money or yourself? If you hold beliefs that inhibit your ability to address the components of a healthy financial situation, your challenge will be greater than necessary. You'll sabotage yourself by neglecting the habits necessary to achieve financial happiness.

Positive Money Beliefs

There are also beliefs that will speed you along the path to financial independence. These positive habits make it easier to have a positive financial future.

These beliefs can make you rich:

Money results from providing value to the world.

It doesn't matter how smart or educated you are. It doesn't matter what you look like. The universe isn't out to get you. If you provide value and charge people for it, you will receive a corresponding level of money.

Brain surgeons make more money than your average store clerk because the surgeon is providing more value. A CEO of a large corporation earns more than a brain surgeon for the same reason.

Money provides freedom and choice.

Money is great for solving problems and providing you with options. Maybe money can't buy you love, but enough of it can fix a bad transmission, buy a ticket to Fiji, or allow you to play golf all day instead of working.

I can help others with my money.

After your own needs have been tended to, you have the ability to help others with their challenges or assist them in attaining their goals.

My financial freedom will happen when I have effective beliefs, thoughts, and habits.

Be less spectacular. Simple actions, taken on a regular basis, will result in great wealth. But it all starts with your beliefs.

Saving money is easy and enjoyable.

How would your savings activities change if you believed this?

A budget is easy to create and follow.

If you can't create or stick with a budget, this belief will help.

I only buy things I need.

How would your bank account look if you lived this belief?

There are numerous others, but you follow the idea. Do you have more positive or negative beliefs about money? Can you see how your beliefs about money are affecting your financial situation?

Do the Work!

If you want to enhance your finances, eliminating negative beliefs and replacing them with positive beliefs is an effective plan of attack.

How to Change a Belief

There are many ways to address harmful beliefs and replace them with positive ones. Many times, all that's required is a little attention and an open mind.

Many of our beliefs are created during childhood and are never questioned.

At one time, you believed in the Easter Bunny. Likely, you have several beliefs about money that are impractical, too.

The experts can't agree whether beliefs can be changed in an instant or whether it takes a significant amount of time. As the old Chinese proverb states, "The best time to plant a tree was twenty years ago. The second-best time is today."

Neuro-Linguistic Programming

John Grindler and Richard Bandler developed Neuro-Linguistic programming (NLP) in the 1970s. You're probably familiar with Tony Robbins, who made the technology popular.

Though there are many facets to NLP, we're most interested in the use of language and perception to change beliefs. For instance, if you imagine something that frightens you, the way you imagine it has an impact. There is an infinite number of ways to think about a spider, for example.

If the image of a spider in our mind is very large and colorful, it will have a different impact on your emotions than an image that's small and lacking color. The characteristics of a mental image include the visual, auditory, and kinesthetic details of a mental image.

Follow this process to change a belief with NLP:

1. **Identify a belief you'd like to change.** Let's pretend you believe that you can't save enough money each month to ever make a difference.

2. **Consider an old belief that you no longer consider to be true.** Perhaps you once believed in Santa Claus or that your high school girlfriend was the only woman you'd ever love. Notice the subtle difference of this once-held belief.

- Are you in the image or viewing it like you're watching a movie?
- Is it in color or black and white?
- Is there a border around the image?
- Is the image centered?
- What do you hear?
- Can you feel anything? Hot? Cold? Sick to your stomach?

3. **Think of something you know to be true.** It could be the belief that Christmas is on December 25th or that a dropped bowling ball will fall. Take note of the subtle differences in this belief.

4. **Think of a belief that you'd like to add.** For our example, it might be the belief that every penny saved is adding to your fortune. Find the most advantageous counter-belief to the belief in step #1. Notice the subtle differences.

5. **Eliminate the belief in step #1.** Take the subtle differences you found in step #2 and apply them to the image in step #1. You're applying the mental characteristics of a belief you no longer hold to the belief you'd like to eliminate.

6. **Now alter the subtle differences of the belief you'd like to add to match those of the belief in step #4.** Make your desired belief have the same mental characteristics of the belief you know to be 100% absolutely true.

7. **Test.** How do you feel about the original belief and the new belief? Can you sense a change? The ultimate test is to observe your behavior. If your behavior changes, you know you're on the right track.

Many people find this process highly effective. You can quickly change a belief with NLP.

Do the Work!

If NLP doesn't seem to work for you, though, search out other options.

Change a Belief with Logic

Humans are thinkers, and we can use logic to our advantage. Beliefs are funny things. Though we can be influenced to believe anything, we're ultimately the creators of our beliefs. You can't see or touch a belief in the real world.

No one can give you a belief you don't accept.

Use the power of logic to shake the foundation of your harmful beliefs:

Choose a belief you'd like to change.

For this example, we'll look at the belief, "Money is the root of all evil."

Where did this belief come from?

Did it come from your parents? A minister? A teacher? Neighbor? Did you read it somewhere? Knowing the origin can help to change the belief.

Is this source an expert?

In reality, only a person that's had a lot of money would have the experience to make such a statement.

Your parents might have had authority over you, but did they really have authority and expertise when it came to wealthy behavior?

What is another possible explanation?

It's possible that money holds root in evil, but what other explanation could there be? Maybe your current belief is just one possible explanation.

Maybe you just heard the saying so many times you've believed it without questioning it.

Maybe money gives evil people the chance to be evil. But does that mean that all people are evil?

Have you ever actually seen money causing evil? Money is just an object. Have you ever seen another object create evil?

Is it possible that the reasons for this belief only exist in your mind and not in the real world?

Realize we form many beliefs in childhood that fail to hold up to examination.

It's understandable why a child forms some specific beliefs under the conditions of childhood. Those in similar situations would likely draw the same conclusions.

Can you see that any of the other interpretations could also be "the truth?"

So, what is the truth? The truth is whatever you choose it to be. You are the creator, and your belief is merely your creation. You interpret ideas and experiences and assign value to these things. Find an interpretation that makes sense but also works for rather than against you.

Faulty beliefs can be easy to change because they have the disadvantage of being incorrect. Most of the beliefs that stand in your way can't stand up to scrutiny.

Do the Work!

Examine your beliefs around money and put them to the test.

Cost-Benefit Analysis

You've undoubtedly made lists in the past listing the pluses and minuses of your available options. Why don't do the same with your beliefs?

If you realize what a particular belief is costing you, you'll have greater motivation to address it.

Realize what you gain from beliefs to understand how you hold yourself back. Follow these steps to analyze the cost and benefit of your challenging money beliefs:

Choose a belief you wish to change.

Consider the belief, "I'll never make $100,000 per year."

What is this belief costing me?

A few examples might include:

If I don't believe I can make $100,000, likely I never will.

I'll be stuck in my current income bracket for the rest of my life.

I don't have hope for the future.

I'll never be able to buy the house I've always wanted.

I'll have to work until I'm much older than I'd like.

How is this belief unreasonable?

Few things in life are 100% true all the time. How is this belief ridiculous?

I can't predict the future, so how could I possibly know how much I'll make someday?

If I have the skills and work hard, then my current limits are irrelevant.

Other people with fewer skills, less intelligence, and less education have made over $100,000 per year. In fact, some of the wealthiest people in the world dropped out of high school.

There's nothing magical about $100,000. It's just a round number that looks good to my brain.

What do I gain by holding this belief?

In most cases, you'll find those seemingly harmful beliefs have an advantage. That advantage is often avoiding fear or getting to be lazy. If you don't think you can make more money, you don't have to try. Harmful beliefs are often excuses used to avoid taking action.

What would I gain by adopting a more helpful belief?

How would you benefit if you believed you could make $100,000 in the future?

I would greatly increase the likelihood of reaching this income level.

I would have hope and enthusiasm for the future.

I would work harder, and my job would be more secure from my increased effort and contribution.

Create an affirmation.

State your new belief in a positive, present way. "I earn $100,000 per year."

Repeat the affirmation 20 times each morning and evening while in bed.

Avoid discounting the effectiveness of affirmations. Try a simple experiment and apply affirmations to a simple task you routinely avoid, perhaps getting up the first time your alarm goes off. When you hear the alarm, turn it off and repeat, "Getting up, getting up, getting up" over and over again. You'll find it much easier to put your feet on the floor!

Do the Work!

One of these methods will work better than the others for you. The key is to try all three. Changing your beliefs takes effort. Merely understanding the processes won't accomplish anything. Apply them consistently.

A Simple Plan of Action

It is time to determine the part of your financial life that's causing the most grief.

Suppose that you have no retirement savings.

Make a list of the beliefs that are having the greatest negative impact.

Which belief is hurting you the most?

- I'll have plenty of time later.
- I'm too young to worry about it.
- I have to buy a house first.
- I won't live long enough to enjoy it.
- I can't afford to save money now for something I won't need for 40 years.
- Things are too complicated for me.
- I'll inherit all the money I could ever need.
- The amount I'm able to save won't make a difference.

Address them one at a time.

Pick the belief that you think is creating the biggest obstacle and apply one of the techniques to eliminate the belief and create a new, more supportive belief.

Keep going until your behavior matches your wishes.

It's possible to feel better but not take action. Keep going until you're taking real action. You might have to try all three techniques to have an impact.

Continue addressing your beliefs that don't support your financial future.

This will take time, but it's time well spent.

Do the Work!

A few simple steps taken each day will have a very positive impact on the future. Start by taking the first step.

Financial Therapy

Congratulations!

You have completed all the sections of:

Financial Therapy: Change Your Money Beliefs and Change Your Life

Follow up your work with this thought: Are your beliefs about money supporting you or acting like a boat anchor? You often know what to do, but struggle to follow through and take the appropriate action. Faulty beliefs inhibit your ability to address your finances effectively.

Your beliefs alter your perception, behavior, and ultimately, your financial future.

Determine these beliefs and evaluate them. Consider how these beliefs negatively impact your financial future. What would you gain by eliminating these beliefs and instilling more helpful beliefs?

Changing your money beliefs can be accomplished by a variety of methods. Finding the optimal method is a matter of trial and error. Start immediately. Financial challenges seldom happen overnight. The cure will take time, too.

Give yourself financial therapy. Change your money beliefs and change your life.

CONQUER YOUR MONEY

"Money isn't the most important thing in life, but it's reasonably close to oxygen on the 'gotta have it' scale." - ZIG ZIGLAR

What are your money blocks? Money blocks are beliefs and behaviors that limit your ability to earn and/or keep money.

Everyone has money blocks. Even a billionaire can have them. There's a reason why they don't have even more money, and many billionaires would like another billion. They didn't achieve their wealth by accident. Money was a priority for them. Their money blocks are just less limiting than those of most of us.

Money blocks can take a variety of forms, but beliefs and behaviors are the most common. Some examples of each include:

Beliefs

- "Earning money is too hard."
- "I'm too old to become wealthy."
- "It's too late for me to save enough money for retirement."
- "I won't have any free time if I make earning money a priority."
- "The taxes will kill me."
- "Good people don't care about money."
- "People won't like me anymore."
- "I don't deserve it."
- "I'm not enough."
- "People like me never get ahead."
- "This is the best job I can get."
- Fear of success
- Fear of failure

Behaviors

- Overspending
- Procrastinating
- Poor financial priorities
- Exercising excessive generosity

A lack of knowledge can also be a money block. If you want to invest your money, but don't know anything about investing, you're blocked from investing successfully.

Money blocks can keep you from earning, saving, and investing money wisely. Money blocks can prevent you from even believing these things are possible for you. Money blocks have the power to wreck your finances and your financial future.

Money blocks can be deep-seated or simple to change, depending on the particular block. One thing is for certain: they're unlikely to leave on their own, and it's your responsibility to deal with them if you wish to make more money.

Consider these topics as a way to learn more about your money blocks and your opportunities for success:

1. **Section 1: Sources of Money Blocks.** Money blocks can come from several sources. Do you know the origin of yours? Understanding the sources of money blocks will demonstrate how pervasive they can be.

2. **Section 2: Releasing Money Blocks.** Money blocks can take more than one form, but the method for dealing with them is similar. Whether your block is a belief, habit, or other behavior, you'll learn how to address it.

3. **Section 3: Try a 30-Day Challenge.** Is a permanent change too intimidating for you? The answer is a 30-day challenge. A month isn't a long time, but you can accomplish more than you think.

4. **Section 4: Affirmations.** Positive affirmations about money tackle your money blocks by changing your thoughts. They can make a huge difference. Changing your thoughts also changes your beliefs and actions that precede and follow your thoughts.

5. **Section 5: How to Prepare Your Children for Financial Abundance.** Maybe you got the short end of the stick in your childhood as it relates to money blocks. You can avoid doing the same to your children. Use this information to help your children thrive financially.

#1 SOURCES OF MONEY BLOCKS

There are many sources of money blocks. Many of them might be a surprise to you.

Understanding the many sources of money blocks will show you how long you've been struggling with them.

It will also demonstrate the importance of keeping yourself aware of when you may be facing a potential new money block.

Money blocks are created from a variety of sources:

Family upbringing.

Everyone has money blocks, including your parents. You may have many of the same money blocks they do. Unless you were incredibly fortunate to be born with parents that had a minimal number of money blocks, you have some work to do.

- It's unlikely that your family made a point of teaching you an abundance mindset.
- Most "polite" people avoid talking about money and money management. It's considered a taboo topic whether the discussion happens at home with loved ones or outside the home with strangers.

Religion.

Many religions, intentionally and unintentionally, consider money as bad. The poor are held in a rather high regard.

- Wealth is commonly viewed as an obstacle to faith and enlightenment. Even a middle-class lifestyle is viewed as excessive in some religions.
- Studies have shown that those who place a high priority on religion often feel uncomfortable and guilty if they are financially well off.

Low self-esteem.

Feelings of self-worth and self-esteem aren't always easy to come by. Unless you were successful as a child and had parents that made a point of building these qualities in you, you could use a boost.

- Unless you actively work on these traits, your money blocks will continue to affect your financial life.
- If you feel unworthy of success and comfort, those things will prove elusive.

Guilt.

Most of us are good people. It can be challenging to drive around in a car that costs $100,000 without any guilt. You could instead house several homeless families with that money and drive a 5-year old Honda Civic instead.

- This is a personal decision. At the very least, eliminating your money blocks would allow you to attract more abundance and help more people.
- There's a difference between self-love and narcissism. There's a difference between being happy with yourself and lacking empathy for others. You can hold yourself in high regard and still care about others. As adults, we're each responsible for our own success in life.

Fear of success.

Success is attractive, but at the same time, it's not for most people. We've been taught to fit in and conform. Our school years teach us that being just like everyone else is a comfortable place to be.

- Most of us are wary of having power and the responsibility that comes with it.
- We also don't want to be noticed too much. We want a little attention, but not a lot. It feels safer and more comfortable to be inconspicuous.
- If you're going to be "big" in life, it requires dealing with attention and responsibility.

The media.

Whether you're watching the news or a movie on Saturday night, the financially strapped are portrayed as the underdog. The wealthy person or company is often considered the villain.

Money blocks come from a variety of forms.

What do you think was the primary source of yours?

Only a few people possess the right mindset, beliefs, and behaviors to build and maintain wealth. Luckily, even though it may take some work, you can undo your money blocks and move toward prosperity.

#2 RELEASING MONEY BLOCKS

Clearing money blocks requires a multifaceted strategy. It's important to address beliefs, habits, and assumptions. Each of these can be attacked from a variety of angles. It's a lot of work but consider the payoff that lies ahead.

When you reduce your number and severity of money blocks, anything becomes possible.

With money blocks, becoming wealthy is like running a marathon with a broken leg -- painful and unlikely.

Beliefs

Your beliefs form the foundation of your abundance mindset. Your beliefs can vary from "I don't have what it takes to be wealthy" to "I'll have plenty of time when I'm older to save money." Money blocks at this level affect your ability to create and hold wealth more than any other type of block.

Your beliefs influence your decisions, actions, and habits. These are the things that ultimately determine whether you become financially successful. Perhaps the most important step in this journey is to create a compelling future. When you know where you want to go, it's easier to identify your money blocks. The person that wants to live the life of a jet-set billionaire doesn't have all the same money blocks as someone that truly just wants to live in a three-bedroom ranch in Cheboygan.

There's no right or wrong answer but figure out what kind of life you want to live. Be able to describe it in detail.

Use these strategies to change your beliefs and your financial future:

Identify your beliefs.

Take a look at every belief you have about money -- good or bad -- and write them down. You should end up with quite a long list.

- Take at least 60 minutes to do this. Then, spend a few minutes each day for the next several days adding to your list. New ideas will come to you.
- Be expansive in your consideration. Don't look at just obvious beliefs. Look at the beliefs you have regarding success and achievement, too. Your overall philosophy of life could be a source of money blocks.

Determine which blocks are harming you the most.

Look over your list of beliefs and ask yourself, "Which of these beliefs is limiting my financial health the most?" Listen to the response you get.

Create a Top-10 list of your negative beliefs. It's important to attack the most crucial beliefs first, so figure out which are causing you the most harm.

Examine the belief.

Choose the most harmful belief and examine it. Begin by identifying the source of the block.

- "How did I acquire this belief?"
- Where did you get this belief? Did you acquire it as a child from your own powers of reasoning? Is it something you gleaned from TV? Parents? Did you get it from a fictional movie or book? Did it come from church?

Consider the quality of the source.

Is your Aunt Betty really a great source of financial wisdom? How successful is the person that gave you this idea? Is a fictional story the best place to acquire a belief?

"Is the source of this belief reliable?"

Consider the intention of the source.

If you were told by someone that this belief was a good idea, ask yourself what their intention was. Were they trying to help you or limit you? Did they have your best interests at heart?

Question the validity of the belief.

Upon close examination, you might find that the belief isn't true.

Is it possible this belief isn't true? Why or why not?

What is this belief costing you?

Make a list of all the challenges and negative outcomes that result from this belief. The longer the list the better.

Create a new, positive belief.

What is a new belief that serves you in your quest to attain wealth? Here are a few examples:

Old belief: "It doesn't matter if I pay my bills on time. It's only an extra $30 if I'm late."

New belief: "$30 invested today is worth over a thousand dollars in the future. There's no reason to waste money. It only takes a few minutes to pay my bills on time."

Old belief: "Earning a lot of money takes too much time."

New belief: "If I make enough money, I'll have all the free time in the world. Besides, by prioritizing my time, I can make plenty of money and still have time for the important things in my life."

Try out the new belief in your life.

There are few things certain in life. Life is more of an experiment. Approaching life with this attitude makes it more enjoyable and interesting. It's also easier to try new beliefs and behaviors. It doesn't have to be a permanent change; you can just experiment.

- Give yourself 90 days to try out a new way of approaching the world with your new belief. Just try it. You can always go back or try something else. What do you have to lose?
- You already know that what you're currently doing isn't working. Take a chance on something that might work.

Make the belief part of you.

Keep a list of your new beliefs with you at all times. A small notebook or your smartphone is perfect. Look at your list of new, positive beliefs several times each day. Read your list to yourself in bed in the morning and evening. Any other time would be a bonus.

Act as if.

Our beliefs change to explain our behavior. When you act differently, your beliefs change to accommodate that behavior. It's too uncomfortable otherwise.

- If you start acting like $10 matters, you'll begin to believe that $10 matters.
- If you save money from each paycheck for a couple of months, you'll believe that saving is important.
- If you study investing each day for a few minutes, you'll believe that you can build an understanding of investing.

Beliefs form the foundation of behavior.

Identifying and changing one belief can change numerous behaviors. You get a lot of bang for your buck when you address your beliefs. Keep this in mind.

Behaviors and Habits.

After addressing your beliefs, it's necessary to take a look at your behaviors and habits. Beliefs influence the actions you take, and it's your consistent actions that determine your long-term results.

This means that you likely have some habits you'll want to eliminate and others you'll want to build. The process of modifying your behaviors and habits is similar to modifying your beliefs. It all starts with identification.

These techniques will help you to change your behaviors:

Identify your behaviors that affect your finances.

Some of these are obvious, while others are more challenging to identify. If you've never thought about it, there are plenty of things you do that you don't realize affect your finances. Think carefully.

- **Saving.** What are your current behaviors and habits around saving

money? How much of your paycheck do you currently save? How easy is it for you to take money out of your savings and spend it on something unnecessary?
- **Earning.** Do you have any behaviors or habits that can lead to increased earnings? For example, do you spend some time each week looking for a better job? Do you research investment opportunities? Are you building websites on the weekend to sell or lease?
- **Spending.** How much money do you spend that you don't need to spend? How do you make spending decisions? Do you go out to eat a lot? Do you buy coffee at Starbucks instead of making it at home? Do you buy things you don't really need?
- **Investing.** How do you make investment decisions? Do you take stock tips from your butcher? Are you conservative or aggressive? Do you invest in things you understand?
- **Giving.** How much do you spend on gifts? Do you loan money to friends? How much do you give to charity? Does the amount of money you give away impact your finances significantly? How do you decide how much to give?
- **Leisure time.** You might wonder how your leisure time is relevant but remember that is time that you can spend however you like. Is that time being spent in a way that helps or harms your finances? Are you using that time wisely?

Identify changes that you want to make.

Everyone's time is limited. Spend your time on the behaviors that are going to make the biggest difference in your life.

Identify the five most important behaviors you want to change. Think both short and long term. Imagine the impact that making this behavioral change will have on your life in a month and over 10 years.

Make a list of the benefits of making this change.

Give your brain some good reasons for making this change. Imagine that you wanted to create a habit of saving 10% of your income:

- It would help to cover emergencies, such as a new furnace.
- It would give peace of mind. It's not always easy to sleep at night with little savings.
- It would eventually result in saving thousands of dollars.
- Retirement would be more enjoyable and stress-free.
- You could help others with some money.
- You could take that trip to Rome you've dreamt about for the last decade.

Start small. Make a small change and build upon it.

For example, you could start by saving 1% of your paycheck and save an additional percent each month or each paycheck until you've reached your goal.

Interrupt your thinking before taking negative action.

For example, suppose you're about to spend money. Rather than just spend it without further thought, you might follow a new pattern:

- Ask yourself, "Is this something I need?"
- "Why do I want to buy this?"
- "How much money will this cost me over 20 or 30 years? Use a financial calculator online.
- What could I do instead of spending this money?
- If you still want to spend it, you might require yourself to wait a week and re-gauge your interest.

Reward yourself for compliance.

Behaviors that are rewarded tend to recur. Obviously, it's important to be careful about spending too much money as a form of reward. Find something that will make it a little more worth your while to change your behavior.

Be patient.

Many of our behaviors are to avoid discomfort in one form or another. By changing your behavior, you're likely to feel uncomfortable. Be strong but be patient with yourself. Change can take time.

Your behaviors are where the rubber meets the road. Your actions create the results you experience in your life. Your beliefs influence your behaviors. Your behaviors build your life.

#3 TRY A 30-DAY CHALLENGE

A 30-day challenge can be a powerful way to alter your thinking and behavior. It's easy to get started on something that only lasts for 30 days. Making a long-term change is much more intimidating. Getting started is half the battle, so a 30-day challenge has a big advantage.

You're going to try a new behavior for the next 30 days.

For many people, this is long enough to create a new habit. Some people require a bit more but it's a great start, nonetheless. It's also long enough to judge if the behavior is helpful to you.

Imagine the impact of doing twelve 30-day challenges each year. Not only would it keep life interesting, but you'd make some incredible changes, especially as the years added up!

Use this process to try an effective 30-day challenge:

Choose wisely.

What will be the focus of the next 30 days? Avoid spending too much time on this. If you've made it this far, you know where you need some work. Pick something and get started.

- Take on something challenging, but not too brutal. Give yourself a great opportunity to be successful. It's human nature to want to push things to the limit, but the words "extreme" and "progress" rarely go together. Don't underestimate the power of incremental change over time.
- Be sure to choose something beneficial. The years are passing by, so make the most of the next month.
- What will your challenge be? What benefits do you expect to gain?

Define your objective clearly.

Know what success will look like. It shouldn't be questionable.

- "Spend less money" is not well-defined.
- "Bring my lunch to work each day" is easy to measure and interpret.

Figure out the potential obstacles.

If you know where the challenges lie, you can prepare for them in advance. Let's stick with our "bring lunch to work each day" example. What are the potential obstacles?

- Not having food at home to pack.
- Dealing with Jim - we go out to lunch at least three times each week.
- I need to get out of the office during lunch to preserve my mental health.
- I don't have a good way to carry my lunch to work.

What are some possible solutions?

- Go to the grocery store every Sunday and buy enough for the week.
- Have Jim meet you at the park for lunch, and he can carry his food out. Explain to him what you're doing. Encourage him to do the same.
- Eat at the park. Eat at the mall. Eat in your car. Eat at your desk and then take off for 30 minutes.
- Buy an adult lunch box or small cooler.

Generate enthusiasm.

Get yourself psyched up. Imagine how great it will feel to show yourself that you have enough control to change your behavior. Think of the benefits you'll gain. Remind yourself that it's only 30 days. You can do it!

Have a plan for dealing with a bad day.

Bad days happen to everyone. There will be a day you want to cheat on your 30-day challenge. Just do your best and keep going.

- Tell yourself that you're going to stick with it today, but you can cheat tomorrow if you still really want to. You'll be likely to survive another day, and tomorrow you'll likely feel better without having to resort to cheating.
- If you do slip one day, avoid feeling too bad about it. Twenty-nine days out of 30 is still a pretty good average!

Evaluate.

Evaluate how things are going throughout the 30 days. What can you do to make the process easier? Where are your sticking points?

- In the end, evaluate your results. Is this something that would be worthwhile to continue?
- Does it give you some ideas for additional 30-day challenges?

A 30-day challenge can create significant change in a hurry. It's only 30 days, so you can do it! You're free to go back to the way things were before, but you won't. Give a 30-day challenge a test-run.

#4 AFFIRMATIONS

Affirmations are familiar to everyone, but few people actually use them consistently, if they use them at all.

Affirmations take time to create results, but you can't help but be influenced by positive messages you read, speak, and hear over and over again.

Affirmations are a simple, non-threatening tool that can really help.

Effective affirmations share several characteristics, such as:

Positive.

Avoid stating affirmations in the negative. Your brain doesn't work that way, and you'll get unreliable results. For example:

- Not this way: I don't spend money that I don't have to spend.
- Yes, say this: I only spend money when necessary.
- Not this way: I am no longer a poor person.
- Yes, say this: I am becoming wealthier each day.

Present tense.

Avoid the words will, was, have been, and so on.

- If you say, "I will be wealthy," you're never going to be wealthy. You're always going to be just before the stage of wealth.
- Instead, say, "I am wealthy."

Simple.

The part of your brain we're addressing is powerful but simple. Avoid confusing it.

- Avoid: I am comfortable with wealth, and I like to save money and invest it to the best of my ability.
- Keep it super simple. Pick one thought: I am comfortable with wealth.
- A 2nd affirmation could be: I like to save money.
- A 3rd affirmation could be: I invest wisely.

Now that you know to create an effective affirmation, choose an area of your financial life and create 5-10 affirmations that will help you. Better yet, create or look up a huge list of affirmations and choose 5-10 that work for you.

When using affirmations, avoid these common affirmation errors:

Too many.

Affirmations require repetition. You can't repeat 300 affirmations very many times each day. How many are too many? More than ten.

Too few.

It's hard to know if a particular affirmation will stick, so avoid limiting yourself to just one. Pick one area you'd like to work on, such as saving, and create several related affirmations. Five to 10 works well.

A lack of focus.

Rather than have one affirmation on saving, one on investing, one on spending, and so on, choose one area of focus.

A lack of consistency.

Affirmations require a lot of repetitions. Morning, noon, and night is a good start. It's important to say them daily.

A lack of patience.

It's going to take time. It's only a few minutes each day, so you have little to lose. Expect it to take months to see benefits and be pleasantly surprised when it takes less.

A lack of visualization.

The words alone are not enough. Instead of just telling yourself, "I like to save money," imagine saving money and how great it feels. Your brain likes pictures and feelings, so give it some to work with.

Affirmation errors are critical in nature. Any of these errors is enough to make your efforts a waste of time. Double-check all of your affirmations and how you use them in your life.

Now that you have a list of affirmations and know the common errors, make a plan for implementing affirmations into your life.

Try these techniques to be successful with affirmations:

Put your list of affirmations into multiple formats.

Put them on your phone, write them down, and record them so you can listen to them. Keep them handy in a variety of formats.

Write your affirmations at least once each day.

Put them in a notebook so you can keep track of them each day. Write them out by hand. Typing into a word processor doesn't work as well.

Read your affirmations for at least five minutes each day.

Just keep reading the list over and over. Best case, you will do this aloud for half of the time and silently for the other half.

Repeat this five-minute routine at least twice each day.

Listen to your affirmations as much as possible:

In the car, waiting in line, and lying in bed. Listen as much as you can stand.

Right before sleeping and right after waking up are the most effective times. Avoid having your affirmations play while you're asleep. Studies show that it doesn't help and can disturb your sleep.

Remember to visualize.

You don't have to lie down in a trance but have a picture in your mind for each affirmation as you repeat them.

That's it! This makes for a great 30-day challenge, too. It only requires a few minutes each day and will work if you put in the time and effort.

Do the Work!

Create a few affirmations and see what happens. What do you have to lose? Use them daily and watch what happens. Be patient and you'll be sure to see positive results.

#5 HOW TO PREPARE YOUR CHILDREN FOR FINANCIAL ABUNDANCE

You now know the basics of money blocks. You know about a compelling future, beliefs, poor behaviors, habits, and affirmations. How can you use this to help your children avoid the negative effects of money blocks?

Fortunately, you can do a lot for them!

Give your children the beliefs about money and wealth they need to thrive financially.

Avoid any talk or behavior that will limit them. Watch your words and behaviors around them.

- Avoid foolish spending.
- Show them how you save money.
- Explain the ideas of abundance, consistent work, and a positive attitude.
- Have regular talks with them about money.
- Work hard to build their self-esteem and confidence.

Your children are always watching and listening. Set a good example for them and you'll be happy with the results.

They might even thank you someday.

Summary

Money blocks can take many forms. Your beliefs, attitudes, behaviors, and knowledge base can be money blocks. A dead-end job can be a money block if you stick with it. Think of a money block as anything that inhibits your ability to build and maintain financial wealth.

Money blocks are acquired from a variety of sources. Your parents and upbringing are the biggest sources of money blocks, but you may have also made incorrect judgments of the world based on your own reasoning and experiences. TV, books, and other sources of media can also be sources of money blocks.

Addressing your limiting beliefs can be the most effective way to deal with money blocks because changing a single belief can alter multiple behaviors.

Beliefs have far-reaching consequences. Self-esteem is another area of major importance. If you doubt your capabilities or your worthiness, you're going to struggle with building wealth. You'll sabotage your efforts if you can even get started in the first place.

If you strive to prosper but get lackluster results, you likely have money blocks. Overcome these blocks and you'll be on an exciting journey to claim the financial abundance you deserve.

BE A PRODUCTIVE ENTREPRENEUR

Every entrepreneur wants to be productive. It feels good to look at something tangible and say, "I created this. I made this. I did this."

Productivity looks different to different people, but the feeling is universal.

To get things done. To check things off a list. To make a serious dent in your checklist. For one person, creating an incredible presentation or meeting the needs of a specific client can make them feel amazing. For another, it may mean developing a new product or coming up with a new design.

For you, it may be completely different, but you know the good feeling you get by putting on a productive day.

Let's look at what it takes to be productive every day as an entrepreneur.

The Battle for Productivity

Productivity encourages a true sense of purpose. It offers a deep feeling of accomplishment, which is important to a happy and fulfilled life.

Being productive also gives you the freedom to spend more time with the ones you love and less time worrying about the things that are left unfinished.

If you're looking for that sense of purpose and happiness that can come from being productive, this section, Being a Productive Entrepreneur, can help you focus on the things that will get you there.

Productivity isn't always easy.

There are so many things that can cause your productivity to falter and even come to a complete stop.

As an entrepreneur, your constant battle is a thousand distractions that can block creativity and derail a productive morning, afternoon, or evening. These distractions may stem from your personal life, or they may be work-related.

All day long, you're receiving:

- Notifications
- Texts
- Slack messages
- Emails
- Social media pings
- Calls
- And a lot more!

Just as you start getting to important matters, your phone dings. It's a new message that you feel like you should probably check. You look at your phone and, the next thing you know, 45 minutes have passed. You've been sucked into the black hole of social media.

And even if you're able to set aside distractions, you may still feel like you're not really accomplishing anything.

You're busy... but you're not productive.

You're getting things done...but you're not getting the right things done.

You answer a lot of emails, reply to a lot of texts, and message a lot of people on Slack...but still, come away each day feeling like you didn't accomplish what you wanted to.

Have you ever felt like you were working *really* hard, but getting nowhere? You go to bed exhausted, wake up exhausted, but you don't feel like you have anything to show for it. You know there has to be a better way, but you just don't know where to start.

Get ready for the Four Pillars of Productivity

These four pillars will help you achieve the sense of accomplishment that you're really striving for. Instead of going to bed feeling defeated, with piles of work still sitting on the table, you can go to bed knowing that you've done enough for the day.

You've put in the work, and you can be fulfilled in what you've completed.

Systems over Goals

You've probably been told that to be productive, you should set goals. Big goals. S.M.A.R.T. goals. Stretch goals. The belief is that in order to achieve anything meaningful, you need to turn it into a goal. Well... maybe.

While goals can be really helpful, they aren't always ideal.

The Problem with Goals

Goals have one big problem: they have a termination point. In other words, you're not successful until you've actually reached your goal, and until you've reached the goal you might feel like:

- You're spinning your wheels, not going anywhere.
- You're a failure.
- You haven't achieved anything since the goal seems so distant.

Measuring success this way can make you feel defeated when you have big, ambitious goals.

For example, if you want to own a Fortune 500 hundred company, nothing you do until you reach that goal will make you feel like you're succeeding. You may be making incredible strides in your business, but they will fall flat compared to your hard-to-achieve goal.

Since goals have an "end", you never feel like a success until you've actually achieved your goal. And even when you achieve your goal, you simply have to start all over again with the next goal.

And the reality is, you might not even know what the "next" goal should be. So, you feel aimless. You know you should be seeking to accomplish something, but you're not sure what that something should be.

Even worse, you might feel like since you already accomplished your goal you can go back to your old habits instead of pushing and growing. You lose all the forward progress that you made. It's a setup to make you feel like a consistent failure.

The Power of Systems

There is another, better way. They're called systems. Systems allow you to:

- Make progress on your goals *every single day*
- Guarantee your success
- Help you reach your milestones
- Avoid the feeling that you're just spinning your wheels

What are Systems?

Scott Adams, who you may know as the author of the famous *Dilbert* cartoons, wrote about systems in his book, *How to Fail at Almost Everything and Still Win Big: Kind of the Story of My Life*.

He explained the difference between systems and goals like this: "Losing ten pounds may be a goal, while the system is learning to eat right."

Here's another example. Suppose your goal is to clean the house from top to bottom. You've spent the whole day cleaning, and you momentarily feel satisfied with what you've done. However, if you have no system in place, your home will quickly go into disarray shortly thereafter.

After a few days...the dishes will overwhelm the sink, the laundry will pile up, and the floors will be a mess.

A system, on the other hand, would be a cleaning routine. Instead of cleaning the entire house in one day, you train yourself to do small tasks each day. The result is a house that's tidy for more than a few hours.

Here's a business example:

- Goal: Generate $50,000 in revenue over the next two months.
- System: Every morning you make three cold calls (or however many is necessary) to potential new customers.

The system ensures that you reach the end result. Using a system doesn't mean that you have no goals. It just means that you start to focus more on the process than the final destination.

So, What's Wrong with Goals?

You've probably been told your whole life to set lofty goals and work really hard to achieve them. On its face, there's nothing wrong with having goals. Goals can inspire, motivate, and challenge us. They give us something to look forward to and a reason to continue striving. But goals can also be rigid and unmoving.

Let's imagine you've set a firm goal for your company. You would like to make X amount of sales by a certain date. You really hustle to make those sales. You push your employees to do the same. You may make a lot of sales.

But what happens when you don't reach your goal amount?

Chances are...you'll feel like a failure.

All the sales that you *did* make won't bring you joy because you didn't sell *enough*. You'll feel unproductive and you may even want to quit. What's really unfortunate about this scenario is that you may have missed many opportunities along the way.

Bottom line? Being overly focused on a distant goal can easily give you tunnel vision. Your determination to complete a singular goal may have kept you from taking the time to develop a new product that could be sold for twice as much.

Scott Adams writes:

> *"...if you focus on one particular goal, your odds of achieving that goal are better than if you have no goal. But you also miss out on opportunities that might have been far better than your goal... With a system, you are less likely to miss one opportunity because you were too focused on another. With a system, you are always scanning for any opportunity."*

Goals Limit Your Threshold for Happiness

The big issue with goals is that you're so narrowed in on a future time that you aren't happy until you hit that mark.

Once you reach a goal:

- The feeling of happiness will likely fade quickly.
- You'll then feel the need to achieve the next goal and the next.
- You're chasing something that is, at its best, fleeting.

Productivity expert James Clear has also written extensively about systems versus goals. In his book, *Atomic Habits*, he explains:

> *"When you fall in love with the process rather than the product, you don't have to wait to give yourself permission to be happy. You can be satisfied anytime your system is running. And a system can be successful in many forms, not just the one you first envision."*

What Happens When You Reach Your Goal?

You may also realize that once you've achieved a certain goal, you have nothing else to work towards. For example, let's suppose you set a personal goal to run a marathon. To achieve your goal:

- You forced yourself to go to the gym four times a week.
- You went running even though you didn't feel like it.
- You cut things out of your diet even though you didn't want to.

You worked *really* hard, but you didn't enjoy the process that got you there. Once you met your goal, you couldn't stand the thought of going back to that regimented schedule. Pretty soon, you've abandoned your running routine and you've gone back to your former lifestyle. Your muscles soften, you put the weight back on, and you can't stand to look at your running shoes.

What went wrong? You were focused on the goal, but the system was unbearable. You probably started training for a marathon because you wanted to be healthier and stronger.

Scott Adams explains that while you can set a goal to exercise three to four times a week on a rigid schedule if you're not enjoying the exercise, there's a much higher risk that you're going to give it up. You may do it for a time, but in the long run, you'll lack the willpower to continue because it feels like a punishment.

Instead, he suggests choosing to be active each day to a level that feels good. In this scenario...

- You're training yourself that being active is positive.
- You're going to get a psychological lift from the exercise.
- You're slowly training your body and mind to enjoy being active as opposed to hating it.

You'll naturally want to challenge yourself as you continue to enjoy being active more. Your original activity level may start with short, slow walks, but you may eventually find that you like running as well.

You'll do so because you want to, and not because you're forcing yourself to.

How Do Systems Help Entrepreneurs?

First and foremost, systems are much more flexible than goals. If you have a type-A personality, this shift may make you feel a little uncomfortable at first. It may feel like you're giving up control by not focusing so much energy on a future outcome.

The big question you have to ask yourself is: What happens when you shift your focus from a concrete goal to the process that gets you there?

If you're focused on the system, does that mean you're abandoning your goals and wandering aimlessly? The short answer is no. Here's why. Suppose a sports coach chooses to focus on picking great players, developing incredible plays, and creating effective practice routines instead of winning.

What would be the result? They'll have a winning team.

James Clear writes:

> *"Every Olympian wants to win a gold medal. Every candidate wants to get the job. And if successful and unsuccessful people share the same goals, then the goal cannot be what differentiates the winners from the losers... The goal had always been there.*

It was only when they implemented a system of continuous small improvements that they achieved a different outcome. "

In order for your business to be successful, it's vital to understand what is working and what isn't working in your *process.*

Think about the things in your system that are working and the things that are not. What does your hiring process look like?

- Do you have strong employees that fit your vision?
- If not, what practices can you change to hire better employees?

Think about your marketing campaign and the system that drives it.

- Is it working?
- What changes can you implement in your system to reach more customers and drive more business?

Now think about your products or services and the systems you have in place to support them.

- What can you do to improve your product?
- How can you streamline the process and make things more efficient?
- Are your products or services testing well?
- If not, what can you do to improve them?

These small, day-to-day improvements will make you feel successful, fulfilled, and productive. Learning how to push through daily struggles will bring you confidence and happiness in a way that hard to reach goals never will.

A system teaches you how to become better at what you do, and it develops your skill level. If something isn't working well, you have the flexibility to change it and move on. You still have the skills that you developed, but you can now use them in a new direction. That's the gift of a system.

The Early Bird Gets Everything Done

There's nothing quite like the peaceful calm of the early morning hours. And the fact is, rising early is one of the key things that most successful entrepreneurs do. The early morning hours are one of the best times to tackle the most important tasks. Rising early allows you to accomplish great things before most of the world has even woken up.

This "mind over mattress" thinking has been around for a long time. You may even be familiar with Benjamin Franklin's quote, "Early to bed and early to rise, makes a man healthy, wealthy, and wise."

There are numerous successful entrepreneurs who are early risers:

- Apple CEO Tim Cook gets up as early as 3:45 am.
- Michelle Gas, CEO of Kohl's department stores, gets up at 4:30 am to go running.
- Former PepsiCo CEO Indra Nooyi rises at 4:00 am and is in the office by 7:00. In 2012, she told Fortune, "They say sleep is a gift that God gives you...That's one gift I was never given."
- Twitter co-founder, Jack Dorsey, wakes up at 5:30 am to meditate and go for a six-mile jog.
- Starbucks CEO, Howard Schultz, is up at 4:00 am and in the office by 6:00 am.
- Richard Branson, a business entrepreneur behind the Virgin group of companies, rises at 5:45 am for an early morning workout and breakfast.

And there many more examples of these early bird business machines. What makes early risers successful, and how do you become an early riser?

What Does the Science Say?

You may be wondering if this old adage is actually true. Do early risers *really* live happier more productive lives?

Here's what the researchers have to say about it.

Night Owls are More Prone to Negative Thought Patterns

In 2014, the Department of Psychology at Binghamton University completed a study that included 100 undergraduate students. Their study found that both people who get less sleep, and those who delay sleep, are prone to Repetitive Negative Thinking (RNT).

RNT is a transdiagnostic disorder that can be observed in other disorders such as depression and anxiety. It's correlated with high levels of worry and negative thought patterns.

Early Risers Increase Their Chance of Success

In 2010, Harvard Business Review released a study by biologist Christoph Randler about early risers.

367 university students participated in his survey, and they were asked what times of the day they were most energetic. They were also asked how willing and able they were to take action or change a situation to their advantage.

Randler reported, "A higher percentage of the morning people agreed with statements that indicate proactive behavior, such as 'I spend time identifying long-range goals for myself' and 'I feel in charge of making things happen.'"

He went on to say:

> "My earlier research showed that they tend to get better grades in school, which get them into better colleges, which then leads to better job opportunities. Morning people also anticipate problems and try to minimize them, my survey showed. They're proactive. A number of studies have linked this trait, with better job performance, greater career success, and higher wages."

A similar study was conducted in 2008 by Kendry Clay at the University of North Texas. The study focused on 824 undergraduate students who were enrolled in psychology classes at the university. They were asked questions about their sleep habits and daytime functioning.

The study found that students who preferred the morning had higher GPAs, and those who preferred the evening had lower GPAs.

Both of these studies had the same conclusion: Early risers have a higher chance of success.

7 Ways to be an Early Riser

Rising early might sound like a fantastic plan, but it's not always as easy as it sounds. Fortunately, there are many things you can do to jump-start the day and ditch the bed.

Tip #1: Go to Bed Earlier

One of the easiest ways to get out of bed in the morning is to go to bed earlier at night. The late evening hours might feel like a good time to be productive, but the truth is:

- You have a limited threshold for productivity.
- Your progress is going to stall.
- Your work is probably going to get sloppy.

Instead, do your most productive work during the daytime hours and leave the evening for rest and time with family and friends. Some people are more prone to staying up late and sleeping in late, but this sleep pattern can be modified. Try going to bed one hour earlier and getting up one hour earlier to start.

Tip #2: Turn off the Screens

We live in a world full of screens--smartphones, tablets, computers, and televisions. We're surrounded by screens. While these tools can be extremely helpful for business, they can also affect your sleep.

The National Sleep Foundation says that technology/screens can affect our sleep in three very big ways:

- They suppress melatonin, the hormone that controls your sleep/wake cycle.
- They keep your brain active. By keeping your mind engaged with television or work, you're telling your brain that it's time to stay awake.
- Your alerts can wake you up at night. If you keep your mobile phone next to your bed, the sounds of emails, texts, and notifications can disturb your sleep.

To prevent technology from disturbing your precious sleep, turn it off or put it away a few hours before you go to bed. This will help your mind unwind and get you ready for sleep.

While many people use their phone for an alarm clock, this creates a huge temptation to check social media or try to fit in a few more minutes of work late at night. Do yourself a favor and go buy an alarm clock. Charge your cell phone in another room and get rid of the nighttime distractions.

Tip #3: Create a Sleep Routine

Creating a sleep routine is what pediatricians recommend to parents that desperately want their babies and toddlers to go to bed at night. However, this idea is not limited to children. A sleep routine is an outstanding way for anyone to get the sleep they need.

If possible, pick the same time to go to bed and to rise every day. Your body will adjust to this schedule and you may find that, eventually, you won't even need an alarm clock to wake up.

The National Sleep Foundation suggests:

- Finding a relaxing routine activity away from bright lights
- Trying to avoid activities that can cause excitement or stress

If you need something to occupy your thoughts before bed, try reading a book instead of watching a movie. Reading is known for reducing stress and helping you get a good night's sleep. According to a study conducted by Cognitive Neuropsychologist Dr. David Lewis, reading can reduce stress by 68%.

Other things you can include in your nighttime routine are:

- A warm, non-caffeinated drink
- Meditation or prayer
- A warm bath
- Breathing routines
- Using an app like "Calm", which helps you wind down each night

Tip #4: Get Some Exercise

Getting a good night's rest can be as easy as putting in some good exercise during the day. Intense exercise is the most conducive for a good night's rest, but any level of activity is helpful. Exercise has been found to increase time spent in deep sleep, improve the quality of sleep, and it can help you sleep longer. In addition, physical activity is known to reduce stress and anxiety -- two things that can greatly affect someone's ability to fall asleep and stay asleep.

Tip #5: Keep Your Alarm Clock at a Distance

If your number one difficulty is simply waking up in the morning, set your alarm clock out of reach. If you can't keep your hands off the snooze button, this will force you to get out of bed. Once you're up, ensure you don't crawl back into the covers.

Tip #6: A Splash of Cold Water

If you're extra groggy in the AM, you can always try splashing cold water in your face. This cold water will help energize you and snap you into an awake mode.

Tip #7: Give Yourself a Reason to Get Up

Thinking of a compelling reason to get out of bed in the morning might be your strongest motivator for early rising. Your reason for getting up in the morning may vary from someone else's but give yourself a good reason to wake up. Choose something that will be effective day after day.

Knowing that you can be more productive early in the morning may be enough to get out of your warm blankets. If not, maybe the thought of a tasty breakfast or a hot cup of coffee might be your reason for leaving your cozy covers.

Kill Your Distractions

You know the feeling. You've prepped yourself to buckle down and start crossing things off your to-do list. It's a mile long, and it just keeps growing. You're finally in the right mindset and you're ready to fly.

You're completely geared up to knock out your list, and you're 100% ready for that feeling of relief and satisfaction you'll have at the end of a full productive day.

- Then the phone buzzes—it's a text message.
- Your laptop dings with a new email.
- Your phone lights up with a new Slack message.
- An employee walks into your office with an important question.
- Your phone rings—it's a non-work-related call.
- You need a cup of coffee. You have to use the bathroom. You're starting to get hungry.

Before you know it, the whole morning is blown, and you don't really have anything to show for it.

Unfortunately, distractions are one of the main killers of productivity. You have a lot of things coming at you, and many of them are keeping you from focusing on what truly matters. While you're busy with these distractions, you're not actually accomplishing anything. So how can you eliminate these distractions and get to the most important stuff?

Here are 5 tips to get rid of the distractions and get back on track.

Tip #1: Make Plans the Night Before

Making plans the day before can be a really helpful trick to help you stay focused on the following day. You don't have to plan out every decision but make choices about simple things that might be distractions during the day.

For example:

- What you'll wear for the day
- What lunch you'll eat
- The way you'll get to work

When you're tired in the morning, these decisions are going to be harder to make and can continuously occupy your thought processes. You can also set a rough schedule for yourself. For example, you may decide that you won't check your e-mail or answer text messages until you've completed two important tasks. From 8 a.m. to 10 a.m. you'll focus solely on a specific project.

Tip #2: Cut Out Social Media

It's now estimated that people are spending 2 hours and 22 minutes a day on social media. That's a great statistic if you're trying to reach customers, but a terrible one for productivity.

Yes, social media can be a necessary resource for marketing and sales, but...

- Constantly checking your personal notifications
- Taking the time to respond to various rants
- Endlessly scrolling through pictures on Instagram

...Isn't going to help your business. Social media is a black hole and a major time suck. Notifications, and social media in general, can be incredibly addictive.

Here are some strategies to help you manage your social media time:

- Set a schedule for when you'll go on social media - for example, between 10 - 11 a.m. and 4 - 5 p.m.
- Use built-in tools like "iOS Screen Time" and "Android Digital Wellbeing" to monitor or restrict social media use on your phone.
- Turn off all non-business-related notifications so you're not feeling the constant pull of "*dings* " distracting you.

Use your business social media accounts to engage with real customers, tweet about your newest products, and post beautiful pictures. After that, put your phone away and focus on your other tasks.

Tip #3: Create Boundaries

In any given workday you'll have to field important calls. There may be some lines of communication that are necessary to your workday, but there are others that can be set aside. Give yourself periods during your day when you don't check your phone, emails, or Slack messages.

Some entrepreneurs choose the early morning to return emails and engage with customers on social media. Others choose to focus on their list of tasks before creating new tasks introduced by outside messages.

Choose the rhythm that works best for you but ensure that you stick to it. It's vitally important to set times of the day when you're not in constant contact with outside interruptions. If possible, it's also a good plan to leave at least one day a week when you're not scheduled for a meeting. This can give you a free day to complete tasks and stay productive.

Tip #4: Create a Productive Space

If you're working at home or in an office, it's important to create a space where you can feel productive. Productivity produces productivity.

In other words, if you were productive in a particular space, your brain will want to be productive there again. You'll associate that place with the good feeling that you had the last time you were able to crush it at work.

Likewise, if you have a certain space that you associate with entertainment -- perhaps the living room where the TV is -- you'll want to do those fun things when you're there. Keep your fun places and your workplaces separate and make your workspace conducive for work.

If you want your workplace to promote work, keep it tidy. A cluttered or messy space will distract you. Even if you don't feel like you have to clean it up, the disorganization will keep you from getting to your tasks. Keep your work area simple and easy to maintain and ensure that it has a door so you can shut out distractions when necessary.

Tip #5: It Can't All Be Work

While there are a few successful individuals who are all work and no play, most human beings aren't geared that way. In fact, we're not really meant to be.

Psychiatrist Stuart Brown, the founder of the National Play Institute, understands the importance of taking time to play. In his book *Play: How It Shapes the Brain, Opens the Imagination, and Invigorates the Soul*, he writes, "The truth is that play seems to be one of the most advanced methods nature has invented to allow a complex brain to create itself."

The act of play opens up a person for creativity and relieves us of our heavy workloads. Some workplaces like Google have even built-in areas at work for play. These spaces are meant to foster creativity and relieve stress in the workplace.

Dr. Brown also explains in his book:

> "...there is a kind of magic in play. What might seem like a frivolous or even childish pursuit is ultimately beneficial. It is paradoxical that a bit of "nonproductive " activity can make one enormously more productive and invigorated in other aspects of life."

Most human beings grow frustrated and unproductive when they force themselves to work constantly and enjoy very little. This is a *system* that is ultimately unsustainable.

There are several things that an entrepreneur can do to combat this:

1. Make work enjoyable. Find ways to make the things you do at work pleasurable and exciting as opposed to drudgery work.

2. Plan to have breaks during the day. Walk around the building, eat a good lunch, or take a coffee break.

It may seem like these things are distractions on their own, but when coupled with more intense sessions of work, they are simply something to work forward to.

3. Choose a quitting time. Choose a part of the day to set aside work and be *finished*. It's extremely important to have time set aside in the day to give attention to friends and family.

It's also important to enjoy relaxation, play, and leisure. This gives you time to bounce back from the workday and start fresh the next day.

4. Take a vacation. Plan for certain times of the year to be non-work times. Enjoy your relationships with others and find ways to have fun. Set aside the phones, emails, and messages and focus on the other things in life that matter to you.

You may never be able to cut out all distractions but limiting them can greatly enhance your chances of success. Reduce social media, limit communication, and make time for play, and you'll soon see that your productive periods are a lot more successful.

Slay Your Dragons

The final pillar we will focus on is prioritizing your workday. While it's easy to start the day with low hanging fruit, like email, the most productive entrepreneurs focus on getting their most important task done first.

Experts always recommend that you slay your dragon (hardest task) first.

Mark Twain said, "If it's your job to eat a frog, it's best to do it first thing in the morning. And If it's your job to eat two frogs, it's best to eat the biggest one first."

In other words, tackle the hardest things before you do anything else.

What Does the Research Say?

How does this theory stack up in real life? Does it really make sense to do the hard things first?

In 2017, Harvard Business School released a working paper called *Task Selection and Workload: A Focus on Completing Easy Tasks Hurts Long-Term Performance*.

The study discussed in the working paper was conducted in an emergency department in a metropolitan hospital. They..." assembled data from the emergency department for twenty-four months in fiscal years 2006-2007 involving over 90,000 distinct patient encounters."

The study was meant to discover how starting with easier tasks versus harder tasks might affect productivity.

The study concluded that completing easier tasks does create a short-term sense of satisfaction, but it can negatively impact long-term productivity.

The paper explains:

> "By selecting the easier task (exploitation) an individual gets work done quicker and likely feels good doing it. However, by choosing the harder task (exploration) one creates an opportunity to learn. Although always selecting the harder task may be sub-optimal, if one continually chooses the exploitation path then longer-term performance suffers. "

In other words, a short-term victory feels good at the moment. It makes a person feel productive when they accomplish something. However, because they are not pushing themselves to learn and overcome the harder tasks, they're actually limiting their potential.

Not only that, but the study found that the physicians who habitually chose the easier tasks first were less profitable to the hospital in the long run.

Put That Plan into Action

Only you know what your most difficult or complicated tasks are but do your best to take on those jobs first. Hit them first thing in the morning when you're at your strongest. Even if your difficult tasks don't take you the longest, they're going to take a lot more effort.

As the day goes on, your ability to focus diminishes. Your willpower may fall apart, and you'll want to avoid your work and put it off until the next day.

If you choose your hardest jobs first, you'll be able to finish the day up with your easiest work. That feeling of productivity from easy tasks will help propel you into the next day when you're ready to slay your dragons once again.

Productivity Is in Your Grasp

The fresh fruit of productivity is well within your grasp. You want that good feeling of productivity and it's entirely in your control.

The four pillars included in this book are actionable ideas that you can start today:

Pillar #1. Develop a system that works for you. Make it sustainable and continue tweaking it for the best results.

Pillar #2. Wake up early in the morning, ready for the day while the rest of the world sleeps.

Pillar #3. Cut out the countless distractions that prohibit your work instead of enhancing it.

Pillar #4. Overcome your most difficult tasks first. Afterward, enjoy the fruits of your labor with an easier afternoon or evening.

Your new and productive work style will help you live that happy and fulfilled life that so many people are seeking.

At the end of the day, you can put your work aside and invest in the relationships in your life that are most meaningful. You can rest easy knowing that you gave your best effort and put in a productive and fruitful workday.

* * *

Complete the *Be a Productive Entrepreneur Worksheet* in the tools section.

GO HEAD TO HEAD WITH DEBT COLLECTORS AND PLAN TO COME OUT SMILING

Debt is one of the most stressful situations anyone can face. Dealing with collection agencies or debt collectors is even more unpleasant. The constant phone calls and letters can have a negative psychological impact. Even though you may have significant financial challenges, you still have options. There are many things you can do to reduce your debt and stop the daily harassment.

It's important to address your debt and debt collectors directly.

The common response by most debtors is to go into hiding. They don't want to answer the phone or open the mail. It doesn't take long to recognize a collections letter from 10 feet away.

But while you're in hiding, the debt isn't going away and the damage to your credit report is only increasing.

You have more options and a stronger negotiating position than you think.

There is actually very little a debt collector can do if the debt is unsecured. Knowing this puts you in a powerful position.

The next four sections will help you deal with debt collectors.

#1 Your Rights and the Law

Knowing that you have debts you're unable to pay can be unsettling. Debt is stressful, especially when you start receiving a constant stream of letters and phone calls from your creditors. The phone calls are less than pleasant. The threats can even be frightening.

Within 5 days of the initial contact with you, the collection agency is required, in writing, to provide information regarding the debt.

This includes information about the nature of the debt and your right to dispute it. The notification will include the debt amount, the original creditor, and information on how to dispute the debt within 30 days. The 30-day mark begins when you actually receive the notification, not when the letter is sent.

If you think the debt is an error, you have 30-days to dispute the debt, in writing. No further collection attempts or communication may occur until the debt has been verified in writing.

Knowing your rights is the best way to fight back against debt collectors.

There are laws that dictate what collection agencies and creditors can and cannot do.

Understanding these laws is important. In most cases, the Consumer Credit Protection Act (CCPA) contains the rules that you'll find most useful. This act only applies to secondary parties, such as a collection agency. It doesn't apply to the original creditor. There are many limitations set by the CCPA that are helpful to debtors.

The Fair Debt Collection Practices Act (FDCPA) is part of the CCPA. The FDCPA sets forth the following guidelines:

It's illegal for a collection agency to threaten you with arrest for your debt.

You won't go to jail for the inability to pay a debt.

Collection agencies can only make phone calls between the hours of 8 a.m. and 9 p.m. in your time zone.

If you're receiving calls outside of the designated times, the collection agency is breaking the law.

It's a good idea to keep a log of the phone calls and other communication you receive. Include the date, time, and name of the caller.

The collection agency isn't allowed to use inappropriate language or unreasonable threats.

Nearly anything beyond informing you that your credit will be further damaged would be an unreasonable threat.

Swearing and racial slurs would be examples of inappropriate language.

It's not permissible for a collection agency to contact your friends, family, coworkers, employer, or neighbors to discuss your debt.

The collection agency can only deal directly with you regarding your debts. They may contact others to determine your location or contact information. But they may only approach a particular person one time.

They may contact your employer to verify your employment, but that's all they may inquire about.

No one from a collection agency can pretend to be a court employee or an attorney.

This includes any communication attempts or materials that would lead a reasonable person to assume that the communication originated from an attorney or court employee.

One of the most powerful features of the CCPA is your ability to write a letter and stop all communication from the collection agency regarding your debt.

Identify yourself and the debt by listing the original creditor and the account number. Mention the FDCPA and inform the collection agency that you don't want to be contacted regarding the debt under any circumstances. You must do this in writing. Verbal communication is insufficient under the law.

The FDCPA is a powerful act, and many collection agencies violate the terms from time to time. Document any infractions. It's possible to file a lawsuit against the offending debt collectors and win.

You might be wondering what the collection agency can do beyond calling and writing. It's possible for your wages to be garnished -- up to 25% in most cases. However, the creditor must file and win a lawsuit in order to garnish your wages. For smaller debts, this rarely happens. The time and cost to go this route aren't worth it in most cases.

#2 When Debt Collectors Break the Law

Debt collectors are notorious for violating the law when attempting to collect a debt.

Now that you know what is and isn't permissible, you can fight back when the law has been broken.

A minimal amount of documentation and courage are required. Steps you can take when debt collectors have crossed the line:

Document any illegal communication or behavior.

In many states, you can record a phone conversation without notifying the other party. However, in some states, this is illegal. Be sure to know the laws in your state. If possible, have a third party on the phone with you to act as a witness.

At the very least, make note of the date, time, and name of the caller when you're contacted by a creditor or debt collector. Make notes regarding the nature of the call and what was specifically said.

File a complaint with the Federal Trade Commission (FTC).

The FTC regulates collection activities. You can file your complaint at www.ftc-complaintassistant.gov. The government makes it easy for you.

Make a copy of the complaint and send it to the state-level agency that regulates debt collection.

This might take a little investigation to find the right agency. The state government website will have the information.

Send a copy of the complaint to both the creditor and the collection agency.

It's not unusual for the original creditor to cancel the debt due to liability concerns.

The collection agency might also toss the debt back to the original creditor.

Sue the collection agency.

Any violation of the FDCPA results in a $1,000 fine. It's not unusual for debtors to be awarded several thousand dollars in the case of multiple violations.

You can also recover any financial losses you may have suffered. This can include any medical or therapy fees incurred from stress and anxiety due to unreasonable collection efforts. Perhaps you had to pay for an unlisted number to stop harassing phone calls.

Small claims court is usually the best option, but you'll have to represent yourself.

The regular court is another option, but the cost of an attorney and the court fees could add up to more than your settlement.

Remember that debt collectors are only interested in collecting money, not losing it. Any reasonable threat of a lawsuit is cause for serious concern. Many collection agencies are barely viable enterprises. It's not difficult to get the space you need to breathe.

#3 Negotiating with Debt Collectors

It's possible to negotiate with debt collectors regarding your debt. In most cases, debt collectors are only paid when they collect on the debt. Usually, they receive a percentage of the amount collected. In other cases, they may purchase the debt from the original creditor.

Most debts that find their way to debt collectors are unsecured debts.

If the debt was secured, as in the case of a home or car loan, the original creditor would take legal steps to seize that asset. Keep these facts in mind when negotiating with debt collectors:

The debt collector didn't loan you any money.

In many ways, the collection agency isn't concerned with how much you owe. It has minimal, if any, skin in the game. Their only concern is quickly collecting as much as possible.

The collection agency wants to minimize its costs.

Calling and sending letters isn't free. They have to pay someone to make those phone calls. There are manpower and postage fees associated with any mail communication.

Collection agencies would rather get a reasonable amount today than the full amount in 6 years.

Know your financial situation.

If you don't have the financial resources to make a lump sum payment or keep up with a payment plan, there's little point in attempting to negotiate.

You can actually create more issues for yourself. For example, you don't want to incur new debt with a fresh statute of limitations.

Ensure that you fully understand the position of the debt collector. They don't have a lot of power, and they haven't lost any money due to your inability to pay the original debt. They want to collect as much as possible but will often accept much less. Options for negotiating your debt:

Eliminate your debt with a one-time lump settlement.

Every collection agency will likely accept a reduced amount as payment in full. It's just a matter of how low they'll go. Each agency may have its own criteria. The more recent the debt, the more they'll want.

- If a collection agency has given up on your ability to pay, they might take as little as 20% of what you originally owed.
- For newer debts, expect 75% or so. Many others are happy with 50%. The important thing is to stick with your number. They'll obviously try to talk

you into paying more. Avoid agreeing to an amount you're unable to afford.

Remember your credit report.

Your credit and credit score have certainly taken a hit if your debt has reached the collections phase. If you're willing to pay something to settle your debt, the collection agency and the original creditor are often willing to clean up your credit issue.

- You'll have at least two account lines associated with the debt. One for the original creditor and one for the collection agency. There will be an account line for each collection agency that has collected on your debt.
- The collection agency typically can only alter the information associated with their account line. They're unable to change the information in your credit file related to the original creditor. Therefore, you'll need to approach both parties.
- Once your debt is paid, insist that the collection agency have its entry deleted or reported as "satisfied in full," and get it in writing.
- Contact the original creditor and plead with them to have the original account deleted or listed as "satisfied in full." Deletion is much better!

Set up a payment plan.

If you decide to go this route, understand that you'll likely be on the hook for the full amount. In most cases, debtors will only make a few payments and then stop. For this reason, there's not a lot of incentive for debt collectors to settle for less than the full amount.

- Beware! They'll ask for a list of your assets, income, expenses, employer information, and maybe even your banking information if you choose to be put on a payment plan.
- If you're unable to make the payments, they'll have even more information than they did before.
- Avoid lying. You'll have to sign documents under the penalty of perjury. While you probably won't end up in jail, if you ever have to go to court, the courts won't view lying under the threat of perjury very favorably.

Any agreement with a collection agency needs to be in writing.

No exceptions! You're likely to get nothing out of the deal if it's not in writing, including any agreed-upon debt reduction.

Assuming you don't have the funds to eliminate your debt, it will be necessary to increase your income or raise additional funds. Finding the money to satisfy your debt:

Get a second job.

Most think having one job is bad enough, but it might be necessary to get a second income to pay off your debt. Take your time and find something that's worthwhile.

A second job doesn't have to mean minimum wage. Find the best paying option.

Ask family and friends.

It isn't easy to ask a family member or friend for money, but it's an option. Ensure you both understand whether it's a gift or a loan. It's also especially important that you follow through with your side of the agreement.

Losing the admiration of your credit card company is easier to swallow than having tension with friends or family.

Cut your expenses.

Do you have cable TV or an expensive cell phone plan? Do you eat out regularly? Some things are more important than an expensive coffee every morning.

It might be time to trim your expenses to free up some extra cash.

Sell some assets.

Whether it's junk in the garage or the stock shares of Coca-Cola your grandma gave you, selling a few items to pay off your debt is an option. Do a little brainstorming and see what you can unload.

Do everything you can to adjust your cash situation.

Be wary of taking on additional debt to pay off old debts. Your discipline will be tested with any new loans. Try to handle the situation yourself but keep friends and family in mind as a source of funds.

#4 Creating a Positive Future

Fixing the present is important, but creating a positive future is also imperative.

Developing good habits and fixing your credit issues are the keys to your financial future.

Both will take time, so get started now. Initial steps to a positive financial future:

Understand your missteps.

Did you fail to notice the signs that you were about to lose your job? Was your spending out of control? Were you amiss when keeping track of your spending? Did you avoid making your payments on time, even though you may have had the funds?

- If you understand why you developed debt issues in the first place, you can take steps to avoid repeating them.
- Develop a plan or take the necessary steps to avoid future debt. It would be a shame to have such a painful learning experience and then fail to benefit from it.

Create a budget.

Many individuals don't have a budget. If you've had financial issues, it's vital that you have this financial tool in place.

Is your budget reasonable for your income and expenses?

Increase your income.

Most financial gurus are focused on the expense side of things, but making more money is a good thing too. Ask for a raise, consider a second income, or seek a better paying position.

Pay your bills on time.

Some of us procrastinate when it comes to paying bills, even if we have the money available. Set up a schedule to sit down and pay your bills each week. Try to avoid being late ever again.

Be careful with new debt.

Those with debt issues tend to repeat their mistakes and get into trouble all over again.

- While most of us need a loan to purchase a house or car, most other debt is caused by impatience.
- If you have to borrow money or use a credit card to pay for a TV or vacation, then you just can't afford it.

Taking these initial steps will get your finances back on track. A bright financial future, free of future debt collections, requires the proper foundation. Avoid repeating your missteps and set the stage for future success.

The next step? Change the negative information in your credit reports.

Depending on the state, negative credit information will stay with you for 7 years or longer. There are ways to speed up the process if you don't want to wait that long. Remove negative credit information with these simple steps:

Get copies of your credit reports.

There are three major credit-reporting agencies. Get copies of your credit report from all three. You can get a free report from each agency once a year.

Circle every negative item on your report, whether it's accurate or not.

Dispute the negative information.

Even if the information is accurate, you still have the right to have the information verified. If they fail to verify the information on time (30 days) or don't have the supporting information, the item must be removed from your credit report.

- Avoid disputing incorrect information via the online tools that are available. This makes things very easy on the credit-reporting agency. Send your disputes by mail. This requires more effort on the part of the agency, and things are more likely to fall between the cracks.
- There is little benefit in disputing negative items that are still current. For example, if you still owe $5,000 on your credit card, the information will just reappear the next time the debt is reported. Only dispute active accounts if the information is inaccurate.
- After 30 days, you ought to either receive a response from the credit bureau or the item should be removed.

Get a new copy of your credit report to verify that the deleted items have been removed.

Wait a few weeks before checking. It can take a little time for the reports to be updated.

To double the effectiveness of your credit score improvement efforts, it's also important to add good information to your report.

Getting rid of the bad information is great, but it's much more effective to load your credit report with as much good information as possible. Adding positive information to your credit report:

Make your payments on time.

Simply paying your bills on time has a hugely positive effect on your credit score.

Take out a loan.

While having a loan doesn't boost your credit, paying off a loan does. There's an old trick for quickly establishing positive credit. Deposit $1,000 into a savings account and use that as collateral for a $1,000 loan. Then go down the street to another bank and use that $1,000 to get another loan. Repeat.

- You can use the proceeds from the last loan to make a few payments. Then pay off one of the loans and release the funds in the corresponding savings account. Take that money and pay off the next loan. Repeat.
- It's a quick way to add several positive items to your credit report.

Get a credit card and be responsible.

Credit cards have the potential to be positive or negative, depending on your ability to use them responsibly.

If you're unable to qualify for a traditional credit card, consider a secured card. You'll have to put down a deposit equivalent to the amount of credit you want. Many creditors will allow you to move to a more traditional card after effectively managing your account for a period.

Avoid applying for too much credit.

When you apply for credit, your potential creditor will do a credit check. Credit checks lower your credit score.

Keep your credit card balances low.

If you're using more than 30% of your available credit, it's hurting your credit score.

Suppose you have a credit card with a $10,000 limit. It's important to keep the balance below $3,000. Otherwise, your score is negatively impacted. Check monthly to ensure your utilization rate is below 30%.

Ask to become an authorized user on someone else's credit card account.

If you know someone with stellar credit, ask to be listed on their account. Tell them you don't even need a card. You just want to be associated with their credit report.

In essence, you inherit their positive credit. Practically overnight, your score can increase dramatically.

It's not difficult to rebuild your credit, but it takes time. There are many ways to remove negative credit information and to add positive information. Get started immediately and your credit future will be bright.

Summary

Debt collectors are a tiresome burden, and they can really detract from the quality of your life!

Remember the reality of the situation. Debt collectors wouldn't be so threatening if they could actually do something.

Intimidation is the name of the game. You're not going to prison just because you're unable to pay your debts. If you truly lack the money or assets to pay the debt, there is little a debt collector can do other than driving you crazy.

You can easily stop all communications from debt collectors by making the request in writing. You'll find that many of them will kick the debt back to the original creditor at that point. Then, the game starts all over again.

Your wages can be garnished up to 25%, but the creditor will have to win a lawsuit first. For smaller debts, this rarely occurs. It's simply not worth the time, cost, and hassle.

If you have significant debts, bankruptcy might be another option to consider.

It would be worth contacting an attorney to explore the possibility of eliminating much of your debt. For your own peace of mind and a secure financial future, it's important to address your debts directly and start working on solutions to both eliminate your debt and boost your credit score. There's no time like the present!

CHAPTER FOURTEEN, SUPPORT

Gratitude is just as important as knowledge. Be sure to remember that your ability to survive the matrix and be the best version of yourself is not only a gift to your life but something you deserve because of your constant effort. Choosing to be the best version of yourself and having the support to be more each day of your effort is a tremendous reason to be grateful. Keep up the work, you are doing great.

Getting Started

Remember, read through each section. Find the ones that you are already utilizing and pat yourself on the back. Spend time daily reviewing these thoughts until they become comfortable and natural to you. Be sure to come back in three months and read through your notes to make sure you haven't strayed from the work you need to make your life great.

Enjoy the Rewards

The labor of my journey is bearable when I pause to enjoy the rewards.

Use this self-affirming language to teach your thoughts a new habit:

- How wonderful it is to take a moment to say thanks for my successes. When I measure the rewards, I accept that each bit of labor along the way is worth it.
- Ultimate success is a long road, yet it is one with several victories along the way. I am deliberate in identifying those victories because they make the journey sweeter. Even taking a moment to acknowledge my perseverance a joyous thing.
- The road to my ideal career is a long one with many junctures. When I plot them out, the overall goal feels more attainable.
- Each course that I complete brings me a feeling of success. It reminds me that I have one less step to take before stepping through the last door. Instead of looking at what is ahead of me, I pat myself on the back for getting this far.
- The challenges that I encounter give me a chance to be creative. Finding solutions to challenging situations is fulfilling.
- I know that each season has its beginning and end. When I remind myself of the limited time of my trials, I gain peace of mind and deeper resolve.
- Today, I am a success story because I make it past each obstacle on my way to greatness. My commitment lies in remaining steadfast so that I am able to enjoy small rewards along the way.

Do the Work!

Take time for self-reflection:

1. How do I compensate myself for making it through difficult times?

2. What are some things I learn about myself when I persevere?

3. How do I encourage myself to push through when I feel weary and demoralized?

Wise Spending

I am committed to spending my money wisely.

Use this self-affirming language to teach your thoughts a new habit:

- I believe that developing financial wellness starts with a small step. It begins with cultivating good spending habits.
- One good habit is to spend my money on necessities first. I have the discipline to focus on what is important.
- My priority expenditures include savings and fixed expenses. I continuously put those things first when I spend my paycheck. When I focus on my necessary expenses, I avoid becoming stressed. When the basics are taken care of, I can rest easier.
- When my expenses are high, I prioritize my purchases. I take care of the important ones first and delay the others until my financial situation allows me to take care of them.
- Spending wisely boosts my net worth. My spending history reflects the story of a financially sound individual. It shows that I am reliable and can handle the responsibility that comes along with having credit.
- When I make wise spending decisions, I reap the benefits. I become a positive example to my friends and family. My actions show them the rewards that come from maintaining financial soundness.
- Because of today's good spending habits, I am excited about the financial options that my future holds!
- Today, I commit to spending my money wisely. I understand that unexpected situations sometimes occur, but my financial preparedness helps me handle those situations maturely.

Do the Work!

Take time for self-reflection:

1. How well do I handle financial emergencies that require a dip into my savings?

2. Why is it important to set financial goals based on my spending habits?

3. When have I given good financial advice to a loved one?

I am Fortunate

I attract prosperity into my life.

Use this self-affirming language to teach your thoughts a new habit:

- I am truly fortunate. Prosperity comes to me in a variety of ways, and I take full advantage of those opportunities that come into my life. I am a magnet for prosperity.
- I receive wonderful financial opportunities each week. I have multiple options for increasing my income. My income is growing and expanding. I am building additional streams of income that are ensuring my prosperity now and in the future.
- Everything I want and need in life is attracted to me. All of my hopes and dreams are being delivered to me.
- Occasionally, I receive what I want or need in the form of a challenge. These are lessons I need to learn to take my life to the next level. I am open to receiving and mastering these challenges. I trust that the universe knows what I need.
- I keep my mind open to all the ways prosperity can arrive in my life.
- Possibilities are presented to me, and then it is my responsibility to make the most of them. I take responsibility for my actions. I attract possibilities and then act on them with my full focus and effort.
- Today, I have the attitudes and beliefs of a prosperous person. I am attracting all forms of prosperity into my life. I am open to receiving the best that life has to offer.

Do the Work!

Take time for self-reflection:

1. What is my definition of prosperity? How would I know if I am prosperous?

2. Am I open to receiving the things and the life that I want to attract?

3. What is my general attitude toward money? How can I bring more money into my life?

Success

I embrace success.

Use this self-affirming language to teach your thoughts a new habit:

- I ask myself sometimes whether I do everything I can to be successful. I think about all the things I do to invite success into my life. I work hard. I establish networks of supportive people at work and at home. My eyes are open to new opportunities.
- If someone offers me a part-time temporary job and I have time for it, I take it. I worry less about how much I am getting paid for a particular job and think more about how the experience of the work could benefit me. I keep my résumé current, adding jobs and projects as I go.
- I set small goals and try to meet them quickly, so I can continually build momentum. To me, embracing success is not just a challenge; it is exciting, fun, and part of my every-day experience!
- Keeping myself open for new accomplishments brings fascinating possibilities into my life. Not knowing what is around the next corner brings uncertainty, but also excitement. My life is beautiful because I am open to opportunities.
- Today, I choose to embrace success. I plan to step forward and accept everything that comes my way. I know I can turn most opportunities into successful ventures.

Do the Work!

Take time for self-reflection:

1. Do I keep myself open to success?

2. What are my fears about embracing new opportunities that come my way?

3. Is there something I am doing to prevent myself from being successful? How can I be more accepting of success?

New Experiences

I make room in my life for new experiences.

Use this self-affirming language to teach your thoughts a new habit:

- I spend my days in search of new experiences. Although I appreciate the familiarity of my routine, I am open to switching things up.
- I keep my mental health in check when I exercise my brain. Being a part of something new challenges my mind. It allows me to explore the extent of my wisdom and intelligence. I love putting myself to the test.
- New experiences introduce me to new people. I am open to learning more about others. Sharing thoughts and ideas is a great way to achieve brotherhood.
- When I try something fresh and unfamiliar, I come face to face with my fears. Being brave allows me to confront whatever keeps me from excelling. It is when I display the courage that I am able to push through challenges.
- My strength of character grows with each new event that I am involved in.
- I share memorable moments with friends and family. It is important to embrace their passions even if I am less interested in the activities than they are. Making room for their desires is an indication that I am making room for them in my life.
- Today, newness is more exciting than intimidating. I know that the only thing to fear is fear itself. When I commit to putting doubts aside, I open myself up to blessings in many forms.

Do the Work!

Take time for self-reflection:

1. How do I determine when an upcoming experience is unsuitable for me?

2. How do I prepare myself to make use of new experiences?

3. How do I keep myself engaged when I am having emotional difficulty?

New Year Finances

I am financially strong as I move into a new year.

Use this self-affirming language to teach your thoughts a new habit:

- The coming of a new year provides me with great opportunities. I make my New Year better by improving my finances. I am capable of improving my financial life!
- I am strong and can take on anything that comes my way. I see financial challenges as opportunities to work smarter and harder so I can better myself.
- Finances are important to me because it provides me with security for the future. My future is a valuable thing. I care about making both my present and future the best they can be. When I focus on my finances, I see ways in which I can improve in the New Year. Because I work to improve, my finances continue to get better and better.
- How I make and spend my money is important. I am strong in a financial sense because I know that money is a valuable commodity. In the New Year, I see how I am able to do even better when it comes to my finances. I enjoy working with my finances to see what I can do with them. It's fun to work with figures and new ideas.
- My financial strength comes from dedication to my work and from making good choices. If I make a mistake, I correct it and avoid making it again. Through learning and growing, my financial picture is bright. The future looks good because I remain financially healthy and strong.
- Today, I am strong and capable financially as the New Year arrives.

Do the Work!

Take time for self-reflection:

1. What can I do to move forward financially in the New Year?

2. How can I avoid getting into old financial patterns from previous years?

3. What should I do to ensure I'm staying on the right financial path?

15

TOOLS

Here's where you will find the questionnaires that support your *Do the Work!* for the units. Answer the questions in writing either by hand or on a text app like Microsoft Word or Google Docs. Keep your answers and go back to them to refresh and make sure you stay on track with your development.

Getting Started

If, while answering the questions, you find them difficult or confusing, don't worry. You may need a refresher of the information. Go back and read the unit again to clarify your thoughts. Dive back in when you are ready.

TURN YOUR PASSION TO PROFIT QUESTIONNAIRE

Section #1: Prepare Yourself

Are you prepared to put in the hard work that is necessary to create a profitable side hustle? How will you generate the motivation necessary to get things done?

What keeps you from starting your side hustle? How can you overcome this?

How would your life change if you were doing work that made you happy? What would your best life look like? Write out your vivid vision of your life.

Section #2: Identify Your Passions and Interests

What are you most passionate about? What do you absolutely love to do?

What are you really good at? What are people constantly asking you to help with?

What do you lose track of time doing?

When do you find yourself in a state of "flow"?

Section #3: Validate Your Side Hustle

Why is it so important to validate your side hustle? How will you validate your side hustle?

What audience will you use to give you feedback on your side hustle idea?

If it seems like your side hustle won't work, how could you adjust your product or service to make it more marketable? Would a different side hustle work better for you?

Section #4: Determine What Sets You Apart from Your Competitors

Why is it so important to differentiate yourself from your competitors?

What specific ways will you be different from your competitors?

Why should customers purchase from you and not someone else?

Section #5: Define Your Goals

How does defining your goals help you make your side hustle a reality?

What goals do you need to set in order to start your side hustle?

Why is it so important that goals be realistic? How will you ensure that you're making progress on a daily, weekly, and monthly basis?

Section #6: Create Milestones

Why is it so tempting to put off actually launching your side hustle?

Why are milestones so important and how do they help you achieve your goals? Are your milestones both achievable and realistic?

How does achieving your milestones encourage you to keep going?

Section #7: Determine How You Will Sell

How will you sell your product?

If you plan on selling online, what is the best platform(s) for you to use?

What steps do you need to take to get selling ASAP?

Section #8: Start Selling

Will your side hustle be perfect when you first launch? After you launch, how can you improve and refine your sales process?

What questions can you ask your friends, prospects or existing clients to help you improve your product messaging and sales?

Section #9: Market Yourself

Why is marketing so important for your side hustle? What specific ways will you market your side hustle?

Do you feel awkward about marketing yourself? How can you move past that?

Why are people more likely to buy from you when you provide them with maximum value?

Section #10: Get Feedback from Customers

Why is it necessary to consistently get feedback from your customers?

How does asking for feedback make you seem more authentic and transparent to your customers?

What feedback strategies will you implement in your side hustle?

Section #11: Provide Amazing Experiences for Your Customers

Why should you create amazing experiences for your customers? What are some simple ways you can create these experiences?

What is the connection between delighting your customers and getting referral business?

Section #12: Build Sustainable Income

How do you know when you're ready to make the leap from side hustle to full-time gig?

Do you have enough sustainable income to enable you to take your side hustle full-time? What expenses do you need to account for?

Is fear keeping you from following your dreams? If so, what are you afraid of? How can you get past this fear?

You're done! Keep up the great work.

WRITE A HIGHLY EFFECTIVE BUSINESS PLAN

This business plan template will guide you in creating your business plan. Once you've filled in the appropriate information, remember to thoroughly proofread it so that it is free from spelling and grammatical errors.

Business Information

Date

Company name

Street address 1

Street address 2

City, state, ZIP

Business phone

Website URL

Email address

Table of Contents

Include all the Bold Titles below in your table of contents.

Executive Summary

Mission Statement: A brief statement of what your business seeks to accomplish

Company Information: Founding date, names/roles of founders, number of employees, number of locations

Company Highlights: Growth highlights of the company (financial or other), along with hard numbers and charts

Product/Service: Short description of what you sell and who you sell to

Financial Information: Financing goals and any current sources of funding

Future Plans: Quick glimpse of where you're headed (expansion, new products)

Company Description

Industry: A quick description of the industry you're in

Target Market: Your primary customer base

Competitive Advantages: Describe any competitive advantages you may have, such expertise or location.

Market Analysis

Industry Information: Size of industry, past growth, projected future growth, current trends

Competitors: Top competitors, strengths and weaknesses, total market share

Target Market: Specific customers you are targeting (current needs and existing solutions, demographic information)

Target Market Size: Amount target market spends, frequency and timing of purchases

Market Share Potential: Amount of market share you believe you can acquire

Barriers to Entry: Things that would make it difficult to succeed, such as strict regulations or high-tech costs

Organization and Management

Key Stakeholders: Who are the key stakeholders in the business and how do they relate to one another (include organizational chart)?

Legal Structure: Describe whether your company is an LLC, S-Corp, C-Corp, or other legal entity.

Employee Background: Background information about key stakeholders that demonstrates expertise/value

Key Hires: List any key hires that you will need to make in order to succeed

Products and Services

Description of Product/Service: A clear description of what your product/service is

Benefits: A thorough description of how your product benefits customers and stands apart from the competition

Pricing Structure: Explanation of how you will price your product

Proprietary Information: Any intellectual property, patents, or proprietary information you possess that will contribute to your success

Supply Chain: Suppliers/vendors you rely upon, along with key information like how often you receive supplies and the method by which you receive them

Marketing and Sales

Positioning: How you will position yourself relative to your competitors (lower cost, superior quality, superior service)

Promotional Methods: Specific tactics you'll use to spread the word about your product or service

Success Metrics: How you will evaluate the results of your marketing efforts

Sales Strategy: Method(s) you will use to sell to customers (cold calling, in-person meetings, other strategies)

Sales Team: Description of who will be selling to customers

Budget: Amount of money to be spent on marketing and sales efforts

Financial Projections

Current Financial Status: Income statements, balance sheets, cash flow statements, debt documentation, and other pertinent details

12-Month Financial Projection: Projected sales, cost of goods sold, profit, expenses, net operating income

Cash Flow Projection: Projection of how much cash you'll have on hand at given points over the next 12 months

Projected Balance Sheet: Projected balance sheet in 12 months

Break-even Calculation: Projection of how much sales volume you'll need to cover costs

Funding Request

Request Details: Type of funding you are requesting along with the amount of funding and terms

Use of Funds: How you will be using the funding (inventory, payroll, other)

Future Plans: How and when you will repay the investment, any plans to sell the business

Appendix

Table of Contents: Make it easy to connect information in the appendix to specific sections of the business plan.

Supporting Information: Key information that supports previous sections

You're done! Keep up the great work.

THE BATTLE FOR PRODUCTIVITY, WORKSHEET

Section 1: The Battle for Productivity

On a scale of 1-10, how would you rate your current levels of productivity?

What are the biggest productivity challenges you face right now?

What specific distractions or activities keep you from being productive?

Who do you know that is very productive? What makes them productive?

What does an ideal day look like for you in terms of productivity?

Section 2: Systems Over Goals

What has been your experience in setting goals?

What are your current goals?

Why are systems more effective in helping you achieve your goals?

What systems will you set up to help you achieve your goals?

If you stick with your systems, what will the end results be? Will you achieve the goals you want?

Section 3: The Early Bird Gets Everything Done

What keeps you from rising early? If you are able to rise early, what makes it possible for you?

Does your bedtime reflect your desire to wake early?

What can you do to minimize the amount of technology you use at night?

What would an ideal sleep routine look like for you?

Do your exercise habits reinforce or hurt your sleep routines?

Section 4: Kill Your Distractions

On a scale of 1-10, how distracted would you say you are during your workday?

What are the primary things that cause you to get distracted?

How can you create space and time for uninterrupted work?

How much more would you accomplish if you had an undistracted day?

What steps will you take to incorporate rest and play into your life?

Section 5: Slay Your Dragons

Do you gravitate toward doing the hard or easy things first at work?

Why is it so tempting to do the easiest things first at work?

Why is doing the easiest things first usually a bad strategy in terms of productivity?

What steps can you take to ensure that you do the more difficult tasks first?

If you do your most difficult tasks first, how will that improve the rest of your day?

You're done! Keep up the great work.

THE BATTLE FOR PRODUCTIVITY, OVERCOME DISTRACTIONS SUPPORT

Here are the most common distractions that can keep you from being productive. Along with each distraction is a suggested set of solutions to help you overcome the distractions and be more productive.

Distraction: Social Media

Solutions:

- Use an app like "Rescue Time" to physically limit how much you can be on social media.
- Delete social media apps from your phone.
- Turn off all social media notifications.
- Set a social media schedule and only allow yourself to use social media during the allotted times.

Distraction: Email

Solutions:

- Avoid responding to email first thing in the morning.
- Only open your inbox at specified times of the day.
- Turn off all email notifications on your phone and computer.
- Create an auto-response that tells others you're only able to respond to email on particular days of the week and then stick to that schedule.

Distraction: Slack, Skype, Messenger
Solutions:

- Turn off all notifications on your phone.
- Close apps and only respond to messages at pre-specified times.
- Snooze notifications on desktop versions of the chat app.

Distraction: Text Messages
Solutions:

- Put your phone in a drawer and only take it out at specified times.
- Disable text notifications on your phone.
- Disable text notifications on your smartwatch and laptop.
- Only respond to text messages during specific times of the day.

Distraction: Phone Calls
Solutions:

- Put your phone in a drawer and only take it out at specified times.
- Respond to voicemails at the end of the day after you've done your most productive work.
- Put your phone on silent mode during your focused periods.
- Disable notifications on your smartwatch and computer.

Distraction: People Interrupting You
Solutions:

- Close your office door.
- Put on headphones.
- When someone asks for a minute of your time, ask if you can catch them at a later, specified time.

A BRIGHT FINANCIAL FUTURE, QUESTIONNAIRE

Creating and implementing effective financial habits one step at a time is the key to long-lasting change.

Use these questions to gain a clear perspective of your situation and plan for positive changes:

1. What aspect of your financial life requires the most attention?
2. What are the most important habits you could put into place to enhance this part of your financial life?
3. Limiting yourself to only one, which habit would have the greatest impact?
4. What are the steps you could take to implement this habit without causing yourself an unmanageable amount of stress?
5. What is an appropriate amount of action to take during the first week?
6. After that habit is complete, what is the next best habit to acquire?
7. How can taking these baby steps work better for you than the methods you've tried for making financial changes in the past?

Do the Work!

To create change, it is important to actually do the work. Answer the questions.

DECLUTTER YOUR MIND, QUESTIONNAIRE

Your mind is filled with clutter. Daily stress, poor mental habits, and unfinished business are a few of the causes of mental clutter.

Just as a cluttered home can be decluttered, so can a cluttered mind.

Use these questions to gain insight toward reducing your mental clutter:

1. What are the excess items in my home and work environment that contribute to my mental clutter?
2. Are there unnecessary people in my life that create additional clutter? Who are they? How can I lessen their impact?
3. How do I distract myself? What do I do when I procrastinate?
4. When I can implement focused breathing into my routine?
5. How can I add at least one 20-minute daily meditation session into my life?
6. How would my life change if I were able to reduce my mental clutter by at least 50 percent?
7. What are the negative thoughts I experience regularly? How do these impact the rest of my day?

Do the Work!

To create change, it is important to actually do the work. Answer the questions.

ENHANCE YOUR CHARISMA AND YOUR LIFE, QUESTIONNAIRE

Enhance Your Charisma and Your Life, Questionnaire

Enhancing your level of charisma can pay off in multiple facets of life. Becoming more charismatic is possible for anyone. Answering these questions will help you in your quest to develop greater charisma:

1. How would an increased level of charisma affect my life? What would change?

2. Who is the most charismatic person I know? What makes them so captivating?

3. Of the four components of charisma, where are my strengths and weaknesses?

- Presence: List your strengths. List your weaknesses.
- Kindness: List your strengths. List your weaknesses.
- Confidence: List your strengths. List your weaknesses.
- Power: List your strengths. List your weaknesses.

4. What four small goals am I going to set to enhance my level of charisma?

- Presence: List your goal.
- Kindness: List your goal.
- Confidence: List your goal.
- Power: List your goal.

5. What do I need to be successful at these goals? How will I know when I've achieved success?

6. When and where am I going to visualize my goals each day? What are the details in my visions, using as many of my senses as possible?

- Presence: List your vision.
- Kindness: List your vision.
- Confidence: List your vision.
- Power: List your vision.

7. Which of my current habits is limiting my ability to be more charismatic? How can I change it to one that supports my goal?

Do the Work!

To create change, it is important to actually do the work. Answer the questions.

TAX-ADVANTAGED RETIREMENT INCOME YOU CAN'T OUTLIVE, QUESTIONNAIRE

These days, it's challenging to figure out ways to set up an income after you retire. Complete this questionnaire to learn more about how you can take advantage of life insurance and annuities and the low or no-tax privileges they offer.

What kind of life insurance do you have?

What do you know about it?

Do you have an annuity?

What is your understanding of an annuity?

What is a whole life insurance policy?

What is a universal life insurance policy?

What is a variable life insurance policy?

Mention the guarantees for each type of insurance here:

- Whole Life:
- Universal Life:
- Variable Life:

What are two ways to get tax-free gains on life insurance?

Next, list 2 downsides of using life insurance as a tax-free investment.

When is life insurance investing particularly advantageous?

Name the two phases of annuities. Tell what occurs during each of those phases.

- Phase 1.

- Phase 2.

What is the difference between fixed and variable annuities?

What is the main benefit of an annuity?

In what situations is it wise to choose life insurance as your investment?

In what situations is it advantageous to have an annuity?

Describe each of these strategies:

- Strategy #1. Using Life Insurance Cash Value for Tax-Free Income
- Strategy #2. Using an Annuity to Guarantee Income for
- Strategy #3. 1035 Exchange: Life Insurance Cash Value into an Annuity
- Strategy #4. Using an Annuity + Life Insurance

Discuss the age issue related to purchasing life insurance policies versus annuities.

Which of the 4 tax strategies is completely tax-free?

Which strategies delay taxes until retirement?

What steps can you take to get started on creating your own tax-advantaged retirement income stream with life insurance and annuities?

Do the Work!

Take the time to answer the questions and evaluate your position. Your understanding could change your financial future.

DECORATE YOUR TAX RETURN WITH RED FLAGS AND GET AUDITED!

There is no foolproof way to avoid being audited. The IRS makes most of its selections either based on the fact that the filer is part of a targeted group or because a computer program picked out the tax return.

Even though many of the returns are chosen by random means, there are certain red flags that make a return more likely to be audited.

If you don't want the IRS knocking on your door, avoid these red flags:

Arithmetic errors:

If you make an addition or subtraction error, you're going to hear about it. This usually doesn't result in a full-blown audit but check your math before filing your return.

If you do get a letter from the IRS about your perceived mistake, double-check. Sometimes a number was read or keyed incorrectly.

Mismatched numbers:

For example, if the numbers on your 1099 form don't match the entries on your return, the IRS will notify you. Again, double-check and be sure that the error was yours, not theirs. Sometimes an IRS employee will enter a social security number as income!

You get most of your income in cash.

The IRS will be looking for unreported income, and any cash deposits made to your accounts will be scrutinized. If those deposits aren't being reported as income, you'd better be able to explain it.

Self-employed and small business owners are particularly targeted.

Keep excellent records, especially about your deposits.

You talk too much.

If you're ever foolish enough to try to pull a fast one on the IRS, keep your mouth closed. You'd be surprised how many neighbors, friends, and even family members report what they've heard.

Remember that the IRS gives 15-30% of the additional tax collected to the whistle blower!

There's even a form, Form 211, to report those not paying their taxes properly. A large number of serious crimes are solved because the perpetrator told someone what they did.

You're out of the ordinary.

When your deductions are considerably greater than others at your income level, the computer will flag you.

Keep in mind that the IRS doesn't have unlimited time and resources. They target the returns likely to result in the biggest collections. Don't pay more tax than you have to, but don't go too far and cross the line in your deductions.

This can even include things like charitable donations. If you claim you're giving 50% of your income to charity, it looks odd to the IRS. They're going to take a closer look at everything on your return. That doesn't mean you can't give 50% of your income away - it simply means that everything else will be scrutinized.

Your tax preparer is questionable.

Not all tax preparers are created equal. Some simply aren't very good. Others are intentionally breaking the law. They may promise a large refund and then claim false deductions on your return. While you're not entirely at fault, the IRS will be coming after you, too.

Do the Work!

Being audited is never a positive experience. On the other hand, if you act in good faith, it's unlikely that anything bad will happen beyond an increase in your tax bill.

The tax code is complicated - everyone knows that, even the IRS. Be honest and you have little to fear. However, keep these red flags in mind before filing your tax return!

SURVIVE AN IRS AUDIT

The vast majority of us get through our tax return without any major problems. Most of us figure the IRS has bigger fish to fry. You would be right most of the time; the odds of the average person being audited are quite slim in any given year.

Hope for the best and be prepared for the worst.

Let's looks a few things you can do to be well-prepared in case you're chosen for an audit.

Before You Get Audited

Keep good records.

If you're not organized, now is the time to start. Keep at least 3 years of tax returns and all the associated documents, bills, receipts, and other items as appropriate. This would include any items related to your income, investments, or tax deductions.

- If the IRS disputes any of your figures, you'll have to have the documentation to back them up. If you don't have the documentation for a deduction, for example, they may disallow that deduction altogether.
- Organization is an ongoing process. Take care of your records daily, as you accrue them, rather than just once a year.

Watch your red flags.

Here are 5 of the things the IRS tends to look for when choosing tax returns to audit:

- **Large business expenses.** Small business owners sometimes try to get

away with deducting nearly every expense they have. The IRS knows this. Be careful.
- **Your "friends."** If you're trying to pull a fast one, it's not uncommon for the IRS to get a tip from a friend, family member, or co-worker. The solution is to not do anything wrong in the first place. In lieu of that, don't tell anyone anything that can come back to haunt you.
- **Complexity.** If you're business or investment transactions are very complex, the IRS might believe that it's likely you made a mistake somewhere.
- **Large Charitable Deductions.** If you give significantly more to charity than others in a similar financial situation, the IRS will take pause. Also, if your charitable donations increase dramatically, the IRS will be curious.
- **Inaccuracies on your W-2 or 1099.** They figure if the basic documentation is wrong, there must be other things wrong as well.

Be prepared.

In the event that you are chosen for an audit, you should immediately prepare yourself. Review your tax return and associated records. Don't hesitate to get expert advice if you need it; a CPA can provide valuable insight and information.

During the Audit

At the time of the audit, do not volunteer more records than the auditor requests. Extra records will never help you but do provide the opportunity for the auditor to find something else wrong.

Keep the auditor honest. They can only request information and records related to the official request that you received in the audit notification. If they stray from that, don't be afraid to politely tell them 'no'. They have the option of filing a second official request, but many won't bother and will simply let it go.

While the odds of being audited are generally quite small, it is unlikely that you'll exit an audit without paying some additional tax or penalty. The IRS wants to generate as much income as it can.

However, having the proper documentation for every item on your return lessens the probability that you'll have to pay. So regardless of which item they question, you have the paperwork to back up what you claimed on the return.

Do the Work!

Provided you haven't intentionally done anything wrong, there is usually nothing significant to worry about. The key is to be honest when filing your taxes and keep your records up to date. If you do these things, you will survive an IRS audit.

RECOGNIZE FAKE IRS COLLECTION CALLS

Fake IRS money collection calls are on the rise. The number of victims continues to grow, but you don't have to be one of them. Remember these important tips from the IRS:

- The IRS doesn't call taxpayers about questions, debt, or late payments. This is the most important thing to remember.
- The IRS sends mail. If there is a problem with your taxes and the IRS, you will receive a letter from them.
- The IRS doesn't ask for payments using pre-loaded debit cards or wire transfers. You have a choice of payment methods.
- The IRS doesn't call to ask for your debit, credit card, or bank information. Avoid sharing this financial information with anyone over the phone.
- The IRS won't call you to ask for personal information. Don't share details like your mother's maiden name, social security number, or other personal information over the phone.

Do the Work!

The IRS warns that fake collection calls are becoming more popular. You must be careful when handling these calls.

INCOME TAXES AND LIVING OUT OF THE COUNTRY

Living in a foreign country holds a lot of appeal. It gives an exotic impression and seems like a never-ending vacation. But it doesn't matter where you go, because the US government still expects you to file a tax return and pay taxes. This is true even if you become a citizen of the other country and live there full time.

For your peace of mind and to keep you out of jail, become familiar with the income tax rules that apply to you as a citizen of the United States living outside the country.

Income tax rules for US citizens living abroad:

No matter where you live, you must file a tax return.

It's entirely possible that you won't owe any taxes, but you must file an income tax return each year.

You're still subjected to all US tax laws.

This includes income tax rates and the same credits and deductions.

There are 2 primary ways to reduce your taxes owed in the United States.

The United States has a reputation for double taxation, but in practice that only applies above certain income limits.

- Foreign tax credit: This credit is intended to protect American citizens from paying taxes twice on the same income. In essence, you can deduct any income taxes you've paid in the foreign country from your taxes owed in the US. There is a limit, however.

- If you paid $12,000 in foreign taxes, you could reduce your US tax bill by $12,000. Simple enough.
- Income exclusions: This is the other option. You can't claim both. The income exclusion allows you to reduce your gross income by up to $97,600. You can also subtract housing costs up to a maximum amount.
- As an example, if you earned $100,000 in a foreign country, your taxable income would be only $2,400. It would be even less after the housing cost credit.
- The housing credit is equal to the cost of housing minus $15,216. The maximum is 30% of $97,600. If your housing costs were $25,000, you could claim an additional deduction of $9,784 from your gross income.
- Self-employed folks are not eligible for this housing exclusion.

Any gross income above and beyond these deductions will likely be taxed in both countries.

Those with significant incomes can expect to have a portion of their income double taxed.

Many wealthy and not-so-wealthy people are choosing to renounce their US citizenship. In many cases, this is due to the tax situation. Over 3,000 people did exactly that in 2013. Even if you don't owe taxes, the cost to have your income tax return prepared in a foreign country can range from $3,000 to $7,000! That's a lot of to pay, especially if you're under the income limits.

The laws surrounding the reporting of foreign investments and bank accounts are very arduous. The banks themselves have to report your accounts. You also have to individually report each account holding $10,000 or more.

It's important to file your US tax returns. The penalty for failing to file while living abroad starts at $10,000 and can go as high as $100,000. This can be true even if you don't owe any taxes.

If you're under the income limit, your US tax bill is likely to be zero. However, the cost and hassle of filing that return can be significant.

Do the Work!

File your US tax return, no matter where you reside!

10 AMAZING LIFE LESSONS YOU CAN APPRECIATE

There are things that everyone learns about life eventually. The sooner you learn them, the better off you'll be. There's no reason to waste any more time! You can learn these valuable lessons the easy way or the hard way.

- **Failure is a necessary part of life.** You can't expect everything to work out 100% of the time. The only way to avoid failure is to never leave the house, and that assumes that you live alone.
- **You get what you tolerate**. Do you have a horrible job, relationship, or waistline? Do your friends mistreat you? The quality of your life drops to the level you're willing to tolerate. If you're willing to tolerate certain behavior from others, you're certain to receive it.
- **Resilience is the key.** Talent and luck are nice, but you can't choose your talents. Luck is hit or miss. But, if you are resilient, you can accomplish anything. How could you fail if you always bounce back to life? Sooner or later, you'll find success.
- **Think before you speak.** How many times in your life do you wish you could take your words back? Many challenges can be avoided by resisting the urge to open your mouth.
- **Life is short.** Worried about keeping up with the Jones's or making a fool out of yourself? Before you know it, your life will be coming to an end. You can be sure you won't care about such things then. Why not stop caring about silly things today?
- **Focus on you.** You're worried about what everyone thinks. You want to impress others. The trouble is, most people spend so much time worrying about themselves that they aren't focusing on you at all.
- **You can't do it all alone.** People are frustrating sometimes, but you can accomplish much more with a little help. Be choosey whom you let into your life, but allow someone in.

- **Repeating actions repeats the results.** If you tried something and it didn't work, try something new. New actions give new results. If you're not happy with the outcome, change your approach.
- **The truth is easier.** Lying can be easier in the short-term, but it's often a disaster in the long-term. You probably don't lie as well as you think you do, and it's difficult to hide a lie indefinitely. Once you're caught lying, the situation worsens. You also ruin your credibility.
- **You control how you feel.** Despite what you might think, the people around you and your circumstances don't control your emotions. Only you have the power to make yourself feel one way or the other. So, why not choose to feel good?

Do the Work!

Create a list and add to it as you learn more about life. Recognizing a lesson is the first step to remembering it in the future when you need it. Life has plenty of valuable lessons to teach, but it's up to you to get the message.

CHAPTER FIFTEEN, SUPPORT

Let's wrap up the book with some final self-affirmative talk. It's been great sharing this journey towards financial health and wealth with you. I am impressed that you did all the work and made a conscious effort to change your life into your thoughts and desires of abundance.

Keep up the good work!

Conscientious

My conscientiousness is evident.

Use this self-affirming language to teach your thoughts a new habit:

- When I take part in a task or project, I do everything I can to do it well. I show extreme care and effort in what I do. It is important for me to be conscientious about anything I am involved in. I am thorough, involved, and hard-working.
- When I am conscientious, those I work with and relate to also enjoy the benefits of my hard work. So, it's a win-win situation for all. I get to be proud of myself and they see benefits as well.
- Being conscientious also means I consider my own ideas about doing the right thing.
- My conscience comes into play regardless of the task. I think about what I believe in when taking part in a project and stay true to my beliefs. Considering what I feel is the right thing matters greatly to me.
- I am energized by the idea that others can learn from my conscientiousness. I engage in my tasks with an open heart and a sense of care and effort.
- Today, I intend to put forth my most conscientious efforts for all my tasks. I care about demonstrating to others that I follow my conscience and one tenet of my beliefs is that hard work and excellence are important. I want my conscientiousness to be evident in whatever I do.

Do the Work!

Take time for self-reflection:

1. Can other people see that I am conscientious?

2. What does it mean to me to be conscientious?

3. How can I foster a greater focus on being more conscientious in my everyday life?

Opportunity to Improve

Having less means more opportunities to improve my circumstances.

Use this self-affirming language to teach your thoughts a new habit:

- I am a positive thinker. I look at even the most intimidating circumstances as opportunities to come out on top. I am unlimited in my self-confidence and the knowledge that I am worthy of winning.
- I embrace challenging circumstances. Sometimes, I would like to be more capable than I am, but I also know that I have what it takes to open other doors to help me achieve my goals.
- I am creative with my talents and can convert any circumstances to opportunities for indescribable success.
- Even if I lose out on one opportunity, I can certainly prepare myself for the next.
- I give thanks for what I have and what I continue to receive. I know I am better off than many others, and for that, I am continually grateful. I avoid taking anything that is given to me for granted. I treasure it and also share what I have with those around me.
- Today, my life is all about making the most of what I have. I am happy with what has been given to me because I know I have the drive and determination to use my talents and abilities to go for more. I see what I want and am committed to going after it with gusto.

Do the Work!

Take time for self-reflection:

1. Is it difficult for me to teach my children to be satisfied with what they have?

2. Do I share my talents and possessions with others?

3. Are there times when I am saddened because I lack sufficient resources?

Count My Blessings

I feel wealthy when I count the blessings that many take for granted.

Use this self-affirming language to teach your thoughts a new habit:

- Blessings come in many forms. I am convinced that all the small ones add up enormously. They combine to help me live a truly privileged life.
- Each day I wake up is a chance to make a difference in the world. That, in itself, is something to be thankful for. I look for opportunities to encourage positivity all around. Seeing someone smile because of my actions is a wonderful blessing.
- My friends are treasured miracles in my life. I enjoy being there for them in the same way they are there for me.
- Having the use of my hands gives me the chance to extend them to someone in need. Each time I look at my hands, I see vessels for a better quality of life. I use them to give, lift, and hold up anyone who needs that help.
- My words remind me that I have the fortune of being able to promote change. I feel blessed with influence because I know I am able to use powerful words. I use my voice to come to the defense of others. It helps me to protect my brother. Being able to offer that protection is an invaluable gift.
- Today, I look at all my built-in strengths and abilities that are easy to take for granted. They make me feel wealthier than having financial success or material possessions.

Do the Work!

Take time for self-reflection:

1. When am I most aware of my ability to use my blessings to help others?

2. How easy is it for me to identify my blessings when they occur?

3. In what ways can I make adjustments in my life to encourage more blessings?

Remain Fluid

I give in without giving up.

Use this self-affirming language to teach your thoughts a new habit:

- I distinguish between giving in and giving up. I can always adjust my approach while keeping my goals in sight. Giving in can lead me to victory.
- Life is full of beginnings and endings. Leaving the past behind prepares me to move forward. I may exchange something good for something even greater.
- I recognize changing circumstances. If my family grows, it may make more sense for me to continue working rather than return to school. Some changes take place within my own mind. My thoughts and opinions shift. I may support a different political candidate while maintaining the same principles.
- Accommodating others matters to me. Serving people adds meaning to my life and makes me happy. I am open to trying out their suggestions as long as they are constructive.
- I monitor my results. Specific goals and timelines let me measure my progress and adjust my plans to become more productive. A sense of comfort and security also assures me that I am doing the right thing.
- Today, I advance along my chosen path even if I take a few detours. Success requires flexibility, perseverance, and the ability to give in to changing ideas or circumstances.

Do the Work!

Take time for self-reflection:

1. How can pride interfere with my ability to give in?

2. Why is it important to know the reasons behind my decision to give in?

3. What is the difference between giving in and being defeated?

I Am Wealthy in Many Ways

I am spiritually, physically, and emotionally wealthy.

Use this self-affirming language to teach your thoughts a new habit:

- I feel abundance all around me. It pervades my mind, body, and soul, bringing me infinite wealth.
- Spending time with my Creator fills my spirit with His goodness. I express my gratitude for my wealth of blessings every day in my prayers.
- Physical wealth flows to me through my healthy habits. I eat nutritious foods and exercise every day. Just these two things relieve my stress, renew my energy, and strengthen my immune system to ward off disease. They keep me healthy and happy.
- I buy healthy food at the grocery store and plan my meals so I can eat nutritiously. I even make my own "fast food." I cook in large amounts, freezing the extra portions so I have healthy heat-and-eat meals ready at a moment's notice.
- Exercise is a priority in my life. Even on days when my schedule is full, I find ways to exercise. I take the stairs instead of the elevator; I actively play with my kids and pets; I park far away from my destination and walk.
- Emotionally, I am a fountain of optimism, confidence, and positivity. I use positive self-talk throughout my day and affirmations to replace negative thoughts with positive images and feelings.
- I receive many benefits from my daily meditations. I visualize scenes of success, happiness, and joy. This, too, is a stress reliever and provides me with the inspiration and motivation to spur me forward with unlimited passion toward my goals.
- Today, my goal is to share my wealth with others, turning their sadness into joy, desperation into hope, and darkness into light.

Do the Work!

Take time for self-reflection:

1. Do I spend time each day increasing my spiritual wealth?

2. How can I add daily exercise to my schedule?

3. What can I do to bring more positivity to my emotional mindset?

Determination

Determination is my goal in whatever I do.

Use this self-affirming language to teach your thoughts a new habit:

- Regardless of what I am doing at any given time, I strive to be firm in my purpose.
- I am strong and focused. I believe I must be determined in order to complete any task. Determination is the central focus of my life.
- My determination helps me move through challenges. Even if an event progresses in a way contrary to what I choose, my level of determination stays strong. I push forward until I reach a satisfactory conclusion.
- Having determination aids me to achieve success, regardless of my goal.
- I realize sometimes I must alter my path. When a change is imminent, deep inside me my determination grows. I usually experience the outcomes I want because of my determination.
- I am proud that I am a good role model for others by staying firm and focused on my purpose. I keep my eyes on the prize. I reflect on how to best achieve the task.
- Today, I know I can tackle any job and keep working to complete it. I stay hopeful and confident. Being firm and focused increases my chances of success in whatever I do.

Do the Work!

Take time for self-reflection:

1. When I approach any task, how determined am I to complete it?

2. Are there times when I simply give up and avoid finishing something? In what types of situations am I most likely to give up?

3. If I were to be more determined to accomplish goals, how would my life change?

ABOUT THE AUTHOR

Billy Carson, the founder of 4biddenknowledge Inc. and 4biddenknowledge TV, a new conscious streaming TV network. Billy Carson is the Best Selling Author of 'The Compendium Of The Emerald Tablets' and is an expert host on Deep Space, a new original streaming series by Gaia. This series explores the Secret Space Program, revealing extraordinary technologies and their potential origins. Billy Carson also serves as an expert host on Gaia's original series, Ancient Civilizations, in which a team of renowned scholars deciphers the riddles of our origins and pieces together our forgotten history documented in monuments and texts around the world.

Mr. Carson appreciates the dedication and hard work it takes to accomplish great things. Recently, Mr. Carson earned the Certificate of Science (with an emphasis on Neuroscience) at M.I.T.. Mr. Carson also has a certificate in Ancient Civilizations from Harvard University.. Among his most notable achievements, Billy is the CEO of First Class Space Agency based in Fort Lauderdale, FL. Specifically, his space agency is involved in research and development of alternative propulsion systems and zero-point energy devices.

TV & FILM

2022: Chronicles Of The Anunnaki

2021: Black Knight Satellite

2021: The Mystery Of The Gosford Glyphs

2021: The Incarnations Of Thoth

- 2019 American Mystery
- 2019 UFOs The Lost Evidence
- 2019 UFO's: Uncovering the Truth
- 2018 Knowledge For Ascension With Billy Carson (In Production)
- 2017 What If (Documentary)
- 2017 DocUFObia (Documentary)
- 2017 Ancient Civilizations (TV Series)
- 2017 Beyond Belief with George Noory (TV Series)
- 2017 Life beyond Our Existence (Documentary)
- 2017 Buzzsaw with Sean Stone (TV Series)
- 2016 The Anunnaki Series (TV Series documentary short)

- 2016 Deep Space (TV Series documentary)
- 2016 Baltic Sea Anomaly: The Unsolved Mystery (documentary)
- 2015 UFAH Favorites (Video short)
- 2012 Countdown to Apocalypse (TV mini-Series documentary)

facebook.com/4biddenKnowledge
twitter.com/4biddnKnowledge
instagram.com/4biddenknowledge

INDEX

Woke Doesn't Mean Broke	i
Reviews	iii
Also by Billy Carson	v
Title Page	ix
Foreword	xiii
A Note from the Author	xv
Table of Contents	xvii
Prologue	1
Introduction	13
Chapter 1	15
Why It May Be Important to Be Wealthy	16
Wealth is for the Smart!	19
The Wealthy Mindset -- How Your Thoughts Affect Your Financial Future	21
How to Determine Your Financial Health	23
Chapter 2	25
What Twinkies Can Teach About Resiliency	26
What an Olympic Bronze Medalist Can Teach You About Healthy Competition	29
Quick Relief for Information Overload	32
What to Do When You Have No Idea What to Do	35
Chapter Two, Support	37
Chapter 3	48
What is a Role Model?	49
Who Are Your Role Models?	50
Why It's Important to Have Role Models	53
Reasons to Become a Role Model	55
Avoiding Negative Role Models	57
Characteristics of a Positive Role Model	59
What Kind of Role Model Are You?	62
Effective Role Modeling Brings Abundance	64
Chapter Three, Support	66
Chapter 4	71
Improve Your Self-Improvement Efforts	72
Do What You Don't Want to Do	75
Deliberate Practice: How to Use it to Your Advantage	77
Achieve an Abundance of Wealth	79
Create the Life You Want	81
Financial Ideas to Keep You on Track	83
How to Set and Achieve Fulfilling Personal Financial Goals	85

Before You Take Revenge, Read This	87
Ways to Develop Yourself	89
Life Lessons You Weren't Taught in School	92
Ways to Unlock Your Potential	94
Signs You're Headed for Financial Disaster	96
Does Your Spending Reflect Your Priorities?	98
Chapter Four, Support	100
Chapter 5	106
Make Life Easier and Increase Your Success	107
Enhance the Quality of Your Life	109
Break Away from Self-Limiting Thought Patterns	111
Ask Effective Questions	114
Choose Positive Self-Talk	116
The Lies You Tell Yourself	118
Ways to Declutter Your Mind	120
Financial Habits that Help You the Most	123
Create a Wealth Mindset	125
Five Self-Help Recommendations to Ignore	128
Chapter Five, Support	130
Chapter 6	139
Pitch or Keep: Your Tax Documents	140
Records to Keep, Records to Shred	143
Manage Job Search Expenses	145
Early Tax Filing	148
Paying Off Debt in the New Year	150
Lease or Buy? Financing Tips for Automobiles	152
Fuel-Efficient Car or Not	154
Financial Rules You Should Reconsider	157
Financial Habits That Will Keep You Poor	159
Making the Most of a Fresh Start	161
Axe Self-Sabotaging Behavior	162
Keys to Survive a Rough Day	165
Thought Patterns Can Cloud Your Judgment	167
Identify and Address Your Weaknesses	169
You Can Take Charge of Your Life	171
Invite Abundance into Your Life	173
Do It Today: Stop Waiting for the Right Time	175
Discover Taking Chances	177
Reasons You're Not Making Progress	179
Ways to Build Self-Reliance	181
Chapter Six, Support	184
Chapter 7	195
Managing Money by Using a Budget	196
How to Simplify Your Budget	198
What Did You Forget to Include in Your Budget?	201
Slice Up Your Expenses Using a Budget Chart	204
Quick Fixes for a Blown Budget	206
The First Time Mortgagees Budget	208
Plan a Budget That Sets You Free	210

Don't Budget Wipe Your Vacation	212
Round of Your Budget with These Essentials	214
Chapter Seven, Support	216
Chapter 8	224
Constantly Improve Any Area of Your Life	225
Stretch Your Vacation Dollars	227
Money Management Tips for the Holidays	229
Tips for Lowering Your Energy Bill	231
Tips to Stay Cool and Save Money in the Summer Heat	233
Tax Considerations for Married Couples	235
Tax-Saving Tips for Small Businesses	237
Deduct Your Child's Allowance: Tax Advantages of Owning a Small Business	239
Make Your Credit Card Work for You	242
Avoid Paying Banking Fees	244
How to Build Passive Income Online	246
Beat Laziness	248
Enjoy More Peace of Mind	250
Components of Personal Transformation	253
Chapter Eight, Support	255
Chapter 9	267
Move Your Financial Life: Tips for Success	268
Managing Your Money When You're Broke	271
Save Big with a Simple Savings Jar	273
Investing: Make Your Dollars Work for You	275
Debit or Credit - Which Card for You?	278
Your Credit Cards Have Rewards	280
Consider a Home Equity Loan	282
Wise Uses for a Home Equity Loan	284
Renting Out the Extra Room	286
Harvest Your Losses for a Tax Break	288
Sources for Emergency Cash	290
Get Your Student Loans Forgiven	291
Shop for the Best Credit Card	293
Avoid a Prepaid Card Until You Read This	295
All About Credit Card Delinquency	298
Getting Yourself Out of Debt	300
Avoid Interest and Prevent Endless Debt	302
Eliminate Debt with a Consolidation Loan	304
Tips to Create a Bright Financial Future	306
Five Steps to Save $4,000 in a Year	309
Chapter Nine, Support	321
Chapter 10	326
The Power of Giving	327
Go Green to Save Green	329
Send Kids to College and Save on Taxes	331
Pass Financial Habits on to Your Children	333
Tax Tips for Your Charitable Donations	335
Leaving Your 401(k) to Charity	337

Beware of Tax Penalties Before Giving Gifts	339
Charitable Donations and Taxes	340
Get a Tax Break When Donating Your Timeshare	342
Chapter Ten, Support	343
Chapter 11	346
Stick to Your Budget While Eating Out	347
Enjoy Lifelong Learning on a Shoestring Budget	350
How to Budget for a Great Summer	353
A Weekend Without Television	355
Make Life Easier and More Fulfilling	357
Be More Open and Share Your Feelings	360
How to Live Consciously	362
Chapter Eleven, Support	365
Chapter 12	371
Start Them Young	372
Start Success Habits Early	375
Tailored Teen Emerges	378
Credit Use During College	381
Pitfalls of College Credit	384
Rights of a Student Borrower	386
College Credit Building Years	388
Now that You're a Graduate	390
Conquer Your Student Loan Debt	393
A 5-Step Plan for Dealing with Student Loans	396
Healthy Credit Habits for Beginners	398
Financing Options for New Vehicles	401
Buying vs. Leasing a Car	403
Before You Cosign on a Loan - Read This!	405
Marriage and Money Goals	408
Merging Your Finances After Marriage	410
What About Your Marriage Credit?	412
Create a New-lywed Budget	414
Essential Marriage Money Discussions	416
Common Couple Mistakes to Avoid	418
Helpful Money Tips to Heed for Newlyweds	420
Expecting the Stork	422
Prepare for Your Roaring 20's and 30's	424
Challenges for Your Roaring 20's and 30's	427
Are You Ready for Your Blazing 40's?	430
Help Your Children Build Their Credit	432
Getting Married...FINALLY	434
The End is in Sight	437
Life Insurance Investing	439
Annuity Investing	442
Life Insurance or Annuity?	444
Tax-Free and Tax-Deferred Income Strategies	445
Make Your Hobby Your Money-Maker	451
Don't Wreck the Finish Line	453
After Your Loved One Has Departed	456

Give the Gift of Living Inheritances	458
Taxes and Your Inheritance	460
Effective Strategies to Reduce Estate Taxes	462
Chapter Twelve, Support	464
Chapter 13	470
Benefits of Being Alone	471
Advantages and Disadvantages of Automatic Bill Paying	473
Are You Financially Prepared to Relocate?	475
Financial Concerns When Starting a New Job	477
Get the Most from Membership Services	479
Find the Perfect Bank for Your Small Business	481
Eliminate Overdraft Charges	483
Find Out Your Credit Score	485
Credit Score Destroyers	487
Disputing Credit Report Information	489
Errors on Your Credit Report	491
Remove Credit Report Errors	493
Hidden Benefits of Using a Credit Card	495
Win Big with Credit Card Rewards	497
Save Your Estate: Avoid Probate Issues	499
Tax Tips for Homeowners	501
Tax Breaks for Homeowners	503
Get the Facts: Compare Tax-Advantaged Investments	505
Chapter Thirteen, Support	506
Chapter 14	512
Turn Your Passion to Profit	513
Write a Highly Effective Business Plan	529
Happy New You! It's a Brand-New Year!	543
Financial Therapy: Change Your Money Beliefs and Change Your Life	556
Conquer Your Money	574
Be a Productive Entrepreneur	590
Go Head to Head with Debt Collectors and Plan to Come Out Smiling	610
Chapter Fourteen, Support	622
Chapter 15	629

Turn Your Passion to Profit Questionnaire	630
Write a Highly Effective Business Plan	633
The Battle for Productivity, Worksheet	637
The Battle for Productivity, Overcome Distractions Support	639
A Bright Financial Future, Questionnaire	641
Declutter Your Mind, Questionnaire	642
Enhance Your Charisma and Your Life, Questionnaire	643
Tax-Advantaged Retirement Income You Can't Outlive, Questionnaire	645
Decorate Your Tax Return with Red Flags and Get Audited!	647
Survive an IRS Audit	649
Recognize Fake IRS Collection Calls	651
Income Taxes and Living Out of the Country	652
10 Amazing Life Lessons You Can Appreciate	654
Chapter Fifteen, Support	656
About the Author	663